Building Abolition

Building Abolition: Decarceration and Social Justice explores the intersections of the carceral in projects of oppression, while at the same time providing intellectual, pragmatic, and undetermined paths toward abolition. Prison abolition is at once about the institution of the prison, and a broad, intersectional political project calling for the end of the social structured by settler colonialism, anti-black racism, and related oppressions. Beyond this, prison abolition is a constructive project that imagines and strives for a transformed world in which justice is not equated with punishment, and accountability is not equated with caging.

Composed of 16 chapters by an international team of scholars and activists, with a foreword by Perry Zurn and an afterword by Justin Piché, the book is divided into four themes:

- Prisons and racism
- Prisons and settler colonialism
- Anti-carceral feminisms
- Multispecies carceralities.

This book will be of interest to undergraduate and postgraduate students, activists, and scholars working in the areas of Critical Prison Studies, Critical Criminology, Native Studies, Postcolonial Studies, Black Studies, Critical Race Studies, Gender and Sexuality Studies, and Critical Animal Studies, with particular chapters being of interest to scholars and students in other fields, such as Feminist Legal Studies, Animal Law, Critical Disability Studies, Queer Theory, and Transnational Feminisms.

Kelly Struthers Montford is Assistant Professor of Criminology at Ryerson University in Toronto, Canada, situated in the "Dish With One Spoon Territory". The Dish With One Spoon is a treaty between the Anishinaabe, Mississaugas, and Haudenosaunee that bound them to share the territory and protect the land.

Chloë Taylor is Professor of Women's and Gender Studies at the University of Alberta in Edmonton, Canada, situated on Treaty 6 territory, a traditional gathering place for diverse Indigenous peoples including the Cree, Blackfoot, Métis, Nakota Sioux, Iroquois, Dene, Ojibway/ Saulteaux/Anishinaabe, and Inuit.

Routledge Studies in Penal Abolition and Transformative Justice Series
Michael J. Coyle and David Scott

The *Routledge Studies in Penal Abolition and Transformative Justice* book series provides the leading publishing location for literature that both reflects key abolitionist thought and helps to set the agenda for local and global abolitionist ideas and interventions. It fosters research that works toward the systemic and systematic dismantling of penal structures and processes, and toward social living that is grounded in relationships that consider the needs of all. This international book series seeks contributions from all around the world (east, north, south, and west) that both engages and furthers abolitionist and transformative practice, study, politics and theory. It welcomes work that examines abolition and transformative justice empirically, theoretically, historically, culturally, spatially, or rhetorically, as well as books that are situated within or at the interstices of critiques of ableism, capitalism, hetero-normativity, militarism, patriarchy, state power, racism, settler colonialism, and xenophobia.

https://www.routledge.com/Routledge-Studies-in-Penal-Abolition-and-Transformative-Justice/book-series/PATJ#:~:text=About%20the%20Series,global%20abolitionist%20ideas%20and%20interventions.

Building Abolition: Decarceration and Social Justice
Kelly Struthers Montford and Chloë Taylor

Contesting Carceral Logic
Michael J Coyle and Methchild Nagel

Building Abolition

Decarceration and Social Justice

Edited by
**Kelly Struthers Montford
and Chloë Taylor**

Routledge
Taylor & Francis Group

LONDON AND NEW YORK

First published 2022
by Routledge
2 Park Square, Milton Park, Abingdon, Oxon OX14 4RN

and by Routledge
52 Vanderbilt Avenue, New York, NY 10017

Routledge is an imprint of the Taylor & Francis Group, an informa business

© 2022 selection and editorial matter, Kelly Struthers Montford and Chloë Taylor;
individual chapters, the contributors

British Library Cataloguing-in-Publication Data
A catalogue record for this book is available from the British Library

Library of Congress Cataloging-in-Publication Data
A catalog record has been requested for this book

ISBN: 978-0-367-34987-5 (hbk)
ISBN: 978-0-367-77028-0 (pbk)
ISBN: 978-0-429-32917-3 (ebk)

Typeset in Bembo
by Newgen Publishing UK

On a personal note, this volume is dedicated to Jacques, Guillaume, and Noireau, who have shaped us and our will to unsettle dominant forms of relating, autonomy, and care.

Broadly, this volume is a gesture to the praxis of solidarity and world-building. It is dedicated to those who resist, struggle, and live within the metaphoric and literal cages of carcerality.

Contents

Contributors

Fernando Avila is a PhD Candidate at the Centre of Criminology and Sociolegal Studies at the University of Toronto, Ontario.

Vered Ben-David is a PhD student in the Department of Law and Legal Studies at Carleton University, Ottawa, Ontario.

Liat Ben-Moshe is Assistant Professor of Criminology, Law, and Justice at the University of Illinois at Chicago, Illinois.

Danielle Bird (*Nêhiyaw*) is an MA Candidate in Indigenous Studies at the University of Saskatchewan, Saskatoon, Saskatchewan.

Katarina Bogosavljevic is a PhD student in Criminology at the University of Ottawa, Ontario.

Jessica Bundy is a PhD student at the Centre of Criminology and Sociolegal Studies at the University of Toronto, Ontario.

Fran Chaisson is a founding member of the Prison for Women Memorial Collective in Kingston, Ontario.

Lauren Corman is Associate Professor of Sociology at Brock University, St. Catharines, Ontario.

Alexa DeGagne is Assistant Professor of Women's and Gender Studies at Athabasca University, Alberta.

Andrew Dilts is Associate Professor of Political Theory at Loyola Marymount University, Los Angeles, California.

Nirmala Erevelles is Professor in the Social Foundations of Education and Instructional Department of Education Leadership, Policy, and Technology Studies at the University of Alabama, Tuscaloosa, Alabama.

Paula Cepeda Gallo recently completed a Master's degree in Gender and Social Justice Studies from the University of Alberta and is a student in the Faculty of Law at Maastricht University in the Netherlands.

Megan Gaucher is Assistant Professor of Law and Legal Studies at Carleton University, Ottawa, Ontario.

Lisa Guenther is Queen's National Scholar in Political Philosophy and Critical Prison Studies at Queen's University, Kingston, Ontario.

Bobbie Kidd is a founding member of the Prison for Women Memorial Collective in Kingston, Ontario.

Eva Kasprzycka is a PhD student in Interdisciplinary Studies at the University of British Columbia Okanagan, British Columbia.

Jennifer Kilty is Professor of Criminology at the University of Ottawa, Ontario.

Erica Meiners is Professor of Education and Women's and Gender Studies at Northeastern Illinois University, Chicago, Illinois.

Dawn Moore is Professor of Law and Legal Studies at Carleton University, Ottawa, Ontario.

Sol Neely is Associate Professor of English at Heritage University, Toppenish, Washington.

Debra Parkes is Chair in Feminist Legal Studies at the Peter A. Allard School of Law at the University of British Columbia, British Columbia.

Justin Piché is Associate Professor in the Department of Criminology and Director of the Carceral Studies Research Collective at the University of Ottawa, Ontario.

Isabel Scheuneman Scott is a PhD candidate in Sociology at the University of Alberta, Edmonton, Alberta.

Calvin John Smiley is Assistant Professor of Sociology at Hunter College, City University of New York, New York City.

Kelly Struthers Montford is Assistant Professor of Criminology at Ryerson University, Toronto, Ontario.

Chloë Taylor is Professor of Women's and Gender Studies at the University of Alberta, Edmonton, Alberta.

Sarah Turnbull is Assistant Professor of Sociology and Legal Studies at the University of Waterloo, Ontario.

Perry Zurn is Assistant Professor of Philosophy at American University, Washington, D.C.

Foreword

Abolition is a kite-idea

Perry Zurn

In certain circumstances, it is possible to fight aircraft-carrier-ideas with kite-ideas.
—Boaventura de Sousa Santos, 2014

In *Epistemologies of the South: Justice Against Epistemicide*, Boaventura de Sousa Santos writes:

> We are many more than our enemies think, […] we think better than they do about their world and ours, and […] we are bold enough to act under the conviction that, in certain circumstances, it is possible to fight aircraft-carrier-ideas with kite-ideas, even though an aircraft carrier is an aircraft carrier and a kite is a kite. This is exactly what some of us have been demonstrating while venting our outrage at the beginning of the second decade of the millennium, in the streets of Cairo and Tunis, Madrid and Athens, New York and Johannesburg—in a word, in the streets of the world.
>
> (de Sousa Santos, 2014, p. 4)

De Sousa Santos is referring to events surrounding the Arab Spring, the Indignant Citizens Movement, and Occupy Wall Street in 2010 and 2011. Movements explicitly set against authoritarianism, austerity, and radical inequality. Movements for human dignity and voice. Each of these instances of political resistance is remembered as a moment of unexpected strength and unassuming means, marked as much by tweets and tents as by bottle bombs and barricades. Thousands upon thousands slung their smooth stones—weak ideas—against behemoth superstructures, and they cracked.

I want to propose that *abolition is a kite-idea*.

Kite-ideas are floozy and a little cheap, easy to build at home. They can be flown by one or two people or synchronized *en masse*. Each with their own string, kite-ideas are personal. They are childlike, imaginative, and relatively harmless, carrying little but their colors. They are inherently flighty, but equally grounded, tethered in some meaningful sense to people and place. And they take flight only with a willing wind, always working together with the earth. Kite-ideas are graspable but uncontrollable. They may seem indecisive as they wander and waver about. And their capacity to be easily moved tags kite-ideas as feminine, as queer, cutting through space with uncanny intimacy.

Aircraft-carrier-ideas are massively heavy, sluggish, and expensive. They are warships, bearing weapons of mass destruction and they are built of power and of money. Moving against water, rather than with wind, they work on but also despite existing natural forces. The clear product of developed nations and globalized corporations, aircraft-carrier-ideas are highly complex, highly specialized, and therefore difficult to dismantle. Unwavering, stubbornly sure-footed, and seemingly indestructible, they carry all kinds of systemic baggage onboard. Bearing the colors of heteropatriarchy and coloniality, they are isolated and isolating, heavily bordered and border-policing.

And yet, under "certain circumstances, it is possible to fight aircraft-carrier-ideas with kite-ideas." What are the parameters of such a fight? Is it a fight that can be won? Or is it a different sort of struggle? Is the kite's fight merely one of disruption, sowing confusion and irony? Or does its fight succeed on a different terrain, demanding engagement (and mustering support) on a different register? Do kite-ideas simply refuse to play the game they have inherited? A kite can land on an aircraft-carrier uninvited, willy-nilly. It can disrupt flight paths. Or it can simply skip over the giant floating metal bed and continue on its way. And if it is only under certain circumstances that such a fight can take place, what are those circumstances? Are they in the past? Are they only in our dreams? Are they here, walking among us?

Abolition is a kite-idea. The prison industrial complex, ableism, patriarchy and cis-heteronormativity, settler colonialism and white supremacy, these are aircraft-carrier-ideas. Floating freight trains of destruction. How often is the thought of abolition dismissed as insubstantial, uninformed, innocent, or even laughable? What fragility lies there in contrast with the massive material-discursive systems across history that have built the ideas against which it flies? I want to unpack that fragility here by getting behind and beneath abolition. I want to track abolition as a specific kind of movement, noting the way it flies overhead, shimmers in the sun, and tugs at the hand.

What is abolition? The famous *ti esti* question, a Socratic kite-idea turned warship by disciplinary philosophy. I have been combing over the definitions and definitional descriptions of the term "abolition" in the writings of contemporary abolitionists such as Liat Ben-Moshe, Angela Davis, Andrew Dilts, Ruth Wilson Gilmore, Che Gossett, Lisa Guenther, Michael Hames-Garcia, Mariam Kaba, Joel Olson, Dylan Rodriguez, Dean Spade, and Eric Stanley, among others. There are certain limitations to the very project of identifying what abolition is via this methodology. First, there may be definitions and descriptions of abolition that lack the word "abolition" itself and therefore fly under the radar. And, second, there are certainly ways these folks and others understand or do abolition that may not be captured by language at all. Nevertheless, this is one pathway to thinking abolition, its movement, and its kinesthetic signatures.

Eric Stanley (2011), while reflecting on the queer abolitionist legacies of Stonewall in his introduction to *Captive Genders: Trans Embodiment and the Prison Industrial Complex*, describes abolition as follows:

> The time of abolition is both yet to come and already here. [...] As a dream of the future and a practice of history, we strategize for a world without the multiple ways that our bodies, genders, and sexualities are disciplined. [...] This is an invitation to remember these radical legacies of abolition and to continue the struggle to make this dream of the future lived today.
>
> (Stanley, 2011, pp. 8–9)

For Stanley, *abolition*—always already a queer thing—is (1) a practice of history, (2) a dream of the future, and (3) an invitation to continue the struggle lived today. Each of these threads is traceable in other texts, lengthened or foreshortened, differently interwoven and differently inspired, but often with similar touchstones. In what follows, I pick up on abolition's debts to Foucauldian genealogy, the messianism in Derridean deconstruction, and the affective resistance among queer/trans, disabled, and/or of color communities in order to triangulate *how abolition moves*. In doing so, I do not mean to suggest that genealogy, deconstruction, and affective resistance are the only ways to understand abolition's investments in either history, future, or struggle, nor that these are abolition's only investments. But they are some of its investments, and these are some of the ways those investments can be understood.

What surfaces in each case is what I call the *weakness of abolition*. By this term, I do not mean to imply either that abolition has no strength or that abolition's weakness is not also its strength. I do mean to attend to the ways in which the thought of abolition, across these traditions, belies a certain fragility. I mean to grapple with abolition's contingency and its vulnerability. I mean to highlight its kite-likeness.

1. Abolition is a practice of history

This is a kite-idea. Who but a lightweight, a waif of a thing, stands before an institution, decides to dismantle it, and turns tail for the archives? What does the dusty past have to do with a damning present?

Well, everything. As Angela Davis (2005) puts it, part of abolishing prisons is breaking the prison's hold on our imagination, the whole network architecture of our cognitive schemas. *To fly high overhead* and gain perspective. It involves a refusal to separate prisons from the history of slavery, emancipation, the Thirteenth Amendment, and race inequality today. History itself is a palimpsest. It involves the happening of things being eternally rewritten and retold, typically according to reigning logics, dominant discourses, and established structures. The present pile of things seems simply to have appeared, fully formed and fully functional, with roots and scaffolds deeply buried. "Genealogy," Michel

Foucault (1980) pens, "will cultivate the details and accidents that accompany every beginning" (p. 144). It illuminates the messy, multiple, and insufficient threads that create the present. And it does so to show the fragility of things, to crack them open, release possibilities, and shift existing pathways (Dilts, 2017). It is the twine of social and cognitive justice.

But genealogy also tells another tale, a tale of the vulnerability of abolition itself and its tendency toward cooptation. Foucault is no abstract theorist. Having done robust abolitionist work with the Prisons Information Group (GIP) and the subsequent Prisoners Action Committee (CAP), Foucault stared long and hard into the shape-shifting face of carceral logic (Thompson & Zurn, 2021). And he looked up grim and weathered. In his writings, he is gripped less by a faith in abolition than by the fragility of abolition. To "abolish" public executions in favor of prisons, he notes, is simply to mask the same corporeal punishment in new, seemingly less corporeal garb, all while extending the microphysics of power across penal, juridical, and academic institutions (Foucault, 1977). To "abolish" the death penalty in favor of life without parole, he warns, is but to implement a cosmetic improvement, one that solidifies the enmeshment of medical and psychological discourses in judicial decisions (Foucault, 2021a). And to "abolish" prisons themselves in favor of alternative penalties, he insists, could submerge the forces of marginalization in other institutions and "liberate carceral functions" across society, diffusing the work of surveillance, control, and resocialization (2021b; 2009, p. 17).

The abolitionist practice of history is empowering. But it is also deeply humbling. A crack and a caution.

2. Abolition is a dream of the future

This is a kite-idea. Who but a child—or the childlike—stands before an institution, decides to dismantle it, and then lapses into daydreams? What hath whimsy to do with war?

Again, perhaps everything. Institutions do not only determine the present, they also craft the future, a future that is coming, down the pike, as formidable as it seems unstoppable. Any movement toward abolition must necessarily invoke, then, different institutions *and* different futures. It must take a moment *to shimmer in the sun*. Reflecting on both the longstanding practice of incarcerating disability and the impending future of institutionalization via these same oppressive structures, Liat Ben-Moshe (2013) and Chapman et al. (2014) recall Jacques Derrida's (1993) insistence that justice involves a responsibility to "those who are not yet born and who are already dead" (p. xviii). Robert McRuer (2006) likewise leans on Derrida when he dreams of another world, beyond institutionalization, a world that welcomes a disability to come. This, he writes, is "a crip promise that we will always comprehend disability otherwise and that we will, collectively, somehow access other worlds and futures" (p. 208). By mobilizing echoes of Derrida (1994) on democracy—something that "will always remain, in each of its future times, to come" —McRuer emphasizes the perpetual unfinishedness of disability justice and, indeed, of abolition writ large (Guenther, 2015).

If abolition is a practice of history that undoes history, abolition is also a dream of the future that unravels itself. For it, we need, as Friedrich Nietzsche (1878) notes in *Human, All Too Human*, to "become traitors, be unfaithful, again and again abandon our ideals" (p. 198). This is one of abolition's weaknesses. Another—not unrelated—is that its dream of the future is a dream of the heart. In his *Death Penalty* lectures, Derrida (2013) speaks explicitly about abolition. He insists that abolition cannot be modelled after the cold calculation of the death penalty itself. It must come from somewhere else. Refusing the "dis-interestedness" of Kant and the self-interestedness of French Revolutionary abolitionists, Derrida leans into his own inter-ested nature—that is, the fact that he exists in and between others, in a co-constituted affective space. "I protest," he writes, "in the name of my heart when I fight so that the heart of the other will continue to beat—in me, before me, after me, or even without me" (Derrida, 2013, p. 257). The dream of abolition is not a calculative vision, but a felt recognition of interdependence and creaturely solidarity, of affective terrains that exceed themselves. And it is precisely this location that secures abolition's insecurity, its incalculability, its unfinished future.

The abolitionist dream of the future is one of propulsion as much as pathos. A fever and a feeling.

3. Abolition is an invitation to continue the struggle lived today

This is a kite-idea. Who but a trickster stands before an institution, decides to dismantle it, and then returns to eating and drinking with friends? How does that make any sense?

It is, precisely, sense-making. The struggle is lived, today, on the terrain of creaturely desire. Desire for belonging and independence, meaning and memory, food and drink, the sun and the earth. While disciplinary habits are secured by tradition and sedimented by specific institutions, new practices can be planted and cross-pollinated through the poetics of relation. *By a tug at the hand.* While it is true that abolition tracks the material histories and resistance dreams of marginalized communities, it tracks, just as much, the acts of love—queer love, crip love, Black and Brown love—among those same communities. This work involves the death of certain desires and the liberation of others. Recall Sara Ahmed (2016), in "A Killjoy Manifesto," vowing: "I am not willing to get over histories that are not over" (p. 262); "I am willing to cause unhappiness" (p. 258). But remember also Charlene Carruthers' (2018) call for "healing justice," Kai Green's (n.d.) for "black trans love," and Leah Lakshmi Piepzna-Samarasinha's (2018) for "care work," alongside so many others. Abolition is a practice of affective and relational transformation.

In this double helix of breaking and building affective and relational ties, what is broken is not only the grip of aircraft-carrier-ideas on our minds and our hearts. What is broken is also ourselves, those of us standing here flying kites. In *This Wound is a World*, queer, Indigenous poet Billy-Ray Belcourt (2019) explores his experiences of love as a force of undoing. He writes:

> Love [...] "always means non-sovereignty," but only if we think of love as what opens us up to that which feels like it can rupture the ground beneath our feet. [...] [L]ove requires that we violate our own attachments, that we give into instability, that we accept that turbulence is the condition of relationality as such. We might agree, then, that love is a process of becoming unbodied; at its wildest, it works up a poetics of the unbodied.
>
> (Belcourt, 2019, p. 55)

Against the aircraft-carrier-idea of sovereignty, as built and massified by settler-colonial states, Belcourt (2016) pits a queer, Indigenous call to love and desire, to our bodies breaking against one another. The "abolition" of carceral logic writ large, he elsewhere states, "is a mode of becoming and being-with" that requires not the "disappearing of others" or the "blocking of worlds," but rather the affective worlding that repeatedly breaks open not just that out there, but us, us here (2016, 11:07). If abolition is anything, besides a practice of curiosity and a practice of hope, it is a reimagination of how to be with one another, to be done and undone by one another.

The abolitionist invitation to lived struggle is a (re)turn to relation and desire. A tear and a tug.

Abolition is never completed; it is only ever in motion. What, then, is the shape of that motion? What are its arcs, its trajectories, its kinesthetic signatures? Tracing the abolitionist signatures active within the theoretical and activist traditions of genealogy, deconstruction, and queer/trans liberation, I have begun a preliminary sketch of an architecture of change, charged, as it is, with a hope as fierce as it is fragile.

Abolition is a kite-idea. A queer thing. It is a triangulation of fabric, wind, and string. Its attention to material histories illuminates the need and the pathways for change, while its commitment to dreaming and struggling, amid the crosscurrents of what is and what might be, is guided by a poetics of relation. Abolition's fabric, its wind, and its string are as forcefully as they are fabulously pitched against the ahistoricity and urgency of the now that serve to isolate us from one another and from ourselves. The question that remains is this: What will the fight look like? What weakness does it risk? What irony does it sow? What other terrain does it insist upon occupying? What refusals does it make to the aircraft-carrier-ideas of settler colonialism and white supremacy, ableism and cis-hetero-patriarchy, and to their prized aircrafts? And what is it—in the past, in our dreams, and walking among us—that conditions those refusals? It is for us to follow the line and watch as it winds overhead and take after it, running.

References

Ahmed, S. (2016). A Killjoy Manifesto. In *Living a feminist life*. Duke University Press.

Belcourt, B. (2016, April 20). Indigenous feminism as abolitionist praxis: An essay in ten parts [Paper Presentation]. The Society for Radical Geography, Spatial Theory, and Everyday Life [Symposium]. https://www.youtube.com/watch?v=Cgkclk6AyvA.

Belcourt, B. (2019). *This wound is a world*. University of Minnesota Press.

Ben-Moshe, L. (2013). The institution yet to come: Analyzing incarceration through a disability lens. In Leonard Davis (Ed.), *The Disability Studies Reader* (4th ed., pp. 132–46). Routledge.

Carruthers, C. (2018). *Unapologetic: A black, queer, and feminist mandate for radical movements*. Beacon Press.

Chapman, C., Carey, A., & Ben-Moshe, L. (2014). Reconsidering confinement: Interlocking locations and logics of incarceration. In *Disability incarcerated: Imprisonment and disability in the United States and Canada* (pp. 3–24). Palgrave.

Davis, A. (2005). *Abolition democracy: Beyond empire, prisons, and torture*. Seven Stories Press.

de Sousa Santos, B. (2014). *Epistemologies of the south: Justice against epistemicide*. Routledge.

Derrida, J. (2005). *The politics of friendship* (G. Collins, Trans.). Verso. (Original work published 1994)

Derrida, J. (2006). *Specters of Marx* (P. Kamuf, Trans.). Routledge. (Original work published 1993)

Derrida, J. (2013). *The death penalty* (Vol. 1) (P. Kamuf, Trans.). University of Chicago Press.

Dilts, A. (2017). Toward abolitionist genealogy. *Southern Journal of Philosophy*, *55*(51), 51–77.

Foucault, M. (1977). *Discipline and punish*. Vintage (Original work published 1975).

Foucault, M. (1980). Nietzsche, genealogy, history. In D. Bouchard (Ed.), *Language, counter-memory, practice*. Cornell University Press. (Original work published 1971)

Foucault, M. (2009). Alternatives to the prison: Dissemination or decline of social control? *Theory, Culture & Society*, *26*(6), 12–24. (Original work published 1976)

Foucault, M. (2021a). Pompidou's two deaths. In K. Thompson & P. Zurn (Eds.), *Intolerable: Writings from Michel Foucault and the Prisons Information Group, 1970–1980*. University of Minnesota Press. (Original work published 1972)

Foucault, M. (2021b). The great confinement. In K. Thompson & P. Zurn (Eds.), *Intolerable: Writings from Michel Foucault and the Prisons Information Group, 1970–1980*. University of Minnesota Press. (Original work published 1972)

Green, K, Evolve Benton, and Dora Santana, Eds. (n.d.). *Black trans love is black trans wealth*. [Manuscript in preparation] http://drkaimgreen.com/black-trans-love-is-black-wealth

Guenther, L. (2015). Abolition statement. *Abolition: A journal of insurgent politics*. https://abolitionjournal.org/abolition-statements-a-collection/.

McRuer, R. (2006). *Crip theory: Cultural signs of queerness and disability*. New York University Press.

Nietzsche, F. (2018). *Human all too human* (R.J. Hollingdale, Trans.; 2nd ed.). University of Cambridge Press. (Original work published 1878)

Piepzna-Samarashina, L.L. (2018). *Care work: Dreaming disability justice*. Arsenal Pulp Press.

Stanley, E. (2011). Fugitive flesh: Gender self-determination, queer abolition, and trans resistance. In E. Stanley & N. Smith (Eds.), *Captive genders: Trans embodiment and the prison industrial complex*. AK Press.

Thompson, K. & Zurn, P. (2021). Intolerable: Legacies of militancy and theory. In K. Thompson & P. Zurn (Eds.), *Intolerable: Writings from Michel Foucault and the Prisons Information Group, 1970–1980*. University of Minnesota Press.

Series editors' foreword

Michael J. Coyle and David Scott

Scholarship in penal abolition and transformative justice is currently undergoing a period of renaissance. The renewed interest in penal abolitionism and the transformative justice model is placing them anew on the intellectual map, and is the result of decades of widening scholarly, policy, activist, and public understanding of the extreme failures of the criminalizing system and the relentless and unceasing impacts of white supremacy, colonialism, patriarchal power, and racial capitalism.

Penal abolition seeks to end the criminalizing system whereas transformative justice strives to recognize (a) the complexity of individual or group experience and identity, (b) how the criminalizing system normalizes only certain experience and identity thus oppressing other experiences and identities, and consequently, (c) how the criminalizing system, as state violence, is not only unable to build a "justice system," but instead actually regularly and widely oppresses, exploits, and harms people, i.e., creates injustice. Transformative justice recognizes the criminalizing system (and the many other expressions of the punitive mentality in education, immigration, or responses to homelessness, poverty, etc.) as inherently unjust, violent and damaging to individuals, group and other identities, and society at large. As such, it works to produce new models of theory and practice that can address what accompanied the rise of criminalizing systems (colonialism), causative forces of harm (e.g., white supremacy, capitalism), as well as to recognize and respond to individual acts of harm (e.g., assault, theft, sexual violence) that require redress, restitution, and a process of recovery for all those involved (victims, transgressors, community members, and sometimes entire communities).

Justice does not simply mean assignment of guilt and punishment, but the *transformation* of environments, settings, practices, and thinking that provide the background and framework for harms to emerge in the first place. As such, transformative justice has the potential to: (1) suggest new thinking for building individual healing, addressing of large-scale inequities, social justice, and liberation wherever oppression exists on the individual, group, or community level; (2) model the building of relationships that move beyond "power-over" dynamics; and (3) foster analysis for building social practices (conditions) that on the one hand leave behind the proven failure of punishment-violence and on the other hand shift the social norms and institutions that are at the root of harms and human capacity to recover. As such, the literature of this series inevitably challenges the language, concepts, culture, and taken-for-granted assumptions about the very existence of law, policing, courts, and prisons, and develops new language, views, models, and praxis.

Both penal abolition and transformative justice are grounded in interdisciplinary study and draw their critiques of the criminalizing system from critical and close readings of history, culture, social theory, and social science; and are foundationally about both dismantling (penal abolition) and rebuilding (transformative justice). In the broadest conception, dismantling in this fashion takes many forms, from intellectual and activist insurrection to more technocratic, although no less important, non-reformist strategies that reject existing institutions (e.g., law, police, courts, and prisons) and logics (e.g., punishment, the carceral state) that are predicated on the violence of unfreedom (e.g., coercion and confinement). Rebuilding is also broad, and includes work that *reimagines* justice as action that transforms the foundation of inequities (e.g., socio-structural imbalances) and transforms the problematic situations that constitute the footing of unfairness (e.g., the preludes to conflicts or personal-structural imbalances), *addresses* the harms and norm violations that humans ubiquitously enact without anew violating persons and communities, and *pushes* programs, organizations and relationships that can alternately harness or operate outside of state power.

The *Studies in Penal Abolition and Transformative Justice* book series provides one of the leading publishing locations for literature that both reflects key abolitionist thought and helps to set the agenda for local and global abolitionist ideas and interventions. It fosters research that works toward the systemic and systematic dismantling of penal and more generally punitive structures and processes, and toward social living that is grounded in relationships that consider the needs of all. This book series publishes contributions from all around the world (east, north, south, and west) that both engage and further abolitionist and transformative practice, study, politics, and theory. Volumes in this series examine abolition and transformative justice empirically, theoretically, historically, culturally, spatially, or rhetorically, as well as situate their analysis within or at the interstices of critiques of ableism, capitalism, heteronormativity, militarism, patriarchies, hegemonic masculinities, state power, corporate harm, racism, settler colonialism, and xenophobia.

The series will attract the widest variety of participants to echo an inclusive community of researchers exploring penal abolition, transformative justice, and related areas from the perspectives of Ableism Studies, American Studies, Anticolonial Studies, Arts and Humanities, Black Studies, Cultural Studies, Feminist Studies, Gender and Sexuality Studies, Global South Studies, Historical Studies, Indigenous Studies, Justice Studies, Literary Studies, Media Studies, Social Sciences, Social Theory, Visual Studies, and more. Thus the

Studies in Penal Abolition and Transformative Justice book series addresses the following:

- Abolitionist <u>explorations</u> of the role of imperialism, colonialism, patriarchal power, and white supremacy in the invention and maintenance of criminalizing logic
- Abolitionist <u>deconstruction</u> of criminalizing assumptions, logic, practices, and policies
- Abolitionist <u>investigations</u> of the development, failure, and costs of the punishment-violence paradigm
- Abolitionist <u>studies</u> of the historic impact of criminalizing ways of seeing, thinking, theorizing, and practicing
- Abolitionist <u>analyses</u> of "crime" theories, paradigms, and their inventors and promoters
- Abolitionist <u>evaluations</u> of the prison industrial complex, the criminalized (youth, adults and communities), and media constructions and representations (of danger, fear, and threat as it relates to "crime")
- Abolitionist <u>historical studies</u> of abolition history, social and transformative justice movements, and cultural expressions of violence and oppression through criminalization
- Abolitionist <u>dissections</u> of the individual, communal, cultural and social destruction wrought by the criminalizing practices of law, police, courts, prisons, probation, parole, rehabilitation motifs, and the ever-expanding tropes emerging in time (e.g., moralism, managerialism, psychologizing, technology, etc.)
- Abolitionist <u>theorizing and proposals</u> for the abolition of law, police, prison, punishment, or other criminalizing practices and institutions
- Transformative justice proposal <u>interventions</u> for the historic inequities and injustices wrought by centuries of "law and order" imperialism, colonialism, patriarchies, slavery, white supremacy, racial capitalism, ableist/cultural/ethno-racist/gender/political oppression, and more
- Transformative justice <u>examinations</u> by and about communities that have formed and form the targets of the violent criminalizing system
- Transformative justice <u>investigations and proposals</u> by and about traditionally excluded/ignored communities (in the global south, Indigenous groups, queer identifying, racial/ethnic minorities, etc.) impacted by criminalizing processes
- Transformative justice <u>empirical studies</u> and <u>case studies</u> demonstrating:
  - The power, effectiveness and use of critical listening and creative solutions to the problems of everyday human conflict and everyday human transgression
  - The differences between the approaches of retributive justice, restorative justice and transformative justice

- The challenges of transforming criminalizing practices in the face of the territorial, defensive and possessive temperament of criminalizing culture, institutions, and workers
- Transformative justice <u>studies</u> for new theories, paradigms and practices for responding to the ubiquity of interpersonal harm and conflict.

Introduction

Doing abolition

Kelly Struthers Montford and Chloë Taylor

The completion of this volume has occurred during a time marked by the COVID-19 pandemic and in which issues of state-organized race crime and carceral abolition have come to the fore. These are issues that might seem separate: ecological destruction and the exploitation of non-human animals driving the pandemic, and state-organized racial crime marked by continued mass incarceration and police killings of unarmed Black, Indigenous, and Latinx individuals (see for example, American Civil Liberties Union, 2020; Flanagan, 2020). Yet race and species are intimately tied in projects of white supremacy. Cageability and killability unite and find different expressions at the intersections of the pandemic and the carceral. State-organized race crime is both slow and fast, always attritional and nefarious, with sensational events, such as police killings, explicit expressions of the state's sanctioning of group-based "vulnerability to premature death" (Gilmore, 2007, p. 247). At the same time that Black persons and Indigenous persons are more vulnerable to contracting, experiencing more severe symptoms, and dying from COVID-19 as a result of colonialism, racism, and poverty (African-Canadian Civic Engagement Council & INNOVATIVE, 2020; Coleman, 2020; Curtice & Choo, 2020), they remain targeted and killed by police and subjected to hyper incarceration. This is also a political moment of intense resistance to state perpetuated race-based crime, with global expressions of solidarity with #BlackLivesMatter following the movement's resurgence in response to the police killings of Breonna Taylor and George Floyd, and the murder of Amaud Arbery, by white men, for jogging while Black (Black Lives Matter, 2020).

This is, then, a time galvanized by social movements and public opinion to defund and abolish policing, in which criminology departments have ceased student field placements with police and corrections (Mills, 2020; Whistle, 2020), and in which calls for the immediate decarceration of prisoners and immigration detainees to reduce the spread of COVID-19 are common. The spread of COVID-19 inside prisons is accelerated and deadly: physical distancing is impossible, hand sanitizer is often prohibited, living conditions are unhygienic, and healthcare is difficult to access at best (Criminalization and Punishment Education, 2020; Van Beusekom, 2020; Williams et al., 2020). Some have argued that "the post-pandemic future" will result in significant decreases of persons in jails and prisons, especially those remanded to pre-trial detention as they are given bail instead. In this sense, some see the pandemic as transforming the criminal legal system, with the ultimate result that community safety is enhanced (Osmok, 2020). These social movements, premised on the urgency of the pandemic combined with the routine killing of Black individuals, raise an enduring tension about how to advocate for justice within the constraints of systems so deeply embedded in our social contexts.

At the same time that social movements committed to racial justice call for the defunding of police, some also call for the arrest and prosecution of police officers responsible for killing Black citizens. Such tensions reveal the pervasiveness of the criminal legal system in constraining our imaginations and mediating "mattering." It is this prevention of alternative normativities that Robert Nichols (2014) argues is the prison's ultimate purpose in settler colonial contexts: the attempted suppression of Indigenous sovereignties in order to reproduce the settler state as legitimate. This is a project that requires continuous effort as it remains confronted by the alternative normativities called forth by an Indigenous political critique. Prison abolition is, then, decolonization.

Whereas Nichols urges critical prison studies scholars to critical settler colonial frame which then leads prison abolition to "announce itself as decolonization" (p. 455), there remains a tendency for penal abolitionists to refer to the project as "abolition." For some Black studies scholars this reveals a historical and racial innocence premised on the idea that plantation slavery and its attendant logics and ontologies have been abolished. Inasmuch as "abolition" in U.S. contexts refers to the abolition of slavery, and given that "'the after-life of slavery' is instantiated in a racial order that is essentially and enduringly antiblack" (Kim, 2018, p. 26)—most notably through state violence and the carceral system—abolition *continues* to be the "effort to dismantle the antiblack racial order and secure meaningful freedom for black people for the first time" (p. 29). To borrow from Sexton's (2010) writing on the political ontology of race, prison abolition is, then, at once about the end of the old order and the "creation of an entirely new world."

It is with this essentially constructive aspect of prison abolitionism in mind that we title this volume *Building Abolition: Decarceration and Social Justice*. As we strive to eliminate the carceral, and the ontologies of race and species upon which it is premised, we also imagine and construct possibilities for their replacement. It is for this reason that we focus on how to *build, generate, and transform* the ways in which we prevent and respond to harm and violence. It is because prison abolition is generative, imaginative, context specific, creative, and undetermined that praxis so often takes the shape of transformative justice. Transformative justice contributes to the constitution of a new world inasmuch as it is a simultaneous undoing and a building that is untethered to the settler colonial state and its criminal punishment system, responsive to the structural conditions that allowed the event(s) in question to occur, and seeks to improve social conditions and contexts in ways that are anti-colonial and anti-racist. Rather than ensnaring individuals in punishment systems that perpetuate the civil, social, and premature deaths of those detained, these practices transform and improve how we relate to one another on a daily basis, build community capacity with a view to improving overall conditions and keeping one another safe, while combatting sexual, gender, racial, colonial, ableist, sanist, speciesist, and class-based violence. In this sense, the "doing" of abolition is the everyday resistance of racist political ontologies that are manifest and produced through our reliance on the carceral and its cages.

It is on the impetus to *do* abolition that this volume is premised. By bringing together scholars and activists proposing feminist, anti-racist, anti-colonial, anti-nationalist, crip, queer, and anti-speciesist possibilities for prison abolition that this volume provides us with new directions for praxis. It takes a wide scope, covering institutions of policing, immigration detention, prisons, as well as prisoner and animal experimentation, to examine how the carceral positions itself as the indispensable arbiter of innocence, guilt, mattering, and punishment. The analyses undertaken by the authors herein unpack the conditions in which such claims are made, with the aim of undoing the supposed "certainty" of the carceral. The authors included in this volume suggest new forms of relationality, responses to harm, and practical measures that can be taken to decolonize, decarcerate, and build community capacity in the immediate. In this sense, the authors propose alternative normativities that unsettle the carceral—at once a project as emergent and unknowable as it is resistant.

In their chapter that is included in this volume, criminologists Fernando Avila and Jessica Bundy argue that "abolitionism is a continuous task and requires keeping one's feet on the ground and one's eyes on the horizon." They moreover argue that prison abolition scholarship should incorporate "the theoretical and methodological tools employed by other critical perspectives, as this "may allow this movement to produce better grounded and more specific descriptions of the realm of prisons and possibly more efficient strategies to achieve the goal of shaking the foundation of the current prison system." The incorporation and expansion of critical theory into prison abolition scholarship is precisely what this volume achieves. Divided into four sections, each part of this book situates prison abolition within larger social justice movements and fields of social justice scholarship: anti-racism, anti-colonialism, feminism, and interspecies justice. Because of the interlocking of oppressions with which all of the chapters in this book engage, several of the chapters could have been placed in more than one of these sections; these intersectional chapters bridge, for instance, anti-colonial scholarship and anti-carceral feminism, or critical race theory and critical animal studies. Many of the chapters also draw upon and contribute to other areas of social justice scholarship beyond those flagged in the section titles, such as queer, critical trans, anti-poverty, critical disability, and critical childhood studies.

We open the volume with a Foreword, "Abolition is a kite-idea," by philosopher Perry Zurn, a meditation on the kite's flight, ungovernable and merely needing a "willing wind" to skip over or usurp the state's aircraft carriers, at once ideological, material, and stubborn. Abolition attends to the archive as a warning and hope for another world, and a call to struggle in the present for affective, relational and embodied ways of being and caretaking that are as pragmatic and achievable as they are unfinished.

Zurn's Foreword is followed by Part I, a set of chapters on the topic of "Prisons and racism." Other than the complete failure of prisons to serve any of the purposes they purport to accomplish, the racism of prisons is the most widely known argument for the abolition of this institution. Governments, oversight bodies and academics have demonstrated that the criminal punishment system is racist at every level—from policing, to courts, to severity of sentences, to the security level of institutions in which individuals are placed, to conditions of probation and parole—people of color are discriminated against (Australian Bureau of Statistics, 2020; Hannah-Moffat & Struthers Montford, 2019; Harcourt, 2020; Hernandez et al., 2015; Kutateladze et al., 2014; Maynard, 2017; Nellis, 2016; Office of the Auditor General of Canada, 2017, 2017; Office of the Correctional Investigator Canada, 2020; Owusu-Bempah, 2017; Prison Reform Trust, 2020; Struthers Montford & Hannah-Moffat, 2020; Vecchio, 2018). Prisons are also racist, however, because of their role in perpetuating slavery (Davis, 2003), Jim Crow (Alexander, 2010), residential schools (Nichols, 2014), the reserve (Struthers Montford and Moore, 2018), eugenics (Guenther, 2016), and racialized ghettoes (Wacquant, 2009). The four chapters in this section of the book introduce and contribute to this critical race literature on prisons, with two chapters focusing on immigration detention centers and the experiences of immigrants vis-à-vis the police, and two chapters that consider the interlocking of racial, LGBTQ2S, ableist, and childhood oppression in the context of the carceral state.

Chapter 1, Avila and Bundy's "Prison abolitionism and critical race theory," is a useful essay for opening both the volume overall and the section on racism in particular, as it provides a brief introduction to and overview of both critical race theory and prison abolition. Avila and Bundy's chapter considers the ineffectiveness of prison abolition scholarship produced within traditional criminology relative to the inroads made by critical race theory, and urges abolitionists in criminology to ground their research in critical frameworks, and critical race theory in particular. Chapter 2, Sarah Turnbull's "Racial innocence, liberal reformism, and immigration detention: Toward a politics of abolition" extends Murakawa's (2019) work on racial innocence in the U.S. context to show how immigration in the United Kingdom at once brands itself as culturally sensitive and inclusive while at the same time targeting racialized immigrants for detention and deportation. Chapter 3, Megan Gaucher and Alexa DeGagne's "The thin blue line between protection and persecution: Policing LGBTQ2S refugees in Canada," considers recent political resistance on the part of queer and trans refugees to the inclusion of police in Pride parades across Canada, situating this resistance in histories of police harassment and brutality against racialized, queer, and trans people. Finally, Chapter 4, Erica Meiners, Liat Ben-Moshe, and Nirmala Erevelles' "Abolishing innocence: Disrupting the racist/ableist pathologies of childhood," bridges the critical race, critical disability, queer, feminist, and critical childhood studies backgrounds of the three authors to elucidate and problematize the concept of innocence as it functions within both carceral logics and abolition praxis.

Part II of the book, "Prisons and settler colonialism," is closely related to Part I, since what Robert Nichols (2014) has called the "colonialism of incarceration" is, like the racism that is indissociable from the carceral state, a tool of white supremacy. At the same time, however, as Nichols has also demonstrated, decolonial critiques of the prison make normative and abolitionist claims than are distinct from the more familiar abolitionism of anti-racism activists and scholars. Specifically, many critiques of the prison from anti-racism perspectives have focused on the "overrepresentation" of people of color in prisons, and the mass incarceration of Black people in the U.S. in particular, and have situated the prison in the history of Euro-American slavery and Jim Crow. These critiques have often highlighted the utter failure of the prison to accomplish any of the goals that it claims, such as preventing crime or making societies safer. Somewhat differently, however, from an anti-colonial perspective, any application of settler colonial law to Indigenous persons, as well as the very existence of settler colonial institutions on stolen land, are fundamentally contested due to the sovereignty of Indigenous nations. Even if prisons "worked" (which they don't), and even if prisons incarcerated and killed white people and people of color equally (which they don't), the anti-colonial critique of the prison would be unimpacted. Although based in different histories of oppression and different normative claims, the anti-colonial critique of the carceral state bolsters rather than conflicts with anti-racist versions of abolitionism that focus primarily on the hyperincarceration of Black people. That is, while the chapters in the first section of this book have reinforced Davis' assertion that, from an anti-racism perspective, prisons are indeed obsolete (Davis, 2003), the anti-colonial perspectives in the second section demonstrate that this institution, which mass-incarcerates Indigenous persons in settler colonial states, is, in fact, *doubly obsolete*.

Chapter 5, Sol Neely's "*Aan yátx'u sáani!* Decolonial meditations on building abolition," draws on the author's involvement in prison education in Juneau, Alaska, and is offered as a series of meditations on the notion of an "Indigenous cosmopolitanism." Grounded in Indigenous oral literary traditions and cosmology, Indigenous cosmopolitanism, Neely asserts, is a uniquely suited means to build abolition and respond to the inter-related imperatives to decolonize and decarcerate. Chapter 6, Lisa Guenther's "Settler colonialism, incarceration, and the abolitionist imperative: Lessons from an Australian youth detention centre," resonates strongly with Neely's chapter. Guenther examines an abusive incident involving Indigenous youth that occurred at an Australian prison, as well as the response it generated, and argues that calls for greater Indigenous participation in corrections fall short of what is actually necessary: the decolonization and abolition of prisons. Chapter 7, Danielle Bird's "Settler colonialism, anti-colonial theory, and 'Indigenized' prisons for Indigenous women," also argues forcefully against increased Indigenous involvement in prisons,

Indigenous programming, and the supposed Indigenizing of prisons as a solution to the settler colonial violence of incarceration. In particular, Bird offers a compelling critique of efforts to "Indigenize" prisons for Indigenous women in Canada, arguing that these reforms continue to construct Indigenous cultures as both the cause and solution to Indigenous women's imprisonment, thereby failing to see settler colonialism as the cause and decolonization as the solution. Finally, Chapter 8, Isabel Scheuneman Scott, Fran Chaisson, and Bobbie Kidd's "'The women that died in there, that's all I could think of': The P4W Memorial Collective and Garden initiative," consists of an interview between Isabel Scheunemann Scott, Fran Chaisson, and Bobbie Kidd regarding the latter two women's experiences at the infamous Kingston Prison for Women, and their work creating a memorial garden on the grounds of this site where numerous Indigenous women committed suicide. The interview is framed by introductory remarks and a closing discussion by Scheunemann Scott on some of the topics covered in the interview.

In addition to being central to an anti-racist and decolonial agenda, prisons are a feminist issue for a number of reasons. Indeed, it is only white, upper- and middle-class, cis, heterosexual, able-minded/bodied women who have ever been unaware that prisons are a feminist issue, since women in this category have been largely immune to the criminalization and incarceration of themselves and their loved ones. For feminists who experience racial, classist, transphobic, homophobic, ableist, and saneist oppression at the hands of law enforcement and the carceral state, prisons have always been a social justice issue (INCITE!, 2006). Prisons are also a feminist issue because they are sites of extreme gender oppression and ubiquitous sexual violence, which they reinforce and perpetuate both within and beyond their barbed wire and walls (Arkles, 2014, 2015; Lydon, 2016; Kunzel, 2010; Backhouse, 2012). Finally, prisons are a feminist issue because white feminists have been complicit and sometimes instrumental in the justification for and expansion of the institution, with feminist anti-violence movements being continually co-opted by the carceral state (Gottshalk, 2006; Bumiller, 2008; Bernstein, 2007, 2010, 2012). As such, feminists have a responsibility to address the issue of incarceration, and to resist the co-optation of feminist causes. Part III of the book, "Anti-carceral feminisms," includes four chapters by feminist scholars that critique prisons and carceral feminism, and contribute to the feminist literature on penal abolition.

While prison abolitionists frequently set aside cases of violent offences, focusing instead on decarcerating those convicted of non-violent crimes, murder and rape are the two crimes most frequently invoked to suggest the impossibility of prison abolition, and are hence crimes that prison abolitionists must address in order to be convincing. Appropriately, then, these are the offenses on which the first three chapters in the "Anti-carceral feminisms" section of the volume focuses. In Chapter 9, "Starting with life: Murder sentencing and feminist prison abolitionist praxis," Debra Parkes attends to which women are convicted of murder, and the colonial and patriarchal contexts in which these offenses occur, to make a persuasive case for an anti-carceral feminism that begins with the most serious crimes. Chapter 10, Dawn Moore and Vared Ben-David's "Looking from northwest to southeast: Feminist carceralism, gender equality and global responses to gender-based violence," presents the failure of incarceration to address global problems of sexual and domestic violence, and explores non-carceral and survivor-centric responses to gender-based violence through a transnational feminist lens. The remaining two chapters in this part of the book mobilize the work of particular feminist theorists to prison abolitionist ends. In Chapter 11, Jennifer Kilty and Katarina Bogosavljevic take up the somewhat neglected scholarship of early feminist critical criminologist Carol Smart to renew critiques of carceral feminism in the age of #metoo, and explore non-carceral, community-based responses to violence as alternative praxis for penal abolitionist feminism. In Chapter 12, "Carceral enjoyments and killjoying the social life of social death," Andrew Dilts applies feminist theorist Sara Ahmed's notion of the feminist killjoy to advocate for an anti-carceral feminism that kills the (white) joys of carceral feminism and carceral society generally. While scholars have focused on the civil and social death drive of prisons, Dilts argues that we need to not only attend to what prisons foreclose, but also to what they produce: parasitic life resulting from the carceral's making of race as it coalesces around the figure of the slave/convict. This parasitic life is a carceral enjoyment that upholds white supremacy, settler colonialism, anti-Black social orders, civil liberties, and private property relations.

Finally, Part IV of the book, "Multispecies carceralities," includes four chapters that contribute to the growing literature at the intersections of critical prison studies and critical animal studies. Prisons, as this section of the book demonstrates, are a critical animal studies issue for a number of reasons. First, white animal activists, like white feminists, have regularly sought carceral solutions to the oppressions against which they struggle, demanding greater law enforcement and more frequent prison sentences for individuals who abuse animals. As in the case of white feminism, the investment of white animal activism in the carceral state has disproportionately harmed people of color, and white animal activism has been most "successful" when mobilizing cases of animal abuse that reinforce racial stigma. Second, prisons are a critical animal studies issue because the carceral state has deployed animals in its ongoing racial warfare, most notably in the weaponization of canines against people of color. Third, prisons are a critical animal studies issue because animals are themselves frequently incarcerated (Gruen, 2014; Morin, 2018; Guenther K., 2020), and the oppression of caging is so deeply linked to animals that incarceration is commonly critiqued as dehumanizing. Finally, prisons are a critical animal studies issue because human-animal relations do not end at the prison gates. On the contrary, people in prisons interact with animals in many ways. To name only a few, prisoners are guarded by dogs as well as humans; prisoners historically and today have been exploitatively employed in animal agriculture and animal slaughter (Struthers Montford, 2019); other forms of animal oppression, such as rodeos, also exist within prison walls (Gillespie, 2018); and prisoners have few choices but to eat animals within prisons (Struthers Montford, 2016). Arguably more positively, prisoners are involved in animal rehabilitation programs (Furst, 2006); and prisoners interact with so-called pest animals who cohabitate with them inside prisons (Moran, 2015). Indeed, in conditions of solitary confinement, these animals may be the only companions that prisoners have.

Chapter 13, Kelly Struthers Montford and Eve Kasprzycka's "Carceral enjoyments of animal protection," builds on Dilts' argument in the previous chapter to show that the animal protection movement's ongoing carceral appetite, most recently evident in the passing of federal felony laws for animal cruelty, is antithetical to the social justice advocacy the movement is premised upon and will fail to improve the lives of non-human animals. Chapter 14, Paula Cepeda Gallo and Chloë Taylor's "Carceral canines: Racial terror and animal abuse from slave hounds to police dogs," traces the brutal history of canines being deployed to control and incarcerate racialized human beings, as well as the contemporary usage of misleading representations of police dogs and puppies to rehabilitate the stained reputation of the police. Chapter 15, Lauren Corman's "Trauma as a Möbius strip: PTSD, animal research, and the Oak Ridge prisoner experiments," draws on the theoretical frameworks of "taxonomies of power" (Kim, 2015), "zones of exception" (Agamben, 2005), and "black spaces" (Wadiwel, 2017) to examine human and animal experimentation in contexts of incarceration, and concludes with reflections on structural and postcolonial trauma. In the final chapter of the volume, "Coexistence as resistance: Human and nonhuman animals in carceral settings," Calvin Smiley considers fictional as well as real life accounts of positive relationships that incarcerated humans have with animals in prison settings, and how these interactions with animals constitute a form of resistance to the social death of incarceration.

The book closes with an Afterword by Justin Piché, "Building abolition in pandemic times." Here, Piché reorients our attention to the "pandemics of inequality" predating and shaping COVID-19, the carceral responses levied in an attempt to control its spread, and the ongoing racialized violence enacted against Indigenous, Black, and other marginalized persons at the hands of the state through its various institutions. While brutal and suppressive, this moment is also an invitation, Piché argues, that brings into sharp focus the requirements and urgency to abolish the harmful structures that we internalize and that are externally imposed. Deeply personal and inescapably structural, to abolish is to build, actions as inextricably linked as they are liberatory.

References

African-Canadian Civic Engagement Council, & INNOVATIVE. (2020). *The impact of COVID-19 on Black Canadians*. Innovative Research Group. https://innovativeresearch.ca/the-impact-of-covid-19-on-black-canadians/

Agamben, G. (2005). *State of exception*. (K. Attell, Trans.) University of Chicago Press.

Alexander, M. (2010). *The new Jim Crow: Mass incarceration in the age of color blindness*. The New Press.

American Civil Liberties Union. (2020). *The other epidemic: Fatal police shootings in the time of COVID-19*. ACLU. www.aclu.org/report/other-epidemic-fatal-police-shootings-time-covid-19

Arkles, G. (2014). PREA litigation and the perpetuation of sexual harm. In *Journal of Legislation and Public Policy*, *17*, 801–34.

Arkles, G. (2015). Regulating prison sexual violence. *Northeastern University Law Journal*, *7*(1), 71–130.

Australian Bureau of Statistics. (2020, September 17). *Corrective services, Australia, June quarter 2020*. www.abs.gov.au/statistics/people/crime-and-justice/corrective-services-australia/latest-release

Backhouse, C. (2012). A feminist remedy for sexual assault: A quest for answers. In Elizabeth A. Sheehy (Ed.), *Sexual assault in Canada: Law, legal practice, and women's activism* (pp. 725–40). University of Ottawa Press.

Bernstein, E. (2007). The sexual politics of the "new abolitionism." *differences*, *18*(3), 128–51.

Bernstein, E. (2010). Militarized humanitarianism meets carceral feminism: The politics of sex, rights, and freedom in contemporary antitrafficking campaigns," in *Signs*, *36*(1), 45–71.

Bernstein, E. (2012). Carceral politics as gender justice? The "traffic in women" and neoliberal circuits of crime, sex, and rights. *Theory and Society*, *41*(3), 233–259.

Black Lives Matter. (2020). *News*. Black Lives Matter. https://blacklivesmatter.com/news/

Bumiller, K. (2008). *In an abusive state: How neoliberalism appropriated the feminist movement against sexual violence*. Duke University Press.

Coleman, A.R. (2020, June 5). Black bodies are still treated as expendable. Vox. www.vox.com/2020/6/5/21277938/ahmaud-arbery-george-floyd-breonna-taylor-covid

Criminalization and Punishment Education. (2020, April 19). Imprisoning the pandemic: COVID Cases in CDN Prisons. CP-EP. https://cp-ep.org/imprisoning-the-pandemic-confirmed-covid-19-cases-in-canadian-prisons/

Curtice, K. & Choo, E. (2020). Indigenous populations: Left behind in the COVID-19 response. *The Lancet*, *395*(10239), 1753. https://doi.org/10.1016/S0140-6736(20)31242-3

Davis, A. (2003). *Are prisons obsolete?* Seven Stories Press.

Flanagan, R. (2020, June 19). What we know about the last 100 people shot and killed by police in Canada. CTV News. www.ctvnews.ca/canada/what-we-know-about-the-last-100-people-shot-and-killed-by-police-in-canada-1.4989794

Furst, G. (2006). Prison-based animal programs: A national survey. *The Prison Journal*, *86*(4), 407–30.

Gillespie, K. (2018). Placing Angola: Racialisation, anthropocentrism, and settler colonialism at the Louisiana State Penitentiary's Angola Rodeo. *Antipode*, *50*(5), 1267–89.

Gilmore, R.W. (2007). *Golden gulag: Prisons, surplus, crisis, and opposition in globalizing California*. University of California Press.

Gottschalk, M. (2006). *The prison and the gallows: The politics of mass incarceration in America*. Cambridge University Press.

Gruen, L. (2014). *The ethics of captivity*. Oxford University Press.

Guenther, K. (2020). *The lives and deaths of shelter animals*. Stanford University Press.

Guenther, L. 2016. Life Behind Bars, in H. Sharp and C. Taylor, eds., *Feminist philosophies of life*. McGill-Queens University Press: 217–38.

Hannah-Moffat, K. & Struthers Montford, K. (2019). Unpacking sentencing algorithms: Risk, racial accountability and data harms. In J.W. de Keijser, J.V. Roberts, & J. Ryberg (Eds.), *Predictive sentencing: Normative and empirical perspectives* (pp. 175–98). Bloomsbury Publishing.

Harcourt, B.E. (2020). Risk as a proxy for race. University of Chicago Public Law & Legal Theory Working Paper No. 323. University of Chicago: Chicago Unbound.

Hernandez, K.L., Muhammad, K.G., & Ann Thompson, H. (2015). Introduction: Constructing the carceral state. *Journal of American History, 102*(1), 18–24. https://doi.org/10.1093/jahist/jav259

INCITE! Women of Color Against Violence. (2006). *The color of violence: The INCITE! anthology.* South End.

Kim, C. J. (2015). *Dangerous crossings: Race, species, and nature in a multicultural age.* Cambridge University Press.

Kim, C.J. (2018). Abolition. In L. Gruen (Ed.), *Critical terms for animal studies* (pp. 15–32). University of Chicago Press.

Kunzel, R. (2010). Rape, race, and the violent prison. In *Criminal Intimacy: Prison and the Uneven History of Modern American Sexuality* (pp. 149–89). University of Chicago Press.

Kutateladze, B., Tymas, W., & Crowley, M. (2014). *Race and prosecution in Manhattan.* Vera Institute. www.vera.org/downloads/Publications/race-and-prosecution-in-manhattan/legacy_downloads/race-and-prosecution-manhattan-summary.pdf

Lydon, J. (2016). "Once there was no prison rape": Ending sexual violence as strategy for prison abolitionism. *philoSOPHIA: A Journal of Continental Feminism,* Spring: 61–71.

Maynard, R. (2017). *Policing Black lives: State violence in Canada from slavery to the present.* Fernwood Publishing.

Mills, S. (2020, August 12). *Carleton criminology department cuts ties with police, prisons.* CBC. www.cbc.ca/news/canada/ottawa/carleton-criminology-police-ottawa-1.5683717

Moran, D. (2015). Budgie smuggling or doing bird? Human-animal interactions in carceral space: Prison(er) animals as abject and subject. *Social & Cultural Geography, 16*(6), 634–53.

Morin, K. (2018). *Carceral space, prisoners and animals.* Routledge.

Murakawa, N. (2019). Racial innocence: Law, social science, and the unknowing of racism in the US carceral state. *Annual Review of Law and Social Science, 15*(1), 473–93.

Nellis, A. (2016, June 14). *The color of justice: Racial and ethnic disparity in state prisons.* The Sentencing Project. www.sentencingproject.org/publications/color-of-justice-racial-and-ethnic-disparity-in-state-prisons/

Nichols, R. 2014. The colonialism of incarceration. *Radical Philosophy Review, 17*(2), 435–55.

Office of the Auditor General of Canada. (2017). *Report 5—Preparing women offenders for release—Correctional Service Canada.* [Independent Auditor's Report]. www.oag-bvg.gc.ca/internet/English/parl_oag_201711_05_e_42670.html

Office of the Correctional Investigator Canada. (2020, January 21). Indigenous People in Federal Custody Surpasses 30%. www.oci-bec.gc.ca/cnt/comm/press/press20200121-eng.aspx

Osmok, P. (2020, August 19). The post-pandemic future: We will drastically reduce the number of people in Ontario jails—and prevent more crimes in the process. Toronto Life. https://torontolife.com/city/the-post-pandemic-future-we-will-drastically-reduce-the-number-of-people-in-ontario-jails-and-prevent-more-crimes-in-the-process/

Owusu-Bempah, A. (2017). Race and policing in historical context: Dehumanization and the policing of Black people in the 21st century. *Theoretical Criminology, 21*(1), 23–4.

Prison Reform Trust. (2020). Race. Prison Reform Trust. www.prisonreformtrust.org.uk/WhatWeDo/Projectsresearch/Race

Sexton, J. (2010). People-of-color-blindness: Notes on the afterlife of slavery. *Social Text, 28*(2 103), 31–56. https://doi.org/10.1215/01642472-2009-066

Struthers Montford, K. (2016). Dehumanized denizens, displayed animals: Prison tourism and the discourse of the zoo. *PhiloSOPHIA, 6*(1), 73–91.

Struthers Montford, K. (2019). Land, agriculture, and the carceral: The territorializing function of penitentiary farms. *Radical Philosophy Review, 22*(1), 113–41.

Struthers Montford, K. & Hannah-Moffat, K. (2020). The veneers of empiricism: Gender, race and prison classification. *Aggression and Violent Behavior*, 101475. https://doi.org/10.1016/j.avb.2020.101475

Struthers Montford, K. & Moore, D. (2018). The prison as reserve: Governmentality, phenomenology, and "indigenizing" the prison (studies). *New Criminal Law Review, 21*(4): 640–63.

Van Beusekom, M. (2020, July 9). US prison inmates among those hit hard with COVID-19. University of Minnesota Center for Infectious Disease Research and Policy. www.cidrap.umn.edu/news-perspective/2020/07/us-prison-inmates-among-those-hit-hard-covid-19

Vecchio, K. (2018). *A call to action: Reconciliation with Indigenous women in the federal justice and correctional systems: Report of the Standing Committee on the Status of Women* [42nd Parliament, 1st Session]. Standing Committee on the Status of Women.

Wacquant, L. (2009). *Punishing the poor: The neoliberal government of social insecurity*. Duke University Press.

Wadiwel, D. (2017). Disability and torture: Exception, epistemology and "Black sites". *Continuum, 31*(3), 388–99.

Whistle, W. (2020, June 3). Schools Cut Ties with Police Departments After Recent Killings. Forbes. www.forbes.com/sites/wesleywhistle/2020/06/03/schools-cut-ties-with-police-departments-after-recent-killings/

Williams, T., Weiser, B., & Rashbaum, W.K. (2020, May 20). "Jails are petri dishes": Inmates freed as the virus spreads behind bars. *The New York Times*. www.nytimes.com/2020/03/30/us/coronavirus-prisons-jails.html

Part I
Prisons and racism

1 Prison abolitionism and critical race theory

Fernando Avila and Jessica Bundy

Critical race theory and prison abolitionism are both academic and activist movements, and both share a critical attitude towards the dominant power relations and social structures that created, and have since legitimized, existing social inequalities in which colonialism and anti-Black racism are foundational. With critical race theory focusing on the relationships between racial power and legal systems, and prison abolitionism focusing on the elimination of the ultimate mechanism of punishment, both aim to achieve social change by dismantling the sophisticated and deeply embedded discourses and practices that justify, support, and re-create these realities. While critical race theory has made various incursions into academia and politics, prison abolitionism has largely remained in a marginal position and has been widely characterized as idealistic, naïve, or too radical to ever achieve its goal.

In this chapter, we describe how the lack of an analysis of grounded systems of oppression within the theoretical framework of prison abolitionism as used in the academic field of criminology at a global level, is a fault that should be addressed in order to advance the deconstruction of the features that define the ubiquity of punishment institutions in different societies. By examining the intersection between critical race theory and prison abolitionism in the United States, we aim to show how prison abolition can expand its discourse beyond traditional audiences and can ask more grounded and critical questions of the current prison system. To do so, abolitionism should be understood from the perspective of specific systems of oppression. We argue that critical perspectives such as critical race theory could provide the contextualized and situated sociohistorical analyses of the carceral power that a solid abolition stance requires to move beyond its marginal position.

Since critical race theory is a U.S.-based theory that has mainly explored the experiences of Black peoples and the literature on U.S. prisons that has followed suit, much of this paper will focus on the Black/white dichotomy in the United States. We acknowledge, nonetheless, that critical race theory has also been adopted by Indigenous scholars, Latinx scholars, and many other minority groups in Canada and the U.S. We further acknowledge that the incarceration rates for minority groups in North America are also disproportionate. Moreover, critical race theory has contributed valuable knowledge about these groups in the prison system (Aylward, 1999; Latty et al., 2016). Nonetheless, while there is an unequivocal relationship between the carceral state, settler colonialism, racism, patriarchy, and white supremacy in the U.S., this chapter focuses mainly on how exposing the pervasiveness of racism has enabled a better understanding of the concrete function of prisons in U.S. society, and has thus provided more solid grounds for the abolitionist cause and brought increased attention to abolitionism in major periodicals, academic conferences and social organizations (Coyle & Schept, 2018, p. 320). Though much remains to be done to advance prison abolitionism in the U.S., the use of critical race theory—which is focused on how law is integral to white supremacy—is required for this movement. Finally, abolitionism is a polysemic term and a heterogeneous movement both in its academic and activist expressions. Multiple ends, discourses, and methods coexist under the abolitionist umbrella. In this chapter we will mainly consider the classical European tradition of prison abolitionism within the academic field of criminology.

Critical race theory

In discussing the current and potential relationship between critical race theory and the prison abolition movement, it is first essential to detail the nature of critical race theory as well as its origins in critical studies and law. We can trace critical race theory to critical legal studies, a critical theory that challenged the objectivity of law and tenets of legal liberalism. Scholars of color were attracted to critical legal studies as it challenged the laws that oppressed persons of color. Racial oppression, however, was not central to critical legal studies work. For example, it was not until the tenth national critical legal studies conference in the 1980s, that a group of scholars of color presented papers on racism and the law. Alienated from existing legal discourse, specifically critical legal studies, these scholars left the conference and went on to conceive critical race theory (Aylward, 1999). As one of the founders of this field, Richard Delgado, stated: "Critical legal studies has not paid much attention to minorities, not placing racial questions on its agenda until this year, ten years after its formation as a legal movement" (Aylward, 1999, p. 27). Other foundational critical race theory scholars include Derrick Bell, Mari Matsuda, Kimberlé Crenshaw, Charles Lawerence, and Patricia Williams. Despite these scholars' criticisms of critical legal studies, critical race theory draws on aspects of critical legal studies, including its intense scrutiny of the criminal justice system and hidden relations of power (Giwa et al., 2014).

Critical race theory examines notions of race, law, and power within society (Delgado & Stefancic, 2001). It further challenges liberal concepts such as objectivity and neutrality as they further conceal and obscure power relations that oppress people of color. In practice, critical race theory broadly addresses issues of race through a critical lens, posing questions about the persistence of race and racism and about race-based oppression in modern "liberal democracies" such as Canada, the United States, and Australia (Williams, 2013; Giwa et al., 2014; James, 1998; Razack, Smith, & Thobani, 2010; Tator & Henry, 2006). Critical race theorists argue that racism is "ordinary" as it "remains hidden beneath a veneer of normality" (Giwa et al., 2014, 278) and that this racism is a daily experience for people of color.

While there are no set core tenets of critical race theory, those most authoritative within the field have identified a similar set of characteristics and components (Bell, 1992; Crenshaw et al., 1995; Delgado & Stefancic, 1998, 2001; Solórzano & Yosso, 2002). One key tenet is that "race" itself is a social construct created, perpetuated, and enforced by humans based on history, location, and social contexts (Omi & Winant, 2005, 2015; Markus, 2008). How we understand race and racialization is not inevitable but the result of various categorizations that over time have been largely accepted as objective: "racial categories and the meaning of race are given concrete expression by the specific social relations and historical context in which they are embedded" (Omi & Winant, 2015, p. 11). Critical race theory takes "Whiteness" to be a socially constructed identity, often based on skin color, that represents the "normal" or "everyday" standard (Gillborn, 2015; Saleh-Hanna, 2017). White supremacy is not simply manifest in explicitly tangible or sensational events—such as the use of racial slurs or race-based physical assaults—but entails "the operation of much more subtle and extensive forces that saturate the everyday mundane actions and policies that shape the world in the interests of White people" (Gillborn, 2015, p. 278). White supremacy operates under the "faulty and violent premises" (Saleh-Hanna, 2017, p. 420) that there are inferior people, that these groups of inferior people can be identified through shared characteristics and histories that are different from and not shared with the "superior" group, and that these groups or inferior categories of people are a threat to civilization; which we know is characterized by the normalcy of Whiteness. While we can clearly identify white supremacy in the actions of the Ku Klux Klan, critical race theory points to the less obvious, semi-concealed prioritization of the interests of white people, often at the cost of those not in power and people of color. Closely related, critical race theory uses the notion of "interest convergence" (Bell, 1980) to describe the perplexing fact that the advancement of civil rights of Black people and some of the legal reforms aimed at reducing racial inequality were only possible because these reforms actually advance the interests of white elites. This idea was conceptualized by Bell (1980), who argued that it was actually the convergence of Black and white interests that made possible the renowned U.S. Supreme Court decision *Brown v. Board of Education* that ruled racial segregation in public schools unconstitutional in 1954.

White supremacy permeates practices, policies, ideologies, and values not only explicitly but also in a veiled and seemingly non-racialized manner through coded language and terminology (Satzewich & Liodakis, 2013). While it is a social construct, "race" has concrete effects on people's lives through racism both in overt and unintended ways. Importantly, "race" is habitually used without any critical thought (Omi & Winant, 2005; Hylton, 2012; Williams, Priest, & Anderson, 2016; Markus, 2008), and when uncritically invoked, "race" works to "differentiate, (dis)advantage, and (dis)empower" (Hylton, 2012, p. 36). Race and racism are embedded in all aspects of society. These systems are complex, flexible, subtle, and they manifest differently based on the context. In a society where "race," especially "neutral" norms of Whiteness and the maintenance of white supremacy, shape laws and policies, this in turn influences most aspects of life—positively for some, negatively for others—including employment opportunities, housing, educational access, and involvement with the penal system. Within the discussion around prisons, we can see the manifestation of racism in the mass incarceration of Black persons, Indigenous persons, and other minority groups.

Though race is foundational to critical race theory analysis, there are critical race scholars who also explore how other dimensions and axes of oppression shape racial inequities. The term "intersectionality" was first coined by Kimberlé Crenshaw (1991), another founder of critical race theory, though the notion itself can be linked to Black feminist politics of the 1960s and 1970s. Nevertheless, this connection is often overlooked (Collins, 2012). Intersectionality analyzes the connections between the shared experiences amongst those marginalized on the basis of race, gender, sexual orientation, socioeconomic status, ability, and other axes of oppression.

Critical race theory advocates for the voice of marginalized individuals and recognizes "that stories or discourses have been a privilege of those historically influential in knowledge generation and research. Counter-stories, however, can present views rarely evidenced in social research" (Hylton, 2012, p. 27). As Parker and Lynn argue, critical race theory aims to "present storytelling and narrative as valid approaches through which to examine race and racism in the law and society" (2002, p. 10). To counter dominant narratives that distort and silence the experiences of people of color, critical race theory often uses storytelling (Solórzano & Yosso, 2002). Storytelling, while at times viewed as a less valid form of data or research, is a profoundly political act as "there is much at stake in how stories are told, by whom, and whether and how they historicize, contextualize, and explain equity and existing social relation" (Razack, Smith, & Thobani, 2010, p. 43). Through the lens of critical race theory, the stories of marginalized groups contribute to the grand narrative and begin to counter the dominant narrative. Additionally, critical race theory "embraces the realization that knowledge comes from thinking and feeling bodies, from bodies that are raced, gendered, and sexualized among other subjectivities, from bodies that are located in hierarchical relations and places of difference" (Baszile, 2014, p. 239). Critical race theory argues that some will always have a positivist view of 'legitimate' or neutral knowledge; however, it does not claim to be neutral but rather puts the voices of racialized people at the center of its agenda.

Prison abolitionism meets critical race theory: Situating punishment

The number of people held in penal institutions worldwide continues to increase. In 2018, there were more than 10.7 million people under custody (Walmsley, 2018). This increasing trend[1]—and the observed proliferation of broader carceral controls[2]—have triggered profuse and global scholarly work around concepts such as the *penal state* and *the carceral state* (Rubin & Phelps, 2017). Prisons persist and propagate despite being supported by ambiguous, unsubstantiated, and contested justifications (deterrence, rehabilitation, incapacitation, and retribution), and entail illegal conditions and detrimental outcomes such as human rights violations, violence, abuse, suicides, and recidivism (Bottoms, 1999; Inter-American Commission on Human Rights, 2011; Cullen, Jonson, & Nagin 2011; Scott, 2013; Darke & Karam, 2016; Woods, 2016; Fazel, Ramesh, & Hawton 2017).

Figures and deficits can fluctuate over space and time, but since their inception as institutions of modern punishment, prisons have been subject to constant debates and movements for their reform. Far from the explicit goals used to openly justify their existence, prisons in reality succeed at inflicting pain and reproducing violence. When faced with this truth, liberal prison reformers advocate for the improvement of prison conditions, for reforming operations and built environments, or even for reducing the use of prison. This perspective is primarily based on an understanding of prisons as an unavoidable reality with a social function in the criminal justice system. However, what if prisons are adequately fulfilling a different set of functions? In fact, their survival despite their supposed failure may be due to the fact that the carceral system is deeply rooted and actually has a different set of precise functions, and their supposed failure is part of their functioning (Foucault, 1977, p. 271). Many scholars have linked the origin of prisons with the need to control and manage undesirable or surplus populations (Rusche & Kirchheimer, 1939; Rothman, 1971; Foucault, 1977; Ignatieff, 1978; Melossi & Pavarini, 1981).

An alternative response towards this same grim reality is provided by prison abolitionism, a movement that was sparked by Mathiesen's *The Politics of Abolition* (1974). Rooted in a broader understanding of crime and punishment as socially constructed concepts (Christie, 1977; Hulsman, 1986), prison abolitionism contests liberal reforms because of their role in the consolidation of the ideological foundations of punishment and in legitimizing prisons as a social response to human conflicts. Although it should be noted that abolitionists recognize that some reforms are needed to improve conditions of imprisonment in the short term, they claim that those reforms should be *negative* or *non-reformist reforms,* and should be in line with a broader and longterm abolition strategy (Mathiesen, 1974). Abolitionists assert that prisons are a fiasco in terms of their purpose and that it is irrational to rely on them, since none of the existing theories that justify prisons as a response to crime have solid grounds or evidence of success: prisons do not rehabilitate offenders, they do not create safer communities, and they fail at deterring future criminal behaviors (Mathiesen, 2006).

But prisons—and the carceral system in general—are more complex than just globally well-established institutions of punishment and control. In addition to carceral expansion and the increasing number of prisoners around the world, we cannot overlook the characteristics shared by those who are criminalized and incarcerated. Specifically, prisons in "liberal democracies" and in settler colonial societies have a disproportionate number of poor, Black, Indigenous, racialized, migrant, foreign national, and asylum-seeking individuals (Pager, 2008; Phillips, 2012; Scott, 2013; Nichols, 2014; Cunneen & Tauri, 2016; Earle, 2016; Baldry, Carlton, & Cunneen, 2015). To better understand the persistence and ubiquity of prisons, we need to develop granular explorations of the carceral power within specific sociohistorical contexts. In the U.S., critical race theory has provided prison abolitionism with that valuable analytical dimension: when the critical perspectives of critical race theory and prison abolitionism intersect, the associations among racism, capitalism, white supremacy, settler colonialism, and state-organized violence via the criminal justice system are starkly revealed.

Possibly the most studied and astonishing case of prison expansion and overrepresentation of Black people in the prison population is the United States (Alexander 2010; Tonry 2011). One report showed that African Americans are 5.1 times more likely to be sent to prison than white people (Nellis, 2016). The mass incarceration of Black people in U.S. prisons evidences one of the essential claims of critical race theorists: that racism is profoundly embedded in society. It is so deeply embedded that even though on paper the criminal justice system is designed to preserve equality and fairness in its procedures and outcomes and is "color-neutral," racism and discrimination filter through each stage of the process, directly (conscious decisions) and indirectly (through proxies for race), accumulating the sediments of racism and ultimately packing prisons up with racialized people. Even the use of algorithms and artificial intelligence as objective and neutral tools in policing and sentencing has been proven to capture and reproduce biases through seemingly innocuous proxies, and to deepen the racial disparities (Ferguson, 2017; Angwin et al., 2016). Further, these racial disparities must be analyzed as the result of the continuous pipeline that starts well before imprisonment. Black communities—mainly Black youth—are strongly affected by racialized and cumulative disparities at every level of the criminal legal system, from over-policing in the community to more severe sentencing at trial (Davis, 2017).

Michelle Alexander, one of the leading scholars who describes the racial dimensions of U.S. mass incarceration, explains this is a clear continuum of the Jim Crow laws that legalized racial segregation. According to Alexander, the "proponents of racial hierarchy found they could install a new racial caste system without violating the law or the new limits of acceptable political discourse, by demanding 'law and order' rather than 'segregation forever'" (2010,

40). Scholars have documented how this demand for law and order was promptly fueled by the criminal justice system through the *war on drugs*. Although this campaign was publicized as seemingly fair, racially neutral, and equal, it in fact led to an exponential increase in the number of people behind bars and a disproportionate targeting of Blacks and Latinx people (Tonry & Melewski, 2008; Alexander, 2010; Tonry, 2011; Provine, 2011). From a critical race theory perspective, Alexander argues that the racial caste system in the U.S. was actually never dismantled, and therefore there is no such thing as a post-racial state in which there is no racism or racial discrimination; the racial caste system was simply redesigned and repackaged in the new form of the penal system. This new configuration of the same old story was made possible through the creation and enforcement of color-neutral laws that functioned as social makeup, banning the explicit use of race as a formal way of discrimination but leaving untouched the insidious social organization that continues racial discrimination, segregation, and ultimately the imprisonment of people of color.

The intersection between prison abolitionism and critical race theory provides the former with a vital analytical category that was "generally absent in the leading contemporary abolitionist texts" (Davis, 2007, p. 365). This has since been pointed out and developed further by multiple scholars, such as Angela Davis, Michelle Alexander, and Ruth Gilmore Wilson. The absence of a racial and class domination perspective at the onset of abolitionism may be explained by its primarily white European origins. In fact, several years after *The Politics of Abolition* (1974), Mathiesen recognized that it was possible to see more clearly that prisons were part of the state's apparatus for political repression, integrated into the political system, than at the time he wrote the book (Mathiesen, 1986, p. 84). While scholars who study the prison industrial complex in the U.S. have increasingly tried to address and reduce the gap described by Davis and others, it remains largely true that dominant threads of criminology require sustained analyses of the ultimate punishment institution attentive to racial oppression and grounded in the concrete experiences of racial, ethnic, gender, and class discrimination. There is room for further inclusion of critical race theory within the prison abolition movement within the U.S., and for aspects of critical race theory to be used to further prison abolition globally. As scholars have noted, in order to advance the realization of prison (and penal) abolition, the continuity of white supremacy, colonialism, slavery, and racial capitalism must not be overlooked (Davis, 2005; Saleh-Hanna, 2015; Coyle, 2018).

The absence of an analysis of grounded systems of oppression within the theoretical framework of prison abolitionism is a weakness that resonates at a global level. The realities in Africa or Latin America are different from those in the Global North, which continue to have a hegemonic role in the production of knowledge. In the case of Latin America, scholars have linked the marginal or null presence of prison abolitionism in the region mostly to the lack of a situated dimension that takes into consideration the political, social, and historical conditions of the region including the colonial legacy, the structural social inequality, the genocide of Indigenous people, the impact of neoliberal policies, the specificities of the punitive institutions, the dictatorships, and the prevalence of informal state violence. In fact, Latin America is one of the most unequal regions in the world where poverty rates in the overall population are about 30% and are 23% higher among Indigenous persons[3]. It is also one of the regions with the most significant increase in the prison population, and continuous violations of prisoners' human rights over the last decades. Local academic scholarship on prison abolitionism in the region, nevertheless, is mostly limited to an acritical importation and reproduction of the core tenets of the classic European litera-ture. As a result of this reproduction, a grounded theoretical framework built from a conscious recognition of the colonial roots of the punishment institutions and the overwhelming social inequity that characterizes the region has yet to be developed (García Méndez, 1986; Postay, 2012; Avila, 2012).

From a prison abolitionist perspective, the mass incarceration of Black people in the U.S. is the most compelling proof that prisons are "useful" tools for maintaining and reproducing social order through the segregation and dis-posal of the "unwanted" population; in other words, surplus, powerless, and disadvantaged minorities. However, a word of caution is necessary. Even though powerful for advancing prison abolitionism and exposing how racial inequality and inequity are mirrored from the current image of society, most criticisms of the prison industrial complex in the U.S. have "largely focused on the racist and capitalistic uses of criminalization and incarceration, rather than on crim-inalization and incarceration as such" (Carrier, Piché, & Walby, 2019, p. 328). Hence, a limited understanding of the relationship between racism and prison that focuses only on who ends up in prison and why may in fact fuel narrow reformist agendas. Mass incarceration of certain social groups in the prison population displays vividly how punishment and social control are inextricably linked, but focusing on overrepresentation in itself is insufficient to deconstruct the prison as a means to handle specific social conflicts (Nichols, 2014). Ruth Wilson Gilmore (2017) cautions how some narratives that focus on *degrees of innocence* may help to consolidate as a hard fact that some people should be sent to *cages*. She states, in fact, that the slavery–imprisonment continuum only explains part of the mass incarceration phenomenon.

Abolitionism is a continuous task, a perpetual movement towards the *unfin-ished* (Mathiesen, 1974). This perpetual movement depends on two analytical dimensions: one that relies on the classic tenets of prison abolitionism and questions punishment in itself, the other that relies on situated and granular knowledge of experiences of oppression. Ruggiero suggests (2014) that in this continuous quest abolitionism should take advantage of negative reforms, in other words, short-term reforms that contribute to the erosion of the penal order. Incorporating the multiple dimensions and axes of oppression within the abolitionist program creates fertile ground for developing short-term strategies for negative reforms. In this regard, the methodological and theoretical tools developed by other critical perspectives may also be relevant. Intersectionality and storytelling as used by critical race theory have a valuable role to play in the prison abolition movement: prisoners are not a homogenous group, their experiences are shaped by multiple identities, and their voices tend to be silenced or mediated in such a way that their experiences are blurred. Abolition of segregation, detention, or imprisonment for certain disadvantaged groups, such as Indigenous people, is a more feasible objective than abolition of prisons as an institution in the short term, and may contribute to eroding the use of prisons as a natural response for certain social conflicts. In fact, a number of scholars have challenged the use of punitive frameworks on specific disadvantaged groups, including the abolition of immigration detention (Garcia Hernandez, 2017), of juvenile prisons (Bernstein, 2015), or the suggestion to start with women's imprisonment as a first feasible step in moving prison abolitionism forward (Carlen, 1990).

Conclusion

Prison abolitionism as a radical movement and theoretical perspective has been historically criticized as impracticable, utopic, and somehow naïve. In fact, fairly little has been achieved or developed since the onset of the classic European prison abolitionism, and its academic and political influence has mostly been peripheral. We have shown how the firm and widely documented link between United States prisons and racial discrimination is an example of how the prison abolition cause can be expanded and deepened when the analysis incorporates concrete and situated historical social and political dimensions. From a critical race theory perspective, which posits race as central to the existence, creation, and enforcement of social and political structures and policies, prisons are another mechanism for racial discrimination and inequality. The connection between critical race theory and the prison abolition movement in the U.S. stresses the importance of localized and situated knowledge that would be beneficial to prison abolition in other contexts. Punishment and social control are, after all, *localized* instruments and *situated* experiences.

Prison abolition—and penal abolitionism broadly—require creativity and deconstructing certain naturalized or engrained concepts that distract us from considering deeper social structures; it is a fact that we (as a society) take prisons for granted (Davis, 2003). Mathiesen described the abolitionist stance as an attitude of saying "no" (2008). Nonetheless, abolitionism goes beyond the elimination of the unjust and unwanted: it must aim at deep structural change that entails dismantling systems of subjugation (Fernandez, 2019) and the creation of more just and ethical communities. A solid abolitionist stance, therefore, also requires granular and situated knowledge of lived experiences and of the concrete systems of oppression at specific historical moments and at specific geographical locations.

In order to move forward and break from this apparent passivity and ideological inertia, the traditional white Euro-centered criminological concerns that shaped the core tenets of prison abolition may find fresh air in other critical perspectives, such as critical race theory and feminist, postcolonial, and queer theories, among others. Given the multifaceted and inclusive nature of abolitionism (Ruggiero, 2010), incorporating the theoretical and methodological tools employed by other critical perspectives may allow this movement to produce better grounded and more specific descriptions of the realm of prisons and possibly more efficient strategies to achieve the goal of shaking the foundation of the current prison system. Moreover, abolition of carceral institutions or punishment in general is not possible without expanding the strategies and the theoretical tools so that they include a specific representation of sociohistorical contexts and individuals. This certainly requires deconstructing the "coloniality of knowledge" (Lander, 2000) to avoid uncritical importation of concepts and arguments built around the problems and processes in hegemonic centers as if they were universal, placeless, and timeless. It is important to bear in mind that abolitionism is a continuous task and requires keeping one's feet on the ground and one's eyes on the horizon. Advancing prison abolitionism by focusing on localized and contextualized systems of domination should be conducted with caution so as not to fuel narrow reformist agendas but to remain focused on the fundamental goal of abolitionism: to dismantle the sophisticated and pervasive social order that supports the ultimate institution of punishment.

Notes

1 Although the absolute figures indicate that the world prison population is higher than ever before, it is also true that incarceration rates have not increased in every national context in recent decades. While most Latin American countries have imprisonment rates that are much higher than three or five decades ago, countries like Canada, India, Sweden or Denmark have shown stable incarceration rates over the years, and others like Netherlands, South Africa and many Baltic and Eastern European countries have shown a sharp increase in imprisonment followed by a significant decrease. These differences in national trends call for localized and grounded analyses (Sozzo, forthcoming).

2 Of note, and in some way indicative of the fluidity and plurality of prison abolitionism, decarceration is seen by some scholars as an abolitionist strategy, while others will claim that it is only an expression of penal minimalism and not a means for a long-term abolition strategy (Carrier, Piché, & Walby, 2019). Current decarceration trends observed in some states of the U.S. and other Global North countries have been described as linked to financial crises (Gottschalk, 2015), and even to a process of net-widening and expansion of the penal control (Cate, 2016; Martin, 2016). CRT's notion of convergence of interests is useful to analyze these processes of localized decarceration.

3 For further information see the U.N. Human Development Report for 2019 (http://hdr.undp.org/en/2019-report) and the 2019 Social Report from the Economic Commission for Latin America and the Caribbean (ECLAC) (2019).

References

Alexander, M. (2010). *The new Jim Crow: Mass incarceration in the age of colorblindness.* New Press.

Angwin, J., Larson, J., Mattu, S., & Kirchner, L. (2016). Machine bias: There's software used across the country to predict future criminals. And it's biased against blacks. ProPublica. www.propublica.org/article/machine-bias-risk-assessments-in-criminal-sentencing.

Avila, K. (2012). ¿Abolicionismo penal Latinoamericano? In R. Bergalli & I. Rivera (Eds.), *Louk Hulsman: ¿Qué queda de los abolicionismos?* (pp. 143–54). Anthropos.

Aylward, C.A. (1999). *Canadian critical race theory: Racism and the law.* Fernwood Publishing.

Baldry, E., Carlton, B., & Cunneen, C. (2015). Abolitionism and the paradox of penal reform in Australia: Indigenous women, colonial patriarchy, and co-option. *Social Justice, 41*(3), 168–89.

Baszile, D.T. (2014). Rhetorical revolution: Critical race counterstorytelling and the abolition of white democracy. *Qualitative Inquiry, 21*(3), 239–49.

Bell, D.A. (1980). Brown v. Board of Education and the interest-convergence dilemma. *Harvard Law Review, 93*(3), 518–33. https://doi.org/10.2307/1340546.

Bell, D.A. (1992). *Faces at the bottom of the well: The permanence of racism.* Basic Books.

Bernstein, N. (2015). *Burning down the house: The end of juvenile prison.* New Press.

Bottoms, A.E. (1999). Interpersonal violence and social order in prisons. *Crime and Justice, 26,* 205–81.

Carlen, P. (1990). *Alternatives to women's imprisonment.* Open University Press.

Carrier, N., Piché, J., & Walby, K. (2019). Abolitionism and decarceration. In M. Deflem (Ed.), *The handbook of social control* (pp. 319–32). Wiley. https://doi.org/10.1002/9781119372394.ch23.

Cate, S. (2016). Devolution, not decarceration: The limits of juvenile justice reform in Texas. *Punishment & Society, 18*(5), 578–609. https://doi.org/10.1177/1462474516642860.

Christie, N. (1977). Conflicts as property. *The British Journal of Criminology, 17*(1), 1–15. https://doi.org/10.1093/oxfordjournals.bjc.a046783.

Collins, P.H. (2012). Social inequality, power, and politics: Intersectionality and American pragmatism in dialogue. *The Journal of Speculative Philosophy, 26*(2), 442–57.

Coyle, M.J. (2018). Transgression and standard theories: Contributions toward penal abolition. *Critical Criminology, 26*(3), 325–39. https://doi.org/10.1007/s10612-018-9404-0.

Coyle, M.J., & Schept, J. (2018). Penal abolition praxis. *Critical Criminology, 26*(3), 319–23. https://doi.org/10.1007/s10612-018-9407-x.

Crenshaw, K. (1991). Mapping the margins: Intersectionality, identity politics, and violence against women of color. *Stanford Law Review, 43*(6), 1241–99. https://doi.org/10.2307/1229039.

Crenshaw, K., Gotanda, N., Peller, G., & Thomas, K. (Eds.) (1995). *Critical race theory: The key writings that formed the movement.* New Press.

Cullen, F.T., Jonson, C.L., & Nagin, D.S. (2011). Prisons do not reduce recidivism: The high cost of ignoring science. *The Prison Journal, 91*(3_suppl), 48S–65S. https://doi.org/10.1177/0032885511415224.

Cunneen, C., & Tauri, J. (2016). *Indigenous criminology.* Policy Press.

Darke, S., & Karam, M.L. (2016). Latin American prisons. In Y. Jewkes, B. Crewe & J. Bennett (Eds.) *The Routledge handbook on prisons* (pp. 460–75). Routledge.

Davis, A.Y. (2003). *Are prisons obsolete?* Open Media Book. Seven Stories Press.

Davis, A.Y. (2005). *Abolition democracy: Beyond empire, prisons, and torture.* http://site.ebrary.com/id/10428695.

Davis, A.Y. (2007). Racialized punishment and prison abolition. In T.L. Lott & J.P. Pittman (Eds.), *A companion to African-American philosophy* (pp. 360–9). Blackwell Publishing. https://doi.org/10.1002/9780470751640.ch23.

Davis, A.Y. (Ed.) (2017). *Policing the Black man: Arrest, prosecution, and imprisonment.* First edition. Pantheon Books.

Delgado, R., & Stefancic, J. (1998). Critical race theory: Past, present, and future. *Current Legal Problems, 51*(1), 467–91. https://doi.org/10.1093/clp/51.1.467.

Delgado, R., & Stefancic, J. (2001). *Critical race theory: An introduction.* New York University Press.

Earle, R. 2016. Race, ethnicity, multiculture and prison life. In Y. Jewkes, B. Crewe & J. Bennett (Eds.), *Routledge handbook on prisons* (2nd ed., pp. 568–85). Routledge. https://doi.org/10.4324/9781315797779-33.

Fazel, S., Ramesh, T., & Hawton, K. (2017). Suicide in prisons: An international study of prevalence and contributory factors. *The Lancet Psychiatry, 4*(12), 946–52. https://doi.org/10.1016/S2215-0366(17)30430-3.

Ferguson, A.G. (2017). *The rise of big data policing: Surveillance, race, and the future of law enforcement.* New York University Press.

Fernandez, L.(2019). Presidential address: Abolitionist approaches to social problems. *Social Problems, 66*(3), 321–31. https://doi.org/10.1093/socpro/spz012.

Foucault, M. (1977). *Discipline and punish: The birth of the prison.* Penguin Books.

Garcia Hernandez, C.C. (2017). Abolishing immigration prisons. *Boston University Law Review, 1,* 245–300.

García Méndez, E. (1986). La dimensión política del abolicionismo. *Nuevo Foro Penal, 12,* 178–87.

Gillborn, D. (2015). Intersectionality, critical race theory, and the primacy of racism: Race, class, gender, and disability in education. *Qualitative Inquiry, 21*(3), 277–87.

Giwa, S., James, C.E., Anucha, U., & Schwartz, K. (2014). Community policing- a shared responsibility: A voice-centered relational method analysis of a police/youth-of-color dialogue. *Journal of Ethnicity in Criminal Justice, 12*(3), 218–45.

Gottschalk, M. (2015). *Caught: The prison state and the lockdown of American politics.* Princeton University Press. https://doi.org/10.1515/9781400880812.

Hulsman, L.H.C. (1986). Critical criminology and the concept of crime. *Contemporary Crises, 10*(1), 63–80. https://doi.org/10.1007/BF00728496.

Hylton, K. (2012). Talk the talk, walk the walk: Defining critical race theory in research. *Race Ethnicity and Education, 15*(1), 23–41.

Ignatieff, M. (1978). *A Just measure of pain: The penitentiary in the industrial revolution, 1750–1850.* Pantheon.

Inter-American Commission on Human Rights. (2011). *Report on the human rights of persons deprived of liberty in the Americas.* Inter-American Commission on Human Rights.

James, C.E. (1998). 'Up to no good': Black on the streets and encountering police. In *Racism & Social Inequality in Canada: Concepts, Controversies and Strategies of Resistance,* (pp. 157–76). Thompson Education Publishing.

Lander, E. (Ed.) (2000). *La colonialidad del saber: Eurocentrismo y ciencias sociales. Perspectivas Latinoamericanas.* Clacso.

Latty, S., Scribe, M., Peters, A. & Morgan, A. (2016). Not enough human: At the scenes of indigenous and black dispossession. *Critical Ethnic Studies, 2*(2), 129. https://doi.org/10.5749/jcritethnstud.2.2.0129.

Markus, H.R. (2008). Pride, prejudice, and ambivalence: Toward a unified theory of race and ethnicity. *American Psychologist, 63*(8), 651–70.

Martin, W.G. (2016). Decarceration and justice disinvestment: Evidence from New York State. *Punishment & Society, 18*(4), 479–504. https://doi.org/10.1177/1462474516642857.

Mathiesen, T. (1974). *The politics of abolition.* Wiley.

Mathiesen, T. (1986). The politics of abolition. *Contemporary Crises, 10*(1), 81.

Mathiesen, T. (2006). *Prison on trial.* Waterside Press.

Mathiesen, T. (2008). The abolitionist stance. *Journal of Prisoners on Prisons, 17*(2), 58–63.

Melossi, D., and M. Pavarini. 1981. *The prison and the factory: Origins of the penitentiary system.* Critical Criminology Series. MacMillan.

Naciones Unidas, and Comisión Económica para América Latina y el Caribe. (2019). *Panorama social de América Latina 2019.* Santiago, Chile: Comisión Económica para América Latina y el Caribe.

Nellis, A. (2016). The color of justice: Racial and ethnic disparity in state prisons. The Sentencing Project. www.sentencingproject.org/wp-content/uploads/2016/06/The-Color-of-Justice-Racial-and-Ethnic-Disparity-in-State-Prisons.pdf.

Nichols, R. (2014). The colonialism of incarceration. *Radical Philosophy Review, 17*(2), 435–55. https://doi.org/10.5840/radphilrev201491622.

Omi, M., & Winant, H. (2005). The theoretical status of the concept of race. *Race, Identity, and Representation in Education,* (pp. 3–12). Routledge.

Omi, M. & Winant, H. (2015). *Racial formation in the United States.* Routledge.

Pager, D. (2008). The Republican ideal?: National minorities and the criminal justice system in contemporary France. *Punishment & Society, 10*(4), 375–400. https://doi.org/10.1177/1462474508095317.

Parker, L., & Lynn, M. (2002). What's race got to do with it? Critical race theory's conflicts with and connections to qualitative research methodology and epistemology. *Qualitative Inquiry, 8*(1), 7–22.

Phillips, C. (2012). *The multicultural prison: Ethnicity, masculinity, and social relations among prisoners.* (1st ed.) Oxford University Press.

Postay, M.E. (Ed.). (2012). *El abolicionismo penal en América latina: Imaginación no punitiva y militancia.* Editores del Puerto s.r.l.

Provine, D.M. (2011). Race and inequality in the war on drugs. *Annual Review of Law and Social Science, 7*(1), 41–60. https://doi.org/10.1146/annurev-lawsocsci-102510105445.

Razack, S.H., Smith, M., & Thobani, S. (Eds.) (2010). *States of race: Critical race feminism for the 21st Century.* Between the Lines Press.

Rothman, D.J. (1971). *The discovery of the asylum: Social order and disorder in the new republic.* Little, Brown and Company.

Rubin, A., & M.S. Phelps. (2017). Fracturing the penal state: State actors and the role of conflict in penal change. *Theoretical Criminology, 21*(4), 422–40. https://doi.org/10.1177/1362480617724829.

Ruggiero, V. (2010). *Penal abolitionism.* Oxford University Press.

Ruggiero, V. (2014). Utopian action and participatory disputes. *Social Justice: A Journal of Crime, Conflict & World Order, 41*(3), 89–106.

Rusche, G., & Kirchheimer, O. (1939). *Punishment and social structure.* Columbia University.

Saleh-Hanna, V. (2015). Black feminist hauntology. *Champ pénal* (August). https://doi.org/10.4000/champpenal.9168.

Saleh-Hanna, V. (2017). An abolitionist theory on crime: Ending the abusive relationship with racist-imperialist-patriarchy [R.I.P.]. *Contemporary Justice Review, 20*(4), 419–41. https://doi.org/10.1080/10282580.2017.1377056.

Satzewich, V., & Liodakis, N. (2013). *"Race" and ethnicity in Canada: A critical introduction.* OUP Canada.

Scott, D. (Ed.) (2013). *Why prison?* Cambridge University Press.

Solórzano, D.G., & T.J. Yosso. (2002). Critical race methodology: Counter-storytelling as an analytical framework for education research. *Qualitative Inquiry, 8*(1), 23–44.

Sozzo, M. (forthcoming). Imprisonment: Making sense of trends. In M. Valverde, C. Kamari, E. Darian-Smith & P. Kotiswaran (Eds.), *Routledge handbook of law and society*. Routledge.

Tator, C., & Henry, F. (2006). *Racial profiling in Canada: Challenging the myth of "a few bad apples."* University of Toronto Press.

Tonry, M. (2011). *Punishing race: A continuing American dilemma.* Oxford University Press.

Tonry, M., & Melewski, M. (2008). The malign effects of drug and crime control policies on Black Americans. *Crime and Justice, 37*(1), 1–44. https://doi.org/10.1086/588492.

Walmsley, R. (2018). *World prison population list (12th Edition).* Institute for Criminal Policy Research.

Williams, D.R., Priest, N. & Anderson, N.B. (2016). Understanding associations among race, socioeconomic status, and health: Patterns and prospects. *Health Psychology, 35*(4), 407–11.

Williams, M.Y. (2013). African Nova Scotian restorative justice: A change has gotta come. *Dalhousie Law Journal, 36*(2), 419–59.

Wilson Gilmore, R. (2017). Abolition geography and the problem of innocence. In G.T. Johnson & A. Lubin (Eds.), *Futures of black radicalism.* Verso.

Woods, C. (2016). Addressing prison overcrowding in Latin America: A comparative analysis of the necessary precursors to reform. *ILSA Journal of International and Comparative Law, 22*(3), 533–62.

2 Racial innocence, liberal reformism, and immigration detention

Toward a politics of abolition

Sarah Turnbull

In the legal infrastructure and practiced fantasies of racial innocence, to ignore race is to end racism.

(Murakawa, 2019, p. 475)

Ultimately, [immigration] detention is an expression of the inequality of noncitizens [… and] racialized immigrants [… in particular]. Used to discipline and refine the citizenry, it is a feature of the racial hierarchy from which dominant society benefits. The detention of […] racialized immigrants helps constitute the normative white citizen and white nation.

(Hernandez, 2008, p. 49)

On a wall of one of the activity corridors at Colnbrook Immigration Removal Centre (IRC), located near London's Heathrow Airport in the United Kingdom (UK), hung a framed (ostensibly earnest) poster of the comic strip cat Garfield. Garfield faces the viewer with an apparent smile, his elbows perched on the round, blue and green globe of planet Earth, his chin resting on his paws. Behind him are an array of flags of the world. In bold, orange capital letters above Garfield's head, the poster reads: "DISCOVER A WORLD OF CULTURES." During my fieldwork at Colnbrook IRC,[1] this poster always struck me as farcical and an apt symbol of the contradictory nature of immigration detention: a racist, gendered, and classed policy and practice that claims to be otherwise (i.e., race, gender, and class neutral). While the poster is near comical in its absurdity, it is suggestive of the liberal idea that anyone could face detention and deportation, rather than the reality that immigration detention centers of the global north largely incarcerate poor, racialized men and women (Bhui, 2016). And it connects to the broader tendency within many public, political, and academic discourses to disavow—or sideline—how race, gender, class, religion, sexuality, and other social relations of power shape systems of immigration detention and deportation and their interconnection with the carceral state. The poster suggests instead that immigration detention simply reflects human "diversity," rather than producing and sustaining fundamental inequalities.

Although immigration detention is not the same as criminal/legal imprisonment and its prevalence varies from country to country, it is a policy and practice that is enmeshed in the carceral state (Loyd, 2015) and is thus fundamentally about race—as it intersects with gender, class, and other social relations of power. Racism is central to the processes of dehumanization that make detaining non-citizens and migrants a reasonable "solution" to the "problem" of migration and non-citizenship. Racism is also pivotal to who gets identified and policed as detainable and deportable (Hester, 2015) and, ultimately, to who is detained and deported (Golash-Boza, 2016). Indeed, just as "[s]urveilling and holding brown and black bodies has become an acceptable method for dealing with the 'problem' of brown and black 'criminality,'" with the prison as the logical "answer" (Hernández, 2012, p. 355), immigration detention has emerged over the past few decades as a central tool of numerous countries' border and immigration control systems, primarily targeting poor and racialized peoples. As Miller (2003, p. 216) observed in the early 2000s, "[i]ncreasingly, the immigration system functions—like the criminal justice system—to socially control through confinement in secure, disciplinary facilities the unpopular and the powerless, which in this case are undocumented [and/or migrant] people of color."

This chapter is inspired by recent work on racial innocence and the carceral state by Murakawa and Beckett (2010), Murakawa (2019), and others (e.g., Struthers Montford & Hannah-Moffat, 2020) that demonstrates the necessity of centering race and racism within studies of punishment and rejecting the idea that "social institutions, policies and practices are all race neutral" (Ugwudike, 2020, p. 485). The chapter has several interrelated aims. First, it seeks to respond to calls by Phillips, Earle, Parmar, and Smith (2020) and Garner (2015), among others, for criminology to stop "turning away from race" and address the "carelessness" by which the discipline treats race and racism (Phillips et al., 2020, p. 429). Second, the chapter aims to examine how racial innocence is embedded in and shapes the parameters of responses to, and reform efforts around, immigration detention. Using the UK as an example, it considers the importance of race and racism—while cognisant that these intersect with other social relations of power—for understanding the policy and practice of immigration detention and recent events and reforms. Finally, the chapter attempts to show how the abolition of immigration detention is intricately bound to prison abolition and broader movements toward racial and social justice. Immigration detention thus must be understood as an increasingly vital part of the carceral state that also produces and maintains systemic racism and white supremacy.

Drawing on Murakawa (2019) in particular, in this chapter I suggest that racial innocence is perpetuated by systems of immigration detention in which race and racism tend not to be adequately recognized and examined, including within the burgeoning criminological literature on the subject (exceptions of course exist; see, e.g., Bhui, 2016; Bosworth, 2018; Golash-Boza, 2015; Hernández, 2012; Hernandez, 2008; Turnbull, 2017a) and within public and political debates around immigration detention's (mis)use and the need for reform. More specifically, Murakawa (2019, p. 474) shows how the carceral state (re)produces racism, defined as the "production and exploitation of group-differentiated vulnerability to premature death." Racial innocence, she argues, is the "practiced blamelessness for the death-dealing realities of racial capitalism" and is "maintained through willful ignorance, blame displacement, and liberal reforms" (Murakawa, 2019, p. 474). The concepts of willful ignorance, blame displacement, and liberal reforms outlined by Murakawa (2019), as I aim to show, map fittingly onto the functioning of immigration detention, particularly in jurisdictions like the UK, where I have conducted research, as well as in other countries of the global north such as Canada, the United States (US), and Australia.

This chapter begins with a brief review of the criminological literature that directly addresses race, racism, and immigration detention.[2] I then draw on Murakawa (2019) to examine the British immigration detention system, showing how the racial innocence of the British carceral state is maintained through the confluence of willful ignorance, blame displacement, and liberal reformism. Echoing others (e.g., Loyd, 2015), I argue that to understand and work to dismantle and abolish immigration detention, it is necessary to illustrate how race and racism—as they intersect with other markers of power like gender, class, sexuality, religion, and so forth—are integral to its functioning and continuance and to im/migration and border control more broadly. Additionally, the policy and practice of immigration detention, along with im/migration and border control, need to be recognized as part and parcel of the carceral state. Issues of migrant justice and the abolition of immigration detention are thus an integral part of broader movements toward racial and social justice and prison abolition.

Race, racisms, and immigration detention

As Bhui (2016, p. 269) cogently argues, "it is not possible to fully understand the dynamics of immigration detention without also understanding debates about race, ethnicity and racism within and across national boundaries." Despite the centrality of race and racism to our understanding of immigration detention, scant criminological scholarship has, to date, directly engaged with these issues (but see Bhui, 2016; Bosworth, 2018; Golash-Boza, 2015; Turnbull, 2017a), even as the criminological literature on immigration detention has grown. Little attention has been paid also to how colonial histories have shaped and continue to shape immigration detention through lingering impacts on migration patterns, contemporary racisms, and anti-migrant sentiment, which are "illustrated by the persistence of abusive and casually dehumanizing behaviors in immigration control and detention" (Bhui, 2016, p. 270; Loyd, 2015; Loyd & Mountz, 2018). Criminology's lack of attention to race and racism has been brilliantly outlined by Phillips et al. (2020), as has the inadequate engagement with race by the nascent crimmigration literature (Garner, 2015). Murakawa and Beckett's (2010) concept of the "penology of racial innocence" is helpful for understanding the lack of criminological engagement with race in work on immigration detention.

One of the most direct engagements on the topic of race and immigration detention is by Bhui (2016), in which he considered the various factors that produce racialized immigration detention. He identifies colonialism as a key factor shaping contemporary racisms and immigration policies, arguing that the "colonial experience is a powerful subtext in the modern immigration debate, especially as prisons and immigration detention centres in Europe are disproportionately filled with nationals of previously colonized countries" (Bhui, 2016, p. 270). Bhui (2016) discusses the example of the UK, showing how colonial policies and notions of race have factored into British immigration policy over time, producing a racialized system of immigration control. A second factor relates to new racisms that are not so explicitly "color-coded" such as *xeno-racism*, a term discussed by Fekete (2001), in which people are discriminated against based on other identities (e.g., class, poverty, religion, culture, etc.) beyond race (Bhui, 2016, p. 274). More specifically, the production of "white suspect populations" reflects the malleability of whiteness as Eastern European migrants are subject to racialization (Bhui, 2016, p. 275; see also Turnbull, 2017a in relation to immigration detention)—they are, in Hernandez's (2008, p. 57) words, at "the margins of whiteness"—and racialized anti-Muslim sentiment and Islamophobia tend to be articulated in terms of undesirable "cultures." To understand the place of race in immigration detention, Bhui (2016) reminds us, it is necessary to recognize the broader context in which race and racism intersect with debates about migration and migration control policies. Indeed, the broader literatures on migration and border control have reinforced the argument that im/migration controls both produce and assemble race and racisms (see, e.g., de Noronha, 2019).

Less research has explored the impact of racism on people in immigration detention or how immigration detention has impacted racialized communities. Hernandez (2008), for instance, has considered the racialized effects of detention on Latino non-citizens and citizens in the US. He observes that the "stigma of criminal foreignness and 'illegality,'" which includes detention and deportation, "are facets of immigration policy [with] which many immigrant communities, in particular Latino communities, have been intimately acquainted for generations" (Hernandez, 2008, p. 37). Fear of detention and deportation amongst Latino communities is not new, despite the ramping up of border control in recent decades, and is not limited to non-citizens (see also Parmar, 2020). Hernandez (2008) argues that the long-standing racialized criminalization of Latinos as "illegals" means that detainability and deportability affect citizens as well. This history is key to understanding racialized immigration detention in the U.S. today and how detention works to continually reinscribe "the racial hierarchy from which dominant [white] society benefits" (Hernandez, 2008, p. 49).

Bosworth (2018) has examined issues of race and racism in relation to staff working in British IRCs. She observes that "IRCs are sites where race and ethnicity are primarily decoded and understood through national stereotypes" (Bosworth, 2018, p. 214–15). In her research, staff drew on implicitly racialized stereotypes about different detainees' nationalities to manage the diverse detainee population and make sense of their work (Bosworth, 2018; see also Bosworth & Kellezi, 2014). Bosworth (2018, p. 214) argues, however, that although nearly all detainees are racial minorities and most of those tasked with guarding them are white, "race in detention, as elsewhere, is rarely a simple binary matter." She suggests that British immigration detention is racially complex in the sense that some staff are minority ethnic British citizens or recent migrants and those who are detained are culturally and linguistically diverse (Bosworth, 2018).

Elsewhere I have examined immigration detention as a racialized practice, drawing on ethnographic research I conducted across four British IRCs (Turnbull, 2017a). This work shows how issues of race and racism in immigration detention are largely disavowed institutionally and only emerge tacitly in the management of "diversity." Like Bosworth (2018; Bosworth & Kellezi, 2014), I found that detainees were governed largely in terms of their nationalities, which presented some interesting paradoxical encounters when issues of "race" surfaced but were met with institutional discourses and practices of diversity (e.g., "celebrating" Africa as part of Black History Month). Importantly, many of those who are detained present their own analyses of the racialized nature of immigration detention, linking their confinement and deportability to British empire and to racism (Turnbull, 2017a; Turnbull & Hasselberg, 2017).

As this brief review illustrates, there is significant scope for race and racism—and related intersections—to be centered in studies of immigration detention, particularly as the topic is garnering increased criminological attention. Likewise, there is an urgent need for anti-racist abolitionist analyses of immigration detention given criminology's entanglements with state institutions, policies, and discourses (Brown & Schept, 2017).

Racial innocence and immigration detention

Racial innocence, according to Murakawa (2019, p. 474), is "a way of knowing fueled by the desire for unknowing." It is linked to "willful ignorance" in the sense that "to ignore race is to end racism" (Murakawa, 2019, p. 475) and relates to Goldberg's (2015) notion of the postracial (i.e., that race and racism are matters of the past). Ignorance, Murakawa (2019, p. 475) reminds us, "is no absence of knowledge; it is, rather, the cultivation of institutions, ideologies, and rhetorical mazes that unwitness racism." Secondly, as Murakawa (2019) argues, racial innocence is further enabled by the creation of "the Negro problem" in which blackness and criminality are conflated, thus both entrenching and justifying racialized and anti-black criminalization and incarceration. Lastly, liberal reformism is an essential part of racial innocence as it helps "secure illusions of racial progress without paying the price of the ticket" (Murakawa, 2019, p. 475). That is, reformism individualizes racism such that "its remedy requires no redistribution of resources," nor radical change, nor protest (Murakawa, 2019, p. 475). Murakawa (2019, p. 474) argues that each mechanism of racial innocence "enables our collective unwitnessing of carceral devastation." Law, policy, social institutions, and social science are all implicated in constituting and sustaining racial innocence (Murakawa, 2019; Murakawa & Beckett, 2010) and thus white supremacy.

Murakawa's (2019) analysis, and Murakawa and Beckett's (2010) notion of the penology of racial innocence, are useful tools for examining immigration detention, particularly as the policy and practice of detention are garnering significant public, political, and academic attention in many jurisdictions. In what follows, I draw on the example of British immigration detention and how recent events and reform efforts can be understood through a critical race analysis, thereby centering race and racism and recognizing the white norms upon which this policy and practice is based and enacted.

Murakawa (2019) argues that the willful ignorance is maintained through a denial of the proof of racial disparity, ongoing racial profiling, and social science research that relies on a narrow definition of racism. In the context of British immigration detention, the racial disparities reflecting the population of those detained and made deportable have been routinely disregarded. As de Noronha (2019, p. 2414) contends, "[t]he claim that the exclusion of immigrants has nothing to do with race is central to the justification for bordering in contemporary Britain." Until recently, the vast majority of those detained were racialized men from Britain's former colonies including India, Pakistan, Bangladesh, Jamaica, and Nigeria. This was the case when I undertook ethnographic research in four IRCs in 2013–14 (e.g., Bosworth & Turnbull, 2015). Since the mid-2010s, however, there has been an increasing number of European Union (E.U.) nationals—and Eastern Europeans in particular—detained in the UK, likely linked to Britain's escalating rejection of the European project as reflected in Brexit (Turnbull, 2017a). As I have argued elsewhere (Turnbull, 2017a), the racialized nature of immigration detention was primarily a non-issue until media reports and statistical data releases began documenting the growing number of EU citizens being detained in the UK. Immigration detention was thus problematized when its "natural" racial character began to change.

Another recent example of willful ignorance, including the unnameability of racism and disavowal of its structural, systemic features, relates to a BBC documentary exposé of conditions at Brook House IRC, located near London's Gatwick Airport, that was broadcast in the UK on September 4, 2017. Secretly recorded video footage captured racist language and abuse of detainees by IRC staff (Canning & Bhatia, 2017). G4S, the private security contractor responsible for operating the IRC, suspended nine staff members and launched an independent investigation into the allegations of abuse raised by the documentary (Canning & Bhatia, 2017), which resulted in a report (see Lampard & Marsden, 2018). Several of the detainees who were subject to abuse also began legal proceedings against the Home Secretary. Additionally, the British Parliamentary Home Affairs Committee launched the Brook House Immigration Removal Centre inquiry on September 13, 2017 and the Home Office tasked the Prisons Probation Ombudsman (PPO) with undertaking an investigation. This latter investigation was then converted into a full public inquiry in November 2019 to "investigate mistreatment of detainees" as a means "to understand what happened at Brook House IRC, to identify learning and to make recommendations that would help to prevent a recurrence of such events" (Brook House Inquiry, n.d.).

Despite racist abuse being captured on video, issues of race and racism quickly retreated into the background. While the Home Affairs Committee's Brook House Immigration Removal Centre inquiry scope included "racial abuse" of detainees by G4S staff, the full public inquiry, which is ongoing at the time of writing, is examining *mistreatment*. As defined by the inquiry's terms of reference, mistreatment is "decisions, actions and circumstances" contrary to "Article 3 ECHR [European Convention on Human Rights], namely torture, inhuman or degrading treatment, or punishment" (Brook House Inquiry, n.d.). Direct reference to racial abuse is not part of the inquiry's terms of reference. In addition, the independent report produced for G4S only mentions racism in four instances and all relate to the use of racist language by individuals. Through these framings, racism is individualized and viewed as connected to a few bad apples, rather than as systemic and reflecting a system predicated on white supremacy. Consequently, the typical solution is improved staffing and better training.

The problem with defining racism narrowly as intentional and the product of bad apples is that it can be hard to "see" in sites like British immigration detention. I found this during my own ethnographic research. Looking back, I realize how my own observations were unwittingly affected by the *penology of racial innocence*: "the presumption that criminal justice is innocent of racial power until proven otherwise" (Murakawa & Beckett, 2010, p. 695). In short, I often found it difficult to "see" exactly how racial power was operating— and to find empirical "proof" to support my observations. The narrowing of racism to intentionality and causation deflects away from the myriad ways that racism is a structural and systemic aspect of immigration detention (Murakawa, 2019; Murakawa & Beckett, 2010). Indeed, in my research, immigration detention center staff were rarely overtly racist. Racism was primarily implicit and disguised through talk of nationalities or cultures rather than race or ethnicity. As Bosworth (2018) notes, most staff know how to act in front of university researchers, and racism occurs subtly in interpersonal interactions through body language and tone of speech (see also Godshaw, 2020). Racism is, however, entrenched in immigration detention as a social institution and in the broader immigration system through the normalization of whiteness and white, western modes of thought as reflected in state policies, practices, and logics. Racist staff are just one part in the larger project of white supremacy as manifested in immigration detention. The dehumanization produced and maintained by racism enables primarily people of color to be detained in the first place. The search for intentionality and causation, along with the unnameability of racism, thus contributes to willful ignorance and the racial innocence of immigration detention.

A second mechanism maintaining the racial innocence of immigration detention relates to blame displacement. The racialized criminalization of migration is akin to what Murakawa (2019, p. 482) discusses as *the Negro problem*—or racial criminalization (i.e., "the conflation of blackness with criminality and the simultaneous minimizing of white criminality as the transgression of white individuals, not a reflection on the white race")—in that migration and migrants deemed problematic and "unwanted" are predominately racialized as non-white and coming from "shithole" countries. That immigration detention is naturalized as "appropriate" for largely non-white migrants—as opposed to white "expats"—reflects the extent to which racism is structured into the immigration and carceral systems of the global north. As Weber (2002) observes, the securitized architectural features of spaces of immigration detention (e.g., perimeter fences, razor wire, entry gates, CCTV cameras, etc.) can give the impression that people who are detained are dangerous and thus worthy of exclusion and confinement; race and detention are thereby further entrenched. Various "laws, policies, and institutional practices generate and reify ideas about racial difference, contributing to processes of racialization," yet are viewed as neutral and nonracial (Armenta, 2016, p. 83). The problem, then, is not racist immigration and border control systems, but rather racialized people who do not follow these ostensibly race-neutral laws and policies.

Indeed, race and ethnicity are denied except as demographic categories in immigration detention (Bosworth, 2018). Within British IRCs, as in other neoliberal institutions (Ahmed, 2012), discourses of "diversity" pervade, supplanting explicit discussion of race and racism (Turnbull, 2017a). "Culture" and "nationality" are seemingly non-racial stand-ins for race and ethnicity and are used to manage extremely heterogeneous detainee populations (Bosworth & Kellezi, 2014; Turnbull, 2017a). Normative perspectives of border control that treat breaches of im/migration law as "fundamentally interpersonal, individualized, and natural deny the multiple forms of structural violence inflicted by the neoliberal state" (Brown & Schept, 2017, p. 445) as well as the "global hierarchy of mobility" (Bauman, 1998, p. 151) and its attendant inequalities (see Anderson, Sharma, & Wright, 2009). Blame is displaced onto racialized people through the racialized criminalization of migration.

Liberal reformism is the third mechanism sustaining the racial innocence of the carceral state (Murakawa, 2019). In particular, reformist practices that target the "non-non-nons" (i.e., non-serious, non-violent, non-sexual offences or individuals) work to reinforce dichotomies of good/innocent and bad/criminal. These sorts of dichotomies, Hernandez (2008, p. 56) argues, "are misleading because not only are 'good' and 'bad' detainees often from the same communities, if not the same families, but the undue processes which harm them usually harm all immigrants." Again, these framings individualize and personalize fundamentally unequal systemic and structural relations of power. As Murakawa (2019, p. 485) puts it, "[a]dvocating for the relatively innocent legitimizes the idea that the relatively guilty deserve what they get," which, in this case, is indefinite immigration detention.

In the context of British immigration detention reform, there has been a move towards the recognition of "vulnerable" detainees through the Adults at Risk policy and social movements to end the detention of women.[3] Such reform efforts have largely meant separating out the vulnerable and "genuine"— most often asylum seekers (good/innocent)—from "foreign criminals" (bad/ guilty). These dichotomous categories are heavily gendered and racialized and reflective of normative understandings of vulnerability. The primary hier- archy of deservedness positions detained female asylum seekers as particu- larly undeserving of detention, with racialized male former prisoners as the most deserving of detention. The latter group are "doubly damned" due to their presumed foreignness and criminality (Griffiths, 2017) and constituted as especially unworthy of empathy. Racism is central to their constitution as for- eign criminals (de Noronha, 2019). Many of these men are long-term British residents whose lives have been significantly shaped by the expansive reach of the carceral state—along familiar lines of gender, race, and class—through edu- cation, welfare, policing, and criminal justice institutions (Godshaw, 2020; de Noronha, 2019). The former group of female asylum seekers are precariously positioned as good/innocent; because they are largely "[w]omen who do not 'fit the traditional image of the innocent victim'—that is, black women, women of color, poor women, sex workers, lesbians, and trans women" (Murakawa, 2019, p. 485), their acceptance as vulnerable—and thus undeserving of detention—is not guaranteed. However, much of the rallying for the end of detention is centered around the closing of Yarl's Wood IRC, Britain's infamous detention center primarily for women, which suggests the idea that decarceration should start with women immigration detainees.

As a reform, the Adults at Risk policy aims to reduce the numbers of "vulner- able people" being detained without, of course, ending detention. Administrative convenience—the desire of the British government to deport people—is prioritized over the mental, physical, and emotional health of detained people and their families and communities. Race, class, gender, sexuality, ability, and other social relations of power shape how vulnerability is defined and assessed and thus cannot be a remedy for the plethora of harms that detention both exacerbates and causes. Tinkering with the system through such reforms also cannot address how detention sustains the "racial hierarchy from which dom- inant [white] society benefits" (Hernandez, 2008, p. 49). It is necessary, Kalir (2019, p. 21) argues, to avoid "reproducing and reasserting a false notion of a humane Western governing regime that is incomplete or has gone astray, and is simply in need of correction or fine-tuning." Rejecting liberal reformism helps us reject racial innocence.

Conclusion: Toward a politics of abolition

The issue of immigration detention is increasingly relevant to prison abolition and social justice. As Loyd (2015, p. 2) reminds us, the boundaries between domestic/national and international issues and policies are ever more blurred and carceral in character. The categories of "criminal" and "non-citizen" are likewise more and more conflated. The domestic infrastructures that enable immigration detention—crime policies, policing, detention centers, prisons, and "the methods for moving people within this network or removing them through deportation"—are part of the carceral state, which should be considered global in nature and function (Loyd, 2015, p. 2). As Loyd (2015, p. 15) argues, "[i]n a globally carceral era, one of the most important tools for ending how prisons and deportation [and, I would add, detention] separate families and communities is to link together what many regard as separate issues." Indeed, the British government's domestic carceral interests are increasingly global— and colonial—through its linking of foreign national prisoner and deportation policies with its development work in former colonies such as Nigeria and Jamaica in what has been termed *penal humanitarianism* (Bosworth, 2017) and *carceral colonialism* (Corporate Watch, 2018).

Furthermore, Hernández (2012, p. 358) observes that the "method perfected in the context of criminal law enforcement for sifting through the masses to identify the undeserving is to target people marked by symbols of race and class-based otherness." Criminal/legal imprisonment and immigration detention are thus intricately connected to each other and to racism and inequality. Like the prison, immigration detention needs to be extracted "from its narrow place in the popular imagination as being just about" im/migration control and relocated instead "in conversations about employment, economies, imperialism, racial justice, uneven development, public health, climate change and environmental justice, land use, and neoliberal ideology" (Brown & Schept, 2017, p. 448), as well as empire and colonialism (Bhui, 2016).[4] This wider perspective also helps move us away from racial innocence.

It is, in sum, important to include immigration detention and border control within movements toward social justice and prison abolition for several reasons. First, there is "the relationship between the detention processes and other forms of structural and cultural inequality affecting" racialized non-citizen and citizen communities alike (Hernandez, 2008, p. 41), such as policing (Parmar, 2020) and incarceration (Sudbury, 2005). The systemic racism of the criminal legal system has ever-expanding detention and deportation consequences (de Noronha, 2019), both as more and more criminal infractions render people deportable and as what Yuval-Davis, Wemyss, and Cassidy (2018) term *everyday bordering* functions to further marginalize and exclude racialized people. Expansive, intertwining carceral and bordering regimes have had, and are having, devastating effects (Kalir, 2019; Murakawa, 2019) that need to be urgently addressed.

Second, immigration detention has "political currency":

> For politicians, the appearance of being tough on crime, immigrants, and terror—for the moment all linked—is valuable, and draws easily on and contributes to popular criminalized perceptions of immigrants. Detaining immigrants, then, assists in creating an illusion of security. In this sense, the noncitizen is an instrument and constitutive factor of our security state,

legitimizing its expansion, and drawing support from voters and popular opinion.

(Hernandez, 2008, p. 49)

Immigration detention is thus part of the diverse processes that also produce and sustain racialized incarceration and social inequality. The political currency of immigration detention is enabled through the fantasy of white supremacy and the idea that it, along with broader bordering regimes, is an "act of self-defense against those who are seen as invading Western states" (Kalir, 2019, p. 20).

Like prisons, immigration detention centers "normalize the practice of creating separate and subordinate spatial, legal, and political universes for whole categories of people" (Murakawa, 2019, p. 468). As Murakawa (2019, p. 468) concludes, "no amount of improvement can secure the innocence of the carceral state." Immigration detention cannot be reformed to reduce the myriad harms it causes. As this chapter has shown, a wider analysis is needed to connect immigration detention—and im/migration and bordering policy more broadly—to criminal legal incarceration and the racial (and gender) injustice upon which these systems are based and continue to reproduce. It is hoped that this contribution furthers criminological discussions about race, racisms, and immigration detention, the interconnections between racialized border control and criminal justice regimes, and the need for abolitionist strategies to dismantle detention and pursue racial and social justice.

Notes

1 Between 2013 and 2014 I undertook a multi-sited ethnography of four British IRCs (see Turnbull, 2016, 2019).
2 For a review of the connections between immigration detention and punishment, please see Turnbull (2017b).
3 There have also been social movements (e.g., #TimeForATimeLimit) to put a time limit of 28 days for people being detained in the U.K. This reform movement has received bipartisan support, including a joint inquiry led by the All Party Parliamentary Groups on Refugees and Migration (see Joint Inquiry by the All-Party Parliamentary Group on Refugees & the All-Party Parliamentary Group on Migration, 2015). Due to space limitations, I cannot expand further on this reform effort.
4 The "current border regime," Khosravi (2019, p. 409) reminds us, "is part of a larger and older project of colonial accumulation by dispossession and expulsion; stealing wealth, labour force and time." Borders, and associated policies and practices like immigration detention, are part of "the infrastructure of racism" and thus must be denaturalized (Khosravi, 2019). See also Kalir (2019).

Acknowledgement

Many thanks to the editors, Kelly Struthers Montford and Chloë Taylor, for inviting this contribution. I am grateful to Kelly, Chloë, and Alpa Parmar for their helpful feedback on earlier drafts of this chapter.

References

Ahmed, S. (2012). *On Being Included: Racism and Diversity in Institutional Life*. Duke University Press.

All-Party Parliamentary Group on Refugees & the All-Party Parliamentary Group on Migration. (2015). *The report of the Inquiry into the Use of Immigration Detention in the United Kingdom. A Joint Inquiry by All-Party Parliamentary Group on Refugees & the All-Party Parliamentary Group on Migration*. https://detentioninquiry.files.wordpress.com/2015/03/immigration-detention-inquiry-report.pdf

Anderson, B., Sharma, N., & Wright, C. (2009). Editorial: Why no borders. *Refuge, 26*(2), 5–18.

Armenta, A. (2016). Racializing crimmigration: Structural racism, colorblindness, and the institutional production of immigrant criminality. *Sociology of Race and Ethnicity, 3*(1), 82–95.

Bauman, Z. (1998). *Globalization*. Polity Press.

Bhui, H. S. (2016). The place of "race" in understanding immigration control and the detention of foreign nationals. *Criminology and Criminal Justice, 16*(3), 267–85.

Bosworth, M. (2017). Penal humanitarianism? Sovereign power in an era of mass migration. *New Criminal Law Review, 20*(1), 39–65.

Bosworth, M. (2018). "Working in this place turns you racist": Staff, race, and power in detention. In M. Bosworth, A. Parmar, & Y. Vázquez (Eds.), *Race, Criminal Justice, and Migration Control: Enforcing the Boundaries of Belonging* (pp. 214–28). Oxford University Press.

Bosworth, M., & Kellezi, B. (2014). Citizenship and belonging in a women's immigration detention centre. In C. Phillips & C. Webster (Eds.), *New Directions in Race, Ethnicity and Crime* (pp. 80–96). Routledge.

Bosworth, M., & Turnbull, S. (2015). Immigration detention, punishment and the criminalization of migration. In S. Pickering & J. Ham (Eds.), *The Routledge Handbook on Crime and International Migration* (pp. 91–106). Routledge.

Brook House Inquiry (n.d.) *A public inquiry into the mistreatment of detainees at Brook House Immigration Removal Centre in 2017*. [https://brookhouseinquiry.org.uk/

Brown, M., & Schept, J. (2017). New abolition, criminology and a critical carceral studies. *Punishment & Society, 19*(4), 440–62.

Canning, V., & Bhatia, M. (2017). Brutality of British immigration detention system laid bare. The Conversation. https://theconversation.com/brutality-of-british-immigration-detention-system-laid-bare-83396

Corporate Watch. (2018). Prison island: Prison expansion in England, Wales and Scotland. https://corporatewatch.org/prisonisland/

de Noronha, L. (2019). Deportation, racism and multi-status Britain: Immigration control and the production of race in the present. *Ethnic and Racial Studies, 42*(14), 2413–30.

Fekete, L. (2001). The emergence of xeno-racism. *Race & Class, 43*(2), 23–40.

Garner, S. (2015). Crimmigration: When criminology (nearly) met the sociology of race and ethnicity. *Sociology of Race and Ethnicity, 1*(1), 198–203.

Godshaw, D. (2020). Becoming an immigrant? Border harms and 'British' men with previous convictions in British immigration removal centers. *Critical Criminology, 28*(2), 225–41.

Golash-Boza, T. (2015). *Deported: Immigrant Policing, Disposable Labor, and Global Capitalism*. New York University Press.

Golash-Boza, T. (2016). Racialized and gendered mass deportation and the crisis of capitalism. *Journal of World-Systems Research, 22*(1), 38–44.

Goldberg, D.T. (2015). *Are We All Postracial Yet?* Polity Press.

Griffiths, M. (2017). Foreign, criminal: A doubly damned modern British folk-devil. *Citizenship Studies, 21*(5), 527–46.

Hernández, C.C.G. (2012). The perverse logic of immigration detention: Unraveling the rationality of imprisoning immigrants based on markers of race and class otherness. *Columbia Journal of Race and Law, 1*(3), 353–64.

Hernández, D.M. (2008). Pursuant to deportation: Latinos and immigrant detention. *Latino Studies, 6*(1–2), 35–63.

Hester, T. (2015). Deportability and the carceral state. *Journal of American History, 102*(1), 141–51.

Kalir, B. (2019). Departheid: The draconian governance of illegalized migrants in Western states. *Conflict and Society, 5*(1), 19–40.

Khosravi, S. (2019). What do we see if we look at the border from the other side? *Social Anthropology, 27*(3), 409–24.

Lampard, K., & Marsden, E. (2018). *Independent investigation into concerns about Brook House immigration removal centre.* Verita. www.verita.net/wp-content/uploads/2018/12/G4S-version-report.pdf

Loyd, J.M. (2015). Carceral citizenship in an age of global apartheid. *Occasion, 8,* 1–15. http://arcade.stanford.edu/occasion_issue/race-space-scale

Loyd, J.M., & Mountz, A. (2018). *Boats, Borders, and Bases: Race, the Cold War, and the Rise of Migration Detention in the United States.* University of California Press.

Miller, T.A. (2003). Citizenship and severity: Recent immigration reforms and the new penology. *Georgetown Immigration Law Journal, 17,* 611–66.

Murakawa, N. (2019). Racial innocence: Law, social science, and the unknowing of racism in the US carceral state. *Annual Review of Law and Social Science, 15*(1), 473–93.

Murakawa, N., & Beckett, K. (2010). The penology of racial innocence: The erasure of racism in the study and practice of punishment. *Law & Society Review, 44*(3–4), 695–730.

Parmar, A. (2020). Arresting (non)citizenship: The policing migration nexus of nationality, race and criminalization. *Theoretical Criminology, 24*(1), 28–49.

Phillips, C., Earle, R., Parmar, A., & Smith, D. (2020). Dear British criminology: Where has all the race and racism gone? *Theoretical Criminology, 24*(3), 427–46.

Struthers Montford, K., & Hannah-Moffat, K. (2020). The veneers of empiricism: Gender, race and prison classification. *Aggression and Violent Behavior.* Online first 15 July 2020. https://doi.org/10.1016/j.avb.2020.101475

Sudbury, J. (Ed.) (2005). *Global Lockdown: Race, Gender, and the Prison-Industrial Complex.* Routledge.

Turnbull, S. (2016). "Stuck in the middle": Waiting and uncertainty in immigration detention. *Time & Society, 25*(1), 61–79.

Turnbull, S. (2017a). Immigration detention and the racialized governance of illegality in the United Kingdom. *Social Justice, 44*(1), 142–64.

Turnbull, S. (2017b) Immigration detention and punishment. *Oxford Research Encyclopedia of Criminology and Criminal Justice.* doi: 10.1093/acrefore/9780190264079.013.231.

Turnbull, S. (2019). Living the spectre of forced return: Negotiating deportability in British immigration detention. *Migration Studies, 7*(4), 513–32.

Turnbull, S., & Hasselberg, I. (2017). From prison to detention: The carceral trajectories of foreign-national prisoners in the United Kingdom. *Punishment & Society, 19*(2), 135–54.

Ugwudike, P. (2020). Digital prediction technologies in the justice system: The implications of a "race-neutral" agenda. *Theoretical Criminology, 24*(3), 482–501.

Weber, L. (2002). The detention of asylum seekers: 20 reasons why criminologists should care. *Current Issues in Criminal Justice, 14*(1), 9–30.

Yuval-Davis, N., Wemyss, G., & Cassidy, K. (2018). Everyday bordering, belonging and the reorientation of British immigration legislation. *Sociology, 52*(2), 228–44.

3 The thin blue line between protection and persecution

Policing LGBTQ2S refugees in Canada

Alexa DeGagne and Megan Gaucher

In 2017, LGBTQ2S[1] refugee organizations in Vancouver refused to walk in the city's Pride parade with the police due to their continued engagement in deportations of queer and trans asylum seekers and refugees. Rainbow Refugee requested the removal of uniformed police officers from the parade in an open letter to the Vancouver Pride Society. Recognizing that many LGBTQ2S refugees experience multiple forms of state violence both in their country of origin and Canada, Rainbow Refugee explained how the act of its members walking in Pride is quite often a form of sexual liberation. While some members found uniformed police to be reassuring, others continue to feel unsafe and at risk both as a result of their sexual orientation and their being refugees (Rainbow Refugee, 2017). These consultations, along with the Vancouver Police Department's ongoing collaboration with Canadian Border Services Agency and Rainbow Refugee's solidarity with Black Lives Matter, informed Rainbow Refugee's refusal to walk in Pride so long as uniformed police officers also participated.

Similar demands were made by LGBTQ2S organizations in Winnipeg. Following public consultation with community members, Pride Winnipeg announced that uniformed police officers would not be invited to participate in their 2017 parade. In an online survey, one-third of respondents identified police uniforms as a traumatic "trigger point," citing experiences of mistrust, apathy and prejudice among transgender, two-spirit and queer people of color (CBC News 2017). Reaction from the Winnipeg Police Service (WPS) was mixed. Recognizing the measure as reasonable and understandable, Commander of the Community Support Division Gord Friesen responded by drawing parallels between WPS' relationship-building work with the LGBTQ2S community and newcomers to Canada. As Friesen explained, newcomers "come from places where the police don't conduct themselves the way we do," and as such, it is important that WPS "humanize the police force first" (CBC News 2017). Through a discourse analysis of media coverage of this moment, Corinne Mason found,

> While "people of colour, two-spirit, transgender" community members were named by Pride Winnipeg as reporting the most negative experiences

with police, WPS consistently identified the comfort and safety of newcomers to Manitoba as the reason for Pride Winnipeg's decision to disallow uniformed officers to march. In fact, 26% of coverage about police presence at Pride focused on newcomers.

(Mason, forthcoming, p. 7)

The Winnipeg Police Union expressed disappointment, claiming that the exclusionary measure was antithetical to the inclusive spirit of Pride, and that if Pride Winnipeg is trying to "incite hatred, they're being successful" (Grabish, 2017).

These two examples frame our analysis of the engagements between domestic police and LGBTQ2S asylum seekers and refugees in Canada. Rich examination of queer asylum seekers' experiences with the Canadian refugee determination process highlights multiple barriers including, but not limited to, static conceptualizations of sexuality and sexual orientation (Dustin and Ferreira, 2017; Hersch, 2017; Mulé, 2019; Rehaag, 2017); the adoption of Western narratives to assess non-Western expressions of sexuality (Gaucher and DeGagne, 2016; Hersch, 2015; Murray, 2015); and questions of credibility (LaViolette, 2014; Rinaldi and Fernando, 2019). This work speaks to the reality that while, comparatively speaking, lesbian, gay and bisexual asylum seekers are admitted to Canada in higher rates, institutionalized heteronormativity and cisnormativity within the determination system itself presents implications unique to this group. In addition to their physical crossing of the Canadian border being policed, queer refugees have their sexual encounters and behaviors both in their countries of origin and upon arrival in Canada policed in the name of assessing their credibility. Less attention has been paid, however, to the policing of queer and trans refugees—both formal and informal—post-admittance (Mason, forthcoming).

Debates over police participation in Pride parades have become proxies for the long-simmering antagonisms between LGBTQ2S communities and police organizations across the country. Canadian police organizations have a long-standing history of targeting, surveilling, harassing, accosting and criminalizing people on the basis of sexuality, gender and race. Black Lives Matter (BLM) Toronto brought renewed attention to these abuses when they walked in Pride Toronto's 2016 parade as an honored group. After initiating a sit-in, BLM Toronto presented a list of demands to Pride Toronto, asking for support and funding for QTBIPOC (queer, trans, Black, Indigenous, people of color) events at Pride, and for police floats to be removed from future Pride Toronto events. BLM Toronto organizers argued that police organizations were colonial and racist, anti-queer and anti-transgender institutions and, therefore, their presence in queer spaces was threatening to Black, Indigenous, POC, immigrant, and refugee LGBTQ2S people. Following the BLM Toronto sit-in, LGBTQ2S activists in other Canadian cities engaged in counter-police actions, ranging from stopping their own Pride parades, to launching social media campaigns, to creating networks of community patrol and safety. These acts of resistance spurred caustic debates across Canadian LGBTQ2S communities about systemic racism, homophobia and transphobia within police organizations, the role of police organizations in LGBTQ2S spaces, and LGBTQ2S people's safety and equality. Backlash came, in part, from LGBTQ2S people who believed that the criminal justice system, and the police, were the best means for assuring protection of community, self, and property. Those who protested the police held that police should not be able to use Pride parades to deepen their regulation of LGBTQ2S communities because the acceptance of police in the Pride parade legitimizes and normalizes increased police presence and the surveillance of marginalized people in LGBTQ2S communities and spaces (DeGagne, 2020).

Our chapter aims to contribute to this conversation by examining queer and trans refugees' experiences with police and being policed post-arrival, and how these experiences have been taken up in the context of police presence at Pride. We examine cases in which LGBTQ2S refugee organizations, and allied groups—QPOC Winnipeg, Two-Spirit People of Manitoba, Like That @Sunshine House (Winnipeg), Queerview Winnipeg, Rainbow Refugee (Vancouver), No One Is Illegal (Coast Salish Territories, Vancouver), No One Is Illegal (Toronto), Coalition of Queer and Trans People of Colour (Edmonton)— have pushed back against and protested Canadian police organizations' incorporation into LGBTQ2S communities through Pride Parades. In the third section of this chapter, we present a mini case study, consisting of two interviews with LGBTQ2S community members who have been directly involved in debates over police presence in the Edmonton Pride Parade.[2] Using the cases of Vancouver and Winnipeg as a starting point, we argue that these resistances disrupt and challenge homonormal mainstream gay and lesbian organizations' legitimization of the intertwined and mutually reinforcing state-making work of the detention state and the national security state. This will be accomplished through an exploration of both the historical and contemporary role of police in Canada's colonial state project; the implications everyday "disorder policing" presents for LGBTQ2S citizens and non-citizens; interview data that maps LGBTQ2S refugees' encounters with police both domestically and abroad; and a discussion of how these acts of resistance speak to a continued trend of contesting police presence in LGBTQ2S spaces. While not solely focusing on the prison system, we address processes of policing that lead to the detention and incarceration of LGBTQ2S refugees and, as such, this chapter aims to position LGBTQ2S refugees within this broader discussion of policing, colonial state building and prison/penal abolitionism in Canada.

Police buttressing the colonial Canadian state project

Canadian governments—both Liberal and Conservative alike—have used the state's progressive stance on LGBT rights to simultaneously recruit certain queer refugees and justify the continued marking of certain cultures as inherently homophobic and "backward." The Conservative government under Prime Minister Stephen Harper was accused of "pinkwashing," with then-Minister of Citizenship and Immigration Jason Kenney and then-Minister of

Foreign Affairs John Baird touting the government's record on gay and lesbian refugee rights. Kenney and Baird praised the government's "lead in helping gay refugees who have fled often violent persecution in Iran to begin new, safe lives in Canada" (CTV News, 2012), all the while passing punitive domestic legislation (Trevenen and DeGagne, 2015). More recently, the Trudeau government favored women, children, families and gay men (who were not initially part of this plan) in its intake of 25,000 Syrian refugees in 2015, positioning single straight men as potential terrorists (Barton, 2015). Governments have used their efforts to protect certain sexual minorities abroad by pitting certain queer bodies within Canadian borders against each other and juxtaposing the progressive Canadian state against the barbaric, traditional non-Western state, ultimately furthering rationalizations for Canada's ongoing settler colonial project.

Canadian police organizations are positioned within this narrative as emblems of the country's progress, which takes the forms of order and civility, and thus safety, for particular groups of people and the state. In recent decades, police organizations have been cast as protectors of oppressed populations within Canada, for example, charged with intervening in domestic violence cases, and homophobic and racist attacks. Yet Canadian police organizations were established to implement and entrench settler colonization and Canadian state making. Police were used to surveil, target, and stop Indigenous "rebellions" against the Canadian state-making project, which consisted of land theft, child apprehension, and cultural genocide (Monaghan, 2013; Monchalin, 2016). The 2020 Royal Canadian Mounted Police (RCMP) dismantlement of the Wet'suwet'en camp seeks to fortify colonial incursions on Indigenous land and peoples. Throughout colonization, Indigenous people and their practices have been deemed "uncivilized," and therefore claimless to their lands, and unable to raise their children, in part because they did not practice "proper" colonial patriarchal kinship, sexual, and gender relations (Morgensen, 2010). To further disseminate Western colonial power relations—through the reproduction of proper gendered and raced populations—the police enforced various sodomy, obscenity, and gross indecency laws against sexual "deviance" and gender non-conformity (Lenon, 2015). The dominant myth and rallying cry have been that white gay men were predominantly affected by these laws and the attendant police abuse. Yet Indigenous, racialized, immigrant, and refugee LGBTQ2S people—those who hold disruptive positions in relation to the settler colonial project—were and continue to be targeted by police, and disproportionately charged and convicted for such sexual crimes (Mogul et al., 2011).

Canadian state making requires policing of sexual "deviants" not just through sexual crimes but also policing across actions and spaces. We see this logic extended to contemporary refugee legislation. The Harper government's 2012 amendments to the *Immigration and Refugee Protection Act,* specifically the *Balanced Refugee Reform Act,* included multiple reforms focused on enhanced state detention and deportation powers exercised against asylum seekers marked as security threats. For Atak et al., this legislation was the cornerstone of a series of legislative and discursive measures aimed at criminalizing "bogus" refugee claimants, while using the "language of security to rationalize the imposition of disproportionately harsh treatment" (Atak et al., 2018, p. 1). In the government's criminalizing of certain migrant groups, asylum seekers are framed as potential queue jumpers, using fraudulent claims of persecution to exploit the generosity of the Canadian state. In response, the state enacts both stricter measurements of credibility assessment to prevent the intake of "bogus" refugees, and harsher penalties for those accused of compromising the terms of their admissibility. Credibility assessment is thus ongoing, particularly for those deemed a threat to national security; what constitutes threat being open to interpretation. Simply put, the "bogus" refugee is criminalized by virtue of their actions to obtain Canadian citizenship, rather than by intersecting systems of racism, settler colonialism and heteronormativity and cisnormativity used to establish their credibility in the first place. Further, this ongoing assessment is operationalized via multiple sites of surveillance including, but not limited to, border guards, bureaucratic agencies, detention/holding sites, and police organizations.

Just as homonormative queers become invested in the Canadian security state, they are also invested in and legitimize the detention state, offering inclusion and protection to some queer and trans citizens in exchange for the targeting, detriment and exclusion of precarious marginalized populations. Kinsman and Gentile argue that the inclusion of some queers ("mostly but not entirely middle-class white men") into the Canadian "national security state" has resulted in the further exclusion of marginalized queers who are "too queer, too irresponsible, and not respectable enough to be part of this nation" (Kinsman and Gentile, 2010, p. 433). In this light, queer rights and inclusion are often obtained at the expense of "communities who are excluded, overpoliced or exceptionalized through regimes of citizenship, policing, immigration regulation, border control and refugee asylum," ultimately invisibilizing the LGBTQ2S community's experiences of discrimination and violence within Canadian borders (Trevenen and DeGagne, 2015, p. 101). In their call for the removal of uniformed police at Pride, both Rainbow Refugee and No One Is Illegal draw attention to this complex process of "marginalization within marginalization" taking place. While both organizations welcome the celebratory nature of Pride, they identify their responsibility to advocate for those who "do not yet receive equal protection, safety and respect from Canadian law enforcement" (Rainbow Refugee, 2017).

"Disorder policing" and the surveillance of LGBTQ2S precarious citizens and non-citizens

Surveillance of queer and trans spaces by the police and their entrapment of queer and trans people dates back to at least the late 19th and early 20th centuries (Aldrich, 2004). Riots erupted in Montreal in 1975 and Toronto in 1981 as LGBTQ2S people in both cities pushed back against heightened police intervention in gay communities, businesses, organizations, and media (Kinsman and Gentile, 2010). Moreover, the first half of the 1980s was characterized by community- and organization- building as a means to secure safe spaces in the face of police and public harassment (Guidotto, 2011). These protests, marches, and campaigns against police surveillance, raids, sting operations, and criminalization represent critical and galvanizing moments in which LGBTQ2S people fought back in collective ways (Hooper, 2017; Warner, 2002).

While the last large-scale police raid on a gay establishment in Canada occurred in 2002 in Calgary, police across the country continue to orchestrate sting operations against queer and trans people having sex in public spaces, now predominantly relying on the tactic of "disorder policing" to intervene in people's daily lives. Police organizations in Canada adopted new modes of policing in the 1990s which "emphasize[d] the policing of low-level disorder" to ward off higher level criminality and the spreading of disorder (Kaplan-Lyman, 2012, p. 181). At its inception, disorder policing focused on stopping people for lesser crimes who were suspected of higher crimes. The tactic progressed, however, to stopping, carding and frisking people who were thought to be potential offenders (Maynard, 2017). Anti-racism LGBTQ2S activists have long stated that police use disorder policing to target racialized and Indigenous LGBTQ2S people on a more insidious basis than the infamous bar raids. Critics and activists argue that police carding is based on systemic colonial, racist, anti-poverty, heteronormal, cisnormal and saneist profiling. People who are Black, Indigenous, unhoused, poor, disabled, in mental distress, neurodivergent and undocumented within LGBTQ2S populations are targeted, surveilled, and carded as they are assumed to be (or to be always potentially) deviant and criminal.

While efforts have arguably been made to correct these discriminatory practices, anti-carceral advocates contend that such initiatives fail to sufficiently dismantle systemic racism, discrimination and abuse. Practices such as carding, surveillance, and incarceration continue to disproportionately target Black, Indigenous, homeless, poor, Muslim, trans, sex worker, disabled, in mental distress, racialized and undocumented communities in Canada (Maynard, 2017). These marginalized populations are thus more likely to be charged and convicted of crimes, to receive harsher and longer sentences, and to experience discrimination, sexual assault, and violence from police and correctional officers (Cole, 2020).

Commonplace understandings of migrant precarity typically focus on those whose precariousness is determined by their illegal status, the assumption being that one's status within Canadian borders is not precarious if here legally. Critical citizenship scholars have pushed back against this correlation, advocating for a concept of precarious status that accounts for the institutional production of authorized and unauthorized legal, social and political forms of "less than full status" non-citizenship, as well as the "nonlinear trajectories" of precarious and non-precarious status (Goldring and Landolt, 2013, pp. 14–15). Simply put, not all refugees easily transition from non-citizen to citizen; moreover, legal citizenship does not necessarily eliminate precariousness. In analyzing queer refugees' experiences with borders, precarity, and citizenship, we need to think beyond conceptual binaries of citizen/non-citizen, precarious/non-precarious, incarcerated/free, etc. A queer, anti-carceral approach offers such a framework, proposing that we analyze these concepts as being inclusive of "forms of punishment that exist outside of detention centres, jails and prisons—insights that challenge the common sense idea that state penal authority always outweighs everyday forms of policing by non-state authorities" (Musto, 2019, p. 44). We do not address prisons directly in this chapter but analyze the processes of policing, which leads to the detention and incarceration of particular groups of people. This approach allows us to question the role of police in these spaces and communities more generally. The policing of migrant status is not exclusive to immigration-focused legislation; rather, certain migrants—dependent on their race, citizenship status, sexual orientation, etc.—continue to encounter physical and ideological borders post-arrival in Canada. Further, certain migrants have their status called into question in perceived non-legal spaces such as accessing health services, social assistance, and education; taking public transit; or in this case, attending Pride events. In all of these instances, migrants often have their status called into question by both penal-state and supposedly non-penal state authorities, and are subsequently reported to police and/or immigration authorities. An accurate conceptualization of precarity for queer refugees thus requires accounting for complex ways in which the conditions of precariousness are "upheld, breached, or challenged in practice, at various levels and sites, by multiple institutional actors, with variable outcomes" (Goldring and Landolt, 2013, p. 15).

While refugee-focused disorder policing arguably focuses on low-level offences, it potentially presents serious consequences for those being policed (Kinsman, 2018). Asylum seekers and refugee claimants can be refused permanent residence if sentenced for any crime, regardless of time served, often resulting in detention and/or deportation. In their 2015 report "Often Asking, Always Telling: The Toronto Police Service and the Sanctuary City Policy," No One Is Illegal concluded that the Toronto Police Service is actively involved in immigration enforcement, despite their much lauded Sanctuary City legislation. Between November 2014 and June 2015, the Toronto Police reported 3,278 people to Canada Border Services Agency (CBSA); 83% of those reports were not the result of outstanding immigration warrants but, rather, a request to perform a "status check" on persons deemed suspicious (No One Is Illegal, Toronto, 2015). Similarly, Transit Police in Vancouver reported 328 individuals to CBSA in 2013, one in five of those facing an investigation into their immigration status and subsequent deportation (No One Is Illegal, Coast Salish Territories, Vancouver, 2015). Like the data from Toronto, a small fraction of those referred actually had outstanding immigration warrants and the rest were reported out of suspicion following a minor infraction such as fare evasion (Marsden, 2019). Moreover, feelings of suspicion are sparked by a range of criteria from a lack of legal documentation to indicators such as skin color, accent, language proficiency, etc. (No One is Illegal, Toronto, 2015). Available data on carding practices in these cities demonstrates that when racialized people call the police, everyone involved is often carded and those without proper identification or unclear immigration status are reported to border authorities, as was the case with Lilliana Fontes, who challenged a deportation order after the police reported her to CBSA while investigating her ex-partner for domestic abuse in 2011 (No One is Illegal, Toronto, 2015). Disorder policing can therefore present very serious repercussions for refugees, asylum seekers, and others with precarious status.

Two interviews on exporting police racism and anti-LGBTQ2S oppression

While LGBTQ2S refugee organizations and allied groups have articulated their objections to police participation in Pride parades, and queer and trans spaces generally, homonormative LGBT community members have defended police organizations. Such defenses of the police serve to elicit police protection for privileged LGBT people, and to thereby legitimize police presence within LGBTQ2S communities and spaces. In recent decades, the police incorporation of and into LGBTQ2S communities has come in several forms: the establishment of LGBTQ2S police liaison and/or general equity committees; the inclusion of sexuality, and gender identity and expression in federal hate crimes legislation; police recruitment campaigns targeted at LGBTQ people; official apologies from municipal police organizations and the federal government for historical police abuses of LGBTQ2S people; conciliation consultations and processes by police organizations; as well as the inclusion of police organizations and officers in LGBTQ2S spaces, neighborhoods, events, and Pride parades.

Defending the police, LGBT community members argued that: there are LGBTQ2S police officers who deserve to be in the parades; police organizations are not systemically homophobic and transphobic but there may be a few "bad apple" police officers who should be disciplined; it is discriminatory and divisive to exclude police from the parades; the LGBTQ2S community cannot build a good relationship with the police by excluding them from queer spaces; and, a minority of LGBTQ2S people have negative relationships with the police and their voices do not represent the desires of the entire community. In the Winnipeg case, the police connected LGBTQ2S people's objection to the inclusion of police in Pride events to an assumed newcomers' fear in relation to the police in their countries of origin. In interviews conducted with LGBTQ2S community members in Edmonton, we have heard similar defenses of the police emerge, which seek to absolve Canadian police organizations of alleged racism, homophobia, and transphobia by claiming that immigrants and refugees have led the anti-police protests, and that they are doing so based on post-traumatic stress from interactions with police organizations in other, less "progressive" countries.

In 2018, a Coalition of Queer and Trans People of Color stopped the Edmonton Pride Parade and made a similar list of demands to those of BLM

Toronto in 2016, including "that the Pride Society uninvite the Edmonton Police Service, RCMP and Military from marching in future parades" (Pride Action, 2018). Interviews were conducted with Edmonton-based LGBTQ2S community members who have been engaged in these resistances and debates. Two of the interviewees' statements were particularly demonstrative of the tensions discussed in this chapter. Interviewee 1 is a white, cisgender lesbian who was a board chair of the Edmonton Pride Festival Society. Interviewee 2 is a Black, queer trans man who is a refugee and activist with several refugee, POC, queer, and trans organizations, and was a leader in the 2018 Edmonton Pride Parade protest.[3]

Interviewee 1

I feel that some of the [divide over the police in the LGBTQ community] is from individuals that come from different countries where the police are bad people. In Canada, yes there are bad police, there are bad people everywhere, but I don't feel it's to the degree of the protests and what happened last year, in our country. I feel there's a confusion between what police do in other countries—they do not do good things, they do not treat gay people well—in other countries they are killing gay people. But here that's not the case that I know of. Yes, there are things that happen, but I feel like homophobic people are mostly people that are on the street, they're not necessarily police, especially when I see that [the police] have that [Sexual Minorities] Liaison Committee, I was on that for a little while. So [the police] certainly do try to help in the gay community. Now I'm sure they don't all help, but it's like any kind of work—there's good people and bad people everywhere. I feel like young people are coming forward and speaking, but they're not speaking on behalf of everybody. They're speaking on behalf of a smaller number of people.

Interviewee 2

LGBTQ refugees have faced violence back home, and that is lived trauma that has not been addressed. And coming [to Canada] I know some people might think police are different, but there is no difference between the police here and the police back home. This might be a developed country, but whatever actions, whatever [the police] do is completely the same. And some of the refugees have not yet healed. They still have this trauma that keeps them awake all the time, and it is coming from police brutality, from police violence. That takes a while. And it means that they have to heal fast before they can even have conversations with the police. Healing takes time if it is not actually prioritized by organizations which have led to oppression, like the police. If police could prioritize the healing, and give space to people who need space and are still healing I think it can ease up their process of having conversations with folks from Raricanow and other refugees. Some of our [LGBTQ refugee] members are faced with police brutality from Canadian police, and that comes through carding, and [the LGBTQ refugees] not knowing their rights. You find them in conversation with police, and it's hard, if you don't know [your rights] police are going to take advantage of you. As a Black person, [the police] already know I may be affiliated with gangsters and already affiliated with drugs or something like that, which is not right. So they've been carded, some of them have been stopped, asked for their IDs. Many refugees don't have IDs, some of them have immigration IDs, which police are not aware of. So they then take them into questioning, and these are people who have trauma even just talking to cops so whenever they're talking [to the police], they're talking from a scared point of view. They can't even explain the paperwork they have because they don't have IDs. Maybe some don't even have an apartment yet to attain the ID card. Those who don't have a work permit may have a refugee ID. But the police are not aware of that and it is not the job of LGBTQ refugees to make the police aware of something like that.

Interviewee 2 points to the traumatic experiences LGBTQ2S refugees have with police in their countries of origin, and how that trauma is exacerbated and reproduced through interactions with police in Canada. He offers examples of how many LGBTQ2S refugees are racially profiled, targeted, and carded by the police; are questioned because of their lack of access to IDs and police officers' lack of knowledge of available IDs; and ultimately have their safety and refugee status threatened.

Yet through statements like those from Interviewee 1, the problem of the police is reoriented as coming from the outside, as being brought in by refugees and misplaced on Canadian police organizations. Mason (forthcoming) builds on Robyn Maynard's (2017) work on Canada's continued outsourcing of anti-Blackness, arguing:

> Assumed to exist in another time or another place, anti-Blackness is outsourced to historical conditions or to another geography, such as the United States. Despite being 3% of the population, Black people make up one-third of those killed by police in parts of the country and Black people are incarcerated in federal prisons at a rate three times higher than the number of Black people in the Canadian population (Maynard, 2017, p. 5). Extending her work to thinking about state violence against BIPOC communities, and especially 2SLGBTQ individuals, I argue that Canada has no "common sense stock knowledge" of negative police relations with racialized queer and trans people."
>
> (Mason, forthcoming, pp. 4–5)

Thus, the first interviewee displaces and delegitimizes the issues, experiences and grievances of Indigenous and racialized LGBTQ2S people against Canadian police in several ways. First, the protestors are characterized as "speaking on behalf of a smaller number of people," thus implying that the grievances of racialized members of the LGBTQ2S community are not representative of the LGBTQ2S community, and thereby dissociating refugee and racialized LGBTQ2S people from the Canadian community. Such racially-exclusive discourses are particularly damaging to LGBTQ2S refugee claimants who must demonstrate a connection to Canadian LGBTQ2S communities to make the case that they are in fact a sexual minority.

Second, police actions are individualized as "a few bad apples," and no more homophobic than the general public. Third, police actions are excused through police incorporation initiatives like Liaison Committees, which are deemed to be trustworthy efforts to improve relations with LGBTQ2S people. Thus the interviewee positions Canada, and its police organizations, as benevolent and good in comparison to "other" countries where the police are "killing gay people." Given that refugees are racialized, and racialized people are disproportionately considered to be non-citizens, it stands to reason that police organizations in refugees' countries of origin are also assumed to be people of color. As OmiSoore Dryden argued in a research interview, refugees are seen as experiencing violence only from other Black people: police in their countries of origin. In this vein, Canadian colonial civility and order is reinforced.

Conclusion

The acts of resistance at Pride in Vancouver, Winnipeg, and elsewhere that were discussed in this chapter highlight the continued pushing back against the ongoing settler colonial state-building project by members of the LGBTQ2S community who question police intervention in queer spaces. No One Is Illegal, Coast Salish Territories, Vancouver (2017) flipped this question of whether the police should be in parades, asking, "If the police were not to march as an institution in Pride, would anyone feel emotion-ally triggered or physically threatened by their absence? Probably not." Some LGBTQ2S community members argue that the police are needed to provide security in defense of potential homophobic and transphobic attacks. To maintain their relative privilege and status, the accepted and protected LGBT citizens defend Canadian police, the detention state and the national security state by asking for police engagement in their commu-nities. Racialized LGBTQ2S refugees are thereby othered, dissociated from the Canadian LGBTQ2S community, silenced and subjected to heightened surveillance, regulation and deportation.

LGBTQ2S community members have extensive histories of marshaling their own parades, which build on long-running practices of mutual aid and "communities of solidarity": providing supports for mental distress, establishing community-safety patrols, and providing free legal advice and defense funds. All of these practices are based on a rejection of state institutions—police, carceral, immigrant, medical, and legal—which have regulated, threatened, and shortened LGBTQ2S lives. Self-marshaling and safety-patrols during Pride parades provide a micro example of what future space could be without the incursion of state institutions in queer spaces. Building what No One is Illegal refers to as "communities of solidarity," these organizations aim to dismantle the contemporary privileging of police in queer spaces and shed light on racialized LGBTQ2S refugees' daily experiences with borders and border enforcement in their many forms. Acts of resistance at Pride highlight efforts to reclaim space not only from the settler colonial state, but also LGBTQ2S community members who reinforce—either intentionally or unintentionally—these unequal power dynamics.

In positioning LGBTQ2S refugees within this broader discussion of policing, incarceration and detention, colonial state building, and LGBTQ2S communities in Canada, we see the complexity of this resistance at work. The work of Black Lives Matter, No One is Illegal and Rainbow Refugee requires an "unlearning of anti-Black racisms in particular with social justice movements" (No One Is Illegal, Coast Salish Territories, Vancouver, 2015). Racially neutral narratives of queer marginalization—specifically in the context of police at Pride—gloss over the deep-rooted interconnectedness between colonialism, xenophobia, racism, capitalism, transphobia and homophobia, and speak to the reality that decolonization requires the simultaneous deconstruction of these multiple systems of power. Moreover, these debates show the interlocking relationships between the two levels of domestic and immigration policing and incarceration/detention, revealing that any attempt to dismantle one level would require serious consideration of how to dismantle the other level. It is not just about excluding police from Pride; rather, it is about pushing back against disorder policing and immigration enforcement in cities so that LGBTQ2S refugees can "access the safety, services and supports they need to live with dignity, and without fear of detention, deportation or harassment" (No One Is Illegal, Toronto, 2019).

Notes

1   Lesbian, gay, bisexual, transgender, queer or questioning, and Two-Spirit
2   Interviews were conducted by Alexa DeGagne as part of her larger Social Sciences and Humanities Research Council-funded research project, "The changing relationship between LGBTQ people and police organizations in Canada." The plan for this study has been approved for its adherence to ethical guidelines by the *Athabasca University Research Ethics Board.*
3   The interviewees' names are not used. Their self-identified race, sexuality and gender, and their organizational affiliations are used to contextualize their perspectives, experiences and statements.

References

Aldrich, R. (2004). Homosexuality and the city: an historical overview. *Urban Studies, 41*(9), 1719–37.

Atak, I., Hudson, G., & Nakache, D. (2018). The securitisation of Canada's refugee system: Reviewing the unintended consequences of the 2012 reform. *Refugee Survey Quarterly, 37*, 1–24.

Barton, R. (2015, November 22). Canada's Syrian refugee plan limited to women, children and families. CBC News. *www.cbc.ca/news/politics/canada-refugee-plan-women-children-families-1.3330185*

CBC News. (2017, May 26). Police welcome in Pride Winnipeg parade, asked not to wear uniforms. CBC News. www.cbc.ca/news/canada/manitoba/winnipeg-pride-parade-police-1.4134157

CTV News. (2012, September 25). Critics accuse Kenney of 'pinkwashing' in targeted emails. CTV News. *www.ctvnews.ca/politics/critics-accuse-kenney-of-pinkwashing-in-targeted-emails-1.970259*

Cole, D. (2020). *The Skin We're In: A Year of Black Resistance and Power.* Doubleday Canada.

DeGagne, A. (2020). Chapter 12: Pinkwashing pride parades: The politics of police in LGBTQ2S spaces in Canada. In F. MacDonald & A. Dobrowolsky (Eds.), *In Turbulent Times, Transformational Possibilities? Gender and Politics Today and Tomorrow* (pp. 258–280). University of Toronto Press.

Dustin, M., & Ferreira, N. (2017). Canada's guideline 9: improving SOGIE claims assessment? *Forced Migration Review* (56), 80–3.

Gaucher, M. & DeGagne, A. (2016). Guilty until proven prosecuted: The Canadian state's assessment of sexual minority refugee claimants and the invisibility of the non-western sexual non-citizen. *Social Politics: International Studies in Gender, State & Society 23*(3), 459–81.

Goldring, L. & Landolt, P. (Eds). (2013). *Producing and Negotiating Non-Citizenship: Precarious Legal Status in Canada.* University of Toronto Press.

Grabish, A. (2017, May 30). Police union upset by Pride Winnipeg's decision against officers in uniform. CBC News. www.cbc.ca/news/canada/manitoba/pride-winnipeg-police-1.4137548

Guidotto, N. (2011). Looking back: The bathhouse raids in Toronto, 1981. In E.A. Stanley & N. Smith (Eds.), *Captive genders: Trans embodiment and the prison industrial complex* (pp. 63–74). AK Press.

Hersch, N. (2015). Challenges to assessing same-sex relationships under refugee law in Canada. *McGill Law Journal 60*(3), 527–71.

Hersch, N. (2017). Refugee claims and criminalization of same-sex intimacy: The case of Sebastiao. *Canadian Journal of Women and the Law 29*(2), 227–58.

Hooper, T. (2017). Policing gay sex in Toronto Parks in the 1970s and today, Activehistory. ca: History Matters. http://activehistory.ca/2017/02/policing-gay-sex-in-toronto/

Kaplan-Lyman, J. (2012). A punitive bind: Policing, poverty, and neoliberalism in New York City. *Yale Human Rights and Development Law Journal 15*, 177–221.

Kinsman, G. (2018). Policing borders and sexual/gender identities: Queer refugees in the years of Canadian neoliberalism and homonationalism. In Nicol N., Jjuuko A., Lusimbo R., Mulé N., Ursel S., Wahab A., et al. (Eds.), *Envisioning Global LGBT Human Rights: (Neo)colonialism, Neoliberalism, Resistance and Hope* (pp. 97–130). University of London Press.

Kinsman, G., & Gentile, P. (2010). *The Canadian war on queers: National security as sexual regulation.* University of British Columbia Press.

LaViolette, N. (2014). Sexual orientation, gender identity and the refugee determination process in Canada. *Journal of Research in Gender Studies 4*(2), 68–123.

Lenon, S. (2015). Monogamy, marriage, and the making of nation. In O.H. Dryden & S. Lenon (Eds.), *Disrupting queer inclusion: Canadian homonationalisms and the Politics of Belonging* (pp.82–99). University of British Columbia Press.

Marsden, S. (2019). *Enforcing Exclusion: Precarious Migrants and the Law in Canada.* University of British Columbia Press.

Maynard, R. (2017). *Policing Black Lives: State Violence in Canada from Slavery to the Present.* Fernwood Publishing.

Mogul, J. L., Ritchie, A. J., & Whitlock, K. (2011). *Queer (In)justice: The criminalization of LGBT people in the United States.* Beacon Press.

Monaghan, J. (2013). Mounties in the frontier: Circulations, anxieties, and myths of settler colonial policing in Canada. *Journal of Canadian Studies 47*(1), 122–48.

Monchalin, L. (2016). *The Colonial Problem: An Indigenous Perspective on crime and Injustice in Canada.* University of Toronto Press.

Morgensen, S. L. (2010). Settler homonationalism: Theorizing settler colonialism within queer modernities. *GLQ: A Journal of Lesbian and Gay Studies 16*(1–2), 105–31.

Mulé, N. J. (2019). Safe haven questioned: Proof of identity over persecution of SOGIE asylum seekers and refugee claimants in Canada. *Journal of Immigrant & Refugee Studies,* 1–17.

Murray, D. (2015). *Real Queer? Sexual Orientation and Gender Identity Refugees in the Canadian Refugee Apparatus.* Rowman and Littlefield.

Musto, J. (2019). Transing critical criminology: A critical unsettling and transformative anti-carceral feminist reframing. *Critical Criminology 27,* 37–54.

No One Is Illegal, Toronto. (2019). Vision, demands, organizing pillars. Our vision. Retrieved January 30, 2020, from https://toronto.nooneisillegal.org/demands

No One Is Illegal, Toronto. (2015). *2015 in Review.* Retrieved January 30, 2020, from https://toronto.nooneisillegal.org/2015Review

No One Is Illegal, Toronto. (2015) *Often Asking, Always Telling: The Toronto Police Service and the Sanctuary City Policy.* Retrieved January 30, 2020, from https://rabble.ca/sites/rabble/files/often_asking_always_telling_-_kedits_dec_1.pdf

No One Is Illegal, Coast Salish Territories, Vancouver. (2017). Joint open letter to Vancouver Pride Society. https://noii-van.resist.ca/joint-open-letter-to-vancouver-pride-society/

No One Is Illegal, Coast Salish Territories, Vancouver. (2015). Who killed Abdurahman Ibrahim Hassan? Black lives, racisms, police & immigration. http://toronto.mediacoop.ca/blog/hussansk/33683

Pride Action. (2018). Pride Action Press Release. Document circulated by the Queer and Trans People of Colour coalition. In the author's possession.

Rainbow Refugee. (2017). Rainbow Refugee open letter to VPS. www.faceook.com/RainbowRefugee/posts/1811390332234426?__tn__=K-R

Rehaag, S. (2017). Sexual orientation in Canada's revised refugee determination system: An empirical snapshot. *Canadian Journal of Women and the Law 29,* 259–89.

Rinaldi, J., & Fernando, S. (2019). Queer credibility in the homonation-state: Interrogating the affective impacts of credibility assessments on racialized sexual minority refugee claimants. *Refuge: Canada's Journal on Refugees 35*(1), 32–42.

Trevenen, K., & DeGagne, A. (2015). Homonationalism at the border and in the streets: Organizing against exclusion and incorporation. In O.H. Dryden & S. Lenon (Eds.), *Disrupting Queer Inclusion: Canadian Homonationalisms and the Politics of Belonging* (pp.100–15). University of British Columbia Press.

Warner, T. (2002). *Never Going Back: A History of Queer Activism in Canada*. University of Toronto Press.

4 Abolishing innocence

Disrupting the racist/ableist pathologies of childhood

*Liat Ben-Moshe, Nirmala Erevelles
and Erica R. Meiners*

Innocence propels criminal justice reform. Bail reform has advanced, in part, because the people held in jails have not been convicted, only charged: they are still potentially innocent. Exoneration Clinics, Innocence Projects, and other such initiatives have grown at Law Schools across the U.S. in order to rescue individuals who were wrongly convicted. Legal challenges to exempt people from the death penalty have historically turned on proxies for innocence: the person was a juvenile or their "IQ" did not meet a particular threshold. Even the Prison Rape Elimination Act, advanced to protect heterosexual men from the threat of sexual assault in prisons for people the state identifies as men, operationalized a form of anti-queer sexual innocence. As innocence continues to be a central pivot for criminal legal reforms, any movement for abolition requires a critical engagement with this concept.

Intimately connected to forms of social, political and legal recognition, innocence is only conferred on those who are marked as normative. Some can be made to approximate innocence, by growing out of childhood or pathology, and others can be rehabilitated to approximate citizenship, via state violence (assimilation, corrections, medical interventions, etc.). Across both the prison industrial complex and its components and proxies—schools, detention centers, mental health institutions, and nursing homes—and throughout prison reform movements, including some abolitionist endeavors—the discourse of innocence is paramount.

As prison abolitionists, we critique this turn toward innocence in campaigns, movements, and organizations. Yet as scholars and organizers we also recognize the imperative to engage with intersecting movements, often perceived as "outside" of criminal legal mobilizations and abolitionist struggles, to aid in mapping how conceptions of innocence are concurrently shored up, reinforced, or travel across other domains. One of the most obvious, and most difficult-to-challenge sites wherein the artifact of innocence is reproduced is that of discourses about children, childhood, and their proxies.

As historian Robin Bernstein (2011) suggests, childhood not only shaped the artifact of innocence but provided its "perfect alibi." We argue that this ideological work is connected to processes of racial pathologization. Bernstein argues that "libel of insensateness" did not fade with the abolition of slavery but instead "stealthily" moved into "children's culture," where innocence "provides a cover under which otherwise discredited racial ideology survives and continues, covertly, to influence culture" (2011, p. 51). Bernstein suggests that categories such as "children," still widely understood as "race-neutral" developmental markers, function as the perfect containers to house and reproduce deeply racialized, ableist and heterogendered conceptions of innocence.

Childhood is strongly associated with innocence, lack of reason, and an inability to consent (Meiners, 2016); concepts utilized by white supremacist and ableist regimes to mark who is worthy of citizenship. In other words, innocence and childhood are available only to a certain subject, i.e. white, cishetero, non-disabled, and non-Indigenous. Through processes of racial criminal pathologization (Ben-Moshe, 2020), other subjects, especially disabled, Indigenous and racialized Others (particularly Black and Brown people) are not afforded childhood or innocence. On occasion when innocence is accorded to these Others, the "pathologization" of childhood occurs—a process that has critical implications for those located at the intersections of race, class, gender, and disability. Following Ruth Gilmore's exhortation that the problem "is not to figure out how to determine or prove innocence of certain individuals or certain classes of people but to attack the general system through which criminalization proceeds" (Loyd, 2012, p. 43), we argue that any abolitionist practice necessitates an analysis of how white supremacist carceral ableism exploits disability via its pathologization of childhood and its affiliation with innocence.

Much of prison reform, and some calls for abolition, are centered on the figure of the "non non nons" (non-serious, non-violent, non-sex-related) (Gottschalk, 2015) but also, on the more insidious (and equally challenging for building a movement for abolition) figure of the innocent (Gilmore, 2015). In this chapter, each of us, from both separate and overlapping disciplinary locations—critical childhood studies, disability studies, and critical race studies—explores how an abolitionist praxis is shaped by a relationship between childhood and innocence at the intersections of race/class/gender/sexuality/disability. In the first section of the chapter, Erica Meiners demonstrates how the image of the child and the paradoxical invocation of innocence associated with it is used to reproduce, expand, and critique carceral logics. Then in the next section, Liat Ben-Moshe explores the oppressive and often contradictory implications of attributions of childhood to disabled adults in an attempt to abolish certain carceral features (solitary, execution). Finally, in the last section of the paper, Nirmala Erevelles explores how this pathologization of childhood via the exploitation of disability is disproportionately applied to students of color in a non-traditional carceral space—public education. We conclude by underscoring how innocence makes possible racialized ableist/pathologizing notions in complicated ways and interconnected sites. While the point of reference for this analysis is insular and largely where we currently live, study, and organize— the United States—we argue that conceptions of the child and the use of innocence in criminal legal reform movements necessary to the construction of but are not unique to the U.S.

Childhood, carceral logics and the paradox of innocence

From *Good Morning America* to the Catholic Church, the year 2019 focused increased attention on the growing number of unattended non-adult migrants being held in prisons at the U.S. / Mexico border. Mainstream media circulates images of young—generally Latinx—children behind bars, stories of incarcerated babies, coverage that alludes to an increase in child sexual traffickers, and exposés on prisons teeming with cages of children. Largely erased from this coverage: the push and pull of U.S. economic and colonial practices and policies that engineer this political moment.

Unsurprisingly, at the border, childhood—specifically childhood innocence—is a fluid enough artifact to be deployed in support of and against "family separation." Those in support of borders state that detention and separation are required to save the innocent from the legions of voracious child sex traffickers. The implied threat also rests on ableist foundations. Shielding children from (disabling) harm, sexual or otherwise, is an unparalleled primary moral imperative. Children must be removed from their loved ones and caged for their protection. High profile and racist narratives of sexual slavery, often demonizing parents who would subject their child to long migration journeys, justify a child's detention and separation from adults. Yet on the other end of the political spectrum those who do not support endless borders and walls also invoke "protection" and argue against subjecting a child to incarceration. Children do not deserve to be behind bars. Images of small figures in adult orange jumpsuits, tiny hands clasping bars—and the looming sexual damage always implied by incarceration—provoke audiences on the left to act. Public support galvanized some politicians to inspect prisons, protest conditions, and also to organize for monitoring and release.

In these narratives, not unlike at previous political moments, the "child" is a fluid enough artifact to be used both to defend and to challenge the U.S. government's practice of child separation and detention at the border. Perceptions of innocence are always key to these mobilizations.

Less sympathetic? Migrant adults who are clearly not innocent and just may be traffickers. Yet the enduring trope of innocence is masked in all of these campaigns to save young people—from sexual harm or from the ravages of the U.S. government—resulting in the de facto criminalization of the adults in their lives who are often their caregivers. Erased in this context is the asymmetry and porousness of the tie between childhood and innocence. Not only have race, gender, ability, sexuality, and more always marked who "counts" as a child, but also within this fluid category of "childhood," innocence is never equitably distributed. While 15-years-olds at the border might engender support and protection, in classrooms and communities across the U.S., Black, disabled and/or queer 15-year-olds, for example, are rarely imbued with any innocence. Also shielded from critical scrutiny in all of these "child saving" campaigns is the key actor responsible for harm—the state—and its key weapons—a border and legions of law enforcement.

The child—along with all institutions involved in shaping this figure, including schools, families, and juvenile criminal legal systems—is a key technology of an always capacious and shifting carceral regime. New forms of surveillance are minted to safeguard children, and new categories of crime are required to mold the child into an appropriate adult (or to indefinitely mark her as inalienable and less than fully human). This is an old story. Yet the work to challenge or reform this carceral apparatus all too often naturalizes and invokes the very artifacts and technologies—in the form of the child—that reproduce and expand core carceral logics. In other words, if children don't belong in immigration prisons, others do. This is the reformist (or non-abolitionary) approach that rests on the artifact of childhood and innocence.

The ableist politics of innocent childhoods

Childhood has never been available to all. But to some, childhood is an eternal status. This is the case for (some, perhaps most) people with labels of intellectual disabilities, who are often perceived (legally and culturally) as in need of constant protection, as eternal children and vulnerable subjects. (This has caveats, of course, as in the figure of the menacing, especially sexually forward, disabled person, usually a man). Some might think that this permanent state of exception of being perceived as eternally child-like/innocent/vulnerable might lead to more protection and less incarceration. But the category of eternally vulnerable/child-like entails not just innocence and the rights conferred on children but also the taking away of rights and freedoms afforded to *adults* such as voting, parenting, sexual and reproductive freedoms, and freedom of movement, often through incarceration/institutionalization. For many disabled people and especially disabled people of color, incarceration is not an exception but a pervasive reality or fear ("if you don't do x you will end up in the institution/group home/jail") (Ben-Moshe, 2013).

Take, for example, the semi-successful campaign to abolish the death penalty for those with intellectual disability labels. In 2002, a Supreme Court case (Atkins v. Virginia) forbade state executions for those who score under a certain threshold (usually 70) in an IQ test because they supposedly have the judgment of a child. Unfortunately, racial criminal pathologization is clearly exemplified in this attempt at abolition for some but not others. In the years since the Atkins ruling, as legal scholar Robert Sanger describes, "some prosecution experts have begun using so-called "ethnic adjustments" to artificially raise minority defendants' IQ scores." (Sanger, 2015, p. 87). In other words, because pathologization and racialization are interlinked with innocence/danger, the ruling is used not to show the inherent problem with corporeal punishment but to justify, clear the path and ultimately execute *more* people of color with disabilities.

Such assumptions about people's competence or proximity to childhood do not stop at the prison gate, and they have grave consequences. Tying innocence with (eternal) childhood also reifies notions like "low IQ" and "mental illness" as inherent conditions in people and not man-made normative frames for measuring people in relation to others (Intelligence Quotient tests do not measure intelligence; they are standardized tests that crudely score an individual's ability to perform on standardized test on verbal, mathematical and spatial measurements). Intelligence and mental state are culturally normative and subjective terms, what Thomas Szasz called "metaphors" or "myths" (Szasz, 1961).

The trope of innocence undergirds many of these campaigns for so-called abolition (of the death penalty, of solitary confinement, or imprisonment). The assumption is that those with psychiatric or/and intellectual disabilities didn't know what they were doing or were "out of their minds" or "not of sound mind" and therefore did not "really" do the harm (the insanity defense, IQ tests). This slippery slope of the discourse of innocence and pathologization of childhood, can be mobilized to supposedly protect disabled/mad people from carcerality (solitary, execution), but it is then used to take away rights and freedoms by arguing for incarceration by other means—such as incarceration in psychiatric institutions, medicalization, sterilization, and more.

Another example of the mobilization of innocence as a vehicle of abolition in the context of disability is the demand for ending certain practices of incarceration (only) for vulnerable populations. For example, the campaign to abolish the practice of solitary confinement for people with psychiatric disabilities in the U.S. was based on the fact that solitary confinement exacerbates mental ill-health. Some also call for abolition of the practice of confining psychiatrically disabled people altogether and insist on better screening to prevent such incarceration. The alternatives proposed are mental health courts, and referral to psychiatric treatment facilities and follow-up.

But those imprisoned critique what they call "death by incarceration" (life without parole) as a brutal and barbaric practice (Kim et al., 2018). Being sent to a psychiatric facility or "treatment" is also a form of state violence and it is a colonial apparatus (quite literally) with its roots in violent assimilationist practices that were perfected on aboriginal children who were abducted from their families and taken to be "rehabilitated" in boarding schools (Ross, 1998; Chapman, 2014). New forms of mandatory "treatment" like psychotropic drugs or community treatment orders, which enable one to live outside of prison, are not perceived by psychiatrized people as less coercive (Fabris, 2011). By recapitulating to this racist ableist discourse of innocence and eternal protection, partial abolition and suggested "alternatives" to incarceration, solitary, or execution are also carceral violence. Innocence, in this context as pathology, ensures seemingly more benevolent forms of incarceration—ones that may not have any modes of parole and that legitimate intrusive and abusive treatments under the guise of care.

(Non)innocence and race/ability pathologies in public education

The pathologization of childhood via discourses of (non)innocence at the intersections of race, class, gender, sexuality, and disability proliferate in spaces not traditionally identified as carceral. Here drawing on ideologies of racial criminal pathology (Ben-Moshe, 2020), it has mostly been urban schools populated predominantly by low-income (disabled) students of color that are deemed pathologically undisciplined/dangerous (Anyon, 1997). In these schools where it is presumed that there is little innocence to nurture and protect, students learn in dilapidated buildings receiving a sub-standard curriculum under the most punitive conditions that shift the trajectory of their educational lives towards the school-to-prison pipeline (Adams & Erevelles, 2015). Also, particularly troubling is the fact that many of these low-income students of color are given the controversial disability label—emotional disturbance (ED)—a label that rather than enabling supportive services under special education legislation (e.g. the Individuals with Disabilities Education Act) and disability civil rights legislation (like Section 504 of the Rehabilitation Act), instead justifies the segregation and expulsion of students from public educational contexts into alternative carceral spaces.

Section 504 has a broader reach than the Individuals with Disabilities Education Act (IDEA) in its protection of the civil rights of disabled people because it covers students who may not be classified under the 13 specific disability labels covered by IDEA by recognizing impairments that are episodic or are in remission—such as ED. (Zirkel & Weathers, 2014). More significantly, Section 504 requires that students have access to supportive services within the general education curriculum in inclusive settings (Weber, 2010), such as providing extended time for testing and behavior supports in the classroom itself. However, white students are more than twice as likely to have a 504 plan compared to their Black or Latinx classmates (Zirkel and Weathers, 2014). This differential access of Black/Latinx(disabled) students and white (disabled) students to 504 plans also results in differential outcomes. White (disabled) students with 504 plans have the privilege of being supported within inclusive educational contexts. Black/Latinx (disabled) students with behavioral and/or emotional challenges with no access to 504 plans seldom experience support in inclusive classrooms, are pathologized on account of their (non-normative) behaviors, and are often expelled to segregated prison-like settings like the alternative school and the juvenile justice system (Erevelles, 2014).

These racially differentiated experiences are foregrounded by focusing on a particular practice called the manifestation review that is used to determine whether a student's "inappropriate" behavior is manifested because of their disability or whether that behavior was merely a willful manifestation of the self. As such the manifestation review determines whether the student is innocent of any inappropriate behavior on account of their disability. These determinations of innocence are impacted by how Section 504 applies to those students who can avail themselves of this protection. For example, Hill (2017) reports that Black students in K-12 schools are 3.8 times more likely than white students to receive out of school suspensions, to be expelled and/or to be referred to law enforcement. Additionally, students with ED labels, though representing just 12% of the student population, represented more than a quarter of the students referred to law enforcement.

This racist logic is concealed by the so-called objective assessment procedures that determine the eligibility of students under Section 504 and thus their (non) innocence in educational contexts. What is concealed is that these assessment procedures constitute white (disabled) students and Black(disabled) students as two sides of the same coin held together and yet separated by an oppressive yet contradictory logic. According to this contradictory logic Black students are denied eligibility for protection under Section 504 because they are conceived of as "naturally dangerous" (Alexander, 2010), foregrounding a dangerous biological determinism that is absurdly couched in a language of choice (i.e. they choose to act out). On the other hand, a white student's eligibility for a 504 plan is justified on the grounds of having a "natural" deficiency also deploying a different form of biological determinism that is outside the realm of "choice" (i.e. they cannot help their poor choices), and is therefore eligible for protection under Section 504.

Thus, what has just been described here is how the discourse of innocence imbued with racist/ableist tropes constitutes the "justice gap"—the "difference between the civil legal needs of low-income Americans and the resources available to meet their needs" (Alexander, 2010). This justice gap is central to the constitution of this concept of (non)innocence that continues to render Black/Brown subjects pathologically deviant when we foreground how white supremacist carceral ableism exploits disability via its pathologization of racialized childhoods and their affiliation with the socio-political category of innocence.

Abolition beyond innocence

While perhaps more visible as a movement tactic in criminal legal reform contexts, we argue here that innocence proliferates in other sites—particularly those attached to childhood. The thicket of affect surrounding the figure of the Child makes querying innocence in these sites more fraught, often dangerous. Even raising the question of child sexualities, for example, can result in being charged with predation.

Abolitionists continue to push back on the deployment of the artifact of innocence in campaigns related to targeted criminalization. Innocence is perhaps the most persistent reform logic in play—working as the backdrop to justify the release of people with convictions for drug offenses in the federal system, mobilizing the bail bond movement, and spurring differential treatment for some charged while under the age of 18. In all of these movements, like many before, the perception of a sliver of innocence—the "non-violent offender," the person who has not yet been tried, the youth—makes the reform and the campaign feasible. This is the problem with what Knopp et al. (1976) referred to as the attrition model. Decarcerating certain people still reinforces racist-ableist logics of white supremacist normalcy. Carcerality is still perceived and maintained as viable and justifiable, just not for those who are innocent or should not be there.

Yet abolitionists have been less engaged with tracking and engaging how one of the primary entities reinforcing a priori conceptions of innocence—always asymmetrically—is the figure of the child and its attachment to race-ability; and, concurrently, how the production of innocence through this figure shapes organizing and norms in the criminal legal contexts. Innocence makes possible racialized ableist/pathologizing notions in complicated and often contradictory ways. Here disability gets invoked as a naturalized pathologizing force to often justify incarceration. At other times, disability as innocent vulnerability is invoked to foreground the violence of incarceration and by doing so inspires paternalistic actions that once again deny agency to the "innocent" subject.

In each of these contexts, disability is called to perform rhetorical/ideological labor that is nevertheless rendered invisible and immaterial by ableist frameworks propagated by carceral capitalism. Thus, when disability is invoked via a politics of innocence, its absent presence in white supremacist carceral ableism continues to mark (disabled) bodies at the intersections of difference as pathologically dangerous and/or paternalistically innocent and in both cases leads people away from prisons into institutions, psych facilities, and life-long surveillance, leaving the brutal logic of carcerality intact.

Could it be the case that to challenge innocence we have to end childhood? In other words, to build abolition, do we then have to end the child? Over a decade ago Lee Edelman critiqued the Child as "the telos of the social order" (Edelman, 2004, p. 11), and thus ordained to be the "phantasmatic beneficiary of every political intervention" (p. 3). Edelman rejected this coercive impulse that claims that we cannot conceive the future without the figure of the Child. We make a similar rhetorical move, albeit one where we foreground how the discourse of innocence as imbricated in the figure of the child etches out in sharp relief the limits of both carceral and abolitionist logics. While Edelman claims that his notion of the Child cannot be confused with the actual lived experiences of "historical children" (p. 11), his argument has received pushback from such scholars as the late queer scholar of color, José Esteban Muñoz (2009), and feminist disability studies scholar, Alison Kafer (2017), who both claim that not all children's futures are fetishized and/or protected or even imagined. In fact, our argument in this chapter delineates the ways in which innocence, when imbricated in racialized pathologized conceptions of childhood, serves to disrupt both liberal prison reform and its more radical counterpart, abolitionist practices. Ultimately, our aim is to foreground the rhetorical/ideological labor that disability is forced to perform at the intersections of white supremacist carceral ableism that produces a deadly necropolitics (Mbembe & Meintjes, 2003): no future at all, even at the horizon of abolition.

References

Adams, D.L. & Erevelles, N. (2015). Shadow play: DisCrit, dis/respectability and carceral logics. In D. Connor, B. Ferri, & S. Annamma (Eds.), *DisCrit: Disability studies and critical race theory in education* (pp. 131–44). Teachers College Press.

Alexander, M. (2010). *The new Jim Crow: Mass incarceration in the age of colorblindness*. The New Press.

Anyon, J. (1997). *Ghetto schooling: A political economy of urban educational reform*. Teachers College Press.

Ben-Moshe, L. (2013). "The institution yet to come:" Analysing incarceration through a disability lens. In L.J. Davis (Ed.), *The Disability studies reader* (Fourth Edition, pp. 132–43). Routledge.

Ben-Moshe, L. (2020). *Decarcerating disability: Deinstitutionalization and prison abolition*. University of Minnesota Press.

Bernstein, R. (2011). *Racial innocence: Performing childhood from slavery to civil rights*. New York University Press.

Chapman, C. (2014). Five centuries' material reforms and ethical reformulations of social elimination. In Ben-Moshe, L., Chapman, C., Carey, A. (Eds.), *Disability incarcerated: Imprisonment and disability in the United States and Canada* (pp. 25–44). Palgrave Macmillan.

Edelman, L. (2004). *No future: Queer theory and the death drive*. Duke University Press.

Erevelles, N. (2014). Crippin' Jim Crow: Disability, dis-location, and the school-to-prison pipeline. In Ben-Moshe, L., Chapman, C., Carey, A. (Eds.), *Disability Incarcerated. Imprisonment and Disability in the United States and Canada* (pp. 81–99). Palgrave Macmillan.

Fabris, E. (2011). *Tranquil prisons: Chemical incarceration under community treatment orders*. University of Toronto Press.

Gottschalk, M. (2015). *Caught: The prison state and the lockdown of American politics*. Princeton University Press.

Hill, E.V. (2017). *The school-to-prison pipeline at the intersection of race and disability*. Inclusivity Strategic Consulting. Available at https://inclusivity.consulting/2017/12/08/school-prison-pipeline-intersection-race-disability/

Kafer, A. (2013). *Feminist, queer, crip*. Indiana University Press.

Kim, A., Meiners, E., Richie, B., & Petty, J. (Eds.). (2018). *The long term: Resisting life sentences working toward freedom*. Haymarket Books

Knopp, F.H., Boward, B., Morris, M., & Schnapper, M.B. (1976). *Instead of prisons: A handbook for abolitionists*. Prison Research Education Action Project.

Loyd, J.M. (2012). Race, Capitalist Crisis, and Abolitionist Organizing: An Interview with Ruth Wilson Gilmore. In Loyd, J.M., Mitchelson, M., & Burridge, A. (Eds.). (2013). *Beyond walls and cages: Prisons, borders, and global crisis*, 14 (pp. 42–54). University of Georgia Press.

Mbembé, J.A. & Meintjes, L. (2003). Necropolitics. *Public culture, 15*(1), 11–40.

Meiners, E. (2016). *For the children? Protecting innocence in a carceral state*. University of Minnesota Press.

Muñoz, J.E. (2009). *Cruising utopia: The there and then of queer theory*. New York University Press.

Ross, L. (1998). *Inventing the savage: The social construction of Native American criminality*. University of Texas Press.

Sanger, R.M. (2015). IQ, intelligence tests, "ethnic adjustments" and Atkins (2015, November 21). *American University Law Review 65*(1). Available at https://ssrn.com/abstract=2706800

Szasz, T. (1961). *The myth of mental illness: Foundations of a theory of personal conduct*. Hoeber-Harper.

Wilson Gilmore, R. (2015). The worrying state of the anti-prison movement. *Social Justice Journal* (blog). Available at www.socialjusticejournal.org/the-worrying-state-of-the-anti-prison-movement/

Weber, M.C. (2010). A new look at Section 504 and the ADA in special education cases. *Texas Journal on Civil Liberties and Civil Rights, 16,* 1–27.

Zirkel, P.A. & Weathers, J.M. (2014). Section 504-only students national incidence data. *Journal of Disability Policy Studies, 26*(3), 184–93.

Part II

Prisons and settler colonialism

5 Aan yátx'u sáani!

Decolonial meditations on building abolition

Sol Neely

When Columbus came, one thing he didn't find here was prisons.

—Judge Rudy James (Tlingit)

Prologue: Indigenous cosmopolitanism and building abolition on *Lingít Aaní*

At the very edge of Juneau, Alaska—tucked up tight against the dramatic mountains of the Tongass National Forest, the earth's largest remaining temperate rainforest—sits Lemon Creek Correctional Center (LCCC), a multi-functional adult prison that houses both men and women. The prison, located on *Lingít Aaní*—the ancestral homeland of the Tlingit people since time immemorial—boasts a number of education and treatment programs, including the Flying University, a prison education program I started that brings students from the University of Alaska Southeast (UAS) into the prison for mutual and collaborative study. Despite these programs, however, the prison continues to function as an extension of the colonial assault on the Indigenous peoples of Southeast Alaska.[1] In the state of Alaska, Alaska Natives make up about 17% of the general population but comprise 38% of the prison population (Prison Policy Initiative, n.d.). When we contextualize this figure within broader national statistics of the United States, even more sobering trends appear. According to a 2017 report from the U.S. Department of Justice, "From 1999 to 2014, the number of [American Indian and Alaska Native] jail inmates increased by an average of 4.3% per year, compared to an increase of 1.4% per year for all other races combined" (Minton, 2017, p. 1). Lingít Aaní is situated within a broader region described by Andrew Hope III, renowned Tlingit civil rights activist and educator, as the "Raven bioregion,"[2] which is home to the Indigenous nations of the Pacific Northwest, Southeast Alaska, and Western Canada. Lemon Creek Correctional Center, built upon the land of the A'akw Kwáan, houses Indigenous inmates from across the state, most of whom come from communities, homes, and cultural traditions bearing rich systems and protocols of justice broken by colonial and genocidal warfare. Although I have taught at a number of prisons over the years in both Alaska and Indiana, all of my thinking about the intersections of decolonial and decarceral justice is shaped by my work at Lemon Creek Correctional Center while living on Lingít Aaní. As such, this prologue serves as both land acknowledgment and dedication to the Indigenous peoples incarcerated at Lemon Creek Correctional Center. *Yee gu.aa yax̱ x'wán!*[3]

As a citizen of the Cherokee Nation living in the Raven bioregion, I remain indebted to and grateful for the Indigenous communities of Southeast Alaska who have welcomed me, my family, my work, and my activism. The Raven bioregion is home to some of the finest art and cultural accomplishments ever produced in the world. The richness of story and culture that perseveres here carries within it the resources and inspiration for both decolonial and decarceral endeavors. Genocidal and settler colonial violence against Indigenous communities of Southeast Alaska and the Cherokee Nation do not necessarily share the same genealogical contours, but such violence is rooted in the shared structures of settler colonialism as a "transnational formation" (Glenn, 2015). As a *structure* rather than an *event*, the violence of settler colonialism plays out across multiple epistemological, political, ontological, and phenomenological registers. Thus, building abolition requires us to stage multiple decolonial and decarceral sites of intervention, at both the *institutional and political* levels and the *existential and phenomenological* levels. Broadly construed, following Gayatri Spivak, I will refer to these two levels of intervention as the *macrological* and *micrological* (Spivak, 1988), which roughly index to the distinction made by Walter Mignolo and others working in decolonial theory as *colonialism* and *coloniality* (Maldonado-Torres, 2007). The critical potential of these terms, however, undergoes revision simply by resituating them in different contexts. The terms do not stand opposed to one another; rather, they signify tactical moments of critical intervention nested within each other.

Across these sites of decolonial and decarceral intervention, the critical vocabulary I bring to the project of building abolition gets translated by the specificity of place. While my own work draws inspiration from the communities I inhabit—from Cherokee culture of Southeast United States to Tlingit culture of Southeast Alaska—I remain deeply moved by and indebted to practices of Indigenous community justice including those from the Yukon-Kuskokwim River Delta area, particularly the complicated work and life of Harold Napoleon (Yup'ik), as well as the teachings of Randall Tetlichi (former Vunut Gwitch'in chief and elder) who spoke with my students as an "elder-in-residence" at the University of Alaska Southeast on circle sentencing and restorative justice practices.[4] The critical responsiveness I adopt, then, is one that I describe as an "Indigenous cosmopolitanism." Prior to colonial contact, Indigenous peoples across North America were already engaged in a kind of Indigenous cosmopolitanism, which struggles to reassert itself today through language and cultural revitalization that render and articulate ancestral wisdom in ways that are legible and responsive to contemporary exigencies. For example, prior to colonial contact, Indigenous peoples maintained extensive trading networks enabled by the use of trade languages. We had produced rich, culturally efficacious ways of attending to violence, transgression, and restoration. Early waves of colonial intrusion, however, set our cultural practices out of balance. The settler colonialism that arrived from Europe brought vicious economies of violence that have spiraled out of human control. Indigenous cosmopolitanism is uniquely suited to respond to the decolonial imperative that bears within it the decarceral imperative. Building abolition must draw inspiration from such Indigenous cosmopolitanism—focused through the apertures of sovereignty, "Indigenous intellectual authority," and the real political processing required of decolonial justice.[5]

By adopting "Indigenous cosmopolitanism" as decolonial and decarceral tactic, I invoke two iterative developments that have shaped how I understand this work. The first emerged from my theoretical work as a graduate student at Purdue University's Philosophy and Literature PhD program. During these studies, when I also taught as an adjunct faculty member in Indiana State University's now defunct Corrections Education Program, I developed a notion of solidarity and radical praxis built upon on the work of Enrique Dussel, Nelson Maldonado-Torres, Subcomandante Marcos, Craig Womack, and Joy Harjo among others. I also read the decolonial work of these thinkers by appeal to the work of Emmanuel Levinas, whose "ethics as first philosophy" explicitly influenced and shaped the revolutionary work of Dussel, Maldonado-Torres, and Marcos. But the quality of solidarity called for by this kind of Indigenous cosmopolitanism, of which the Zapatista rebellion was an exemplar, was rooted in a literary and cultural separatism called for by Craig Womack in the penultimate chapter of *Red on Red: Native American Literary Separatism*. In this case, the call for separatism does not compromise solidarity. On the contrary, unlike its more secular European variants, an Indigenous cosmopolitanism emerges, in varying ways across historical and contemporary horizons, from a cultural and literary separatism that provides the groundwork for a more radical pan-tribal solidarity. Womack articulates an Indigenous cosmopolitanism of sorts when he appeals to the prevalence of "the spiral" in Muskogean philosophy, by which he invokes the three-dimensional spiral of a ceremonial fire—"the spiral of smoke rising from a fire, its embers slithering up the night sky during a summer evening at the [stomp] grounds" (Womack, 1999, p. 250–1).[6]

The second, and much more important iteration of this sense of Indigenous cosmopolitanism that I have developed, occurred after I arrived to Lingít Aaní, when I began working with my friend and colleague, Ishmael Angaluuk Hope (Tlingit, Iñupiaq). My work with Hope has occasioned two developments in my thinking about the potential for an Indigenous cosmopolitanism in the service of building abolition: (1) with Hope's influence, my sense of Indigenous cosmopolitanism became more explicitly rooted in oral literary traditions that are the source material for writers and activists like Womack and Harjo, and (2) I was moved by Hope's commitment to all expressions—political, phenomenological, and otherwise—of such decolonial and Indigenous cosmopolitanism, including those sources of critique within European literary and philosophical traditions. Hope does not shy away from the work of rescuing Europe's own oral literary traditions from the violence of colonialism—which, as Dina Gilio-Whitaker has noted, "has steered the colonizers away from their own ancestral wisdom" (Gilio-Whitaker, 2020, p. 6). By situating abolitionist endeavors in the concreteness of oral literary traditions, their protocols, and their ceremonies, we are also delivered to a more richly embodied sense of self since, as Womack notes, "in oral traditions, the story literally emanates from the speaker's body" (Womack, 1999, p. 249). With Hope, I have worked to develop a notion of Indigenous cosmopolitanism rooted in an Indigenous phenomenology that draws from many sources of inspiration but is rooted in the intellectual frameworks and protocols of Indigenous oral literary traditions.[7]

Because "Indigenous modes of justice typically reflect a restorative orientation," building abolition by appeal to such Indigenous cosmopolitanism impacts both descendants of victims and perpetrators of settler colonialism, the colonized and the colonizers (Gilio-Whitaker, 2020, p. 26). One of the ways by which white supremacy works is that it fails to account for its own impoverishment. Indigenous, decolonial justice bears abolitionist potential because, as Gilio-Whitaker notes, it restores right relations for all involved (2020). In particular, it restores "systems of responsibility" within both macrological and micrological relations and thus restores what Kyle Whyte describes as "peoples' capacities to experience themselves in the world as having responsibilities for the upkeep or continuance, of their societies" (Gilio-Whitaker, 2020, p. 27). In what follows, I offer a set of two critical meditations, framed by excursuses on the Flying University, that address the decolonial starting points for building abolition. They are not intended to be exhaustive or even comprehensive. Rather, they relate to each other like aphorisms, inviting not so much argument but responsiveness. In the first meditation, I examine the formation of the state not as an accomplishment of peace but as the macrological codification of a permanent war against Indigenous bodies. In the second meditation, I examine the phenomenological and micrological sites of decolonial intervention requisite for building abolition in ways that restore ancestral wisdom to both descendants of perpetrators and victims of colonization (Schroeder & DeLaney, 2019).[8]

Excursus: A brief history of the Flying University

In Fall 2012, inspired by Steven Shankman of the Inside-Out Prison Exchange Program (Shankman, 2017),[9] I started a prison education program at Lemon Creek Correctional Center (LCCC) in Juneau, Alaska, that brings students from the University of Alaska Southeast (UAS) into the prison for mutual and collaborative study. In that inaugural seminar, we primarily studied works by Vaclav Havel and Emmanuel Levinas. I had been teaching two parallel courses, one at UAS and one at LCCC, which we integrated during the last four weeks of that initial 2012 semester. The following semester (Spring 2013), I organized our first sustained seminar of "inside" and "outside" students in which we continued our focus on existential philosophy and literature as privileged sites of political disruption and liberation, folding into our studies select readings from the Zapatista *Other Campaign* (Marcos & Zapatistas, 2008). It is also the semester that we adopted, by mutual consensus, the name *Flying University* for our fledgling program, which is borrowed from the underground philosophy courses taught by Jan Patočka in Prague during the early years of normalization after the 1968 Soviet invasion of Czechoslovakia. Patočka co-authored the Charter 77 manifesto for human rights with Havel, and the Flying University served as a means to enable dissent—what Havel called "living in truth"—through philosophical critique and sober existential activism (Havel & Keane, 2016).

The philosophical genealogy that shaped the early development of our work at Lemon Creek Correctional Center was inspired by my graduate teacher, Martin Beck Matuštík, who attended Patočka's underground classes in Prague as a student and who was later arrested in 1977 with Patočka and others when their Flying University was raided by the secret police. About that early iteration of the Flying University, Matuštík writes, "Patočka's underground Flying University was nurtured on the basis of broad philosophical rights and solidarity among theoretically diverse intellectuals, and provided a model of collaboration that later manifested itself in the revolution of November 1989" (Matuštík, 1998, p. 81). During our first year of Flying University at LCCC, "inside" students really took to this material—and when, in March 2013, Martin Matuštík and Patricia Huntington came into Lemon Creek Correctional Center by my invitation, students of our new program asked Matuštík if they could call our project *the Flying University*. Matuštík generously agreed that our new work was genealogically and philosophically connected to the original Flying University and was, therefore, entirely deserving of the name.

What came to distinguish the Flying University from Inside-Out is that Flying University eventually became a reentry effort as much as a prison education effort. Whereas Inside-Out students are prohibited from contacting "inside" students after the program is complete, the exigencies of our community in Southeast Alaska did not afford that possibility. People incarcerated inside Lemon Creek Correctional Center are the cousins, family members, former neighbors, and acquaintances of Flying University participants. After the first year, some of the "inside" students were released from incarceration—and, rather than pursuing successful reentry through employment as they were generally encouraged to do by their parole officers, some formerly incarcerated students of the Flying University decided to continue their education on campus at UAS. With this development, we organized an on-campus student club—consisting of formerly incarcerated students, student-allies, and supportive faculty, staff, and administration—to build community support for student success. We hosted potlucks, barbecues, film screenings, study groups, food drives, and more. By 2016, the Flying University was well-rooted in our community and enjoyed the support of a growing reputation across the state. As stories of our successes spread, our local public media station produced a documentary about our work (Burton, 2016). At that time, I also served as the chair of the Education Workgroup for the Juneau Reentry Coalition (JREC), which brought me into the prison and halfway house not only as an educator but also as a community organizer. The producer of the documentary, Scott Burton, hosted a screening of the film followed by a community discussion featuring formerly incarcerated students of the Flying University. This event, in turn, inspired community members to donate resources and funds that would eventually allow "inside" students of the Flying University opportunity to take the courses for college credit without incurring debt. In time, and with the inspired support of many, Flying University accomplished what it intended— viz., building *restorative community*.

As all of this was happening, a group of bipartisan legislators in Alaska began to draft some genuinely progressive criminal reform measures that came to be known as "SB 91." When it passed, it signaled a bold new vision for Alaska, one that—to my mind—was as close to a prison abolition bill as you could get away with in the settler-retributive "justice" culture of the United States. The bill intended to start cutting the number of prison beds in Alaska and use two-thirds of that savings to reinvest in our local reentry coalitions to support people exiting incarceration. Working in concert with other states who had success-fully enacted similar legislation, along with the Pew Research Center, Alaska legislators opened opportunity for community testimony. It was, predictably, a heated debate that split the state—with those against SB 91 relying on tired tropes of criminal identity (i.e., the unredeemable "criminal mind") and doub-ling down on their calls for retributive as opposed to restorative justice. I had arranged for formerly incarcerated supporters of Flying University to receive legislative advocacy training to show up at the State Capitol and tell their stories. In the end, SB 91 passed with bipartisan support. However, even before the provisions of SB 91 would take effect, a coincidental rise in crime invited self-serving politicians to exploit a false correlation between the passage of SB 91 and the rise in property crimes. Riding that kind of anti-SB 91 public sen-timent, several Alaska legislators and a candidate for governor, Mike Dunleavy, campaigned on the promise to repeal SB 91. Additionally, parts of SB 91 required that local reentry coalitions develop partnerships with the AK Department of Corrections—which, from my perspective, compromised the integrity of our reentry coalitions as grassroots, restorative projects in the interest of community healing. In November 2019, Mike Dunleavy—supported by the Koch brothers and Donald Trump—won election as governor. With supporters in the legis-lature, SB 91 was systemically dismantled even before all its provisions could take effect.

This brief history of the Flying University helps frame the critical meditations that follow. As a continuing mercantile economy, the history and aspirations of the Alaskan political economy remain firmly entrenched in its colonial purpose. After only one month in office, Governor Dunleavy delivered his first "State of the State" address in which he emphasized his "free-market, tough-on-crime" campaign rhetoric, specifically announcing this: "Number one, we're going to declare war on criminals" (Brooks, 2019). This "war" sent shockwaves through the Alaska prison system, as top administrators in his new Department of Corrections began to cut prison education opportunities and suspend community volunteerism. Dunleavy's "war on criminals" is, of course, nothing new. He did not invent it. He simply recycled it. It bears its own genealogy that needs to be articulated and situated. Its predictable effectiveness rests on two axes. The first is a radically impoverished political imagination characteristic of settler colonialism, which is buttressed by an impoverished relation to *story* itself. Such an impoverished political imagination makes it difficult to *imagine otherwise* than the retributive system of mass incarceration we've inherited. Alaska is not an exception when "the answer" to the problem of the prison crisis is simply to imagine *more prison*. The second axis of this "war on criminals" hinges on Alaska's fragile "boom-or-bust" political and economic infrastructure maintained by Alaska's colonial-mercantile economy. For decades, Alaska legislators and voters have failed to heed the call to diversify Alaska's state economy. Consequently, the enduring colonial economy produces a false sense of scarcity, which gives an alibi to legislators who do not want to invest in decolonial or restorative justice practices. While Flying University became a thriving prison education program with decolonial roots in local, state, and national abolitionist communities, we encountered our most formidable challenges in the destructive moral and budget agendas of Governor Mike Dunleavy's campaign—which recycled debunked narratives and falsely contextualized "data" in order to restore Alaska's criminal justice system to its previously failed state of limited, if any, educational opportunities; a reliance on private prison industries; and a concomitantly high recidivism rate approaching 70%.

The coincidence of these impoverished cultural and economic fragilities, as legacies and symptoms of colonial violence, engenders opportunity to exploit colonial anxieties and stoke a "war on criminals." But any "war on criminals" is, simply put, a war on our *communities*. Given the overrepresentation of Alaska Natives in the state's prisons, it is also a war on Indigenous bodies. But this "war on criminals" does not issue from a previous peace. It is a direct extension of the wars that make possible settler colonialism. As this brief history of the Flying University reveals, attempts to build abolition must rest on decolonial endeavors mobilized across various political (*macrological*) and phenomenological (*micrological*) registers. Identifying and situating sites of decolonial intervention requires a tactical vigilance for discerning the nuances and needs of such endeavors. A postsecular Indigenous cosmopolitanism bears resources for sustaining such a critical vigilance in the interest of building abolition. In some sense, the political is carried by the phenomenological—and abolitionist endeavors will flounder if the phenomenological is not regarded as a privileged site of intervention (Guenther, 2013).[10] The following critical meditations aim to align abolitionist endeavors across the political and the phenomenological as well as the decarceral and decolonial.

Meditation One: Staging sites of decolonial intervention in a state of war

> *The peace of empires issued from war rests on war. It does not restore to the alienated being their lost identity.*
>
> —Emmanuel Levinas, 2013

Alaska Governor Mike Dunleavy's promise, in his first "State of the State" address, to wage a "war on criminals" must be read not as mere rhetorical trope in the interest of political gain but as a literal war set *against* our communities *within* our communities. This war is a literal war, but it also bears allegorical, moral, and prophetic (or apocalyptic) dimensions that have, historically, adopted multiple strategic configurations with irreversible repercussions. These strategic configurations score as much across the inner contours of self as they indelibly impact place and community, necessitating both phenomenological and political responsiveness. Building abolition, I argue, must begin with a concrete accounting of the *literalness* of this "war on criminals" as an extension of the settler colonial wars that forged the laws of a nation. Abolitionist campaigns cannot adopt a mythic and illusory "peace of empires" as its starting point. To understand the state not as an accomplishment of peace but as the codification of an ongoing colonial war is the necessary "Copernican revolution" we must assume for efficacious abolitionism. Thus, all of my decolonial and decarceral work begins with this starting point, which I adopted after reading Michel Foucault's set of lectures delivered at the Collège de France (1975–76), published in English as *Society Must Be Defended*: The state is not born with the cessation of war but is codified in the mud and blood of war.

Such a "Copernican revolution" intervenes against a widely shared assumption about the relation of war and politics. It was the Prussian general and military theorist, Carl von Clausewitz, who established many of the modern assumptions of war in the early part of the 19th century. Clausewitz's theory of war has sustained critical interest because his analysis of war aimed to develop a comprehensive "modern" philosophy of war in the midst and wake of the Napoleonic Wars. Two enduring claims from Clausewitz's theory of war that deserve attention include: (1) his famous maxim, "War is not an independent phenomenon but the continuation of politics by different means" (Clausewitz, 1984, p. 7); and (2) "War is therefore, not only chameleon-like in character, because it changes its colour in some degree in each particular case, but it is also as a whole, in relation to the predominant tendencies which are in it, a *wonderful trinity*, composed of the original violence of its elements, hatred and animosity, which may be looked upon as a blind instinct; of the play and probabilities and chance, which make it a free activity of the soul; and of the subordinate nature of a political instrument, by which it belongs purely to the reason" (Clausewitz, 1984, p. 89). Christopher Bassford writes that this "wonderful trinity" of war that fascinated Clausewitz could be constitutionally articulated as composing "violent emotion / chance / rational calculation" (Bassford, 2020). While Clausewitz's work, as Sandor Goodhart writes, offers "in somewhat of a rational Aristotelian fashion" an attempt "to develop the principles of warfare as he understood them within the Napoleonic era in which he wrote and fought," more recent—post-Holocaust—theory has asked a different set of questions regarding this relation of war and politics, inverting Clausewitz's original order to interrogate politics as a moment within war (Goodhart, 2014, p. 231).

State of war: From a theory of sovereignty to a theory of domination

Foucault, of course, offers one of the more critically sustained and engaged responses to Clausewitz's well-known dictum that war is "a continuation of politics by different means," inverting the order to argue that "politics" is, in fact, "a continuation of war by other means." For Foucault, Clausewitz's dictum derives from a theory of power that he describes as "the Statist unity of sovereignty" or a "theory of sovereignty." Because such Statist theory of sovereignty emerges in the context of European settler colonial endeavors, it ought not be confused with Indigenous sovereignty claims. One central feature of this theory of sovereignty is the *unity* of power it deploys, particularly among three elements: "subject, unity [of power], and law" (Foucault, 2003, p. 45). Regarding subject, a theory of sovereignty presupposes the existence of a subject, of subject-to-subject relations "naturally endowed (or endowed by nature) with rights, capabilities, and so on" (Foucault, 2003, p. 44). Regarding unity, Foucault writes that a theory of sovereignty:

> [...] assumes from the outset the existence of a multiplicity of powers that are not powers in the political sense of the term; they are capacities, possibilities, potentials, and it can constitute them as powers in the political sense of the term only if it has in the meantime established a moment of fundamental and foundational unity between possibilities and powers, namely the unity of power.
>
> (Foucault, 2003, p. 45)

He goes on to write, "Whether this unity of power takes on the face of the monarch or the form of the State is irrelevant; the various forms, aspects, mechanisms, and institutions of power will be derived from this unitary power" (Foucault 2003, p. 44). In other words, a multiplicity of powers, in a theory of sovereignty, can only be established and function on the basis of this unitary power. And, finally, regarding law, Foucault writes that a theory of sovereignty attempts to show how power can be constituted "not exactly in accordance with the law, but in accordance with a certain basic legitimacy that is more basic than any law that allows law to function as such" (Foucault, 2003, p. 44). According to Foucault's analysis, a theory of sovereignty does three things: (1) it presupposes the subject caught up in such power analysis; (2) its goal is to establish the essential unity of power; and (3) "it is always deployed within the preexisting element of the law: *Subject, unity power*, and *law*" (Foucault 2003, p. 44).

But Foucault asks a series of questions about the underlying assumption and genealogical pressures that privilege a theory of sovereignty as an analytic of power, and these questions reveal to him a genealogy of power relations that he calls, in contrast to *a theory of sovereignty, a theory of domination*. He writes, "Rather than deriving powers from sovereignty, we should be extracting operators of domination from relations of power both historically and empirically" (Foucault, 2003, p. 45). To do this, "we begin with the power relationship itself, with the actual or effective relationship of domination, and see how that relationship itself determines the elements to which it is applied" (Foucault, 2003, p. 45). In contrast to a theory of sovereignty that presupposes subject, unitary power, and the legitimacy of law, Foucault argues that a *theory of domination* offers these critical corrections:

(1) *Regarding subject*: Because we begin with the power relation itself, "with the actual or effective relationship of domination," "[w]e should not [...] be asking subjects how, why, and by what right they can agree to being subjugated, but showing how *actual relations of subjugation* manufacture subjects." (2003, p. 45)

(2) *Regarding unitary power*: In the wake of this, "[o]ur second task should be to reveal relations of domination, and to allow them to assert themselves in their multiplicity, their differences, their specificity, or their reversibility; we should not be looking for a sort of sovereignty from which powers spring, but showing how the various operators of domination support one another, relate to one another, [...] how they converge and reinforce one another in some cases, and negate or strive to annul one another in other cases." (2003, p. 45)

(3) *Regarding legitimacy and law*: Finally, Foucault writes, "revealing relations of domination rather than sources of sovereignty means this: We do not try to trace their origins back to that which gives them their basic legitimacy. We have to try, on the contrary, to identify the technical instruments that guarantee that they function." (2003, p. 46)

Foucault summarizes his shifting analyses of power relations from *a theory of sovereignty* to *a theory of domination* succinctly: "Rather than looking at the three prerequisites of law, unity, and subject—which makes sovereignty both the source of power and the basis of institutions—I think that we have to adopt the threefold point of view of the *techniques*, the *heterogeneity of techniques*, and the *subjugation-effects* that make technologies of domination the real fabric of both power relations and the great apparatuses of power" (2003, p. 46).

Given the relevance of Foucault's work in decarceral endeavors, his shift toward a theory of domination occasions a set of questions that ought to guide, in sobering ways, the starting assumptions of any abolitionist campaign. In summary form, here are some of these questions:

- "If we look beneath peace, order, wealth, and authority, beneath the calm order of subordinations, beneath the State and State apparatuses, beneath the laws, and so on, will we hear and discover a sort of primitive and permanent war?" (2003, p. 46–7)
- "Can the phenomenon of war be regarded as primary with respect to other relations (relations of inequality, dis-symmetries, divisions of labor, relations of exploitation, et cetera)?" (2003, p. 47)
- "We could, and must, also ask ourselves if military institutions, and the practices that surround them—and in more general terms all the techniques that are used to fight a war—are, whichever way we look at them, directly or indirectly, the nucleus of political institutions." (2003, p. 47)
- And, finally, "How, when, and why was it noticed or imagined that what is going on beneath and in power relations is a war? When, how, and why did someone come up with the idea that the civil order is an order of battle? [...] Who saw war just beneath the surface of peace; who sought in the noise and confusion of war, in the mud of battles, the principle that allows us to understand order, the State, its institutions, and its history? (2003, p. 47)

It is with these sets of questions that Foucault began to ask himself, "Who, basically, had the idea of inverting Clausewitz's principle, and who thought of saying: 'It is quite possible that war is the continuation of politics by other means, but isn't politics itself a continuation of war by other means'?" (2003, p. 47–8). These questions are not merely theoretical, and they ought not be kept to the margins of academia or political theory. Foucault gives us the analytic, but the evidence and symptoms of this *state of war* are lived out in the bodies of Indigenous people and the descendants of slaves who continue to suffer the real corporeal legacies of the settler colonial wars that founded the United States.

We have then, a heavy set of theoretical analyses of power that force us to take this question seriously. *The state is not born with the cessation of war but is codified in the mud and blood of war.* We see this war encoded in the very founding documents of the United States, not only in places like the so-called 3/5 compromise clause of the U.S. Constitution or in the history of racial apartheid in the United States, but we see it especially in the whole history of Federal Indian Law through its successive and sometimes contradictory stages:

- "International sovereign to international sovereign" (1770s–1820s)
- "Removal and relocation" (1830s–50s)
- "Reservation" (1850s–90s)
- "Allotment and assimilation" (1870s–1930s)
- "Indian self-rule" (1930s–50s)
- "Termination (assimilation)" (1950s–60s)
- "Tribal self-determination." (Wilkins & Stark, 2018, p. 150)

Politics as the continuation of war is, perhaps, best exemplified in the figure of Andrew Jackson, who moved from soldier and general to statesman and president and signed into law the Indian Removal Act of 1830, which laid the groundwork for dispossessing my own ancestors from their traditional Cherokee homelands.

Returning to matters of Alaska and Lingít Aaní, we can see these economies of violence recapitulated with the signing of the Treaty of Cession in March 1867, which ended Russia's occupation of Alaska and inaugurated a new phase of settler colonialism by the United States—one which has played out much more in line with Foucault's *theory of domination* even as it continues to account for itself as a *theory of sovereignty*. Ishmael Hope has written about this history of warfare as it has been told to him through oral histories from his father and grandfather. In the couple of years immediately following the Treaty of Cession, relations between the Tlingit people and the United States government played out "like a sovereign nation dealing with another sovereign nation" (Hope, 2017). However, almost immediately, the U.S. Navy initiated war with the Tlingit people of Southeast Alaska in what has become known as the Kake War, when the U.S. Navy bombed multiple Tlingit villages in Southeast Alaska beginning in 1869. As Hope points out, the commonplace historical narrative of the U.S. possession of Alaska is a myth—the myth that "the United States purchased the land outright from the Russians" and that "the military occupation was one of law and order [...] rather than what anthropologist and historian Steve Langdon characterize[s] as 'state terrorism' when discussing the bombardment of Kake, the first of the three bombardments in 1869, with one in Wrangell following that same year and the last in Angoon in 1882" (Hope, 2017).

To the extent that the story of the United States taking possession of Alaska is told as a story of law and order, it is told from the perspective of a *theory of sovereignty* rather than that of a *theory of domination*. Hope calls out and names as racist the settler colonial history of Alaska derived from such a theory of sovereignty. Decolonizing entails, on some level, decentering (colonial) sovereignty claims from such history—which are the same claims that still legitimize the prison-industrial complex—in order to better stage efficacious sites of decolonial and decarceral intervention. From the point of view of a theory of sovereignty—which, as Foucault notes, presupposes *subject*, *unitary power*, and the *legitimacy of law*—we witness ways by which the origin story for the state of Alaska articulates itself in terms of peace as opposed to war:

(1) *Regarding subject*: The Treaty of Cession legitimizes the subjugation of Native peoples. However, as Hope notes, "The United States did not purchase the legal title to the land of Alaska. As the Tlingit lawyer and civil rights leader William Paul and his son Fred Paul, also a lawyer, articulated, the Treaty of Cession was an agreement where, according to Fred, 'Russia sold the right to rule Alaska, the right of suzerainty, not the land itself'" (Hope, 2017). Colonial theories of sovereignty leave little room for the legitimacy of Indigenous sovereignty.[11]

(2) *Regarding unitary power.* Foucault calls on a theory of domination that is better suited to critically attend to "various operators of domination [that] support one another, relate to one another, [...] how they converge and reinforce one another." For Hope, the U.S. settler colonial war against Alaska Natives did not end with the literal bombing of Tlingit villages but was maintained and transformed by a focus on education: "After the land was secured in the late 19th century, the movement changed to one of education, led by the missionary Sheldon Jackson, with young Alaska Natives attending boarding schools that emphasized assimilation and leaving the 'old customs' behind" (Hope, 2017, Hope & Neely, 2020). Such genocidal violence is exemplified in an 1892 speech by Captain Richard H. Pratt, founder and superintendent of the Carlisle Indian School, who rationalized the implementation of boarding schools in effort to "kill the Indian [...] and save the man." These boarding schools share a common genealogy with today's prison-industrial complex.

(3) *Regarding legitimacy and law.* About the Kake War, Hope writes, "Recognition of Tlingit ownership and sovereignty changed with the bombardments. While the bombardments were couched in terms of law and order, there was a clear shift in policy. No longer did the U.S. recognize Tlingit land ownership, their laws and way of life. This shift in policy created the means for the state terrorism of the bombardments" (Hope, 2017). Today, there are a number of colonial codes that still bring state terror to Alaska Native villages, whether it occurs in the failing public school systems that bear the genealogy of boarding school violence, or the pandemic of missing and murdered Indigenous women, or in the concern for subsistence and food sovereignty. Shifting toward a theory of domination as opposed to a theory of (colonial) sovereignty means delegitimizing a whole set of political discourses and cultural practices that give an alibi to the colonial-carceral matrix.

Building abolition must adopt the literalness—in all its catastrophic, monstrous, disastrous iterations—of this *state of war*, for the theory of sovereignty that fetishizes *subject, unitary power,* and *legitimacy and law* is the same theory from which the prison-industrial complex, and its function in what Foucault calls the "carceral archipelago," is derived.

As Foucault argues, "No matter what philosophico-juridical theory may say, political power does not begin when the war ends. [...] War obviously presided over the birth of States: right, peace, and laws were born in the blood and mud of battles" (2003, p. 50). But Foucault is also clear that this is not some romanticized or "ideal" battle "dreamed up by philosophers or jurists": "The law is born of real battles, victories, massacres, and conquests which can be dated and which have their horrific heroes; the law was born in burning towns and ravaged fields. It was born together with the famous innocents who died at break of day" (Foucault, 2003, p. 50). He adds, "Law is not pacification, for beneath the law, war continues to rage in all the mechanisms of power, even in the most regular. War is the motor behind institutions and order. In the smallest of cogs, peace is waging a secret war" (Foucault, 2003, p. 50). The point, Foucault contends, is "to *interpret* the war that is going on beneath peace; peace itself is a coded war" (2003, p. 51).

In the interest of building abolition, I propose—first—that we adopt this Foucauldian "Copernican Revolution" that echoes Levinas' historical description, albeit to different ends, "The peace of empires issued from war rests on war" (2013, p. 22). Such a call requires us to examine concrete political histories and violences of the state not from a mythic perspective of peace, law, and order but from the macrological perspective of war and shifting techniques of domination. Foucault's call to interpret this "war beneath peace," however, shifts focus from the political to the phenomenological and requires us to attend to what Spivak calls the "micrological textures of power" (Spivak, 1988). Neither of these colonial-carceral registers—across the macrological and the micrological—can be ignored.

Meditation two: Interpreting the war beneath peace

The numbers of the imprisoned, the disappeared, and the assassinated in different countries also grows.

A world war:
the most brutal,
the most complete,
the most universal,
the most effective.

Each country,
each city,
each countryside,
each house,
each person,
each is a large or small battleground.

—Subcomandante Marcos, 2015

What does it mean to "interpret this war" in the interest of building abolition? If there is no neutral ground on which to stand, building abolition means that descendants of both victims and perpetrators of colonization must take up their responsibility to interpret this war that remains indelibly encoded in the state we call peace. Here, I am inspired by the work of Gabriele Schwab, who identifies as a second-generation Holocaust perpetrator and who has written in eloquent and comprehensive ways about the transgenerational trauma that haunts violent histories and the peoples who suffer them. Much of her work has been composed in consultation with her friend, Puebloan poet, Simon Ortiz—so her own questions attending to European genocide find relevance in the American genocide of settler colonialism. In her book, *Haunting Legacies: Violent Histories and Transgenerational Trauma*, Schwab asks, "How does one think about cultural belonging from the perspective of the victims of colonization, on the one hand, and of the descendants of perpetrator nations, on the other hand?" (2010, p. 98). She argues, "We have arrived at a place in history where we can no longer afford to deal with the histories of victims and perpetrators in isolation" (p. 82). The question for Schwab, which she shares with Simon Ortiz, is, how can such a dialogue occur? Under what conditions would it be possible for descendants of victims and perpetrators of such violence to "translate" their experiences, especially when the circumstances of such "translation" are irrevocably conditioned by centuries of moral, aesthetic, and cultural colonialism?[12] The question, for me, hinges on a question of legibility. What, from Indigenous experiences in the wake of settler colonial wars and their extension through institutions of "education" and "corrections" will remain fundamentally illegible to colonial experiences? The question not only addresses matters of oral histories and cultural practices but also phenomenological modes of consciousness. Efforts to interpret the "war beneath peace" must also contend with the micrological textures of power.

Responding to the decolonial imperative that is central to building abolition requires us to attend to another critical distinction noted at the top of this chapter—that between *colonialism* and *coloniality*. While there is nothing "post" about colonialism in the United States, in this distinction, *coloniality* is typically thought to outlive *colonialism*. For Nelson Maldonado-Torres, who develops the concept as coined by Walter Mignolo, coloniality "refers to long-standing patterns of power that emerged as a result of colonialism, but that define culture, labor, intersubjective relations, and knowledge production well beyond the strict limits of colonial administrations" (Maldonado-Torres, 2007, p. 243). Like a song that plays on long after the instrument is gone, coloniality is "maintained alive in books, in the criteria for academic performance, in cultural patterns, in common sense, in the self-image of peoples, in aspirations of self, and so many other aspects of our modern experience" (Maldonado-Torres, 2007, p. 243). Maldonado-Torres notes that, in a way, "as modern subjects we *breathe* coloniality all the time and everyday" (Maldonado-Torres, 2007, p. 243). And in his own work, Maldonado-Torres looks to three registers of coloniality: the coloniality of *power*, the coloniality of *knowledge*, and the coloniality of *being*. The distinctions nuance sites of intervention while preserving their respective entanglements—and in this way *coloniality* is not just a species of *colonialism* but the very "logic, culture, and structure of the modern world-system" (Cardinal, 2019).

The urgency for staging decolonial interventions against *coloniality* in the interest of building abolition does not come at the expense of interventions against *colonialism*, which is still operative at least in the context of the United States. On this point, I stand with Eve Tuck and K. Wayne Yang who—in their essay, "Decolonization is Not a Metaphor"—insist that their goal is "to remind readers what is unsettling about decolonization" (Tuck & Wayne Yang,

2012, p. 3). They specifically write, "Decolonization brings about the repatriation of Indigenous land and life. Decolonization is not a metonym for social justice" (Tuck & Wayne Yang, 2012, p. 7). Their concern is that increasing references to "decolonization" only play into containment strategies that compromise the real political processing that must occur beyond speaking healing words: "Decolonization, which we assert is a distinct project from other civil and human rights-based social justice projects, is far too often subsumed into the directives of these projects, with no regard for how decolonization wants something different than those forms of justice" (Tuck & Wayne Yang, 2012, p. 3). I entirely agree with the concerns of Tuck and Yang, here. Settler appropriation of the vocabulary of "decolonization" risks recentering whiteness, resettling theory, extending settler innocence, and guaranteeing settler futures (Tuck & Wayne Yang, 2012, p. 4). But what those terms of decolonization entail largely remain, I argue, *illegible* to many descendants of settler culture. Even worse, to the extent that the logic of coloniality bears the capacity even to "colonize the imagination," there are numerous Indigenous folks who bear the sorrows of this impoverished colonial imagination and internalize the values of white supremacy.

This is why staging *coloniality* as a critical site of decolonial and decarceral intervention is crucial, I feel, to abolitionist projects. In some sense, if *colonialism* concerns itself with the *macrological* and institutional instantiations of settler power, *coloniality* tends to the *micrological* textures of power, which requires the critical work of an Indigenous phenomenology, one that adopts many of the same starting points as Levinas' "phenomenology of sociality" (Levinas, 1998, p. 169). That is to say, rather than starting—as the whole history of Western philosophy tends to—with modalities of consciousness predicated on vision and visibility, we start with what Levinas calls a "consciousness termed hearing" (Levinas, 1989, p. 154). Rather than beginning, as Husserl does, with *intentionality* as the starting point, Indigenous phenomenology begins, with Levinas, in *inspiration*—linked to the literalness of respiration—by which we breathe out into exhaustion and breathe in, again, into inspiration (1997, p. 115). This is the honest cadence of our abolitionist lives. And, because Indigenous phenomenology, culled from diverse influences by appeal to contemporary Indigenous cosmopolitanism, better attends to the "micrological textures of power" that score across both descendants of victims and perpetrators of colonialism, it is also better suited to the task of "translating" settler and Indigenous experiences in the interest of restorative justice. This is because the micrological textures of power determine in advance what becomes legible to a person and what remains illegible to them.

The question of legibility and illegibility is a phenomenological one, and it dramatically affects how we interpret "the war beneath peace." For example, my friend and colleague, X̱'unei Lance Twitchell, once described to me the effects of the boarding school experience—a continuation of "war by other means"—in these terms: "They beat our language out of us and replaced it with a language that hates us." It is that intimacy of the inner contours of self, of how we relate to language, story, consciousness, each other—whether it be the irreducibly rich kinship relations of many Indigenous cultures or the possessive individualism and instrumental rationality of settler colonial cultures—it is that *intimacy* of the micrological that must be attended to, so that the terms and imperatives of both decolonial and decarceral endeavors can become politically legible. Key to these shared abolitionist tasks of translating experience, interpreting war, restoring linguistic and cultural vitality, and imagining abolitionist traditions of justice otherwise than what we have inherited is a *quality of story* lost to the settler colonial imagination. The prison-industrial complex persists because the settler colonial political imagination is a radically *impoverished* political imagination, and that imagination will never recover a robust and responsive sense of justice without recovering the richness of story. About "the permanent possibility of war," Emmanuel Levinas writes:

> But violence does not consist so much in injuring and annihilating persons as in interrupting their continuity, making them betray not only commitments but their own substance, making them carry out actions that will destroy every possibility for action. *Not only modern war but every war employs arms that turn against those who wield them.*
>
> (Levinas, 2013, p. 21; my emphasis)

Within and against the micrological textures of coloniality, we are called to interpret "the war beneath peace." But each of us is situated on a spectrum that divides descendants of victims and perpetrators of colonialism, so we must also begin by translating experiences across this spectrum—which includes an accounting not only of the trauma of historical violence levied against Indigenous peoples in settler colonial wars but also, especially, the utter impoverishment of colonial political imaginations that continue to give an alibi to systems of retributive justice.

Excursus: Preface from *Flying in Shackles*, a publication of the Flying University

In Summer 2014, we published our first literary volume of poetry and art for the Flying University. The project was headed by an "outside" UAS student, Emily King, with support from a URECA (Undergraduate Research and Creative Activity) grant. Emily organized creative writing workshops and, by consensus, the publication was titled *Flying in Shackles* (King & Neely, 2014).[13] Reproduced, here, is the preface I contributed to the volume in which I call on readers—across the spectrum that divides descendants of victims and perpetrators of colonialism—*to listen.*

> *If we can defend our humanity, then perhaps there is a hope of sorts.*
>
> —Václav Havel

Václav Havel writes that every prisoner has a story. Emmanuel Levinas tells us that none of us are reducible to our histories. They mean the same thing, that each of us bears a genealogical depth with rich colorations of self that cannot be accommodated by the reductive logic of identity and "choice" that governs our contemporary carceral system. Each of us bears within us a *secrecy* of sorts, an incommensurability with the institutions we inhabit, with our histories, and with the psychological compositions that come to represent our institutional identifications. The work of the Flying University, then, begins with this assumption: When we go inside the prison, we are called to bear witness to lives irreducible to their histories. This irreducibility, this incommensurability between a person's life and their history, is the space of transformation, however small such space might be.

The existential and pedagogical starting points for the work we take up in the Flying University are not the same starting points upon which the contemporary prison system in the United States is built. Ours requires a qualitatively different kind of *vigilance* for attending to our responsibilities, for mustering the pedagogical and material resources that enable us to respond, as Levinas is fond of saying, in response-ability. Levinas, for whom *ethics* is first philosophy, writes that the face of the other calls us toward this responsibility. The face of the other *addresses* us, but this address is two-fold: In one sense, the face of the other *calls* to us (addresses us in the vocative sense); at the same time, we are *situated* by this call—which is to say, we are given address—in our response that gestures, "*Here I am,*" the gesture of witness. Everything about this volume and the Flying University begins in this space of incommensurability, this no-space, this utopia (*ou-topos*) where, paradoxically, we find address. Perhaps this is one way to read the phrase, "Flying University"—which, like Havel's notion of the "parallel polis," stakes out within the prison a place that is *parallel* to it but also *incommensurable with* it.

This volume attempts to collect some of the voices and visions of those incarcerated within Lemon Creek Correctional Center and who have studied as part of the Flying University these last few semesters. Some of the pieces published here have been work-shopped in our Fall 2013 creative writing seminar, led by UAS student Emily King. Others have been composed under different circumstances or at different times, including some photography. All of them, however, contribute to the telling of a story—at times in direct ways and at others indirect. But if it is true that every prisoner has a story, we must take care to qualify how we understand "story" here.

One's story does not begin with one's birth and end with one's death, and it's certainly not reducible to juridical records or court transcripts. Our stories have roots in deep genealogical entanglements of which we are not always author. Our stories emerge in the context of historical violence, racism, poverty, alienation. They speak in the language of symptoms, not of causality, so they are not always reducible to representation. Events and meanings in our lives are saturated with significance in ways that we cannot always attend to or account for. We can think of this in ways similar to Jakob Beer, who observes—in Anne Michael's novel, *Fugitive Pieces*, "I did not witness the most important events of my life." One's story is always *before and beyond* the arrival of the individual—which is not to abstract from the concreteness of one's lived biography; rather, such rich (*diachronic*) sense of story restores a voluptuous sense of self that is otherwise reduced to identity and history. Story, in this sense, means giving back to others what is too frequently stolen from them by the reductive logics that organize the carceral system: one's alterity.

Every prisoner has a story. Yet, it is true that the carceral system—as it is historically constituted—is tone deaf to this quality of story. When our society is structured according to a deep entrenchment of the prison-industrial complex—a situation in which the United States, with 5% of the world's population, houses 25% of the world's prisoners—then real existential horror emerges. Politically speaking, we have built a vast cultural apparatus that is both *tone deaf* to such qualities of story and, worse, *indifferent* to that deafness. Václav Havel in his chapter "Stories and Totalitarianism" writes about the relation of story to history and ideology: "Story has a logic of its own [...] but it is a logic of a dialogue, an encounter, the interaction of different truths, attitudes, ideas, traditions, passions, people, higher powers, social movements, and so on [...] Every story presupposes a plurality of truths, of logics, of agents of decisions, and of manners of behavior." Story, Havel tells us, is constituted "between the inevitable and the unforeseeable"—yet, he adds, we have driven it from our public life. We don't *listen*. Indeed, it might be that we no longer know *how* to listen. And the consequence of this failure to attend to individuals' stories in the terms such stories demand is a pervasive, creeping, one-dimensional thinking that shapes the rationality of our institutions and gives alibi to their failure.

Toni Morrison writes that, for her, all story begins with *listening*. She writes, "When I read, *I listen*. When I write, *I listen*—for silence, inflection, rhythm, rest. Then comes the image, the picture of the things that I have to invent." Similarly, Cornel West tells us that, when we listen to the music of John Coltrane, we have *to hear* through all the music a quality of suffering that emerges through the dissonance of the blue notes. Lucius T. Outlaw, in an essay on "Critical Thought in the Interest of African-Americans," insists that when we read African American literature, we have *to hear* through the text the circumstances and questions that gave rise to that particular expression of life praxis.

All of these admonishments are valid here, and they announce another unexpected temptation. A publication such as this relies too heavily on seeing and on visibility. It is a medium that manifests through vision. One takes it in one's hands, seizes it, and *regards* it with the eyes. Can we take up the book in another way, though? One that accounts, in advance, for this quality of story invoked by Havel and Levinas? If history is governed by a seeing, then story is encountered by listening. As you take up this book in your hand, we implore you, first, *to listen*. Every prisoner has a story.

Epilogue: Abolitionism and restoring the logic of the gift

The world is not made of atoms, but of stories.
—Muriel Rukeyser (Conant, 2010, p. 11)

Foucault is not alone in staging an analytic of power that adopts, as its starting point, a sober appraisal of the state as codified warfare. René Girard also takes this up in his last book, *Achever Clausewitz*, which was translated into English as *Battling to the End* (Girard & Chantre, trans. Baker, 2010). Emmanuel Levinas also writes about "the permanent possibility of war" in his warning that everything Western philosophical traditions have taken for "ethics" has only ever been the confusion of a "politics" whose primary task is comprised of "the art of foreseeing war and of winning it by every reason" (Levinas, 2013, p. 21). For Girard, we are already caught up in apocalyptic economies of violence that escape our control. These economies of violence—across macrological and micrological registers, through colonialism and coloniality—were inaugurated with the advent of modernity in the first settler colonial campaigns against Indigenous peoples of the Americas. As Maldonado-Torres notes, "Enrique Dussel states that Hernán Cortés gave expression to an ideal of subjectivity that could be defined as the *ego conquiro*, which predates René Descartes' articulation of the *ego cogito*. This means that the significance of the Cartesian *cogito* for modern European identity has to be understood against the backdrop of an unquestioned ideal of self expressed in the notion of the *ego conquiro*" (Maldonado-Torres, 2007, p. 244–5). Descartes' inauguration of methodological skepticism, according to Maldonado-Torres, aligned with the colonial skepticism of the state of humanity for Indigenous peoples. Moreover, in settler colonialism, the state as codified warfare adopts what Patrick Wolfe calls "the logic of elimination" (Wolfe, 2006)—or what Maldonado-Torres calls the "death ethic of war" (Maldonado-Torres, 2008). The prison-industrial complex of the United States adopts the same "death ethic," so we can talk about a "death ethic of the prison." Like settler colonialism, it is inherently eliminatory. The "death ethic of the prison" recapitulates the "death ethic of war" in this vicious logic of elimination.

In "On the Coloniality of Being," Maldonado-Torres invokes Fanon's *damné* as "the subject that emerges in a world marked by the coloniality of Being" (Maldonado-Torres, 2007, p. 257). The figure of the *damné* is both "concrete being" and "a transcendental concept," which Maldonado-Torres describes by appeal to Emile Benveniste who shows "that the term *damné* is etymologically related to the concept of *donner*, which means, to give" (Maldonado-Torres 2007, p. 258). In the context of coloniality, the *damné* "is a subject from whom the capacity to have and to give have been taken away" (Maldonado-Torres, 2007, p. 258). What Maldonado-Torres calls "the coloniality of being," which is one dimension of coloniality entwined with the coloniality of knowledge and the coloniality of power, is that dynamic "that aims to obliterate—in its literal sense of doing away completely so as to leave *no trace*—gift-giving and generous reception as a fundamental character of being-in-the-world" (Maldonado-Torres, 2007, p. 258). In this case, not only are Indigenous voices silenced or marginalized, but such silencing radically de-forms settler cultures of usurpation. If the prison system shares with settler colonialism the logic of elimination and a "death ethic," then the same silencing is true for our incarcerated neighbors.

Building abolition through the dual endeavors of decoloniality and decarceration means restoring the *logic of the gift* against *the logic of elimination*. It means hearing the voices of incarcerated people and attending not so much to their *histories* as to their *stories*. It means that abolition takes shape *not* through what Maldonado-Torres calls "racist/imperial Manichean misanthropic skepticism" (2007, p. 245) but through Indigenous protocols of *respect* that recognize and restore the gift-giving capacity of our incarcerated populations. These are revolutionary, literally, starting points for building abolition—and I do not know that settler colonial societies can muster the resources for such revolutionary abolitionist praxis without recognizing their own impoverished cultural and political traditions—which means finally giving up white supremacy—and committing fully to decolonizing across all political and phenomenological registers. Fanon writes:

> Decolonization, which sets out to change the order of the world, is, obviously, a program of complete disorder. But it cannot come as a result of magical practices, nor of a natural shock, nor of a friendly understanding. Decolonization, as we know, is a historical process: that is to say it cannot be understood, *it cannot become intelligible nor clear to itself except in the exact measure that we can discern the movements which give it historical form and content.*
> Fanon, 1963, cited in Tuck & Wang, 2012, p. 2; my emphasis

I take decarceral projects to be similar: The historical processes necessary for building abolition are not intelligible in advance. They can only become clear through a critical vigilance for the micrological textures of power that shape what becomes politically and ethically legible to us, through directly confronting the limits of our shared political imaginations and restoring the quality of story that many Indigenous cultures already bear.

We can close, for the moment, by appeal to two examples. The first is occasioned by a poem, written by an "inside" student of the Flying University, which I frame and interpret through Indigenous protocols of respect which generously receive the gift-giving capacities of incarcerated voices. The poem is simply titled, "Father":

> I've acquired a fire that burns and hides
> deep down inside. Even though I've tried
> with all of my might to extinguish

this light it persists night after night.
Until it's too much to take keeping me
awake it breaks through my soul
exposing a hole that unfolds into an
obscene being with use and abuse not trust
and lust. It thrusts forward and it holds
my every thought.
To become my father is not what I want.
His drunken slurs and abusive terms brought a sudden
urge and submerge my entire being into seeing him
strangled, dangled from a rope
with the hold of a noose around his throat.
What was I, some kind of joke?
Throw me across the room to see if I broke?
Lock me in the freezer to see if I froze?
Sticks and chords bats and boards anything he sees.
Could insanity be the weapon of his desire
with that fire in his eyes, but why?
I don't understand how can one man have so much hate
that he can't wait to see his own child
covered in blood from top to bottom and to think the cops
never caught him infuriates me even more to the fact
that if he ever comes back, I'll do that exact.

Many years have past and the memory
still lasts along with the hate
and internal debate that decides my father's
fate. All this rage can't be displayed on a single page
it streams through my entire soul.
So who knows if I'll explode and display
in a way that's not okay.
So the last wish that I enlist upon myself I cant help
but dream of one thing—Revenge.
After that it will finally end.

As the preface to *Flying In Shackles* calls for, hold this poem in your hand and listen. Imagine this young man in prison. Hear his story, and imagine this: A renowned Tlingit elder—who I adore beyond measure—goes into the prison to address a congregation of men and women who have two years or less to serve. His name is Kingeestí David Katzeek, and he approaches the microphoned lectern and says, "Aan yátx'u sáani! Aan yátx'u sáani!" *Noble people of the land. Beautiful and precious children of the land.* Imagine that. He approaches a congregation of prisoners and addresses them as "noble children of the land." But the phrase literally means "the high caste people of a place"[14]—which elevates the face of the prisoner to a position of height, not unlike Levinas' ethics of the face-to-face relation. I've seen Kingeestí David Katzeek do this in the prison, and the first time he said it, I felt myself split open on the inside. Every time I go into the prison, I think about this gesture. It has become my protocol of respect that prepares me to receive the gift-giving capacity of the students we encounter in the prison. I want us to think about this young incarcerated poet as one such noble and precious child of the land. What this young man possesses, whatever else his crimes or transgression might be, is a source of critique that demystifies the sacrificial logic of the state and restores the moral priority we ought to give his voice in building abolition and abolition democracy. Kingeestí's ceremonial declaration "Aan Yátx'u Sáani!" emerges from centuries of Tlingit protocols for respect. Insofar as protocol is an expression of sovereignty and ceremony is an expression of jurisdiction, we witness in the cry a thundering reterritorializing of relations in the heart of the prison.

The second example of how decolonial and decarceral endeavors coincide in the interest of abolition returns us to the Organized Village of Kake—"a federally recognized tribe that serves Tlingit people living in the Kake region" of Alaska, where in 1869 the U.S. Navy bombed multiple Tlingit villages. Today, this small Tlingit village of under 600 people has adopted "The Circle Peacemaking Program" (Tribal Access to Justice Innovation, n.d.). According to the Tribal Access to Justice Innovation—which records and promotes "promising justice-related programs in Indian Country"—the Circle Peacemaking Program draws its cultural inspiration from "peacemaking" as a "part of the fabric of Tlingit culture and tradition," even as it had not been practiced in Kake for many years due to the imposition of settler colonial "justice" systems. The Kake Circle Peacemaking Program became necessary as tribal members increasingly felt that Alaska's court system was failing to adequately respond to the widespread problems of alcohol abuse and suicide that plague rural Alaska Native communities in the wake of colonial-genocidal war. With the Kake Circle Peacemaking Program, however, we witness the revolutionary restoration of Indigenous values as foundational to systems of justice, for which economies of balance and restoration replace runaway economies of retributive violence. We witness the centrality of *restoring story* to *restorative justice*—of restoration as re-*story*-ation. And one of the major contributing factors to its success is the "enthusiasm of Kake community members to incorporate Tlingit culture into the justice system."

In the end, building abolition must restore the logic of the gift against the logic of elimination. It must give up systems of justice predicated on colonial *theories of sovereignty* and rediscover—across political and phenomenological horizons—a *new* sovereignty (the very oldest will become the newest) within and against *theories of domination* that characterize the genocidal wars of settler colonialism.

A káx̱ ḵugax̱tulagáaw! Ḵusax̱án tin yagax̱toodláak![15]

Notes

1 At top, I want to acknowledge that, like any prison, Lemon Creek Correctional Center is a colonial institution. Within the institution, however, there are a number of people whose good work needs to be recognized. Most importantly, I acknowledge the enduring commitment to transforming lives of the two education coordinators, Paul McCarthy and Kris Weixelman without whom none of my prison education work in Alaska would have taken root.

2 Andrew Hope III, from unpublished manuscript, "Sacred Forms." I use the phrase with permission of Andrew Hope III's son, Ishmael Hope, who tells me the original phrase was "Raven-Creator Bioregion" but this was revised over time in discussions with Richard and Nora Dauenhauer.

3 Translation: "(You all) have strength and courage."

4 See also, Shanti Thakur (Director), Mark Zannis (Producer), & Kirk Tougas (Cinematography). (1997). *Circles* [Documentary]. CA: National Film Board of Canada (NFB). (58 running minutes)

5 I adopt this phrase, "Indigenous intellectual authority," from Ernestine Saankalaxt' Hayes, friend and former colleague from University of Alaska Southeast and Alaska State Writer Laureate (2017–18).

6 Womack's use of the "spiral" is inspired by his reading of Joy Harjo's poetry who, at the time of this writing, presently serves as the 23rd Poet Laureate of the United States.

7 It is beyond the scope of this essay to develop this sense of Indigenous phenomenology and cosmopolitanism, which I am reserving for a manuscript currently in process. However, readers can get a better sense of this project by consulting an interview I conducted with Ishamel Hope and Will Geiger. See S. Neely, I. Hope, W. Geiger, "Within the Whole Body: An Interview with Ishmael Hope and Will Geiger on Tlingit House Screens and Indigenous Phenomenology," *Screen Bodies* 4, no. 1 (2019): 25–47.

8 Some of this material was thought out in discussion with Dr. Elaine Schroeder, who has twice interviewed me for her public radio show, *Mind Over Matter.*

9 I have had plenty of opportunity to work with Steven Shankman over the years on prison education projects and remain indebted to his sustained support of my work.

10 Lisa Guenther has offered one of the more sustained phenomenological endeavors related to building abolition, and I am grateful for her support and encouragement over the years. It has been an honor to teach her phenomenological work in the prison as part of the Flying University.

11 At the 2013 "Rethinking Prisons" conference hosted by Vanderbilt University, there was a conversation among formerly incarcerated descendants of African slaves who argued that the modern prison system is predicated on a social contract theory that slaves to the United States never agreed to, which is related to this point on the legitimacy of subjection according to a theory of sovereignty.

12 I have written about this question of "translating experience" between descendants of victims and perpetrators of colonialism elsewhere. See, Neely, S. (2016). On Becoming Human in Lingít Aaní. *Environmental Philosophy, 13*(1), 83–104. doi:10.5840/envirophil201642634

13 *Flying in Shackles* was published independently by the Flying University. A local print shop printed a number of copies for limited distribution only.

14 I am grateful to my Tlingit colleague and friend, X̱'unei Lance Twitchell, for unpacking the meaning of this important phrase with me in personal correspondence.
15 Translation: "We are going to fight for it! We are going to succeed with love!"

Dedication

Respectfully dedicated to Tlingit elder, culture bearer, and *Shangukeidí* (Thunderbird clan) leader, *Kingeistí* David Katzeek (1942–2020), whose influence is everywhere in this chapter and who walked into the forest just before its publication.

Gunalchéesh ax̱ ee yilatóowu. (Thank you for teaching me.)

References

Bassford, C. (2020, September 20). Tip-toe through the Trinity. Retrieved September 15, 2020, from www.clausewitzstudies.org/mobile/trinity8.htm

Brooks, J. (2019, January 23). In State of the State, Gov. Mike Dunleavy calls for 'war on criminals' and tougher spending limits. Retrieved September 30, 2020, from www.adn.com/politics/2019/01/23/in-state-of-the-state-gov-mike-dunleavy-calls-for-war-on-criminals-and-tougher-spending-limits/

Burton, S. (Producer). (2016). *The Flying University* [Motion picture]. Juneau: 360 North.

Cardinal, P. (2019, November 05). On Global Human rights—Part one. Retrieved September 30, 2020, from www.mcgill.ca/humanrights/article/70th-anniversary-universal-declaration-human-rights/global-human-rights-part-i

Clausewitz, C.V. (1984). *On war.* (M. E. Howard & P. Paret, Eds. & Trans.). Princeton: Princeton University Press.

Conant, J. (2010). *A poetics of resistance: The revolutionary public relations of the Zapatista insurgency.* Edinburgh: AK.

Foucault, M. (2003). *Society must be defended: Lectures at the Collège de France, 1975–.* (D. Macey, Trans.). New York, NY: Picador.

Gilio-Whitaker, D. (2020). *As long as grass grows: The indigenous fight for environmental justice, from colonization to Standing Rock.* Boston, MA: Beacon Press

Girard, R. & Chantre, B. (2010). *Battling to the end: Conversations with Benoit Chantre.* (M. Baker, Trans.). East Lansing, MI: Michigan State University Press.

Glenn, E.N. (2015). Settler colonialism as structure: A framework for comparative studies of U.S. race and gender formation. Retrieved September 29, 2020, from www.sjsu.edu/people/marcos.pizarro/courses/240/s0/200SettlerColonialism.pdf

Goodhart, S. (2014). *The prophetic law: Essays in Judaism, Girardianism, literary studies, and the ethical.* East Lansing, MI: Michigan State University Press.

Guenther, L. (2013). *Solitary confinement: Social death and its afterlives.* Minneapolis, MN: University Of Minnesota Press.

Havel, V. & Keane, J. (2016). *The power of the powerless: Citizens against the state in central-eastern Europe.* London: Routledge.

Hope, I. (2017, March 30). 19th century US military bombardments on Tlingit villages: How land was illegally obtained by the US government. Retrieved September 30, 2020, from http://alaskanativestoryteller.com/2017/03/19th-century-us-military-bombardments-in-tlingit-villages-how-land-was-illegally-obtained-by-the-us-government/

Hope, I. & Neely, S. (2020, August 6–8). *Pedagogy as a Continuation of War by Other Means*. Lecture presented at Culturally Responsive Education. https://conference. sealaskaheritage.org/session/pedagogy-as-a-continuation-of-war-by-other-means/

King, E. & Neely, S. (Eds.) (2014) *Flying in shackles. A publication of the Flying University*. Juneau: AK Litho.

Levinas, E. (1989). *The Levinas reader*. (S. Hand, Trans.). Oxford: B. Blackwell.

Levinas, E. (1997). *Otherwise than being, or, Beyond essence*. Pittsburgh, PA: Duquesne University Press.

Levinas, E. (1998). *Entre nous: Thinking-of-the-other.* (M. B. Smith & B. Harshav, Trans.). New York, NY: Columbia University Press.

Levinas, E. (2013). *Totality and infinity: An essay on exteriority*. Pittsburgh, PA: Duquesne University Press.

Maldonado-Torres, N. (2007). On the coloniality of being. *Cultural Studies, 21*(2), 240–70.

Maldonado-Torres, N. (2008). *Against war: Views from the underside of modernity*. Durham: Duke University Press.

Marcos, S. (2015). Tomorrow Begins Today. In F. Lechner & J. Boli (Eds.), *The globalization reader*. Hoboken, NJ: Wiley-Blackwell

Marcos, S.I., & Zapatistas. (2008). *The other campaign*. San Francisco, CA: City Lights.

Matuštík, M.J. (1998). *Specters of liberation: Great refusals in the new world order.* Albany: State University of New York Press.

Minton, T.D. (2017, September). American Indian and Alaska Natives in local jails, 1999–2014. Retrieved September 29, 2020, from www.bjs.gov/content/pub/pdf/aianlj9914.pdf

Neely, S. (2016). On becoming human in Lingít Aaní. *Environmental Philosophy, 13*(1), 83–104. doi:10.5840/envirophil201642634

Neely, S., Hope, I., & Geiger, W. (2019). Within the whole body. *Screen Bodies, 4*(1), 25–47. doi:10.3167/screen.2019.040104

Prison Policy Initiative. (n.d.). Overrepresentation of American Indians in Alaska. Retrieved September 29, 2020, from www.prisonpolicy.org/graphs/2010percent/AK_American_Indian_2010.html

Schroeder, E. (Writer), & DeLaney, S. (Producer). (2019, February 5). Mind over matter [Radio show]. KRNN.

Schwab, G. (2010). *Haunting legacies: Violent histories and transgenerational trauma.* New York, NY: Columbia University Press.

Shankman, S. (2017). *Turned inside out: Reading the Russian Novel in prison*. Evanston, IL: Northwestern University Press.

Spivak, G.C. (1988). Can the subaltern speak? In C. Nelson & L. Grossberg (Eds.), *Marxism and the interpretation of culture*. Champaign, IL: University of Illinois Press.

Tribal Access to Justice Innovation. (n.d.). Circle peacemaking. Retrieved September 30, 2020, from www.tribaljustice.org/places/traditional-practices/circle-peacemaking/

Tuck, E. & Wayne Yang, K. (2012). Decolonization is not a metaphor. *Decolonization: Indigeneity, Education & Society, 1*(1), 3rd ser.

Wilkins, D.E. & Stark, H.K. (2018). *American Indian politics and the American political system*. Lanham, MD: Rowman & Littlefield.

Wolfe, P. (2006). *Settler colonialism & the elimination of the native*. Kurrajong NSW: Subversion Press.

Womack, C. (1999). *Red on red: Native American literary separatism*. Minneapolis, MN: *University of Minnesota Press.*

6 Settler colonialism, incarceration, and the abolitionist imperative

Lessons from an Australian youth detention center

Lisa Guenther

In August 2014, six boys in isolation at the Don Dale Youth Detention Centre in Australia's Northern Territory were tear-gassed after one of the boys opened his cell door, which had been accidentally left unlocked by a Youth Justice Officer.[1] For 30 minutes, Dylan Voller was banging on the door of the Behavioural Management Unit (BMU), asking how long he had been in isolation and smashing whatever he could with a metal light fixture he had pulled from his cell. After mocking the 14-year-old boy, calling him an "idiot" and a "little fucker," prison staff threatened to turn loose a prison guard dog, then decided instead to spray ten bursts of tear gas into the unit within 90 seconds. Two of the young people, who had been quietly playing cards in their cramped cell when the tear gas flooded in, tried to protect themselves by hiding behind a mattress. Afterwards, they reported that they "thought they were going to die" and had "said their good-byes" (OCC 2015, p. 20). Youth Justice Officers (as they are called) left one boy in his cell for eight full minutes before dragging him outside and hosing the whole group down with water.

Immediately following the incident, Northern Territory Corrections Minister John Elferink congratulated his staff on a job well done: "The staff worked hard, Fluffy the Alsatian worked hard and, as far as we are concerned, it was a problem that was solved quickly."[2] Immediately following the tear-gas incident, the Don Dale Centre was temporarily closed and the youth were moved into Berrimah Prison, a notoriously decrepit and overcrowded adult facility. Eventually, they were moved back to Don Dale, in spite of an official report that found the facility "totally unacceptable accommodation for young people in detention" (Hamburger et al., 2016, p. 21). And so, after being shuffled around like pieces on a chessboard, the boys found themselves back where they had started. The incident took place in a territory that justifies militarized intervention into Aboriginal communities for the sake of child protection since, as the Board of Inquiry into the Protection of Aboriginal Children from Sexual Abuse (BIPACSA) tells us, "Little Children Are Sacred" (BIPACSA, 2007).

Conditions in the Don Dale Behavioural Management Unit are appalling, even without further abuse from staff. Young people are kept for up to 23 hours a day in a windowless concrete box with no running water, no air conditioning or fans, and almost no natural light. There is one shower for the unit, but it is only partially enclosed, exposing the person in the shower to a direct view from three of the cells (OCC, 2015, p. 8). At the time of the tear-gassing incident, some boys were double-celled due to a lack of space, which meant that they at least had human contact, but in a space that was built for one person (p. 35). In a panel on youth justice in 2017, former corrections officer Eliza Tobin listed some of the names staff commonly used to call kids at the Don Dale Centre, including "oxygen thieves," "wastes of space," "little black camp dogs," and "little black poofters."[3] A former teen prisoner reported that guards used to offer them chocolate or Coca-Cola in exchange for fighting or eating bird feces on video for the guards' social media posts.[4]

In the wake of the tear-gassing incident, Northern Australian Aboriginal Justice Agency law and justice manager Jared Sharp said: "When young people are caged up like animals like that, you can understand where their psychological sense starts to deteriorate and things can become more inflamed."[5] The Northern Territory (NT) accounts for 1% of Australia's population and 5% of its prisoners; 85% of the territory's adult prison population, and up to 100% of its youth prison population, are Indigenous, in spite of being only 30% of the overall population in NT.[6] Indigenous children are 26 times more likely to be imprisoned than non-Indigenous children.[7] Once incarcerated, Indigenous people tend to be over-classified as medium or high security detainees, which further restricts their freedom of movement and their access to jobs or programs (Hamburger et al., 2016, p. 9). And Aboriginal communities are affected by high rates of death in custody, whether in prison or at the hands of police.[8]

In spite of the repeated acknowledgement in official inquiries of trauma in Aboriginal communities,[9] and the mandate of youth detention to "address the individual psychological, social and emotional wellbeing of the detainee,"[10] the Don Dale Youth Detention Centre did not employ a clinical psychologist until shortly before the tear-gassing incident.[11] Youth Justice Officers were given only three days' training, with no education in de-escalation techniques and no mention of the historical or political context of Indigenous hyper-incarceration (OCC, 2015, pp. 25–6). In fact, even the numerous government reports on the tear-gassing incident—the Northern Territory Review into Youth Detention Centres in January 2015 (which I will call the Vita report, after its author, Michael Vita), the Office of the Children's Commissioner's report in August 2015, "A Safer Northern Territory Through Correctional Interventions" in July 2016 (which I will call the Hamburger report, after its author, Keith Hamburger), and the interim report for the Royal Commission into the Protection and Detention of Children (March 2017)—routinely fail to acknowledge the impact of colonial violence. This violence includes invasion, mass killings, ongoing displacement from the land, confinement on Aboriginal stations, missions, and reserves, stolen wages on cattle stations and sugar cane plantations, penal transportation to isolated places like Rottnest Island and Palm Island (the latter of which has been described by historians as "a peculiar mix of prison, protectorate and concentration camp" (Finnane & McGuire, 2001, p. 292)), and genocidal policies of child removal—to mention just a few of the sites of traumatic interpersonal, structural, and state violence inflicted by settlers on Aboriginal peoples in Australia.[12]

The closest any of the government reports comes to acknowledging the impact of colonization and its relevance to Indigenous hyper-incarceration is the Royal Commission, which draws a strong connection between high rates of incarceration among Aboriginal youth and the systemic failure of child pro- tective services, going back to the Stolen Generations. These connections are important, and even their passing acknowledgement is preferable to the Vita report's admonition of Aboriginal legal and justice organizations for failing to allocate enough resources to support Aboriginal youth in detention, when Vita must know that these resources are thinly stretched in all directions, and when he does not recommend significant investments in Aboriginal programs or mentorship (Vita, 2015, pp. 15–16). But even the Royal Commission tends to invoke Aboriginal trauma as a psychological issue and a sign of pathology, rather than situating this trauma in relation to a long and unfinished history of colonial violence.[13]

By downplaying settler accountability for state, structural, and interper- sonal violence against Indigenous peoples, the liberal discourse of "inclusivity" remains closer to the racism of poorly-trained Youth Justice Officers than one might like to think. In fact, the word "racism" never comes up in government reports on the tear-gassing at Don Dale, nor do these reports raise fundamental questions about the legal basis for settler jurisdiction.[14] Why exactly should settler law apply to Aboriginal people, when the settler state has a long his- tory of using law as a weapon to decimate Aboriginal communities—not only in the Stolen Generations of the 20th Century, but also in laws like the 1886 Amendment of Victoria's Act for the Protection and Management of Aboriginal Natives (also known as the Half-Caste Act), which eliminated half of the state's Aboriginal population with the stroke of a pen? Other examples of genocidal settler law in Australia include the Aboriginals Protection and Restriction of the Sale of Opium Act which the state of Queensland passed in 1897, allowing the Chief Protector to place Aboriginal Australians on reserves and to separate Indigenous children from their communities, housing them in "reformatories" that are arguably the precursor to today's youth detention centers. Again, with the stroke of a pen, the state appointed the Director of Native Welfare as the legal guardian of all Aboriginal children, whether or not their parents were still living. Western Australia followed suit with similar legislation in 1905, New South Wales in 1909, and South Australia and the Northern Territory in 1911. In Queensland, the fictive kinship of the white settler "father" was not revoked until 1965.

The rhetoric of protection and the different but related rhetoric of interven- tion[15] are crucial for understanding the continuity, not only between the history of settler violence and the tear-gassing of boys at the Don Dale Youth Detention Centre, but also between this violence and the evasiveness of official reports whose purpose is presumably to foster accountability and transparency, so that such incidents are not repeated. It's important to remember that the violence of removing Aboriginal children from their communities was not only *legal*, it was carried out in the name of *protecting* Aboriginal people (Reynolds, 1996). Instead of grappling with this long and complex history of state-sanctioned settler violence, official inquiries into the tear-gassing at Don Dale tend to focus on institutional reform, as if the problem could be addressed through better infrastructure, adequate training and wages for correctional staff, standard operating procedures for behavior management, and so forth. The unquestioned framework for accountability and reform is still the settler criminal-legal system, with tributaries of Indigenous mentorship flowing into the mainstream and enriching its capacity to deliver protective/corrective services.

What if we took a different approach, starting not with the settler state as an unquestioned baseline, but with a critical analysis of the connections between settler colonialism, racism, and the hyper-incarceration of Indigenous people? How might a more direct and comprehensive reckoning with the history and legacies of settler violence help us to address the most pressing problem raised by the tear-gassing at Don Dale, which is not that a few Youth Justice Officers acted in ways that were embarrassing to the state, but that young people, most if not all of whom are Aboriginal, are routinely attacked, harmed, and abused by adults from a settler society in positions of asymmetrical power and authority? What would it take to abolish the conditions under which the liberal democratic settler state inflicts, perpetuates, and disavows genocidal violence against Indigenous peoples?

Settler colonialism and the (carceral) elimination of the native

In his 2006 essay, "Settler Colonialism and the Elimination of the Native," Patrick Wolfe argues that "[i]nvasion is a structure, not an event" (Wolfe 2006, p. 388).[16] In other words, invasion is not something that happened in 1788; it is an ongoing structure that organizes institutions like youth detention centers, incidents like tear-gassing, and discourses like Royal Commissions. The logic of this structure is the elimination of Indigenous peoples and of the alternative to settler dominance that the past, present, and future existence of Indigenous existence represents (Wolfe, 2006, p. 393). Sometimes the logic of elimination takes the form of outright genocide, such as in mass killings, the suppression of birth, or the forced removal of children. But Wolfe argues that assimilation is also a form of elimination, and a particularly powerful one in liberal democracies, because it seeks to dissolve the unique relationship of Indigenous peoples to land and the historical priority of Indigenous laws, customs, and modes of relation, transforming Indigenous nations or peoples into "individuals" with the same rights and status as any other individual (Wolfe, 2006, p. 402; Wolfe, 2015, p. 57). Wolfe calls this "assimilation's Faustian bargain—have our settler world, but lose your Indigenous soul. Beyond any doubt, this is a kind of death" (Wolfe, 2006, p. 397).

Settler colonialism not only seeks to *eliminate* Indigenous peoples, but also to *replace* them (Wolfe, 2015, 33). And yet, the "quest to replace Native territoriality only maintains the refractory imprint of the Native counter-claim" (Wolfe, 2015, p. 36). Even if settlers managed to eliminate every Indigenous person from the land they claim as their own, they could not change the fact that Aboriginal people were there first. The history of Indigenous priority may be scrubbed from school textbooks, sports teams and suburban streets may appropriate the names or symbols of Indigenous peoples, and settlers may proclaim their own Indigeneity (Ben-Zvi, 2018). But none of these "settler moves to innocence" (Tuck & Yang, 2012, pp. 9–10) reverse the priority of native to settler, which continues to haunt the settler nation-state.

A key feature of settler colonialism is the "organizing grammar" of race (Wolfe, 2006, p. 387). For Wolfe, racism is not the cause but the *instrument* of settler violence: "colonizers did not set out to create racial doctrine. They set out to create wealth" (Wolfe, 2015, 52). Nevertheless, settler wealth is predicated on the displacement and dispossession of Indigenous people, so racism is not incidental but precisely *instrumental* to settler economics. Wolfe argues that while Blacks in the United States were racialized through the one-drop rule, such that *any* Black ancestry was sufficient to make someone black, Indigenous peoples in the US and Australia were racialized through the concept of blood quantum, which allowed for a progressive disappearance of Indianness as their "blood" was "diluted" through intermarriage (often a code-word for the rape and kidnapping of Indigenous women). While these racial schemas are very different, even diametrically opposed, they both serve the interests of white settlers; the reproduction of Black slaves gave settlers access to free labor, while the dilution of Native "blood" gave them access to free land (Wolfe, 2006, p. 388). The racialization of Indigenous peoples seeks to undermine their status as sovereign nations and to represent them as "populations" with biological characteristics to be measured, analyzed, and subjected to risk assessment (TallBear, 2013). As Tiffany Lethabo King has argued, the violence of conquest is less intense in this "structural" injustice; it is by no means confined to the "event" of invasion.[17]

The ongoing violence of conquest is clearly visible at the limits of multiculturalism, where settler society meets an internal "frontier" of unassimilable and unruly Indigeneity, and the project of assimilation flips into a project of emergency intervention through the criminal-legal system, the custodial/welfare system, or both. In these moments, as we have seen, the settler state often deploys the rhetoric of protection or care for Indigenous communities— particularly for children—while using physical violence, displacement, forced removal, and detention as strategies for making Indigenous communities live on terms established unilaterally by the state. In a criminal-legal context, the rhetoric of assimilation is reframed as "rehabilitation" for individual "offenders," as if the only way of guaranteeing public safety and their own continued survival were "behavior management programs" modeling "pro-social" (i.e., settler-sanctioned) values and actions.

Race plays a crucial role in the criminalization of Indigenous peoples, or what the Hamburger report calls their "crimina*lity*" (Hamburger et al., 2016, p. 5). In Australia and other Anglo settler states, Indigenous people tend to be criminalized as trespassers, a threat to property, disrespectful to police, "drunk and disorderly," a "burden on society," a public nuisance. Or, as the Youth Justice Officers at Don Dale put it: "oxygen thieves," "wastes of space," and "little black camp dogs." This racialization is reflected in what the Australian Human Rights Commission Report on Aboriginal Deaths in Custody (1996) calls the "trifecta" of charges brought against many Aboriginal people who later die in custody: namely, offensive language, resisting arrest, and assaulting a police officer.[18] The thousands of settlers, immigrants, and visitors to Australia who get drunk and party on the beach during Schoolies week, swearing up a storm in the presence of police officers, are not at great risk of being arrested and dying in custody; an Indigenous Australian with roots going back thousands of years on the continent may not be so lucky.

In light of Wolfe's analysis of settler colonialism, we could understand the incarceration of Indigenous people as a spatial strategy of quarantining the surplus of unassimilated Indigeneity and framing this surplus as a "danger" to (settler) society. But it is also a temporal strategy. Wolfe writes that "the structural [as opposed to punctual] dimension of invasion […] has to suppress—or, at least, contain—the Native alternative across time" (Wolfe, 2015, p. 36). This is why children are so important; they must be "protected" in a way that kills the Indian in the child, or eliminates the prior and ongoing land claims of Indigenous peoples, without saddling settler society with an insupportable burden of guilt. In this sense, the incarceration of Indigenous people also serves to obscure the historical continuity of the past with the present, to orient the meaning of time towards an uncontested future of settler stability, and to eliminate other possible futures rooted in ongoing practices of Indigenous sovereignty.

This is why incarceration and segregation—both in the sense of racial segregation and in the sense of extreme isolation in prison, or "seg"—play such an important role in the neoliberal, post-welfare-state management of Indigenous peoples, reframed as "populations." They are practices that seek to both restrict the movement of Indigenous peoples on (their own) land by confining them to an established spot, and to manage their relation to time through prison sentences that are measured in temporal units of days, months, and years. Many of the Youth Justice Officers interviewed for the Children's Commissioner's report said, "there is no rehabilitation for young persons [at Don Dale] […] [they] just come in and do their time" (OCC, 2015, p. 41). But both rehabilitation and warehousing are ways of making someone "do" time, imposing settler ontologies of segmented time and space. Being forced to do time in a windowless concrete box for 23 hours a day is a standard consequence in settler legal systems, but think of the impact this has on the rhythms of Indigenous life: the constant interruption of police stops for "driving while black," drinking while black, surviving as black; the cycle of being arrested on minor charges, removed from your community, released to dim economic prospects, re-arrested on parole violations, and so forth. The spatio-temporal *structure* of settler colonialism sets a trap for Indigenous peoples to get caught in the eddy of endlessly repeated cycles of trauma, violence, and punishment, while settler society charts a linear trajectory of progress and prosperity for itself, and for Indigenous individuals who manage to assimilate. And when the official report comes down the pipeline, the pattern repeats itself again: more funding for training and infrastructure to expand and entrench the settler criminal-legal system, lukewarm or even resentful acknowledgements of Indigenous suffering, and half-hearted, underfunded gestures towards the "inclusion" of Indigenous perspectives.

The result is something akin to what sociologist Loïc Wacquant calls the "carceral-assistential complex," whose purpose is "to surveil, train and neutralize the populations recalcitrant or superfluous to the new economic and racial regime according to a gendered division of labor, the men being handled by its penal wing while (their) women and children are managed by a revamped welfare-workfare system designed to buttress casual employment" (Wacquant, 2001, p. 97). But in this case, men, women, and children are swept into the penal wing *in the name of* protection and care. What renders Aboriginal people eligible for care, or at least for the rhetoric of protection, is the prospect of their recruitment as what Aileen Moreton-Robinson calls the "good Indigenous citizen," namely one who accepts the permanent authority of the settler state and contributes to the health and prosperity of the population rather than draining its resources and becoming a burden or a menace against which "society must be defended" (Foucault, 2003). In conversation with Michel Foucault, Cheryl Harris, and other critical theorists, Moreton-Robinson argues that "patriarchal white sovereignty, as a regime of power, deploys a discourse of pathology as a means to subjugate and discipline Indigenous people to be good citizens, and that the tactics and strategies deployed within this race war reveal its own pathology" (Moreton-Robinson, 2015, p. 155). It is precisely as *citizens*[19] that Indigenous people may be punished by the state (p. 157), and it is precisely as a *liberal democratic* state governed by the "rule of law" that state agencies arrest and incarcerate Indigenous people rather than killing them outright, even if an astounding number of Indigenous people also die in custody.

To summarize: In the Australian settler state, the hyper-incarceration of Aboriginal and Torres Strait Islander peoples functions as a spatial and temporal strategy for managing the limits of assimilation, and as a criminal legal strategy for the ongoing challenge of eliminating Indigenous peoples and appropriating Indigenous land. At the limits of assimilation, the prison no longer functions as a panopticon. While disciplinary power targets those who are presumed to have a soul that is capable of redemption and a capacity for becoming docile subjects (Foucault, 1979), the neo-colonial prison is designed to contain and control a non-assimilable surplus or remnant. As such, it reinstates the basic logic of the frontier, which is closer in structure to the leper colony in Foucault's *Discipline and Punish* (1979): namely, a binary opposition and spatial separation between us and them, good and bad, "community" and "offender," where good Indigenous citizens are welcome to reside on this side of the line, just as long as they behave like whites and avoid living in "remote" locations where it is difficult and expensive to "protect" them and to stage "interventions" when the settler state deems it necessary (RC, 2017, p. 33).

This distinction between good (read: assimilable) and bad (read: non-assimilable) Indigenous people has roots in 19th-century discourses of protection. For the assimilable, "protection" means the structural violence of social welfare programs, including the forced removal of Aboriginal children from their families and communities, and the genocidal violence of the Stolen Generations. For the non-assimilable, "protection" means the violence of displacement onto increasingly small, prison-like plots of land, segregated from the enterprising activities of settler communities. This connection between the (allegedly) soft power of assimilation and the (unapologetically) hard power of removal, segregation, incapacitation, or death, is *still at work* in the official inquiries into the tear-gassing of children at Don Dale. Everyone agrees that a terrible thing happened, that no child deserves to be attacked with chemical weapons, stripped naked, hooded, or strapped into a restraint chair by adults who humiliate them with no respect for their dignity or fragility. But as soon as this primal scene of settler violence is acknowledged, it begins to fade into the background, giving way to recommendations for better training, higher salaries, and improved infrastructure for the perpetuation of a settler legal system that has not proven itself willing or able to provide even a minimal level of protection for young people.

How do we move beyond this impasse, where the settler state continues to reinscribe a logic of elimination even in official reports designed to promote accountability? Here is a partial and preliminary list of starting points for settlers:

(1) Acknowledge and affirm Indigenous sovereignty and its prior claim to land, before and beyond the settler state.
(2) Acknowledge that Indigenous peoples had, and continue to have, their own legal orders prior to the imposition of settler law. Support the continuation and reclamation of these legal orders.[20]
(3) Resist the equation of punishment with accountability. As Robert Nichols has argued, even the phrase "Indigenous overincarceration" implies that some level of incarceration is appropriate for Indigenous peoples (Nichols, 2014). And yet, we have not even established with any degree of legal or constitutional rigor the applicability of settler law to Indigenous peoples (Reynolds, 1996).
(4) Cultivate abolitionist practices. Scholar-activist Alexis Pauline Gumbs asks:

> What if abolition isn't a shattering thing, not a crashing thing, not a wrecking ball event? What if abolition is something that sprouts out of the wet places in our eyes, the broken places in our skin, the waiting places in our palms, the tremble holding in my mouth when I turn to you? What if abolition is something that grows? What if abolishing the prison industrial complex is the fruit of our diligent gardening, building

and deepening of a movement to respond to the violence of the state and the violence in our communities with sustainable, transformative love?

(Gumbs, 2008, p. 145)

In other words, what if abolition, like settler colonialism, is a *structure* rather than an *event*? If this is the case, then we can't expect decolonization and decarceration to happen as apocalyptic turning-points, and we shouldn't assume the existence of a single, catch-all solution to the intersecting problems of Indigenous hyper-incarceration, the Stolen Generations, and the failure of the settler state to recognize Aboriginal sovereignty and to honor Indigenous claims to the ownership and custodianship of land. Rather, both abolition and decolonization call for everyday practices of unsettling and refiguring our relationships to Indigenous peoples, to land, and to ourselves.

(5) Get out of the way. Don't block Indigenous survival, resistance, and resurgence by insisting that it take a form that is acceptable to the settler state. Social movements like Idle No More and Indigenous practices of resistance and refusal like blockading roads, mines, and pipelines, interrupt the rhythms of settler society and affirm their own temporality of resurgence beyond the settler cycle of violence, "protection," and punishment. As a settler myself, I think we need to find power, and not just deprivation or the sacrifice of "privilege," in the possibility of dismantling white patriarchal sovereignty and the forms of possessive individualism in which it invests (Moreton-Robinson, 2015). This means becoming different kinds of subjects, in relation to different organizing logics, motivated by the desire for a more just and beautiful world, structured not by the logic of elimination, replacement, and racism, but by the promise of decolonization, whatever that looks like and whatever it demands of us.

Notes

1 Thanks to the Department of Philosophy at the University of Queensland in Brisbane, Australia, for hosting me as an Atkins Visiting Professor in July–September 2017, and to the Queensland School of Continental Philosophy for inviting me to present an earlier draft of this chapter in August 2017. My analysis is deeply shaped by conversations with the graduate students in my intensive seminar on Settler Colonialism and Incarceration, by a roundtable discussion with Warraba Weatherall and Debbie Kilroy, and by conversations with Bogaine Spearim, Joanne Faulkner, Marguerite La Caze, and Damian Cox.

2 www.abc.net.au/news/2016-07-25/four-corners-evidence-of-kids-tear-gas-in-don-dale-prison/7656128.

3 www.abc.net.au/news/2017-03-24/don-dale-detainees-called-camp-dogs-by-officers-commission-hears/8384218.

4 www.adelaidenow.com.au/news/national/nt-police-have-launched-a-criminal-investigation-into-the-allegations/news-story/ebfc8109ac57bc6792838656ba0318d4.

5 www.sbs.com.au/news/thefeed/article/2016/07/26/history-allegations-inhumane-treatment-don-dale-juvenile-detention-centre.

6 Hamburger Executive Summary, p. 4; Vita, 2015, p. 10; RC, 2017, p. 9; Anthony, 2018, p. 252.

7 www.sbs.com.au/news/thefeed/article/2016/07/26/facts-about-indigenous-youth-detention-australia?cid=inbody:a-history-of-the-allegations-of-inhumane-treatment-at-the-don-dale-juvenile-detention-centre.

8 See RCIADIC, 1991.

9 This is especially pronounced in the Royal Commission report (RC 2017, pp. 33, 35).

10 https://nt.gov.au/law/young-people/don-dale-youth-detention-centre-darwin.

11 The Vita report refers to the "recent recruitment of the first clinical psychologist [as] an excellent initiative that will provide much needed support" (Vita, 2015, p. 16; see also OCC, 2015, p. 51).

12 See Anthony (2018) for an in-depth critique of the Royal Commission report and of the structural injustice that this report reinforces and disavows. Anthony argues that "the violence perpetrated by guards on Indigenous children in NT detention can be classified as state crimes" (p. 270)—an argument that resonates with Heidi Stark's critique of the settler state as a "criminal empire" (Stark, 2016).

13 See also Sherene Razack's (2015) critique of official inquiries into Aboriginal deaths in custody in Canada.

14 Thalia Anthony notes the absence of any meaningful acknowledgement of racism in the Royal Commission report, suggesting, "Perhaps it did not appear racially discriminatory to the Royal Commission because Indigenous children are the entire detention population and are mistreated and deprived of their rights in equal measure, or that it is discriminatory for Indigenous children to be singled out for detention in the first place" (Anthony 2018, 266).

15 The discourse of intervention is nested within the rhetoric of protection: "New universal and targeted strategies for child protection and youth justice will focus on prevention and early intervention, with increased investment in health and welfare from early childhood" (Hamburger Statement of Response, p. 3). For a critique of the intervention model, see Nicole Watson's work on the NT Intervention (Watson, 2010–11).

16 See Kauanui (2016) for an important critique of the way this phrase has been taken up by settler scholars in American Studies. My own work in this chapter repeats the pattern of engaging with Wolfe at greater length than with the Indigenous scholars to whom his analysis is indebted. With some hesitation, I have retained the basic structure of the paper as I wrote it in August 2017, when I was just beginning to study the connections between settler colonialism and the hyper-incarceration of Indigenous peoples. Wolfe's work set me on the path of learning from the work of Indigenous scholars, and I want to acknowledge both my gratitude for this initial provocation and the imperative of unsettling, and perhaps even abolishing, settler colonial studies as a field that centers the perspectives of white scholars.

17 See Lethabo King (2019) for a brilliant critique of white settler colonial studies as "reproduc[ing] a rigid settler-Indigenous binary that erases Black people and anti-Black violence from its analytical frames" (p. 67). King's critique of the field focuses largely on Veracini's account of settler colonial studies, and she acknowledges a certain proximity between Wolfe's account of the logic of elimination as a broader term than genocide and her own account of conquest as "a larger conceptual and

material terrain than settler colonialism," but Wolfe's account of race should be read in the context of King's work and other work at the intersection of Black Studies and Indigenous Studies, including Karuka, 2017; Kelley, 2017; Leroy, 2016; and Tuck et al., 2014.

18 www.humanrights.gov.au/publications/indigenous-deaths-custody-report-summary In particular, see 2004 death of Mulrunji Doomadgee in Palm Island, Queensland, who was arrested on a public nuisance charge for allegedly swearing at a white police office and singing "Who Let the Dogs Out" while the officer was arresting another Aboriginal person.

19 Moreton-Robinson argues, "[C]itizenship rights are a means by which subjugation operates as a weapon of race war that can be used strategically to circumscribe and enable the biopower of patriarchal white sovereignty" (2015, p. 157). See also Stark, 2016.

20 Thalia Anthony points out that an "alternative vision for justice was outlined by Indigenous witnesses before the Royal Commission. It involves a structural shift in the power relationship that would release Indigenous families and children from state controls and instead empower local Aboriginal communities to look after the care and well-being of their own children" (Anthony, 2018, p. 268). She also notes the importance of treaties, restorative practices, and resistance to primitive accumulation in her sketch of this alternative vision for justice.

References

Anthony, T. (2018). "They were treating me like a dog": The colonial continuum of state harms against indigenous children in detention in the Northern Territory, Australia. *State Crime Journal* 7(2), Special Issue on State Crime and Colonialism (Autumn), 251–77.

Australian Human Rights Commission. (1996). Indigenous Deaths in Custody 1989–1996: Report Summary. www.humanrights.gov.au/publications/indigenous-deaths-custody-report-summary

Ben-Zvi, Y. (2018). *Native land talk: Indigenous and arrivant rights theories.* Dartmouth College Press.

Finnane, M. & McGuire, J. (2001). The uses of punishment and exile: Aborigines in colonial Australia. *Punishment and Society 3*(2), 279–98.

Foucault, M. (1979). *Discipline and punish: Birth of the prison.* (A. Sheridan, Trans.). Vintage Books.

Foucault, M. (2003). *"Society must be defended": Lectures at the Collège de France, 1975–1976.* (D. Macey, Trans.). Picador.

Gumbs, A.P. (2008). Freedom seeds: Growing abolition in Durham, North Carolina. In CR10 Publications Collective (Ed.), *Ten years of strategy and struggle against the prison industrial complex.* AK Press.

Hamburger, K., Ferris, A., Downes, L., Hocken, J., Ellis-Smith, T. & McAllister, N. (2016, July). *A safer Northern Territory through correctional interventions.* Report of the Review of the Northern Territory Department of Correctional Services. BDO and Knowledge Consulting. https://justice.nt.gov.au/attorney-general-and-justice/justice-publications/hamburger-report

Karuka, M. (2017). Black and native visions of self-determination. *Critical Ethnic Studies. 3*(2), 77–98.

Kauanui, J. K. (2016). A structure, not an event: Settler colonialism and enduring indigeneity. *Lateral, 5*(1) (Spring).

Kelley, R.D. (2017). The rest of us: Rethinking settler and native. *American Quarterly, 69*(2) (June), 267–76.

King, T.L. (2019). *The black shoals: Offshore formations of black and native studies.* Duke University Press.

Leroy, J. (2016). Black history in occupied territory: On the entanglements of slavery and settler colonialism. *Theory & Event, 19*(4), 1–12.

Moreton-Robinson, A. (2015). *The white possessive: Property, power, and indigenous sovereignty.* University of Minnesota Press.

Nichols, R. (2014). The colonialism of incarceration. *Radical Philosophy Review,* 17(2), 435–55.

Northern Territory Board of Inquiry into the Protection of Aboriginal Children from Sexual Abuse [BIPACSA]. (2007). *Ampe akelyernemane meke mekarle: "Little children are sacred".* www.inquirysaac.nt.gov.au/

Office of the Children's Commissioner, Northern Territory [OCC]. (2015, August). *Own initiative investigation report services provided by the Department of Correctional Services at the Don Dale Youth Detention Centre.* Accessed on April 20, 2021 https://assets.documentcloud.org/documents/2426631/final-ddydc-report-to-minister.pdf

Razack, S. (2015). *Dying from improvement: Inquests and inquiries into indigenous deaths in custody.* University of Toronto Press.

Reynolds, H. (1996). *Aboriginal sovereignty: Reflections on race, state, and nation.* Allen Unwin.

Royal Commission into Aboriginal Deaths in Custody [RCIADIC]. (1991). *Royal Commission into Aboriginal Deaths in Custody report.* Australasian Legal Information. www.austlii.edu.au/au/other/IndigLRes/rciadic/

Royal Commission into the Protection and Detention of Children in the Northern Territory [RC]. (2017, March) *Royal Commission into the Protection and Detention of Children in the Northern Territory interim report.* Attorney General's Department. https://childdetentionnt.royalcommission.gov.au/about-us/Pages/interim-report.aspx

Stark, H.K. (2016). Criminal empire: The making of the savage in a lawless land. *Theory & Event* 19(4).

TallBear, K. (2013). *Native American DNA: Tribal belonging and the false promise of genetic science.* University of Minnesota Press.

Tuck, E. & Yang K.W. (2012). Decolonization is not a metaphor. *Decolonization: Indigeneity, Education and Society 1*(1), 1–40.

Tuck, E., Smith, M., Guess, A.M., Benjamin, T., & Jones, B.K. (2014). Geotheorizing black/land: Contestations and contingent collaborations. *Departures in Critical Qualitative Research 3*(1) (Spring), 52–74.

Vita, M. (2015). *Review of the Northern Territory Youth Detention System report. January 2015.* www.nt.gov.au/__data/assets/pdf_file/0004/238198/Review-of-the-Northern-Territory-Youth-Detention-System-January-2015.pdf

Wacquant, L. (2001). Deadly symbiosis: When ghetto and prison meet and mesh. *Punishment & Society, 3*(1) (Winter 2001), 95–133.

Watson, N. (2010). The Northern Territory emergency response: The more things change, the more they stay the same. *Alberta Law Review 48*(4), 905–18.

Wolfe, P. (2006). Settler colonialism and the elimination of the native. *Journal of Genocide Research 8*(4), 387–409.

Wolfe, P. (2015). In whole and in part: The racialization of indigenous people in Australia. In *Traces of History: Elementary Structures of Race*. Verso Books.

7 Settler colonialism, anti-colonial theory, and "indigenized" prisons for Indigenous women

Danielle Bird (Nêhiyaw)

According to Canadian national statistics, the annual rates of federally incarcerated Indigenous women are alarming. A 2018 report from the Office of the Correctional Investigator (OCI) indicates that "Over the last ten years, the number of Indigenous federally sentenced women increased by 60%, growing from 168 in March 2009 to 270 in March 2018" (Zinger, 2018, p. 61).[1] Other reports from Public Safety Canada show that there has been up to a 90% increase in federally sentenced and incarcerated Indigenous women over the last 20 years and in 2020, the Correctional Service of Canada (CSC) publicized that Indigenous women now account for 42% of federally incarcerated women across Canada (Wesley, 2015; Correctional Service Canada, 2019; Canadian Association of Elizabeth Fry Societies, 2015). Despite the statistical variability, all reports indicate that there has not been a period of time in the last several decades where Indigenous women were not overrepresented in prisons, nor do prison advocates (like the OCI), anticipate any significant rate decreases in the near future (Office of the Correctional Investigator, 2020). Such dire statistical analyses and revelations forced criminal justice advocates and correctional service watchdogs to re-examine Indigenous women's overincarceration as a human rights issue. This has reignited calls to implement alternatives to imprisonment and increase funding for Indigenous women's healing, rehabilitation, and reintegration programs by 2025 (Mochama, 2018; Lamirande, 2017; Native Women's Association of Canada, 2017; Standing Committee on the Status of Women, 2018). However, Robert Nichols reminds us that the discourse of overrepresentation and disproportionality in criminal justice literature operates in ways that obscure the historical and current function of carceral institutions where "disproportion may be constructed as the result of economic or social pathologies exogenous to the criminal justice system itself" (p. 440). In other words, Indigenous overincarceration, as it is theorized within the criminal justice literature, neatly situates colonialism in the past and it is constructed as an "event" where incarceration is cited as an example of its "legacy" obscuring the violent emergence and expansion of settler colonial carceral logics and structures within settler colonial Canada. This chapter explores the ongoing "Indigenization" of prisons as the primary solution to Indigenous women's imprisonment and examines how efforts to "Indigenize" prison systems reify the centuries-old "Indian Problem" by constructing Indigenous women's criminalization as "Indigenous" problems, requiring "cultural" solutions, rather than as manifestations of ongoing settler colonialism and settler colonial institutions in need of total transformation.

While calls to improve women's experiences within the criminal justice system existed before the 1980s when human and prisoner rights advocates underscored significant abuses taking place inside Kingston's Prison for Women (P4W), the Task Force on Federally Sentenced Women (TFFSW) is considered the first significant feminist-led federal inquiry, which also included the voices of Indigenous women within its investigation of the experiences of federally sentenced women (Hayman, 2006; Barrett et al., 2010). This initiative focused on themes of women's empowerment, creating meaningful choices for women, treating women with respect and dignity, creating a supportive and holistic environment, and sharing responsibility for women's overall well-being within corrections and the community (Hannah-Moffatt & Shaw, 2000). The TFFSW recruited members from various sectors of society to include in their final report diverse perspectives from incarcerated women, scholars, policy makers, correctional staff, and community outreach and advocacy groups.[2] This was a significant feature of the TFFSW as feminist organizations and prisoner advocates insisted on employing a distinctly *"Canadian* solution" to addressing women's issues inside of prisons (Hayman, 2006, p. 9).[3] However, the TFFSW's "Canadian" solution initially overlooked the fact that Indigenous women made up a significant proportion of the prisoner population in P4W. As a result, Indigenous women who were imprisoned in P4W were only invited to participate in the TFFSW as "after-thoughts" when members of the task force highlighted the lack of Indigenous representation within this initiative (Hayman, 2006, pp. 52, 53).[4]

Healing was a central theme in the contributions Indigenous women involved in the TFFSW made to the *Creating Choices* report and their calls for the creation of the Okimaw Ohci Healing Lodge emerged from a larger critique, which questioned the effectiveness of European modes of carceral control on Indigenous peoples' rehabilitation (Hamilton & Sinclair, 1991; Adelberg & the Native Women's Association of Canada, 1993; Monture-Angus, 2006; Bronskill, 2016).[5] The Okimaw Ohci Healing Lodge (OOHL) located on the Neekaneet First Nation near Maple Creek, Saskatchewan, is described as a multi-level security institution, which was designed with a focus on Indigenous women's healing and rehabilitation. The OOHL's operational structure, according to the CSC, is based on the TFFSW's cornerstone principles of creating the conditions for women's empowerment, offering women opportunities to make meaningful and responsible choices, fostering respect and dignity, providing women with a supportive prison environment, and sharing the responsibility of criminalized women with other stakeholders (Correctional Service of Canada, 2017). The federal government and the CSC's creation of the OOHL is considered by many criminal justice agents as a culturally valid response to addressing the needs of federally incarcerated Indigenous women and some Indigenous women agree (Barrett et al., 2010). In fact, Indigenous women fought for decades to ensure that gender responsive and culturally appropriate programs and services were available to Indigenous women in prisons (Dubec et al., 1982; Sugar & Fox, 1990). Indigenous women's calls to exercise their sovereignty by engaging in their own cultures and traditions in prisons should have been honored without criminal justice control and influence. However, government agencies like the CSC responded to Indigenous women's concerns through a pathologizing approach that suggests that Indigenous women's criminalization is a manifestation of "cultural deficiencies" and individual "dysfunctions" rather than an effect of settler colonial dispossession, marginalization, and oppression of Indigenous women (Martel & Brassard, 2008; Struthers Montford & Moore, 2018; Turnbull, 2014).

The criminal justice system's problematic response to Indigenous women's concerns resulted in sweeping "Indigenous cultural reclamation" reforms which overgeneralized the diverse experiences of Indigenous women in prison, and pan-Indigenous cultural reclamation projects inside prisons, being positioned as the primary solution to addressing the issues that contribute to Indigenous women's criminalization (Correctional Service Canada, 2013; Martel & Brassard, 2008, pp. 343, 344). Decades of reports reveal that Indigenous women fare far worse on every social and economic indicator than their non-Indigenous counterparts. Indigenous women are also identified by criminal justice researchers as having lower levels of educational attainment, fewer opportunities for employment, high emotional and personal needs, and higher incidences of substance use, yet criminal justice research fails to fully acknowledge the role racism, misogyny, patriarchy, and settler colonial violence play in these disparities (Bell et al., 2004).

These disparities exist because Indigenous women's ongoing presence and sovereignties present significant challenges to the legitimacy of national founding narratives within white settler states like Canada (Morgensen, 2012). Settlers thrive off the elimination of Indigenous bodies, because the erasure of Indigenous people from Indigenous lands advances settler colonial state-building projects which require state access to Indigenous lands and resources (Wolfe, 2006; Simpson, 2016). Settler colonialism, according to Maile Arvin, Eve Tuck, and Angie Morrill:

> is a persistent social and political formation in which newcomers/ colonizers/settlers come to a place, claim it as their own, and do whatever it takes to disappear the Indigenous peoples that are there. Within settler colonialism, it is exploitation of land that yields supreme value. In order for settlers to usurp the land and extract its value, Indigenous peoples must be destroyed, removed, and made into ghosts.
>
> (Arvin, Tuck, & Morrill, 2013, p. 12)

The Canadian settler state's project of elimination has occurred in a number of ways, but is evident when we examine the multiple ways that Indigenous women are disappeared through targeted acts of colonial violence, caught in state mechanisms of settler colonial social control, and are underprotected by settler laws and criminal justice (Dean, 2015; Simpson, 2016; Million, 2013; Kaye, 2016; Amnesty International, 2004; Palmater, 2016; The Native Women's Association of Canada, 2009; Lawrence, 2003; Suzack, 2010; Razack 2016; Human Rights Watch, 2013). Within settler states like Canada, the removal, destruction, and erasure of Indigenous peoples from the land also occurs, in part, through policing, incarceration, and criminalization of Indigenous people. These settler colonial acts of carceral social control are political projects which only serve to reinforce the settler state's justifications for the theft of Indigenous lands by constructing Indigenous people as "savage" criminals needing containment through decontextualized narratives and negative images (Nichols, 2014; Ross, 1998; Chartrand, 2019). For example, Heidi Stark (2016) reveals how the false discursive construction of Indigenous people as a "savage race" without any social, political, legal, and economic organization justified Canada's theft of Indigenous lands, while simultaneously rationalizing white settler criminal behavior through the unilateral imposition of European laws within Indigenous lands.

Patricia Monture-Angus (1998) challenged the idea that Canadian laws were absolute, underscoring the fact that within Canada's state building project, Indigenous legal systems and ways of knowing and being were excluded, ignored, and deemed illegal based on false notions of white settler superiority. Similarly, John Borrows (2001, 2010) has extensively documented how the purported superiority of Canadian federalism and settler laws has undermined and concealed Indigenous legal traditions in ways that have contributed to and justified settler colonial infringement on Indigenous rights, lands, and bodies. Within this context, definitions of "criminal offending" within criminal justice literature are often conceptualized based on white, heteronormative, and patriarchal understandings of *what constitutes a crime* within Canada.[6] Indeed, Indigenous women have been deemed criminalized based on gendered, racialized, and sexualized social constructs prior to the creation of what is currently known as Canada (Sangster, 1999, 2002; Erickson, 2011; Simpson, 2016). However, Razack reminds us that it is "the settler [that] is not legitimate. The land is occupied and continues to be stolen" (2015, p. 7). The myth that Canada was created from the labor and sacrifices of "hard-working pioneers" remains deeply embedded within Canada's national narrative and constructs the theft of Indigenous lands as a "liberation movement" rather than colonization and Indigenous people's subjugation (Moreton-Robinson, 2015, p. 60). Missing from many Canadian and newcomer perceptions of Indigenous people is an understanding that Canadian state-sponsored acts of genocide, including the legislated imprisonment of Indigenous people in residential schools and on reserves, the prohibition of Indigenous people's social, political, economic, and spiritual practices (such as the potlatch and Sundance), and the ongoing onslaught of settler colonial violence all contribute to the disparities that exist when we examine Indigenous women's involvement with the criminal justice system (Woolford & Benvenuto, 2015; Palmater, 2014; Starblanket, 2018; The Truth and Reconciliation Commission, 2015; Pettipas, 1994; Struthers Montford & Moore, 2018).

Within the criminal justice system, prison-based cultural reclamation projects have become a prominent feature within CSC programs and services for incarcerated Indigenous people with the strategic goal of assisting incarcerated individuals to "successfully reintegrate back into society as law-abiding citizens" (Correctional Service Canada, 2008). Even though CSC representatives maintain that its organization has no control over who is sent to prison and thus has no control over the growing numbers of Indigenous people in prison, the fact remains that prison officials and their policies play an important role in people's transitions from prisons to communities (Harris, 2016). Indeed, in 2007 the Native Women's Association of Canada (NWAC) slammed the CSC, arguing that it continues to fail Indigenous women by ignoring decades of recommendations that:

> have identified where improvements can and should be made [...] [A]lthough these policies and practices have been identified, they are not being implemented. The barriers to their implementation include cultural, racial and gendered discrimination, and decision making based on cost factors or budget considerations rather than on the human rights of Aboriginal women offenders.
>
> (NWAC, 2007, p. 3)

Similarly, Kim Pate, the former Executive Director of the Canadian Association for Elizabeth Fry Societies (CAEFS) argued the Canadian government continues to fail Indigenous women by not offering them protection when they face well-documented lethal levels of abuse and that "too many of the families and friends of Indigenous women and girls who are missing and found murdered are told that their loved ones are likely off partying, prostituting or in jail. The outrageous reality is that too many are forced to defend themselves, and then criminalized for doing so" (Canadian Association of Elizabeth Fry Societies, 2011, paragraph 2). However, Audra Simpson (2014) argues that "the 'phenomenon' of disappeared women, the murdered and missing Native women in Canada, is not a mystery, it is not without explanation [...] Indian women "disappear" because they have been deemed killable, able to be raped without repercussion, expendable. Their bodies have historically [and I argue contemporarily] been rendered less valuable because of what they represent: land, reproduction, Indigenous kinship and governance, an alternative to heteronormative and Victorian rules of descent" (Simpson, 2014, p. 156). Settler colonial Canada has been identified by scholars as hostile towards Indigenous women who fail to conform to white settler standards of femininity, and the criminal justice system, despite all the gender and diversity reforms, remains a violent settler colonial societal structure (Razack, 2002; Simpson, 2016).

While NWAC and the CAEFS have long been critical of Indigenous women's treatment inside Canadian prisons, members of the Standing Committee on the Status of Women have recently argued in favor of advocating for reconciliation with Indigenous women inside federal prisons (2018). This call occurred despite the fact that many Indigenous people have been critical of Canada's efforts to implement all of the Truth and Reconciliation Commission (TRC)'s 94 "Calls to Action" and have questioned the receptiveness of broader society to advancing reconciliation with Indigenous people on an national level (Manuel & Derrickson, 2017; Starblanket, 2018). The committee's report was released after racial tensions flared throughout the country after the high-profile acquittals of Bradly Barton in the murder of Cindy Gladue and Raymond Cormier in the murder of Tina Fontaine.[7] On a larger scale, tensions emerged from debates about who the criminal justice system is intended to serve and raised significant questions about the Canadian criminal justice system's apparent ongoing disregard for Indigenous women (Bird & Kaye, 2020).

Unequal systems of power and domination are embedded within every aspect of settler colonial justice systems and it is through the process of legitimized knowledge production that truth, power, and knowledge are operationalized and deployed to promote the ongoing erasure of criminalized Indigenous women. An anti-colonial discursive framework as a theoretical lens is suitable for disentangling Indigenous women's criminalization from the complexities involved in the construction of the Canadian criminal justice system and the colonial rhetoric that sustains what Patricia Hill Collins describes as "the matrix of domination" (Hill Collins, 1990, p. 246). Dei and Asgharzadeh highlight how anti-colonial frameworks allow the colonized to use Indigenous knowledge within an anti-colonial framework to interrogate "power configurations embedded in ideas, cultures, and histories of knowledge production, validation, and use" (Dei and Asgharzadeh, 2001, p. 300). Anti-colonial theorizing troubles representations of homogenous Indigenous knowledge systems and challenges us to think critically about how power is constructed and employed on the basis of who gets to decide what Indigenous knowledge is, who will have access to that knowledge, and how access is granted or restricted in ways that further marginalize criminalized Indigenous women.

There is no doubt that the manifestations of intergenerational trauma passed down from the residential schools system is an important part of understanding why Indigenous people are the fastest-growing prisoner population in Canada, but such limited discourses decontextualize the current lived realities of Indigenous people within a context of settler colonialism, which asks that Indigenous people "heal" while still being subjected to settler colonial violence on a daily basis.[8] For example, Government officials laud cultural reclamation initiatives inside of prisons as a progressive movement towards the agenda of reconciling with Canada's genocidal tendencies, but only when they are created, controlled, and administered through settler colonial mechanisms of social control (Correctional Service of Canada, 2013, 2014). Paulette Regan notes that within the context of reconciliation, "when non-Native Canadians talk about reconciliation [...] the tendency is to speak solely of the need for Native people to heal themselves and reconcile with us, so that the country can put this history behind it and move forward" (Regan, 2010, p. 59).

The disconnect between the theory of gender and cultural responsiveness and how the CSC employs its programming in practice is reflected in Indigenous women's overt and long-standing lack of faith in criminal justice policies and practices. Interrogating race, class, and gender, and acknowledging the ongoing effects of settler colonialism are imperative within the realm of criminal justice. However, the CSC continues to deflect any responsibility for the growing numbers of Indigenous women caught within the prison cycle while continuing to boast "gender-responsive" and "Indigenous-friendly" prison reforms for prisoner "rehabilitation and reintegration". Similarly, the limited focus on Indigenous women's criminalization as a result of cultural loss grossly oversimplifies Indigenous women's lived realities as they navigate racism, patriarchy, white supremacy, misogyny, and settler colonialism both inside and outside of carceral institutions. As a result, many of the sweeping "Indigenous-based" reforms found within the criminal justice system tend to construct Indigenous people as "different," while ignoring the larger structural failures of the criminal justice system. Prison reforms offer no transformative change and have yet to reduce, reverse, and eliminate the growing numbers of criminalized Indigenous women who are also underprotected by the criminal justice system (Razack, 2002, 2015, 2016; Simpson, 2016; Dhillon, 2015; National Inquiry into Missing and Murdered Indigenous Women and Girls, 2019).[9] Settler colonial carceral systems require abolition and abolition requires an entire restructuring of settler colonial societies, because the power dynamics that are upheld through white supremacy and settler colonialism ensure that Indigenous women bear the mark of stigmatization, regardless of whether they are criminalized or not.

Notes

1 The total female prisoner population in Canada was 684 in 2018.
2 For a detailed examination of the Task Force on Federally Sentenced Women and its members see: Hayman, *Imprisoning Our Sisters*, 2006.
3 Women-led and feminist-inspired organizations such as: Women for Justice, the Legal Education and Action Fund (LEAF) and the Canadian Association for Elizabeth Fry Societies (CAEFS) initiated court challenges and lobbied the federal government for changes in women's correctional policy and practice. For more information see Adelberg & Currie (1993).
4 Representatives from the Canadian Association of Elizabeth Fry Societies and scholars Patricia Monture-Angus and Sharon McIvor were instrumental in ensuring that Indigenous women were included in Task Force deliberations. See Sugar and Fox (1990) and Hayman (2006).
5 Indigenous women who participated in the TFFSW made significant connections between their experiences with colonialism, racism, and violence and questioned the effectiveness of mainstream prison programs in the context of "rehabilitation." For a

summary of Sugar and Fox's survey on federally sentenced Aboriginal women, see Adelberg & Currie (1993).

6 For example, Indigenous women and their choice to engage in sex work has often been constructed as a "criminal activity" see Barman, J. (1997); or as a result of "criminal activity" (e.g., human and sex trafficking) see Hunt, S. (2015).

7 For more information see: McLean, C. (2018, February 22); and Harris, K. (2018, October 11).

8 For example, see: Comments by Erica Violet Lee (p. 464) in Kaye, J. (2016).

9 The Office of the Correctional Investigator releases annual reports detailing prison reforms and initiatives and documents changing prison dynamics, issues, and demographics. For examples see: The Office of the Correctional Investigator, (2020), Ivan Zinger, 2018, 2019.

References

Adelberg, E. & Currie, C. (Eds.). (1993). *In conflict with the law: Women and the Canadian criminal justice system.* Press Gang Publishers.

Adelberg, E. & The Native Women's Association of Canada, (1993). Aboriginal women and prison reform. In E. Adelburg & C. Currie (Eds.), *In conflict with the law: Women and the Canadian justice system.* Press Gang Publishers.

Amnesty International. (2004). *Stolen sisters: A human rights response to discrimination and violence against Indigenous women in Canada.* [Report]. www.amnesty.ca/sites/amnesty/files/amr200032004enstolensisters.pdf

Arvin, M., Tuck, E., & Morrill, A. (2013). Decolonizing feminism: Challenging connections between settler colonialism and heteropatriarchy. *Feminist Formations, 25*(1), 8–34. doi:10.1353/ff.2013.0006

Barman, J. (1997). Taming Aboriginal sexuality: Gender, power, and race in British Columbia, 1850–1900. *BC Studies: The British Columbian Quarterly 115*(6), 237–66.

Barrett, M.R., Taylor, K., & Allenby, K. (2010). *Twenty years later: revisiting the task force on federally sentenced women.* Correctional Service of Canada, Research Branch. www.csc-scc.gc.ca/005/008/092/005008-0222-01-eng.pdf.

Bell, A., Trevethan, S., & Allegri, N. (2004). *A needs assessment of federal Aboriginal women offenders.* Correctional Service of Canada, Research Branch. www.csc-scc.gc.ca/research/r156-eng.shtml

Bird, D. & Kaye, J. (2020) Social control, settler colonialism, and representations of violence against indigenous women. In C. Brooks, M. Daschuk & J. Popham (Eds.), *Critical perspectives on social control and social regulation in Canada.* Fernwood Publishing.

Borrows, J. (2001). Indian agency: Forming first nations law in Canada. *Political and Legal Anthropology Review 24*(2), 9–24.

Borrows, J. (2010). *Canada's Indigenous constitution.* University of Toronto Press.

Bronskill, J. (2016, December 16). Federal study touts Indigenous sentencing regime to address prison numbers. CBC News. www.cbc.ca/news/indigenous/federal-study-touts-indigenous-sentencing-regime-1.3892493.

Canadian Association of Elizabeth Fry Societies. (2011). Canada must correct appalling record of discrimination against Indigenous women. [Press Release]. www.caefs.ca/wp-content/uploads/2013/04/Press-Release-Canada-must-correct-appalling-record-of-discrimination-against-Indigenous-women.pdf.

Canadian Association of Elizabeth Fry Societies. (2015). 2015 Fact Sheet: Indigenous Women. www.caefs.ca/wp-content/uploads/2013/05/FINAL-2015-Fact-Sheet-Indigenous-Women.pdf.

Chartrand, V. (2019). Unsettled times: Indigenous incarceration and the links between colonialism and the penitentiary in Canada. *Canadian Journal of Criminology and Criminal Justice 61*(3), 67–89.

Collins, P.H. (1990). *Black feminist thought: Knowledge, consciousness, and the politics of empowerment.* Unwin Hyman.

Correctional Service Canada. (2008). Speakers binder, section 2: The mandate, mission and priorities of the Correctional Service Canada. www.csc-scc.gc.ca/text/pblct/sb-go/02-eng.shtml.

Correctional Service Canada. (2013). Commissioners directive: Aboriginal offenders. www.csc-scc.gc.ca/acts-and-regulations/702-cd-eng.shtml#D_Aborginal_Corrections_Continuum_of_Care

Correctional Service Canada. (2014). Correctional Service Canada healing lodges. www.csc-scc.gc.ca/institutions/001002-4007-eng.shtml

Correctional Service of Canada. (2017). Indigenous corrections. www.csc-scc.gc.ca/publications/005007-3001-eng.shtml.

Correctional Service Canada. (2019). "Statistics and research on women offenders." www.csc-scc.gc.ca/women/002002-0008-en.shtml

Dean, A. (2015). *Remembering Vancouver's disappeared women: Settler colonialism and the difficulty of inheritance.* University of Toronto Press.

Dei, G.S. & Asgharzadeh, A. (2001). The power of social theory: The anti-colonial discursive framework. *The Journal of Educational Thought 35*(3), 297–323.

Dhillon, Jaskiran K. (2015). Indigenous girls and the violence of settler colonial policing. *Decolonization: Indigeneity, Education & Society 4*(2). https://jps.library.utoronto.ca/index.php/des/article/view/22826.

Dubec, B. & Ontario Native Women's Association. (1982). *Native women and the criminal justice system: An increasing minority.* Ontario Native Women's Association.

Erickson, L. (2011). *Westward bound: Sex, violence, the law, and the making of a settler society.* University of British Columbia Press.

Hamilton, A.C. & Sinclair, C.M. (1991). *Report of the Aboriginal Justice Inquiry of Manitoba: The justice system and aboriginal people. Vol. 1.* Queen's Printer.

Hannah-Moffatt, K. & Shaw, M. (Eds.). (2000). *An ideal prison? Critical essays on women's imprisonment in Canada.* Fernwood Publishing.

Harris, K. (2018, October 11). Top court hears grim details of Cindy Gladue's last hours as it considers new murder trial. CBC News. www.cbc.ca/news/politics/supreme-court-gladue-barton-1.4762680

Harris, M. (2016, December 31). Stone walls do not a prison make: A conversation with CSC Commissioner Don Head. iPolitics. https://ipolitics.ca/2016/12/31/walls-do-not-a-prison-make-a-conversation-with-csc-commissioner-don-head/.

Hayman, S. (2006). *Imprisoning our sisters: The new federal prisons for women in Canada.* McGill Queens University Press.

Human Rights Watch. (2013). *Those who take us away: Abusive policing and failures in protection of Indigenous women and girls in Northern British Columbia, Canada.* [Report]. hrw.org/report/2013/02/13/those-who-take-us-away/abusive-policing-and-failures-protection-indigenous-women.

Hunt, S. (2015). Representing colonial violence: Trafficking, sex work, and the violence of law. *Atlantis: Critical Studies in Gender, Culture & Social Justice 37*(2), 25–39.

Kaye, J. (2016). Reconciliation in the context of settler-colonial gender violence: "How do we reconcile with an abuser?" *Canadian Review of Sociology/Revue Canadienne de Sociologie 53*(4), 461–7.

Lamirande, T. (2017, October 31) Number of Indigenous people in prison now a human rights issue says Correctional Investigator. APTN. https://aptnnews.ca/2017/10/31/number-of-indigenous-people-in-prison-now-a-human-rights-issue-says-correctional-investigator/

Lawrence, B. (2003). Gender, race, and the regulation of Native identity in Canada and the United States: An overview. *Hypatia, 18*(2), 3–31. www.jstor.org/stable/3811009

Manuel, A. & Derrickson, R. (2017). *The reconciliation manifesto: Recovering the land and rebuilding the economy.* James Lorimer & Company.

Martel, J. & Brassard, R. (2008). Painting the prison 'red': Constructing and experiencing Aboriginal identities in prison. *British Journal of Social Work, 38*(2), 340–61. doi:10.1093/bjsw/bcl335

McLean, C. (2018, February 22). Jury finds Raymond Cormier not guilty in the death of Tina Fontaine. CBC. www.cbc.ca/news/canada/manitoba/raymond-cormier-trial-verdict-tina-fontaine-1.4542319

Million, D. (2013). *Therapeutic nations: Healing in an age of Indigenous human rights.* University of Arizona Press.

Mochama, V. (2018. January 4). Treatment of women in Canadian prisons a human rights travesty. The Star. www.thestar.com/opinion/star-columnists/2018/01/04/treatment-of-women-in-canadian-prisons-a-human-rights-travesty.html

Monture-Angus, P. (1998). Standing against Canadian law: Naming omissions of race, culture and gender. *Yearbook of New Zealand Jurisprudence, 2,* 7–29.

Monture-Angus, P. (2006). Confronting power: Aboriginal women and justice reform. *Canadian Woman Studies, 25*(3).

Moreton-Robinson, A. (2015). *The white possessive: Property, power, and Indigenous sovereignty.* University of Minnesota Press.

Morgensen, S.L. (2012). Theorising gender, sexuality and settler colonialism: An introduction. *Settler Colonial Studies, 2*(2), 2–22. doi:10.1080/2201473X.2012.10648839.

National Inquiry into Missing and Murdered Indigenous Women and Girls. (2019). *Reclaiming power and place: The final report of the national inquiry into missing and murdered indigenous women and girls. Volume 1a.* Retrieved from www.mmiwg-ffada.ca/wp-content/uploads/2019/06/Final_Report_Vol_1a-1.pdf.

Native Women's Association of Canada. (2007). Federally sentenced Aboriginal offenders: An issue paper. www.nwac.ca/wp-content/uploads/2015/05/2007-NWAC-Federally-Sentenced-Aboriginal-Women-Offenders-Issue-Paper.pdf.

Native Women's Association of Canada. (2017, August). Indigenous women in solitary confinement: Policy backgrounder. www.nwac.ca/wp-content/uploads/2017/07/NWAC-Indigenous-Women-in-Solitary-Confinement-Aug-22.pdf

Nichols, R. (2014). The colonialism of incarceration. *Radical Philosophy Review, 17*(2), 435–55.

Office of the Correctional Investigator. (2020, January 21). Indigenous people in federal custody surpasses 30%. Correctional investigator issues statement and challenge. www.oci-bec.gc.ca/cnt/comm/press/press20200121-eng.aspx.

Palmater, P. (2014). Genocide, Indian policy, and legislated elimination of Indians in Canada. *Aboriginal Policy Studies, 3*(3), 27–54, doi:10.5663/aps.v3i3.22225

Palmater, P. (2016, July). Shining light on the dark places: Addressing police racism and sexualized violence against Indigenous women and girls in the national inquiry. *Canadian Journal of Women & the Law, 28*(2), 253–84. doi:10.3138/cjwl.28.2.253

Pettipas, K. (1994). *Severing the ties that bind: Government repression of Indigenous religious ceremonies on the prairies.* University of Manitoba Press.

Razack, S.H. (2002). *Race, space, and the law.* Between the Lines.

Razack, S.H. (2015). *Dying from improvement: Inquests and inquiries into Indigenous deaths in custody.* University of Toronto Press.

Razack, S.H. (2016). Gendering disposability. *Canadian Journal of Women and the Law, 28*(2), 285–307.

Regan, P. (2010). *Unsettling the settler within: Indian residential schools, truth telling, and reconciliation in Canada.* University of British Columbia Press.

Ross, L. (1998) *Inventing the savage: The social construction of Native American criminality* (1st ed.). University of Texas Press.

Sangster, J. (1999). Criminalizing the colonized: Ontario Native women confront the criminal justice system, 1920–60. *The Canadian Historical Review, 80*(1), 32–60.

Sangster, J. (2002). ""She is hostile to our ways": First Nations girls sentenced to the Ontario Training School for Girls, 1933–1960. *Law and History Review, 20*(1), 59–96. doi:10.2307/744155

Simpson, A. (2014) *Mohawk interruptus: Political life across the borders of settler states.* Duke University Press.

Simpson, A. (2016). The state is a man: Theresa Spence, Loretta Saunders and the gender of settler sovereignty. *Theory & Event, 19*(4). muse.jhu.edu/article/633280

Standing Committee on the Status Of Women. (2018, June). *Report of the standing committee on the status of women, a call to action: Reconciliation with Indigenous women in the federal justice and correctional systems.* Parliamentary Information and Research Service. http://nccabc.ca/wp-content/uploads/2018/08/A-Call-to-Action-Reconciliation-with-Indigenous-Women-in-the-Federal-Justice-Correctional-Systems.pdf.

Starblanket, T. (2018). *Suffer the little children: Genocide, Indigenous nations, and the Canadian state.* Clarity Press.

Stark, H.K. (2016). Criminal empire: The making of the savage in a lawless land. *Theory & Event, 19*(4) n.p. www.muse.jhu.edu/article/633282;

Struthers Montford, K. & Moore, D. (2018). The prison as reserve: Governmentality, phenomenology, and indigenizing the Prison (Studies) Symposium: The laws of captivity: Critical and humanistic inquiries. *New Criminal Law Review, 21*(4), 640–64.

Sugar, F. & Fox, L. (1990). *Survey of Federally Sentenced Aboriginal Women in the Community.* [Report]. Native Women's Association of Canada.

Suzack, C. (2010). Indigenous women and transnational feminist struggle: Theorizing the politics of compromise and care. *CR: The New Centennial Review, 10*(1), 179–93. www.jstor.org/stable/41949685.

The Truth and Reconciliation Commission. (2015). *Canada's Residential Schools: The history, part 1. Origins to 1939, volume 1. The final report of the Truth and Reconciliation Commission of Canada.* Government of Canada, http://caid.ca/TRCFinVol1Par12015.pdf

Turnbull, S. (2014). Aboriginalising the parole process: 'Culturally appropriate' adaptations and the Canadian federal parole system. *Punishment & Society, 16*(4), 385–405, doi:10.177/1462474514539538.

Wesley, M. (2015). *Marginalized: The Aboriginal women's experience in federal corrections.* [Report]. Aboriginal Corrections Policy Unit, Public Safety Canada. www.publicsafety.gc.ca/cnt/rsrcs/pblctns/mrgnlzd/index-en.aspx

Wolfe, P. (2006). Settler colonialism and the elimination of the Native. *Journal of Genocide Research, 8*(4), 387–409. doi:10.1080/14623520601056240

Woolford, A. & Benvenuto, J. (2015) Canada and colonial genocide. *Journal of Genocide Research, 17*(4), 373–90. doi:10.1080/14623528.2015.1096580

Zinger, I. (2018). *Office of the Correctional Investigator annual report 2017–2018.* Office of the Correctional Investigator. www.oci-bec.gc.ca/cnt/rpt/annrpt/annrpt20172018-eng.aspx

Zinger, I. (2019). *Office of the Correctional Investigator annual report 2018–2019.* Office of the Correctional Investigator. www.oci-bec.gc.ca/cnt/rpt/annrpt/annrpt20182019-eng.aspx

8 "The women that died in there, that's all I could think of"

The P4W Memorial Collective and garden initiative

Isabel Scheuneman Scott, Fran Chaisson and Bobbie Kidd

This chapter is largely framed by a conversation that I (Isabel) had with Fran Chaisson and Bobbie Kidd. Fran Chaisson is originally from Toronto, Ontario. She lives by the seven Grandfather teachings, is a keeper of the big drum, and sits on the board of the Elizabeth Fry Society of Kingston. Bobbie Kidd is originally from Winnipeg, Manitoba. She is a Personal Support Worker and grandmother to three young children whom she loves spending time with. Both Fran and Bobbie are Indigenous: Fran is Ojibwa; Bobbie is uncertain of her exact lineage. Both women currently live in Kingston, Ontario. I am originally from Surrey, British Columbia. My family originates from various European countries; however, I identify as Canadian. I currently live in Edmonton, Alberta, where I am working towards my PhD in sociology at the University of Alberta. My research explores Indigenous women's stories within *Tightwire*, a newsletter produced by prisoners within the Prison for Women (P4W). In February 2021, I accepted an invitation to become a member of the P4W Collective. In our conversation, Fran and Bobbie talked about their experiences of incarceration at the former P4W and how they are working with other P4W Memorial Collective members to develop a memorial garden.

According to the Collective's website, "the P4W Memorial Collective is a group of women ex-prisoners from P4W, Indigenous activists, and prison justice advocates who are working towards obtaining a permanent memorial garden on the grounds of the Prison for Women" (www.p4wmemorialcollective.com). The Collective honors women, girls, genderqueer, and two-spirit individuals who are caught up in Canada's prisons. This is accomplished in two ways. First, the Collective helps raise public consciousness about injustices that continue to be faced by prisoners in Canada. Second, the Collective draws attention to conditions of criminalization that lead to incarceration.

Through the creation of a memorial garden, the Collective seeks to ensure that the histories of P4W and former prisoners are visible to and thus not forgotten by the public. While the garden will memorialize all women who have died in Canadian prisons, it will be especially focused on those who died at

P4W. In this way, the garden "will contribute to a greater understanding of the historical heritage of the Prison for Women beyond the architectural heritage features of the prison" (www.p4wmemorialcollective.com). As tourism in Kingston is on the rise, the Collective also hopes that the garden will play "an important part of presenting a different side of the history in the city" while also providing a beautiful green space to visitors (www.p4wmemorialcollective.com). This different side of history is particularly important in places like Kingston where prison tours are a main draw for tourists and tickets often sell out far in advance (www.tripadvisor.ca).

I open this chapter with a brief history of some of P4W's most critical issues and moments. The next section consists of a conversation I had with Fran and Bobbie in January 2020. I conclude the chapter by providing some brief remarks.

Brief history of P4W

The Prison for Women was the only federal women's prison in Canada prior to the opening of six other federal penitentiaries, beginning in 1995 (Hayman, 2006). P4W, a four-storey prison, opened in 1934 and was in operation until 2000 (Adema, 2016; Hayman, 2006). Prior to its opening, housing women with men within the same prison was a common practice; however, P4W was primarily constructed due to the Correctional Service of Canada's (CSC) administrators' feelings of discomfort regarding this practice (Adema, 2016). Gendered assumptions were even used to guide the physical design of P4W. For instance, P4W lacked surveillance towers—common features of other prisons—because women were perceived as timid (Adema, 2016) and presumably they would not attempt to escape. Ironically, women were simultaneously characterized as hypersexual, transgressive, and threatening—and it was these combined gendered logics that underpinned the operation of P4W (Adema, 2016). Adema (2016) argues that "the decision to build P4W was, therefore, based on sexist assumptions regarding the character of women, specifically delinquent women" (p. 228).

Several overarching problems with P4W were identified almost immediately following its opening. Problems with P4W were first pinpointed in the Archambault Report in 1938—only four years after P4W opened (Adema, 2016). The Archambault Report argued that the responsibility of women's incarceration should fall back to the provinces (Adema, 2016). In returning this responsibility to the provinces, the Archambault Report claimed that CSC would help keep women closer to their families and communities (Adema, 2016). The report also stated that this proposed change made sense given that women's crimes were more likely to merit provincial rather than federal custodial sentences (Adema, 2016). Ultimately, the Archambault Report recommended that P4W be closed (Adema, 2016). Beyond the geographical dislocation of women caused by the impossibility of being federally imprisoned anywhere else, other problems with P4W included the inflexibility of classifications and security levels, difficulty in providing and thus lack of adequate programming, hyper-representation of Indigenous women, and repeated human rights violations against prisoners (Adema, 2016; Hayman, 2006; Kilty, 2018).

The closure of P4W was supported by the Task Force on Federally Sentenced Women which was established in 1989 after the appointment of a new commissioner of corrections, Ole Ingstrup, in 1988 (Hayman, 2006). While the Task Force was initially developed without the explicit guidance and participation of Indigenous women, four Indigenous women (two of whom were federally incarcerated[1]) eventually came onto the Task Force. The purpose of the Task Force was to examine the correctional management of federally sentenced women from the beginning to the end of their sentences, and to develop policies and plans to help guide the process while being responsive to women's unique needs (Hayman, 2006). In 1990, the Task Force released their findings in a report entitled *Creating Choices: The Report of the Task Force on Federally Sentenced Women* (Struthers Montford, 2015). One distinct feature of *Creating Choices* was that it focused on notions of difference to demonstrate diversities between women as a group, Indigenous women and non-Indigenous women, as well as women and men (Hayman, 2006). The report also detailed how these differences ought to be reflected in the treatment of federally sentenced women (Hayman, 2006). *Creating Choices* put forward five principles that the Task Force hoped would guide the federal imprisonment of women: (1) empowerment; (2) meaningful and responsible choices; (3) respect and dignity; (4) supportive environment; and (5) shared responsibility (Hayman, 2006; Struthers Montford, 2015). The report also detailed several recommendations, which included the opening of six new federal women's prisons that would operate under the above principles (Hayman, 2006; Struthers Montford, 2015). These new prisons were perceived as solutions to the problems identified with P4W (Dell et al., 2009; Hayman, 2006).

Creating Choices became a monumental document in Canada's penal history. Some of the reasons for this are that the report drew on radical language (while also conforming to the style of most other government reports), an entire chapter was devoted to the voices of federally sentenced women, and, perhaps most importantly, issues concerning Indigenous women were not confined to a sole chapter, but rather were raised throughout (Hayman, 2006). While the Task Force sought for their report to have an empirical basis by commissioning research regarding federally sentenced women, the research was continually delayed. Consequently, the Task Force began their work well before receiving the findings; thus much of their work was based on unreliable evidence and what they assumed the population of federally sentenced women to be (Hayman, 2006).

One of these assumptions was that all federally sentenced women, but particularly Indigenous women, were victims. Specifically, Indigenous women's victimization was perceived as stemming not only from within the criminal (in)justice system, but from historical impacts of colonialism (Hayman, 2006).

Assumptions of women's (almost) exclusive experiences of victimization are problematic because they tend to erase women's agency and resistance to victimization and oppression (Chesney-Lind, 2006). While I do not question the very real experiences of victimization that incarcerated Indigenous women experience (Comack, 2018), to avoid invisibilizing women's resistance, I believe that researchers must also emphasize women's agency. Indeed, Hayman (2006) argues that the only members of the Task Force who had more than anecdotal experience (and were thus qualified to speak on behalf of federally sentenced Indigenous women) were the two Indigenous women who had served federal time, Fran Sugar and Lana Fox. While some may argue that these two women's stories are in fact anecdotal (which functions as a quick and easy way to dismiss the research, diminish the work of researchers, and downplay the lived realities of those who share their stories), there are others who point to the importance of stories as evidence (McAleese & Kilty, 2019). For instance, McAleese and Kilty (2019) note that while not all stories are evidence of a widespread problem, when individual stories are taken together over time and show similar narratives about different aspects of prison life, these stories are indicative of a larger and significant trend rather than simply being anecdotal. The fact that the Task Force sought out and engaged with Sugar and Fox's stories demonstrates that they took seriously women's lived experiences of criminalization and incarceration.

At the same time, while *Creating Choices* attempted to draw in Indigenous women's voices—and is thus a rare example of women's stories actually being considered in policy making—frequently, when sharing, the women were met with silence by members of the Task Force (Hayman, 2006). The Task Force's lack of response could be indicative of what Sam McKegney (2008) terms "ethical disengagement"—that is, when non-Indigenous people try to avoid doing damage to Indigenous peoples by, for instance, retreating into silence. When non-Indigenous people are silent about Indigenous peoples and stories, McKegney (2008) argues that this signals a lack of deep and respectful engagement which contributes to the obfuscation of Indigenous voices. Despite its problems, *Creating Choices* remains a one-of-a-kind Canadian penal document that espouses gender-responsivity and speaks to the concerns of federally incarcerated women, with particular emphasis on the experiences of Indigenous women (Dell et al., 2009; Hayman, 2006; Struthers Montford, 2015).

However, shortly before the process of P4W's official closure commenced there was a series of events that would culminate in a national Commission of Inquiry. In April 1994 at least three prisoners claimed that one CSC officer, Anne Power, remarked to multiple Indigenous prisoners "Why don't you go hang yourself like the other Native girls" (Adema, 2016, p. 250–1). This rhetorical statement provoked several Indigenous prisoners (Adema, 2016) and on April 22, six prisoners briefly violently confronted CSC staff (Adema, 2016; Kilty, 2018). These prisoners were then placed in solitary confinement (Adema,

2016) for nine months and were criminally charged; five pled guilty (Kilty, 2018). Of note is that during their time in segregation, the women had:

> very restricted access to basic needs, including menstrual and other hygiene products like toilet paper and deodorant, and were denied access to clothes, cutlery and even paper and writing utensils, which is a methodical way to inhibit their ability to file formal grievances about their conditions of confinement and human rights violations.
>
> (Kilty, 2018, p. 140)

The actual events that occurred following this initial incident are unclear as prisoners and CSC staff had competing versions of what happened. The most we know about what happened is contained within the Arbour Report—the document resulting from the *Commission of Inquiry into Certain Events at the Prison for Women in Kingston*, headed by Justice Louise Arbour (Adema, 2016). Two days after the confrontation, on April 24, three women (who were already being held in segregation prior to the incident) self-harmed, took a hostage, and attempted suicide (Kilty, 2018). On April 26, CSC staff demonstrated outside P4W and demanded that the women involved in the April 22 incident be transferred to another prison which meant either moving them back into federal men's prisons or to regional psychiatric treatment centers—neither of which were viable options (Kilty, 2018). The prisoners heard and saw the demonstration from their cells (Kilty, 2018). Tensions were extremely high between prisoners and CSC staff (Adema, 2016). This hostile environment particularly affected Indigenous prisoners because of the Native Sisterhood's[2] political activism, their calls for P4W's closure (especially following the release of *Creating Choices*), the recent suicides of Indigenous women at P4W, and the tense relationship between Indigenous prisoners and CSC staff who perceived Indigenous women as "difficult to control" (Adema, 2016, p. 250).

That same evening (when the prisoners were sleeping), the Warden, Thérèse Leblanc, called in an all-male, all-white Institutional Emergency Response Team (IERT) (Adema, 2016; Kilty, 2018). This IERT was "a team of eight men plus a coordinator, in riot gear and weaponry designed to protect anonymity of the staff and intimidate" the prisoners (Adema, 2016, p. 251). This type of gear prevented eye contact between CSC staff and prisoners while allowing physical and emotional separation (Kilty, 2018), further enabling CSC to treat the prisoners as less than human. The IERT was called in to perform cell extractions and strip searches of the eight women in segregation to search for weapons (Adema, 2016; Kilty, 2018). This search lasted upwards of six hours (Kilty, 2018). During this time, the IERT hit "their batons against concrete walls beside the women's heads in an effort to keep their attention and silence them as they try to warn one another to comply rather than resist" (Kilty, 2018, p. 128). The women were chained to their beds and had their clothing forcibly removed (Adema, 2016). Seven of the eight women were "subjected to body cavity searches on the concrete floors of their cells" after which the "women were left in empty segregation cells wearing nothing but paper gowns, waist-hand restraints and leg irons" (Kilty, 2018, p. 124). Some of the women were left completely naked (Adema, 2016).

When videos of this incident surfaced, they captured national media attention and underlined the problems within P4W (Adema, 2016; Kilty, 2018). Justice Louise Arbour concluded that incarcerating women in segregation for more than nine months and allowing male IERT members to strip-search women broke the rule of law (Kilty, 2018) and was in violation of human rights legislation (Adema, 2016). Specifically, these actions were in violation of the legislation governing CSC operations, namely Sections 46 to 67 of the Corrections and Conditional Release Act, also known as CCRA (Adema, 2016). These violations broke requirements such as for the person conducting the search to be of the same gender and for prisoners to be free of any cruel, inhumane, and/or degrading treatment or punishment (Adema, 2016). CSC was also found to be in violation of the Commissioner's Directive 571 B which included policies to ensure privacy and dignity, as well as for a witness to be present during the search (Adema, 2016). From its opening to its closing, P4W faced relentless criticism. Fran and Bobbie experienced and witnessed the problems firsthand and generously shared some of their experiences with me.

Conversation with Fran and Bobbie

ISS: Back in September 2019 where we first met at the Building Abolition Conference in Banff, I had the opportunity to attend your session which included the screening of a short documentary film entitled "A Memorial Garden." This was the first time that I heard about the P4W Memorial Collective in which you are both members. Before we get too much into the Collective, I wanted to ask you both to tell me a little bit about your experiences at P4W—starting, for instance, with when and how long you were incarcerated there. Bobbie, would you like to start?

BK: Okay, I went in in [19]85 and I was in there for eight years, eight or nine years, something like that. I would sum up [my experiences at P4W] as a private prison. I mean, you didn't talk to the outside world, you didn't, you know what I mean? There was no communication with the community except for the people that came in once in a while, like a volunteer who came in once a month. Communication with anybody was kind of hard in there because they [prison staff] wanted to know everything, nothing was confidential at all. So, you kind of felt isolated from the world, you know. And you made friends, you have relationships in there and stuff like that but they [prison staff] also didn't like that, they would label you, you know? If you were having a relationship just because you like that person, doesn't mean that you did whatever they did, you know what I mean? This is how I felt—they would label you as the same kind of person. So, they didn't, you know, agree with relationships because they say, "oh well she's into drug culture or whatever culture because she's hanging around with a certain person." You never had your own identity.

ISS: What about for you, Fran? I think I remember you said you were first incarcerated at P4W in 1973?

FC: Yes, I went in April of [19]73 right after the riot. [...] I got held back three weeks because of the male prison riot across the street where they smashed it up. I got transferred in '73, I did two years for assaulting police and then I went back in April of [19]83, but it was a lot different in 10 years inside the Prison for Women. When I first went in in '73, I was probably the youngest that had ever gone through the doors at that time, and most of the people that were in there were all lifers. I'll say 98 percent of women that were in there at that given time would have been mostly lifers, and the population had been probably no more than 50 women in there at that given time, in the early '70s. I found the whole system was different than it was when I went back in in '83. [...]

BK: There was a lot of bad, bad karma in the place, a lot of bad energy, and they said this place is not good at all. Actually, it was Kim Pate from E[lizabeth] Fry [Society]—they're the ones that fought to close it [P4W]. I remember it was Joey, Frannie, me, and a couple other girls who fought to keep it open because, like I said, because none of us, we were like the only ones in there right. We knew it was coming but we also didn't know if we were going to be separated from each other. Like, what was going to happen, like we were, you know, change is bad when you're in prison because you're in there for a long time and you have no control, you feel like worthless. [...]

FC: They do what they want with you. Honestly, you know what I think jail is? It's nothing more than a human warehouse, you know. [...] There's nothing good about incarceration. The only thing good about it is shutting it all down. Women should never be in jail in the first place. You've taken them from their kids and their families for no reason but to punish. They're not serial killers, most of them have drug problems or they've been sexually abused—that's why most of them are even in there to begin with; and you know, they [prison staff] need to heal them, not punish them.

BK: There is no healing in prison and there is no reintegration in prison either, that's why people end up always going back because there's nothing in there to really help you, unless you're actually religious when you first go in there because it's all church people and stuff that go there right, so unless you're spiritual or you got a certain religion then you know, you can probably, you know, learn some stuff to get reintegrated right back into the community. But as a person that, you know, trying to understand what's going on with yourself and you're trying to get better but you're being also manipulated by the system because they're saying "you're no good, you deserve to be here" and this and that. The mental abuse in there is horrific in GVI [Grand Valley Institution for Women] because they have male guards in there working in a women's prison who can walk in there at nighttime. So, in the summertime maybe you're in there and you take off your blanket and you're in your bra and underwear, you've been an abused woman all your life. There's nothing good about prison, you know what I mean? Like, there's so many things…

FC: It's dysfunctional.

BK: […] You know, you have people in there that, you know, as I was in there myself so I know, I've seen it for myself, there was a couple of male guards that worked there that had been in the army for 25 years so now they decided they're going to spend their last few years in a women's prison so they come in there and treat you like you're a bunch of guys. "I told you to sit down and shut up," like you know, I said "Listen dude, you're not in the army and this is a women's prison I'll have you know"'cause that could trigger a lot of abused women, right? So they [the Correctional Service of Canada] let them [men] go in there [women's prisons], they let that go, they let everything go, and that's the thing right, you know, about these prisons, and like I said, there's no integration because there's nothing, there's no help in there. They make you feel more worthless than helped, you're not helped. You feel helpless when you get out of there because you don't even know if anybody will like you or want to talk to you because they [prison staff] have made you feel so worthless about yourself just because of the mental abuse that they do. You have to be strong to be in prison because, if you do have mental health [concerns] and stuff like that then that's even worse for you 'cause then they just lock you up but you're so medicated, you don't even know what your name is. So, when you get out, they send you a week's worth of medication; when you come off that medication, you go right into the drugs and back to jail. That [the way medication is allotted to people released from prison] doesn't help either.

FC: It's hard to say who has the answers, you know, but obviously, the system didn't work 100 years ago, and it doesn't work today. All it [prison] is is a multi-billion dollar white-man's game, that's all it is. And we [Indigenous women] are the pawns in the game.

ISS: So, I'm wondering if you can speak a little bit more about—you've started to talk about it already—how, for instance, one of the outcomes of the closure of P4W was the creation and opening of the Okimaw Ohci Healing Lodge in Saskatchewan. You're probably well aware of this, how there's been a lot of attempts in many different institutions to "Indigenize" prisons. One of the ways that CSC was trying to Indigenize the prison system was through the Healing Lodge which, I've heard a lot of women were excited about, and other women were really scared about, so I'm wondering, can you speak more to…

BK: It [the Healing Lodge] can help a lot of people but they only started that like a few years ago right.[3] It wasn't like, they never had that for any of us before. When GVI, yes, when they opened up that place, I seen a few women go there and I've seen it really do a lot of good for people there. But I've also seen that people were scared to go there because, again, it's the unknown, you know what I mean? It's the unknown, like "what kind of place is this going to be?" because it is supposed to be like a kind of jail too right, 'cause they have to have some kind of security 'cause you're leaving from a federal prison to a Healing Lodge.

ISS: Well, just to be clear, the Healing Lodge is still a federal prison, it's just called a "Healing Lodge."

BK: Yeah, that's what I'm saying; this is why I'm telling you this, and that's why I said that's why a lot of women didn't want to go there; but I've seen where a lot of people liked it too and I've seen where it did help change a lot of women. I'm glad that they have that [Healing Lodge] there; but it kind of like, and they also have a house on the grounds of GVI where it's a, before you go to the Lodge, or Healing House they call it, and you can move there but you have to be Indigenous right.

ISS: So, there are obviously problems with, you know, saying "Oh we're Indigenizing the prison," and I wanted to hear more about what you think— do you think the prison system can ever be completely decolonized? Is that even possible?

FC AND BK: No.

ISS: A resounding no.

BK: Absolutely, no.

FC: What part of it, really?

ISS: I was curious about what you think. I mean, on one hand we have, and the Healing Lodge may be the only, at least partially good example of this, of you know, really trying to, at least at the outset, take [incarcerated] Indigenous women's concerns seriously; but on the other hand…

FC: It's to cover their asses and make it look good for the white man—"Hey, look what we got for them, holy fuck, imagine that, they even got their own Healing Lodge" right? Shove it up your ass, it's CSC either way you look at it, it's still the system, you know, like really. You know, these are the issues, this is what the public does not see, Isabel, they don't see the mental abuse that the women go through while incarcerated. They have no idea the fucking mental abuse that the women go through, you know. And really wow, is all I can say because you know what, they've done some things to the women that you know, traumatize them. They'll be traumatized for the rest of their life. Anybody that's in a prison is not going to be normal when they come out. I don't know what "normal" is but I can tell you one thing, you may go in there thinking you've got your shit together, you've got it together, you're not going to come out like that, I don't care who you are because that prison is going to have some effect on your mind, it has to. How could it not? To this day, I still have nightmares of the women screaming in there. No pill is going to take that away—who's going to give me help for that? A psychiatrist? What, give me [psychiatric] drugs? You know what I'm saying?

BK: Even with drugs you don't get rid of that, those nightmares, you don't ever get rid of them.

FC: You know what? I'm not going to take this from the army vets 'cause I know they go to war, but I'm going to tell you one thing, the [incarcerated] women, it's almost the same shit, just a different pile. That's where they're going, they're going to war and they're always watching their backs in there because you never know what's going to happen one way or the other, [...] you understand? 'Cause that's what survival is in there, you know. You'll learn survival ways you never knew you had before, believe me. You know what, they're called coping things, you learn little things that you learn to cope...

BK: Yeah.

FC: ... to get through the day.

BK: Yeah.

ISS: So, we've talked a little bit about, I mean, just the tip of the iceberg about why it isn't possible to decolonize the prison system. I'm wondering, do you have or what are some real or imagined examples of what would actually be considered to you as decolonial responses to harm? What would that look like?

FC: Okay, I'll give an example, okay. If I was running an institution, this is what I would do. I would make the women go to work, pay rent, put them on the street and let them work, then make them come back and pay rent; but let them go out and let them work so they can learn responsibility, ownership, and all of the other stuff that goes with that...

BK: And pride.

FC: ... Dignity, all the stuff that they don't give you in there [prison]. That's what a person needs when they leave there [prison]. 'Cause they don't have it when they leave there, you know what I'm saying?

BK: And I think too, they need more like to have programs that are privatized, not run by CSC...

FC: Yeah.

BK: ... But run by you know actually healing people, you know, people that like, social workers that know their...

FC: Psychologists.

BK: ... Yeah, but you know, stuff like that, but from the street, not from inside...

FC: Yeah.

BK: Because even inside when you see a psychologist because like it's even gotten worse in there since you've been in there, they tell you [that] you can't open that can of worms 'cause they've only got an hour with you. So, then you know, you go back to your cell and you want to slash your throat after that shit, you know what I mean? 'Cause you only got an hour so right away you're like dead in the water, and then you can't talk to them either because then they write reports and then they write things in reports that are not even true that you said that. You know, you might have said it the wrong way because you don't know how to speak anymore in there because you only speak to your friends and guards. You don't see the community to speak properly. So, when you get out, you've gotta go back to school.

ISS: Let's imagine for a second that Canada doesn't have any prisons…

FC: Yay!

ISS: … How would you see a decolonial response to harm if we didn't have prisons?

FC: Well, honestly, it's just like drug addicts. If you treat a drug addict like a person instead of a drug addict, when you give respect, you get respect back. And that, you know what, that's the bottom line. When you treat people right, they treat you right, you know? There's no need to put women in jail; yes, women got to pay for their crimes. Put them in for a year or two and then make them go out to fucking work and know what it's like to live in the community, amongst the community, to stay in the community. They don't give you no tools when you get out, and they don't give you a book either…

BK: None.

FC: … You know, all they do is give you a ticket [to get where you're going] and that's it.

BK: And they figure, like Fran said, they've covered their ass, you know what I mean? They've put you in there, that's all they have to do. They made you do groups […] and, you know, this is the groups you have to do and they don't even have nothing to do with reintegration out into the community. They're [prison programs] there just to cover their [CSC staff] ass so that when you get out and you get in trouble, they say "Well I tried to help her," you know what I mean?

ISS: Yeah.

BK: So, if you were out in the community and they get you to say like treatment, you have to go to treatment for six months you know, or different, open up different community hospitals or like more community programs…

FC: Yeah.

BK: … And stuff like that. That's what I think; women need more support than they do jail.

ISS: Of course.

FC: They need healing.

BK: Yes, and they need to understand what's wrong with them first because they're so insecure and so, you know from their lives and stuff like that, that they need healing, they don't need jail. […]

ISS: Yeah, I don't believe in prison either.

FC: You see? Well that's what I'm saying. […] Like, that little [Ashley] Smith[4] girl, she should have been fucking healed, not punished and shipped around here and there and fucking everywhere. Nobody wanted her. That's why she took her life.

ISS: Yeah.

FC: You know? Come on.

BK: There's a lot of girls that took their lives in there because of that.

FC: Yes. When I was in there, in a two-year period, there was seven hangings. I can't remember if all seven ended up in death, I believe five of them were deaths.[5] But you know what? That shouldn't go on behind bars; they're supposed to be there, that system is supposed to be there to protect us, not fucking destroy us.

ISS: I agree, that should have never happened.

FC: And honestly that's what I find it [prison] does. Women's needs are different than men, okay? I don't believe anybody should be in jail, but women's needs are way different than men, and you know what? Taking a woman from her kids right there is enough fucking mental punishment and then to lock her up in a fucking cage, come on. You know what? You put a dog in a cage and tease it, what's going to happen when you let that dog out of the cage? Well that's what happens when you let the inmates out. They [CSC staff] [...] made us that way.

ISS: I agree, for sure. So, I want to return to the idea of the P4W Memorial Collective. Based on my understanding, it has two primary goals. The first is to contribute to a greater understanding of the historical heritage of P4W beyond its architectural features, of course; and second, to create a green space where people can sit and remember the women who were incarcerated at P4W. Before we get into the garden though, I'm curious about some of your experiences within the Collective. Fran, from what I understand, you were one of the women who initially came up with the idea for a Collective; and at the Building Abolition Conference, you talked about having some uncertainties about creating the Collective yourself and so you reached out to some professors at Queen's University who you believed outside [non-incarcerated] people may be more likely to listen to.

FC: Correct.

ISS: So, I was wondering, Fran, if you could tell me a little bit more about what prompted the idea to create a P4W Memorial Collective?

FC: Okay, like I said, while I was incarcerated, there was seven hangings, right? When I got out, I was still living in Kingston and many times I used to go by on the bus to school and I would look at, think of the women that died in there. That's all I could think of. That's what came to my mind is them, the women that died in there, and I would look at the [P4W] building and think "fuck man, man where are they all?" But when I was incarcerated in P4W, I went to the administration and I asked where these women were buried because I knew a couple bodies were never claimed by the families and I was told Potters Hill, but nobody would answer me. When I asked CSC regional headquarters, nobody could answer the question for me [...] "Where are these women['s bodies]?" Anyway, over the years, long story short, a [CSC] staff member told me, she said "Fran, I'm going to tell you something". She said, "There's two women at Highway 15 that are buried there." So, I went out there to check and there is two fresh stones there definitely. The rest are all dated back to the 1800s so I know this staff member was not lying to me. And I asked her, I said "How is it that you know for sure they're there?" She says "Fran, 'cause I was on the van when the bodies were put into the ground." She was there when they were buried there. […] So I contacted the Pittsburgh Institution, that's across the street from it [the women's unidentified gravesite] on Highway 15. I contacted them there and, but they won't, they haven't responded back to me 'cause I'm inquiring about that guard. To be honest with you, over the holidays, we kind of let things settle down a bit, and we just regrouped as a group this week [January 2020], so we've got everything back on the table again. But where things are at, we're gonna ask for, to hold CSC responsible to have name plates for the two, three women. There's three women, there's two on Highway 15 and there's one woman at Saint Mary's. […] But yeah. So that's where that's standing right now. Now as far as the memorial [garden] goes, like I said, that was just a thought—out of respect for our Fallen Sisters— 'cause that's how I felt, I was in a war in there, honest to God, I can't explain it any other way, you know, I just can't. But anyway, you know, that's how I felt. I just can't leave some place and not have respect for the women that were in there; they were my family.

ISS: Yeah.

BK: Mmhmm.

FC: You know, they were my family.

BK: Yeah.

FC: You know, we don't get to choose our family, but they were our family. They grow on you; you have no choice but live with them, you understand? You can't move to another town. They grow on you, one way or another, they become your family, right or wrong.

ISS: Yeah.

FC: And when somebody hurts in there, everybody hurts. If a woman slashes in there, everybody feels that pain, do you know what I'm saying?

ISS: Yeah.

FC: That's why it's so dysfunctional in there, because you've got so many women incarcerated with so much grief and pain; that's why most of them are there…

BK: Yup.

FC: … Because they turn their grief and pain into anger…

BK: Mmhmm.

FC: … And that's why a lot of them are sitting behind bars today.

BK: Yeah.

ISS: Yeah.

FC: […] So all we're doing now is just regrouping and following up on three issues. We have the 2020 conference coming up, let me see, okay, so we're bringing back to the table the P4W stuff [the memorial garden], and Highway 15 [where the women's bodies are believed to be buried], are the three things that are on our table that we're going to start working on ASAP 'cause we want answers to all three, right?

ISS: Yeah, for sure.

FC: You know, and how Queen's [University] got involved, when I started this, I'm not educated in a university setting, I am street wise, but I'll tell you something, I knew Ann Hansen was [formally educated] so I figured if I can get her on board with me, committed with me, then I'm going to go for this [creating the Collective and memorial garden]. And so, it's been me and Ann Hansen all the way through the whole 30 years. We've had other people come and go in the group and all of the inmate-women are more than welcome to be updated on what we're doing 'cause we never keep nothing from the other inmates, we want them all to know what we're doing and why we're doing it.

ISS: Mmhmm.

FC: You know? Because they [the women who were formerly incarcerated at P4W] have a say in this. You know? This [the memorial garden] is going to help them heal too. What this is, is a healing garden, that's all it is to us, is a healing garden; a place where we can heal and remember our family [Fallen Sisters who died at P4W as well as other women who were incarcerated there], you know?

ISS: Yeah.

FC: If it was a guard that died, [t]he[y] would have got a funeral and everything, but you know what? They throw the bag of women out the fucking door like it's trash…

BK: Yeah. In a hole.

FC: Yeah.

ISS: Yeah, that's really messed up to say the least. I do want to talk about the memorial garden, but first, Bobbie, I just wanted to ask you, when did you join the P4W Memorial Collective and why did you join it? What made it appealing to you?

BK: Well after like, I've always thought the same way about the women [that they're family], like you know like when I left to P4W, but I just had my son then, I just had a baby, 'cause I was the first one in Canada to keep him in prison with me at the minimum [security prison]. So, I fought to keep my son with me, right? So, at that time, you know, I didn't get involved with everything, and I didn't run in to Frannie for years because I was being an at-home mother, and I was trying to work and trying to be done life goals, you know trying to do things, but me and Frannie had run into each other but I never got into any kind of the movement 'cause I was so busy trying to be a mother, right?

ISS: Mmhmm.

BK: So, I got into it a bit more last summer when I ran into Fran because of the [Building Abolition] Conference in Banff. It was about six months, I ran into Fran and she started talking to me about this [the P4W Memorial Collective] and I was really interested because I have the same feelings as her, they [the women who died at P4W] are my Fallen Sisters and it is part of healing to go to that Garden and be able to talk to those women…

FC: Yeah.

BK: Say you know "Listen, we're sorry this [memorial garden] took so long, but we're here, we love you, you know? We want you to know that we remember you"…

FC: "We will never forget you."

BK: … Yeah, you know? And so, I thought it was a great idea and that's why I jumped in, 'cause that's my feelings too, because you do get close to people in there and when they hurt, you hurt. Like I said, women, they're in there [prison] because of emotional stuff, not because they're mass murderers and stuff like that, you know?

ISS: Of course, yeah. So moving on to talk a little bit more specifically about the memorial garden—based on my understanding, the goals of the memorial garden are to honor both the lives that were lived and the lives that were lost within P4W…

FC: Correct.

ISS: … and the garden is believed to be capable of this through its ability to raise public consciousness about injustices that happened…

FC: Yeah.

ISS: … and that continue to be faced by prisoners in Canadian jails, and also that lead to women's imprisonment in the first place.

FC: Yeah.

ISS: Can you tell me a little bit about what the Collective has proposed for the memorial garden? What are you hoping that it looks like? What kind of features do you hope it has?

FC: We've done a whole folder on what it's going to look like. We've laid out the land, had a lady come in and work with us. Her name is Anne [Maxwell],[6] not Ann Hansen, […] she is a professional landscaper. Yeah, we've got it all measured out, everything. We've got what we even want in the garden, everything is right there. We're going to tweak it, 'cause you never get everything you want.

ISS: Of course.

FC: We've got trees there and everything. We got benches in there, it looks beautiful if you were to look at it. […]

ISS: So, I know there are supposed to be some trees and benches, but can you tell me, what is the importance of those features of the garden to you?

FC: Okay, you know what? We really, really thought about the garden for years, what we would want in it, and we want it to be an Indigenous garden, you understand? Now when I say that, this is what I'm saying. We would like to have a bench, an Indigenous bench put there. This guy […] he's already agreed to build this one and put it up for us, for $500, and it's beautiful. Anyway, we want to just make it as safe. You know what? This place is not just for the women; if this [P4W] building turns into a living unit right, it'll be for the people that live there too, but we Indigenize it so that it's recognized for what it really is—it's a[n Indigenous] healing garden. That's all it is. If somebody wants to go in there and read a book, that's great. If somebody wants to go in there and sit there and eat their lunch, that's great, you know?

ISS: Mmhmm. So, how do you see the garden contributing to remembering the women [who were incarcerated at P4W]?

FC: I think it's the most important thing to remember the women. It gives us a way to grieve the women. It's a healthy thing. It's a positive for everybody involved.

ISS: Yeah.

BK: They were your family, like I said. It's like, you know, you're grieving for your family.

FC: [...] The thing is, I've been at it so long, I feel like it [the Collective and its goals] is my life, I owe it to my life, you know? It's going to happen [the memorial garden], there's no two ways about it. This has got to happen, and it's the right thing to do, and you know what? Nobody's disagreed with that, so now it's just getting 'er done right.

ISS: So, from what I understand, I read an article in the National Post [Perkel, 2018] that was quoting the P4W Collective and they said that the garden will be a space that increases public awareness about the women and girls who continue to suffer and die in custody...

FC AND BK: Yeah.

ISS: ... but also, in the same article, the Collective emphasized the garden as a space to celebrate the strength, survival, and resistance of women behind bars...

BK: Yes.

FC: Yeah, yeah.

ISS: ... so remembering the suffering that occurred within P4W is very important to the Collective, as well as highlighting the strengths of women who were incarcerated there. Is that something you agree with?

FC AND BK: Yes.

FC: Yes, 110 percent, yes.

ISS: Okay, so I'm curious—this question is for both of you: What are some examples of strength, survival or resistance that you personally experienced or witnessed during your time at P4W?

BK: I witnessed a lot of strength in women. They have their inner strength, their want to survive for their children, their families, you know, for each other. You know, like, uh, we got a lot of strength from each other, you know, like, when one was down, one was there to bring you up, you know, like, so within each other, within ourselves, our survival was just, you know, surviving for somebody else because we had no self-worth so we weren't trying to survive for us, you know, but we tried to survive for each other, encourage each other, and for our families, the people who had families, you know? And for each other.

FC: You know, it's something in life that you go through, it's a journey...

BK: Mmhmm.

FC: ... and I get all that. Sometimes you have a bad journey, and sometimes you have a good journey. Not everything's bad in prison, okay. For me, what was bad was the mental, the mental stress, I would say, and not so much my own as it is watching what other people were being put through.

ISS: Right.

FC: You know, it really broke my heart. I'll give you an example, if a girl had a family in from out West, I'll give you an example, right, and uh, the institution [prison] allows her to see her family but uh, maybe a week before her family comes, she might have got busted for maybe something stupid like refusing a direct order [from CSC staff] and that could cover anything okay, even swearing. Now, here's the game they [CSC staff] play, they will charge her so she won't get that visit, and you know that's going to drive her fucking insane when she's waiting for her family to come and they've got her in segregation on a fucking charge like that?! And they wonder why she's slashing when she comes out?!

ISS: Yeah.

FC: That's the shit I'm talking about, like the mental abuse…

BK: But we give each other strength, that's how we get our strength, from each other…

FC: We pull each other up. That's why we're out here [in the community]…

BK: … The survival of our families.

FC: Yeah.

ISS: So, how do you think that, in spite of all this negativity, the suffering and very clear examples of colonial and patriarchal harms happening in the prison…

BK: Yeah.

ISS: … how were the women at P4W able to be strong? What does it mean to draw strength from one another? How do you do that?

FC: Well number one, they gotta find the strength from within too, okay?

ISS: Mmhmm.

FC: It [strength] comes from there; and you know what? When you get put through some of those hoops, you get stronger 'cause before you know it, you're not walking through them, you're running through them because you've learned a way to do it [navigate the prison system], you see?

ISS: Mmhmm.

FC: It's called survival, that's what I say, that's where I compare us to the army. We are always surviving in there from day to day, you know? And actually, that's what it is, it's like a survivor fucking game in there and they just play head games with you sometimes, but the head games they play with you are very, very uh disturbing, you know? Like number one, okay, here's where I'm sitting right now—the new Bill I believe is C-83[7]; I read a lot of that Bill, and here's the problem I'm having—they [CSC] talked about the last six months closing down segregation/isolation [Special Handling Units]. Well what did they do? They turn around, oh yeah, they shut down isolation and opened up fucking SIUs [Structured Intervention Units] instead…

BK AND ISS: Yeah.

FC: … what's the difference [between Special Handling Units and Structured Intervention Units]?! You know, like that's what they did to cover their asses and make it look good once again for the public. What the public don't realize is that the SIU they're [prisoners] in are the same as a fucking segregation unit.

ISS: Yeah.

BK: And they made you look like you need that though, they make it sound like you're dangerous and all…

FC: Yeah.

BK: … and that's why the public are so peeved by us, people in prison, because, you know, nine out of ten people, are not violent, if anything, like I said, we're there to support each other and help each other to get through this stuff, you know what I mean?

FC: All the mental anguish, and all the mental games and the head games, and the abuse and everything you go through in there.

ISS: Mmhmm. So, I'm just aware of the time, I know we're coming up to an hour now [the time frame we agreed to speak for this chapter], so I just want to ask one more question and it's related to what we were just talking about—this whole public awareness piece. I know, the P4W Memorial Garden is meant for healing, it's meant for the women that were incarcerated at P4W, but from my understanding it's also meant in some capacity as an educational space for the public. For instance, Linda Mussell wrote an article in the *Journal of Prisoners on Prisons* where she argues that prisons are sites that have the ability to advance particular narratives or stories that contribute to people's understandings of incarceration and punishment [Mussell 2019]. My question is, what kinds of narratives or stories are you hoping that the garden will be able to share with its visitors?

BK: Well like everything that, you know…

FC: It's not for them [the general public/visitors]…

BK: … I don't care about the public either, about knowing, but still at the same time, the public needs to be aware that there is a lot of anguish in prison and that these women, there's still women that suffer today, and that you know, this is what happens when you're in prison. And, also what I do, and what Frannie does, is we enlighten the community ourselves by talking to different schools, going to different places, and doing talks about these kinds of things.

ISS: Yeah. I think one of the things I know that you and I have talked about, Bobbie, outside of this conversation is the importance of sharing our truths…

BK: Yeah.

ISS: … and sharing our stories with people who may not have other opportunities to, you know, learn our truths. You know, learning from textbooks is not necessarily accurate…

BK: Textbooks are nothing compared to the real-life thing.

ISS: That's right.

BK: And the thing is, about this whole thing is that if we don't bring awareness, if you stay silent, more women are going to suffer through the next ten years of their lives...

ISS: That's right.

FC: You know what, Isabel? I don't give a shit what the public thinks, feels, or says about this memorial garden one way or the other because, you know what? We ain't doing it for the public or fucking visitors, we're doing it for the women that died in there...

BK: Yeah.

FC: ... and that's our [the Collective's] goal, and that's our main focus. And you know what? Whoever, whoever looks at this, is going to have their own opinion anyway, right? They're going to walk away with their own thoughts from it, and you know what? You can't change what people think, you know what I'm saying? But you know what, the way I look at it, it's [the garden] a positive thing and as long as it's kept positive, it'll always be positive. It might be painful, but it'll be positive.

ISS: Yeah.

FC: It's a good pain, you know? Like really. Like when we all get together on Prisoners' Justice Day on August 10th, you know what? That's a day when we all feel each other.

BK: Yeah.

FC: We don't even have to explain anything, nothing, there's nothing to explain, we all feel each other, we are all on that page together. And you know what? I can see what it's going to be like at 2020 in Toronto [for the P4W Memorial Collective Conference], it's going to be over the top because there, we're all going to be from all different parts of the globe, you know? And people really want to hear what we've got to say and that's something different for me in my life 'cause usually I'm just told to shut my mouth, right? I'm not an activist, I'll say that right now, I'm not an activist, but I'm an advocate, I will always advocate for women's rights, always, always, always, always have another woman's back...

BK: Yeah.

FC: ... you know? As far as I'm concerned, that's what life is about—you help the other women, that's what it's about, you know?

ISS: Yeah.

FC: And you know, like I've been in, I've done 18-years [in prison] in total. I did seven [years] in provincial while I wasn't in federal so it's not like I went anywhere, I didn't go to university, I just graduated jail, that's all.

ISS: Right.

FC: Like you know, I'm not sorry I was in there for 18 years, I did that 18 years, I turned that around for myself. I got an education out of there, I worked while I was in there, and I worked on my anger while I was in there. So, for me, I took advantage of the situation, and you know what? [...] I was never institutionalized, I just adapted well. [...] They [CSC staff] thought I was [institutionalized], I don't care what they think, they don't pay my rent.

ISS: Yeah.

FC: They said, "oh you'll be back in six months." I've been out 30 years now, you know, and it's been a struggle. Every day is a struggle out here, it's nothing to get out of jail, it's how to stay out of jail, [that] is the issue.

ISS: Yeah. And I think that's, like I really respect that the primary goal of the memorial garden is to heal and remember what happened...

BK: Mmhmm.

ISS: ... and the women who lived there...

FC: Yes.

ISS: ... but it also is a space where others [who haven't experienced incarceration] can learn that truth...

FC AND BK: Yes.

BK: Exactly.

ISS: ... and hopefully move towards being respectful, being more open to listening and hearing the realities of what went on in there...

BK: Exactly.

ISS: ... and the realities that are still happening today.

FC: And, you know what? If one person feels that, then we did our job.

ISS: Yeah.

FC: That's all it takes, is one person to feel that and learn that, then we did our job, you know?

ISS: Well, I think you are doing fantastic work. I am so thrilled to have met you both and to learn so much from you. It's been wonderful to stay in touch and I hope we continue to stay in touch.

BK: Oh yeah, for sure.

FC: It goes both ways, Isabel. We need you guys [academics] as much as you guys need us, and that's really the truth. You know, it was Queen's University that took it [the P4W Memorial Collective] to the level it's at now. You know, that's what they did for us, and they believe in us, and they do, they know we're not lying, you know? These women have seen it for themselves, you know? They got right hands on, you know? Lisa [Guenther] and Jackie [Davies] and all them, you know, they've heard all our stories for years. Well, Jackie has, Jackie's pretty well been in there with us, you know? But yeah, you know. But there's just so much pain there, that's what it is, there's so much pain.

ISS: Yeah. It's important for us to work together.

FC: Yeah. Anyway, that's it.

ISS: Well, I'm really happy I had the chance to talk with you both today. I know, Bobbie, you have to get going to sleep before your nightshift. Is there anything else either of you want to quickly add before we close today?

BK: I think we're good. No, if you've got anything else or if we think about anything else, we'll just be in touch.

FC: But I'll close with this—do you know why the Creator made the sky so high?

ISS: Why's that?

FC: So the little birdies wouldn't bump their heads.

FC, BK, AND ISS: [Laughter].

FC: So they don't run into planes.

FC, BK, AND ISS: [Laughter].

Closing remarks

Despite describing many pains of imprisonment, Fran and Bobbie, alongside others, fought to keep P4W open. On one hand, Fran and Bobbie witnessed and personally experienced the atrocities that occurred at P4W and do not believe in prisons as solutions to crime, but on the other hand, they were afraid of the unknown that came with the opening of new federal women's prisons. They pointed to the total lack of control they had over their lives when they were incarcerated and, in their eyes, moving to a new prison signified even less control for them. Moreover, they did not want to be separated from their fellow-prisoners who, over time, had become their family; the closing of P4W promised to create separation between the families that had formed as a result of being imprisoned together. Women such as Fran and Bobbie who tried to keep P4W open understood any move by CSC to "help" as a strategy to "cover their asses" and expand carceral power. For instance, CSC responded to Indigenous prisoners' complaints by opening the Okimaw Ohci Healing Lodge (Adema, 2016). CSC claimed that the Lodge would be different from other federal women's prisons because of its basis in Indigenous principles and philosophies (Hayman, 2006). However, as Fran and Bobbie would have predicted, the Lodge was quickly coopted by the (neo)colonial punitive logics that underpin CSC (Adema, 2016; Snider, 2003; Struthers Montford, 2015).

Importantly, not all federally incarcerated Indigenous women were on the same page regarding the closure of P4W. There were Indigenous women who played key roles in the closure of P4W as well as the accompanying construction of the Healing Lodge (Adema, 2016). Considering this, I agree with Adema's (2016) argument that CSC's simultaneous processes of closing and opening prisons can be characterized as part of Canada's story of colonization, decolonization, and neocolonialism.[8] That is, Canada's prison system is closely tied to historical and contemporary colonialism, incarcerated Indigenous women worked to decolonize the prison from within it, and the opening of the Healing Lodge (while created with decolonial intentions of both Indigenous and non-Indigenous peoples) represents a move towards neocolonialism as it is impossible to decolonize prisons within a colonized country (Adema, 2016).

Bearing this in mind, it is unrealistic to believe that CSC can undergo changes that are significant and meaningful to federally sentenced Indigenous women because "Indigenizing" and/or decolonizing Canada's prison system is impossible. That said, it is important that we do not discount the tremendous efforts of both previously and currently incarcerated Indigenous women who were and are working towards positive changes for their fellow prisoners. The P4W Collective's proposed memorial garden is an excellent example of this work. While the garden does not intend to change the prison system per se, it provides an Indigenous place to heal from colonial, carceral, and patriarchal harms. Importantly, by incorporating medicinal plants into the garden, the space promotes healing that is specific to Indigenous peoples. Moreover, the garden provides a physical space in a public place. In this way, the garden and what it stands for are publicly acknowledged. Given that Indigenous women experience both current and historical silencing in the Canadian and global contexts (Comack, 2018), an acknowledgment of P4W's history is necessary and well past due. Mussell (2019) supports these ideas by stating that:

> memorializing a prison which has closed means acknowledging institutional histories, as well as the on-going imprisonment of people and associated harms. This includes documenting the experiences of prisoners currently incarcerated, people who are in the process of transitioning back to the community, and people whose life conditions mean that they may become incarcerated for the first time or multiple times over their lives.
>
> (Mussell, 2019, p. 68)

Having said that, the garden is not exclusively for Indigenous women who were previously incarcerated at P4W; everyone is welcome.

To help me envision more fully the proposed memorial garden, Fran and Bobbie put me in touch with one of their friends, another formerly incarcerated woman and member of the P4W Collective, Ann Hansen. Ann kindly provided detailed information regarding the garden and connected me with Anne Maxwell, the award-winning local landscape designer in Kingston, Ontario, who provided the P4W Memorial Collective with computer-generated designs for the garden. From the information provided by Ann and Anne, including written documents and visual renderings that Anne created, we can imagine what the memorial garden will look like. Of course, the garden is currently in the proposal stage, thus anything is subject to change.

The proposed site for the memorial garden is located at the front of P4W. It is envisioned to be large enough (34 foot x 50 foot = a total of 1,702 square feet) to permit visitors not only to sit but walk through. The patio portion of the garden will be made up of limestone slabs that balance with the stonework of P4W. There is space in the center of the patio to add something of the Collective's choice, such as a statue. The seating area will be comprised of a limestone bench, a bronze metal bench, and a single seat. The vegetation will consist of plants that are used for medicinal purposes by Indigenous peoples of the Boreal area in Canada. These may include an eastern white cedar to

Figure 8.1 Anne Maxwell's photograph showing the front entrance of P4W

Figure 8.2 Anne Maxwell's rendering of the front entrance of P4W with the proposed
P4W memorial garden

the right of the garden, a black spruce (already on the property), wild sage, ninebark, bluebell, black-eyed Susan, and many more. All the proposed plants are easy to maintain. There will be a granite plaque of remembrance (2 foot × 2.5 foot) mounted on a pedestal close to the sidewalk of the main entrance to P4W; and there will be a conifer between the plaque and stairs.

As it currently stands, there is nothing on the grounds of P4W that honors those who were formerly incarcerated there. Also absent from the grounds is any formal mention of the women who died inside the walls of P4W. As a result, the women whose lives were lived and lost within P4W are rendered invisible to unaware visitors and community members. A visual signifier of those women's lives, such as the garden, accomplishes several things. First, it helps create public awareness, reflection, and formal acknowledgment of Canada's prison conditions and their relation to Indigenous women, both currently and historically. Second, it provides a formal space where people can go to remember and honor their loved ones—women formerly incarcerated at P4W as well as others who were formerly or are currently incarcerated. Lastly, the garden creates a decolonized space that promotes Indigenous medicines and healing from colonial, carceral, and patriarchal harms. In these ways, the proposed memorial garden represents a critical move by the P4W Memorial Collective towards decolonizing a carceral place.

Notes

1 Interestingly, one of the federally incarcerated Indigenous women on the Task Force, Fran Sugar (Hayman, 2006), was the President of the Native Sisterhood in P4W (Adema, 2015).
2 The Native Sisterhood was founded in 1971. It was a group of similarly motivated women who "responded to intertwined histories of racial and gendered violence" (Adema, 2016, p. 223).
3 The Healing Lodge opened in 1995 (Hayman, 2006).
4 Ashley Smith was a young Indigenous woman who died in CSC custody (McGill, 2008). Ashley was 15 years old when she was "sentenced to one month in juvenile custody for throwing crab apples at a postal worker" (Kilty, 2018, p. 125). During her time in custody, she repeatedly engaged in self-injurious behaviors and resisted correctional officers' attempts to subdue her (Kilty, 2018). As a result, Ashley received numerous institutional infractions and spent nearly three years in custody (Kilty, 2018). When Ashley turned 18, she was transferred to the adult federal corrections system and spent the duration of her time (11.5 months) in segregation (Kilty, 2018). Ashley Smith died due to asphyxiation "from a hand-fashioned ligature she had tied around her neck while correctional staff filmed her from just a few feet away in the hall outside her cell, having been instructed not to enter her cell" until she had passed out (Kilty, 2018, p. 125).
5 All seven hangings resulted in death and six of the seven women who died were Indigenous (Hansen, 2018).
6 Anne Maxwell's renditions as well as more details of the Memorial Garden are displayed and discussed in the closing remarks.

7 Bill C-83, *An Act to amend the Corrections and Conditional Release Act and another Act*, received Royal Assent—meaning it passed into law—on June 21st, 2019 (LEGISinfo, 2020). The Bill eliminated the use of administrative segregation and replaced it with "structured intervention units" (Casavant & Charron-Tousignant, 2019).

8 Neocolonialism is a form of colonialism that is unique to the 20th century (Adema, 2016). According to Adema (2016), neocolonialism is an adaptation of colonialism that masquerades as tolerance and is invisible to non-Indigenous peoples who engage in such practices.

References

Adema, S. (2015). Not told by victims: Genocide-as-story in Aboriginal prison writings in Canada, 1980–96. *Journal of Genocide Research. 17*(4), 453–71.

Adema, S. (2016). *More than stone and iron: Indigenous history and incarceration in Canada, 1834–1996.* Doctoral Dissertation. Wilfrid Laurier University.

Casavant, L., and Charron-Tousignant, M. (2019). *Legislative summary of Bill C-83.* Library of Parliament.

Chesney-Lind, M. (2006). Patriarchy, crime, and justice: Feminist criminology in an era of backlash. *Feminist Criminology. 1*(1), 6–26.

Comack, E. (2018). *Coming back to jail: Women, trauma, and criminalization.* Fernwood Publishing.

Dell, C., Fillmore, C., & Kilty, J.M. (2009). Looking back 10 years after the Arbour Inquiry: Ideology, policy, practice, and the federal female prisoner. *The Prison Journal. 89*(3), 286–308.

Hansen, A. (2018). *Taking the rap: Women doing time for society's crimes.* Between the Lines.

Hayman, S. (2006). *Imprisoning our sisters: The new federal women's prisons in Canada.* McGill-Queens University Press.

Kilty, J.M. (2018). Carceral optics and the crucible of segregation: Revisiting scenes of state- sanctioned violence against incarcerated women. In Kilty, J.M., and Dej, E. (Eds.). *Containing madness: Gender and 'psy' in institutional contexts* (pp. 119–44). Palgrave Macmillan.

LEGISinfo. (2020, May 20). *House Government Bill.* www.parl.ca/LegisInfo/BillDetails. aspx?billId=10078426&Language=E

McAleese, S., and Kilty, J. (2019). Stories matter: Reaffirming the value of qualitative research. *The Qualitative Report. 24*(4), 822–45.

McGill, J. (2008). An institutional suicide machine: Discrimination against federally sentenced Aboriginal women in Canada. *Race/Ethnicity: Multidisciplinary global contexts. 2*(1), 89–119.

McKegney, S. (2008). Strategies for ethical engagement: An open letter concerning non-Native scholars of Native literatures. *Studies in American Indian Literatures. 20*(4), 56–67.

Mussell, L. (2019). After the prison closes: Seeking healing, memory, and awareness at P4W. *Journal of Prisoners on Prisons. 28*(1), 66–73.

Perkel, C. (2018, August 9). Women urge memorial garden at notorious former prison in Kingston. *National Post.* https://nationalpost.com/pmn/news-pmn/canada-news-pmn/women-urge-memorial-garden-at-notorious-former-prison-in-kingston

Snider, L. (2003). Constituting the punishable woman: Atavistic man incarcerates post-modern woman. *British Journal of Criminology, 43*(2), 354–78.

Struthers Montford, K. (2015). Transforming choices: The marginalization of gender-specific policy making in Canadian approaches to women's federal imprisonment. *Canadian Journal of Women and the Law/Revue Femmes et Droit. 27*(2), 284–310.

Part III

Anti-carceral feminisms

9 Starting with life

Murder sentencing and feminist prison abolitionist praxis

Debra Parkes

> We have to do the hardest work first, not when we are done with the rest of the work. We have to do the hardest work first. To me it is a chance to take leadership from edginess, from energetic people who live in ways that are generative of enthusiasm for struggle.
>
> —Beth Richie, 2015, p.268

There is much talk these days of criminal legal system[1] reform and sentencing reform. Policy makers, advocates, and community members from a range of groups and social locations see the harms of punitive sentencing systems. There is growing awareness about the human and fiscal costs of mandatory sentences, about the harms of solitary confinement in prison, and about the truly alarming levels of mass incarceration of Black and Indigenous people in the U.S., Canada, and beyond. When it comes to sentencing reform, advocates often focus their critiques on imprisonment for "non-violent offences."[2] In this vein, advocacy efforts to end mandatory sentences in Canada and elsewhere tend to carve out "serious violent offences," particularly murder, as not the focus of a reform agenda.

However, as Ruth Wilson Gilmore (2015) has forcefully argued, identifying and focusing our decarceration efforts on the "relatively innocent" is a trap. It legitimates carceral logics and punitive policies by implicitly conceding that there is a durable core of punishable subjects, usually those convicted of "violent offences." This chapter sketches out the contours of an argument for why feminists might not want to cede that ground, why anti-carceral feminism might involve centering our analysis on the most, rather than the least, serious crimes[3]—starting with those who are serving life sentences. In Canada, that means starting with everyone convicted of murder.

The chapter opens with a brief review of key concepts such as anti-carceral feminism, (new) prison abolitionism, and the challenge the "dangerous few" pose to abolitionist work. Next it briefly describes Canada's punitive murder sentencing laws and the growing population of lifers that has been created by them. The balance of the chapter traces the contours of a feminist abolitionism that meaningfully includes—even centers—the law's most extreme punishments and the people subjected to them in its theorizing and organizing. In arguing for an anti-carceral feminist praxis that advocates for the abolition of life sentences, the chapter identifies four non-exhaustive reasons for that focus. The first reason relates to the problem of using state violence through incarceration to address interpersonal violence. The second is about who bears the brunt of these sentences. The third is about what we learn, and what informs anti-carceral feminist praxis, when we center the people who are living these sentences. A final reason relates to what we might be able to achieve, in concrete terms, by seeking to abolish these sentences. The chapter concludes with some thoughts on the future of this kind of organizing and scholarship in the current moment.

Anti-carceral feminism and the new prison abolitionism

While some of the foundational prison abolitionist scholarship of the 20th century was written by white, European men (e.g., Mathiesen, 1974), Black women have been central to the development of abolitionist organizing and scholarship (Davis, 2003; Critical Resistance-INCITE!, 2003; Wilson Gilmore, 2007).[4] The so-called "new abolitionism" of the past three decades is often identified with the Critical Resistance conference held at Berkeley in 1998, together with earlier organizing largely by women of color, that was rooted in a long-term political vision to end the prison industrial complex (Roberts, 2019). Dorothy Roberts (2019) outlines three main tenets of this new abolitionism: that the current (U.S.) carceral punishment system is rooted in slavery and the racial capitalist regime that undergirded it; that the criminal legal system functions to oppress Black people and other marginalized groups to maintain racial capitalism; and that it is possible to imagine and build a more humane and democratic society that does not rely on caging people to meet human needs and solve social problems.

Bree Carlton (2016) has described anti-carceral feminism as a unique voice within the prison abolitionist movement, one "grounded in intersectional feminist critiques, strategies, and actions driven to struggle against and undermine structures of oppression that give rise to violence and injustice" (p. 285). She has documented how anti-carceral feminist campaigners in Victoria, Australia, engaged strategically with efforts to reform women's imprisonment in pursuit of decarceration and structural change.

On the crucial question of addressing gender violence, particularly sexual violence, Judith Levine and Erica Meiners (2020) draw on, and amplify, the work of abolition feminists, "women—Black, brown, queer, trans, poor, disabled—whom the state has never protected." Levine and Meiners note that "[t]hese abolition feminists have learned from experience that prisons do not end violence, but instead perpetrate and perpetuate it, while destroying lives, families, and communities" (p. 13). Abolition feminism, including the work of INCITE! Women, Gender Non-Conforming, and Trans People Against Violence, grew out of a desire to create a movement that took seriously the imperative to address gender violence while also, crucially, rejecting the use of state violence through incarceration as an effective means to address that interpersonal violence (Levine & Meiners, 2020, pp. 34–35).

In a similar vein, Chloë Taylor (2018) has argued that it is imperative for feminist prison abolitionists to include sexual assault in our analysis. She points to the increasingly punitive sentences for sexual offences as a driver of mass incarceration; the way sexual violence is ubiquitous in prison life, perpetrated by both staff and incarcerated people; and the particular ways that the despised figure of the sex offender has been mobilized to justify long sentences and prison expansion (Taylor, 2018, pp. 29–30). Taylor notes that sex offenders are, in many respects, more despised than murderers. Yet murder is the most serious offence in Canadian law (and, indeed, in most legal systems) and the most severe punishments tend to be reserved for it.

Prison abolitionists have long debated the place of "the dangerous few" in abolitionist theorizing and movements. As Carrier and Piché (2015) note, "abolitionists have not satisfactorily confronted some critiques that have been forwarded to prison and penal abolitionism, including the irresolution… of the problem of the 'dangerous few'" (p. 3). These "dangerous few" are a "set of constantly updated names and faces associated with acts so revoltingly egregious that they seem to defy the very possibility of language" (Carrier & Piché, 2015, p. 3). In media stories and parliamentary debates about life sentences in Canada, names such as Clifford Olsen, Paul Bernardo, Robert Pickton — men convicted of multiple murders of women and children—regularly feature. The category of people convicted of murder is a large one and many, indeed most, of the people who are sentenced to life for murder are not in the league of Paul Bernardo or Robert Pickton. However, it is crucial that abolitionist movements reckon with the "dangerous few." In fact, challenging the construction of dangerousness is critical and central to abolitionism (e.g., Neve & Pate, 2005; Knopp et al., 1976). For Mariame, Kaba the answer to the question of what to do with the dangerous few is a collective project: "let's figure out together, across our communities, what would be a just system for adjudicating and evaluating harm. […] It's a question that invites people in, that invites people to offer their ideas" (Kaba & Duda, 2017).

Furthermore, there is merit in turning the logic of starting-with-the-easy-cases on its head. A notable exception to the tendency to leave the "dangerous few" or the "most severe" cases to the end, is the approach taken by Liat Ben-Moshe et al. (2015) in drawing on crip theory, queer theory, and the radical deinstitutionalization movement to argue for an inclusive, antinormative abolitionism. They argue:

> [An] antinormative stance, enabled by a queer and disability studies/disability justice position, can be, and should be, the starting point of any abolitionary discussion and action […] A question raised often in the context of abolition of carceral spaces […] is what to do with those deemed as having the most challenging behaviors. In prison abolitionist circuits,

this discussion is known as "what to do with the dangerous few" […] Translated to praxis, some prison abolitionists and activists in the fields of developmental disabilities and antipsychiatry indeed begin their critique and suggestions for alternative social arrangements from the positionality of "severe" cases […] If left to the end, such people would most likely be placed in segregated settings.

(Ben-Moshe et al., 2015, 272–3)

Ben-Moshe et al. provide the American examples of Jerome Miller and Fay Honey Knopp, whom they say "illustrate the ways we should center nonnormativity in general in our discussions […] and begin our conversations from the position of those who are perceived as the most "severe" and defiant in imagining more just futures" (Ben-Moshe et al., 2015, p. 273).

Indeed, Miller was a prison administrator who closed Massachusetts' major youth jails and instead placed young people who were criminalized into community programs or homes, beginning with the youth considered most violent and dangerous (Miller, 1991). In a similar vein, Knopp wrote the prison abolitionist manual, *Instead of Prisons*, in the 1970s and then spent her life working with the "toughest" cases of those convicted of sexual and other violent offences. One of her seven modes of decarceration was abolishing indeterminate sentences and parole. Knopp sought to "demonstrate the ineffectiveness of prisons for this segment of the imprisoned population [such that] there will be no doubt that prisons are also an ineffective response to less criminalizable acts like theft or drug use" (Ben-Moshe, 2013, p. 91).

Starting with who?

Starting with life in Canada means that we start with people convicted of murder. As of 2018 there were 5,619 people serving life or indeterminate sentences (Public Works and Government Services Canada, 2019).[5] During the past decade, there has been a 25% increase in the number of people admitted to prison on a life or indeterminate sentence, such that people under these sentences represent 24% of all individuals under federal correctional supervision in Canada. The vast majority of these people—4,957 individuals—are serving a mandatory life sentence for murder (Public Works and Government Services Canada, 2019, p. 60).

Everyone convicted of murder in Canada gets sentenced to life plus a mandatory period of time, set by a judge, that must pass before the person can apply for parole. That period must be at least ten years but it can be set anywhere from ten to 25, unless the law treats the killing as an aggravated form of "first degree" murder. The killing of a police officer or a prison guard, a murder that is found to have been planned, or one that took place in the course of certain other crimes such as sexual assault, forcible confinement or criminal harassment, is elevated to first degree murder. In those cases, the parole ineligibility period must be set at 25 years.

While Canadian law does not formally provide for life without parole sentences, a law passed in 2011 makes it possible for judges to "stack" parole ineligibility periods if a person is convicted of more than one murder. The judge can make the ineligibility periods run consecutive to one another. Under this law, a number of people have been sentenced to 75-year parole ineligibility periods in the form of three 25-year parole ineligibility periods ordered to run consecutively (e.g., R v. Bourque 2014, R v. Ostamas 2016). This is de facto life without parole. Furthermore, there have been attempts to formally make life without parole sentences a part of Canadian law. In 2015, there was a bill before Parliament called the *Life Means Life Act* (Bill C-53, 2015) that would have made life without parole sentences available for certain murders. That bill died on the order paper when an election was called.

To be clear, the mandatory parole ineligibility periods simply provide a date at which the person becomes eligible to start applying for parole—for example after ten, 20, 25, or 50 years. This does not mean that the person will actually get parole at that time. Only 20% of lifers get parole on their first try (John Howard Society of Canada 2018). It is often only "model prisoners" –usually white, middle-class people—who ever get out at or near their eligibility dates. Indigenous people, for example, spend more time in prison before being released on parole than their non-Indigenous counterparts (The Correctional Investigator of Canada, 2019, p. 65). Some lifers are never released. Crucially, even when someone on a life sentence does get parole, they are under the thumb of corrections for their entire life, such that they can have their parole revoked and be returned to prison at any time until they die—even decades after they are first released on parole. Parole officers have broad discretion to suspend or revoke parole for reasons such as communicating with the wrong person, being high, being homeless, or being depressed—anything that might be considered to "indicate a potential increase in risk" (Correctional Service of Canada, 2019, s. 13).

This happened to a friend of mine, a woman who served 18 years of a life sentence in prison and was on parole in the community for eight years before her parole was revoked for being depressed. She was put in prison over the Christmas holidays and her lawyer was working on getting her released through a habeas corpus legal action. A few weeks later, my friend was moved to a halfway house where she died by suicide. Her husband, also a lifer, did more than 20 years inside before being successfully on parole for a decade. Shortly after the death of his wife, he was charged with a new offence (a charge that was later dropped for lack of evidence) and his parole was revoked. That was eight years ago. He remains in prison.

Why center lifers? Why start with abolishing life sentences?

a. On using state violence to respond to interpersonal violence

Harsh sentences for murder and other forms of interpersonal violence are often defended and justified as protecting everyone, but particularly women and children from violence. Feminist calls to take gender-based violence seriously have been heard as calls for more and longer punishment. The support of some feminists for criminal legal responses to intimate partner violence and sexual violence have lent legitimacy to particularly harsh sentencing regimes and have fueled the harmful policing and mass incarceration that come with these punitive polices (Bumiller, 2008, Kim, 2019a, 2019b). Levine and Meiners (2020) expose the relationship(s) between interpersonal violence and state violence through policing and incarceration, when viewed through an abolitionist feminist lens:

> Interpersonal violence and the violence inflicted by the state are not opposing actors in a moral or political war. Rather, the abuser or rapist and the criminal legal system are a team, the former the bad cop, the latter the good. They speak in unison: *Might makes right.* …[G]etting rid of punishment would be a great blow to the power of the patriarchy, as well as that of white supremacy.
>
> (Levine & Meiners, 2020, p. 5)

We know that the pursuit of punishment has not led to the end of sexual and gender violence (Levine & Meiners, 2020, p. 2). As Jeff Shantz and Eva Ureta (2020) have argued recently in the Canadian context, "[p]roperly assessing calls to defund the police and other carceral institutions means a proper reckoning with what these systems are actually doing—not what we imagine them to be doing." While not to blame for the punitive regime of sexual offences and mass incarceration, some feminists "have played a large role in sketching the blueprint and supplying the parts that make the machine function" (Levine & Meiners, 2020, p. 4). Elsewhere, Lawston and Meiners (2014) provide a thorough, intersectional feminist account of some of the harmful implications of appeals to the carceral state to punish gender violence, drawing attention to the particular ways that women of color are caught in the carceral net. They critique the "pathways to crime" framework and subsequent gender-responsive programming, highlighting their role in expanding the carceral state, their failure to address the structural roots of harm and victimization, and their essentialism.

Prisons are institutions of state violence. As Vicki Chartrand (2015) has explained in the context of women's imprisonment, "violence occurs under a complex rubric of security and institutional order" (p. 6). It is routinized and manifest in such practices as strip searches, special handling units, involuntary transfers, solitary confinement, dry cells, lack of medical attention, self-harm, suicide, assaults, and forced injections. Through interviews with incarcerated women, Vetten and Bhana (2005) have identified similarities between women's experiences of incarceration and abusive relationships. Both include authoritarianism, enforced restriction of movement, violence, and enforcement of trivial and arbitrary demands (p. 265). By punishing interpersonal violence with state violence through incarceration we locate the responsibility for that violence solely in individuals and we leave untouched the structures and cultures that facilitate and perpetuate it, such as heteropatriarchy, colonial dispossession, white supremacy, capitalism, and the like.

b. On who bears the brunt of these sentence

In Canada, Indigenous women make up nearly half of all women sentenced to life in recent years (Public Works and Government Services Canada, 2019), despite this group only comprising approximately 4% of the population of women in Canada. The rate of incarceration of Indigenous women is growing at a rate significantly faster than it is for Indigenous men. Gilmore (2015) argues that a focus on the relatively innocent—those convicted of non-violent offences— "helps to obscure the fact that categories such as 'serious' or 'violent' felonies are not natural or self-evident, and more important, that their use is part of a racial apparatus for determining 'dangerousness'." Campaigns that are focused on decarcerating people serving time for non-violent offences are going to leave out Indigenous women.

Critiques of the mass incarceration of Indigenous people in Canada have largely focused on the "crisis" of Indigenous mass incarceration (Arbel, 2019), as the number and proportion of Indigenous people in prisons and jail rise each year. For example, the rate of federal incarceration (sentences of two years or more) decreased overall by 15% from 2009 to 2018. However, for Indigenous people it increased by 46%, including a 61% increase for Indigenous women (Public Works and Government Services Canada, 2019). As such, it is disturbing that there has been relatively little interrogation of the colonial violence that is at the heart of the history of policing and prison expansion in these lands now called Canada (Nichols, 2014; Arbel, 2019; Chartrand, 2019). Robert Nichols notes that "[w]hen the critique of incarceration rests upon the over-representation of racialized bodies within penal institutions, this tacitly renders carcerality a *dehistoricized* tool of state power—even if distorted by the pathological effects of a racist society—displacing an account of the continuity and links between carcerality, state formation, and territorialized sovereignty" (Nichols, 2014, p. 444). Taking this history, and Indigenous sovereignty, seriously "calls for an alternative normativity that challenges the very existence of the carceral system, let alone its internal organization and operation" (p. 445).

There has been some long-overdue attention in Canada in recent years to the horrifying reality of missing and murdered Indigenous women. In 2019, the National Inquiry into Missing and Murdered Indigenous Women and Girls (MMIWG) released its final report, identifying Canadian state responsibility for MMIWG as a genocide, and issuing 231 Calls to Justice, very few of which have been implemented (National Inquiry into MMIWG, 2019). Those of us who go into prisons to meet with incarcerated people know that the Indigenous women, girls, trans, and two-spirit people whose disappearances and deaths have been largely ignored by law enforcement in Canada are the same people who fill women's prisons in Canada. Indigenous people are, at once, overpoliced and underprotected by law (Dhillon, 2015; Nichols, 2014). The maximum security units of Canadian women's prisons are filled with Indigenous women (The Correctional Investigator Canada, 2019; Parkes, 2016).

The authors of *The Long Term: Resisting Life Sentences, Working Towards Freedom* (Kim et al., 2018) understand the teaching they do in a men's maximum security prison as feminist, abolitionist labor, connected to the labor of families and communities organizing on the outside. This work has made it evident to them that "[a]n abolitionist feminist praxis is needed now more than ever to challenge the indefinite long-term caging of our communities." The brunt of punitive sentencing policies aimed at addressing violence, and murder in particular, is felt most harshly by those who are Indigenous and racialized. It is whole families and communities who are doing these life sentences; and it is whole communities and networks that are seeking liberation through organizing and activism.

c. On what our movement gains by centering lifers

By listening to and centering lifers—and particularly women lifers—in feminist abolitionist praxis we can see how the lives of these women and trans, non-binary, or two-spirit people are so profoundly shaped and harmed by structural and state violence and what Ruth Wilson Gilmore (2011) has aptly described as "organized abandonment." By centering people living under life sentences we do not allow the official stories that are told about them to stand unchallenged. We tell different stories, ones that locate the particular event that led them to be criminalized in a context of state and structural violence, including experiences of trauma, poverty, racism, abuse at the hands of authority, and abandonment to deal with all of this individually. Rejecting carceral responses to violence, particularly murder, is unfathomable to many people. Yet when we actually engage with lifers' lived realities, in their complexity, we tend to think quite differently. We need to start with these stories and not leave them for another day.

For lawyers, who are regularly complicit in what Alec Karakatsanis (2019) has aptly called the "usual cruelty" of the criminal legal system, the abolitionist practice of developing participatory defense campaigns provides a promising model. Groups such as Survived and Punished (S&P) center people charged with serious offences, often women, and build a movement around the task of defending them. S&P is a national coalition that includes survivors, organizers, victim advocates, lawyers, policy experts, scholars, and currently and formerly incarcerated people. S&P organizes to decriminalize efforts to survive violence, to support and free criminalized survivors, and to abolish gender violence, policing, prisons, and deportations. Through campaigns and legal advocacy such as Free Breasha (Breasha Meadows killed her abusive father when she was 14 years old) and Free Marissa (Marissa Alexander was prosecuted and threatened with 60 years in prison for firing a gun to defend herself from an abusive partner), S&P brings attention to, and rallies coalitions of people and broader public support around, individual women's cases, while understanding and locating them within broader prison abolitionist critiques.

Survived and Punished is, crucially, rooted in a rejection of the politics of exceptionalism. As the S&P website says, "[t]he 'politics of exceptionalism' occurs when people advocate for the freedom of an individual only because they are considered exceptional to other imprisoned people—for example, the perfect survivor, the perfect immigrant, etc." S&P rejects that politics, going on to say that "[w]hen we support individual defense campaigns, or when we call for the freedom of 'survivors' in particular, we promote a 'politics of relationality,' or strategies that help people engage the broader crisis of criminalization." The work of Survived and Punished is connected to, and integrated with, other prison abolitionist organizing. It does not see the women and trans folk whose cases S&P champions as exceptional. Their experiences are the result of the system working in the ways that Ruth Wilson Gilmore has laid out so powerfully, through organized abandonment.

d. On what we might achieve by centering lifers

Another way that those of us with legal training can contribute to abolitionist movements is through supporting strategic law reform efforts. Over the past three years I have been supporting the work of an Independent Senator in the Parliament of Canada who has put forward a bill to abolish all mandatory sentences (Bill S-208, 2020; Pate, 2020).[6] The legislative change would allow judges to order a shorter sentence—or no prison sentence at all—instead of the minimum sentence currently mandated. The Bill's sponsor, Senator Kim Pate, who identifies publicly as a prison abolitionist, has insisted that the reforms would apply to all mandatory sentences, including the life sentence for murder, even though the inclusion of murder sentences no doubt makes the bill politically less palatable. I was called as a witness before the Senate committees considering the Bill and I wrote an opinion editorial on abolishing the mandatory life minimum sentence for murder when Senator Pate's bill was being considered in the Senate (Parkes, 2018) in an effort to raise public awareness about the harms caused by these sentences. At the time of writing, Bill S-208 is stalled in Parliament and is unlikely to be passed into law.

From an abolitionist perspective, this legislative proposal involves possibilities but also serious limitations. The amendment would effectively turn mandatory sentences into presumptive sentences, meaning that a judge would not have to sentence everyone convicted of murder to life. And even if they did hand out a life sentence, the judge could order that the person subject to the sentence be eligible for parole at a number of years lower than 10, the current minimum. This is admittedly a relatively small change. And without a significant cultural shift it would not likely benefit many people because life sentences have become normalized in the Canadian criminal legal system. When capital punishment was abolished in Canadian law in 1976, the compromise was to bring in a harsh regime of life sentences and long parole ineligibility periods. Lawyers and judges—even criminal defense lawyers who otherwise advocate for no prison or as little time in prison as possible—tend to accept as unproblematic the idea that a person should be caged or at least under some form of correctional supervision for their entire life.

The proposed legislative amendment, even if passed, remains a long way from actually abolishing life sentences, a goal that seems impossible to achieve in the short term. But that posture of impossibility is exactly what abolitionist thinking and organizing challenges. As Perry Zurn notes in the Foreword to this volume, abolition is a "kite-idea," up against entrenched "aircraft-carrier-ideas." Kites can be built at home. They are child-like, imaginative. They take flight only with a willing wind and are tagged as feminine, queer. By contrast, aircraft-carrier-ideas—punishment, incarceration, white supremacy, capitalism—are floating freight trains of destruction. Ben-Moshe (2018) argues that abolition is a radical epistemology—or what she calls *dis-epistemology*. It is about both knowing and unknowing, "letting go of attachment to certain ways of knowing […] [and] letting go of the idea that anyone can have a definitive pathway for how to rid ourselves of carceral logics" (p. 347). The abolition of life sentences, and the decarceration of people subject to them, are part of the abolitionist alternative that Thomas Mathieson (1974, p. 1) describes as being rooted in "the unfinished, in the sketch, in what is not yet fully existing."

Conclusion

As discussed by Mathieson (1974) and throughout the literature, abolitionists have long wrestled with the challenge of identifying "non-reformist" or positive reforms that pursue decarceration in meaningful ways while not entrenching carceral logics and penal institutions. Notwithstanding these worries and challenges, abolitionist work is productive, generative, difference-making. Berger, Kaba and Stein (2017) put it well:

> Prison abolitionists aren't naive dreamers. They're organizing for concrete reforms, animated by a radical critique of state violence. Central to abolitionist work are the many fights for non-reformist reforms—those measures that reduce the power of an oppressive system while illuminating the system's inability to solve the crises it creates. Rather than juxtapose the fight for better conditions against the demand for eradicating institutions of state violence, abolitionists navigate this divide […] Abolitionists have worked to end solitary confinement and the death penalty, stop the construction of new prisons, eradicate cash bail, organized to free people from prison, opposed the expansion of punishment through hate crime laws and surveillance, pushed for universal health care, and developed alternative modes of conflict resolution that do not rely on the criminal punishment system.
> (Berger, Kaba, & Stein, 2017)

Locating people subject to life sentences at the heart of abolitionist work does at least two things. It creates the potential to alleviate some of the worst harms of incarceration for those doing the longest time. It also reveals and challenges the liberal lie that the criminal punishment system is actually about protecting people from violence and harm. By centering these harshest of sentences and those subject to them in our work we participate in the unfinished business of abolition. For me, that unfinished business includes teaching future lawyers, campaigning for the closure of prisons, and advocating for the freedom of currently incarcerated people.

The law students I teach go on to become defense lawyers, prosecutors, or other participants in the criminal legal system. In bringing an abolitionist vision to my law school teaching, I hope to unsettle my students, these future lawyers, and to provide them with some tools to bring a prison abolitionist ethic to their lawyering work (Parkes, 2017; Karakatsanis, 2019). To close on a hopeful note, each year I meet law students who already identify as prison abolitionists. Admittedly, this is a small minority but I have seen it growing over the past 20 years. In 2020, the #BlackLivesMatter uprising and related work to defund the police and decarcerate our communities have brought prison abolitionist ideas and organizing into the mainstream (e.g., Paiella, 2020). In my view, centering those doing the longest time for the most serious offences will be key to the movement's long-term success. #FreeThemAll

Notes

1 I use the term "criminal legal system" or "criminal punishment system" rather than "criminal justice system" to challenge the assumption that the system delivers justice. See generally Karakatsanis (2019).
2 See, e.g., the website of the Smart Justice Network of Canada http://smartjustice.ca/smart-justice/prison/ ("the Smart Justice approach to prison is to reserve it for violent and dangerous offenders, and as a response of last resort, while aiming to solve the problem of non-violent crime in ways that are effective for people and for the public purse — outside the prison system.")
3 Crucially, abolitionist thought problematizes the notion of crime itself (e.g., Christie 2004).
4 In Canada, Indigenous women such as the late Patricia Monture (2006) have been important voices in the movement.
5 Indeterminate sentences are reserved for people declared by a sentencing judge to be "dangerous offenders" (usually for repeat convictions for violent offences). See *Criminal Code of Canada*, R.S.C., 1985, c. C-46, s. 753.
6 This was the second incarnation of this bill championed by Senator Pate. She put forward a similar bill in 2018, which was not passed but was subject to Parliamentary hearings and significant media attention.

References

Arbel, E. (2019). Rethinking the "crisis" of mass imprisonment. *Canadian Journal of Law and Society, 34*(3), 437–56. https://doi.org/10.1017/cls.2019.37

Ben-Moshe, L. (2013). The tension between abolition and reform. In M.E. Nagel & A.J. Nocella II (Eds.), *The end of prisons: Reflections from the decarceration movement* (pp. 83–92). Rodopi.

Ben-Moshe, L. (2018). Dis-epistemologies of abolition. *Critical Criminology, 26*(3), 341–55. https://doi.org/10.1007/s10612-018-9403-1

Ben-Moshe, L., Gossett, C., Mitchell, N., & Stanley, E.A. (2015). Critical theory, queer resistance, and the ends of capture. In G. Adelsberg, L. Guenther & S. Zeman (Eds.), *Death and other penalties: Philosophy in a time of mass incarceration* (pp. 266–95). Fordham University Press.

Berger, D., Kaba, M., & Stein, D. (2017, August 24). What abolitionists do. *Jacobin.* www.jacobinmag.com/2017/08/prison-abolition-reform-mass-incarceration

Bill C-53: An Act to Amend the Criminal Code and the Corrections and Conditional Release Act and to Make Related and Consequential Amendments to Other Acts (the Life Means Life Act). (2015). 1st Reading March 11, 2015, 41st Parliament, 2nd session. Retrieved from the Parliament of Canada website: www.parl.ca/legisinfo/BillDetails.aspx?billId=7865843&Language=E

Bill S-208: An Act to Amend the Criminal Code (Independence of the Judiciary) (2020). 1st Reading February 4, 2020, 43rd Parliament, 1st session. Retrieved from the Parliament of Canada website: https://parl.ca/DocumentViewer/en/43-1/bill/S-208/first-reading

Bumiller, K. (2008). *In an abusive state: How neoliberalism appropriated the feminist movement against sexual violence.* Duke University Press.

Carlton, B. (2016). Penal reform, anti-carceral feminist campaigns and the politics of change in women's prisons, Victoria, Australia. *Punishment & Society, 20*(3), 283–307. https://doi.org/10.1177/1462474516680205

Carrier, N. & Piché, J. (2015). Blind spots of abolitionist thought in academia: On longstanding and emerging challenges. *Champ Pénal, 12*, 1–38. https://doi.org/10.4000/champpenal.9162

Chartrand, V. (2015). Landscapes of violence: Women and Canadian prisons. *Champ Pénal, 12*, 1–27. https://doi.org/10.4000/champpenal.9158

Chartrand, V. (2019). Unsettled times: Indigenous incarceration and the links between colonialism and the penitentiary in Canada. *Canadian Journal of Criminology and Criminal Justice, 61*(3), 67–89.

Christie, N. (2004). *A suitable amount of crime.* Routledge.

Correctional Service Canada. (2019, April 15). Commissioner's directive 715-2 post-release decision process. www.csc-scc.gc.ca/politiques-et-lois/715-2-cd-en.shtml#5

Critical Resistance & INCITE! (2003). Critical resistance-incite! Statement on gender violence and the prison-industrial complex. *Social Justice, 30*(3), 141–50.

Davis, A.Y. (2003). *Are prisons obsolete?* Seven Stories Press.

Dhillon, J.K. (2015). Indigenous girls and the violence of settler colonial policing. *Decolonization: Indigeneity, Education & Society, 4*(2), 1–31.

Gilmore, R. W. (2007). *Golden gulag: Prisons, surplus, crisis, and opposition in globalizing California.* University of California Press.

Gilmore, R.W. (2011). What is to be done? *American Quarterly, 63*(2), 245–65.

Gilmore, R.W. (2015, February 23). The worrying state of the anti-prison movement. *Social Justice.* http://www.socialjusticejournal.org/the-worrying-state-of-the-anti-prison- movement/

John Howard Society of Canada. (2018, May 30). *Canada gives less parole despite excellent results.* John Howard Society of Canada. https://johnhoward.ca/blog/less-parole-despite- excellent-results/.

Karakatsanis, A. (2019). *Usual cruelty: The complicity of lawyers in the criminal injustice system.* The New Press.

Knopp, F.H., Boward, B., Brach, M.J., Christianson, S., Largen, M.A., Lewin, J., Lugo, J., Morris, M., & Newton, W. (1976). *Instead of prisons* (M. Morris, Ed.). Prison Research Education Action Project.

Kaba, M. & Duda, J. (2017, November 9). Towards the horizon of abolition: A conversation with Mariame Kaba. The Next System Project. https://thenextsystem.org/learn/stories/towards-horizon-abolition-conversation-mariame-kaba

Kim, A., Meiners, E.R., Petty, A., Petty, J., Richie, B.E., & Ross, S. (Eds.). (2018). *The long term: Resisting life sentences working toward freedom.* Haymarket Books.

Kim, M.E. (2019a). The carceral creep: Gender-based violence, race, and the expansion of the punitive state, 1973–1983. *Social Problems, 67*(2), 251–69.

Kim, M. E. (2019b). Anti-carceral feminism: The contradictions of progress and the possibilities of counter-hegemonic struggle. *Affilia: Journal of Women and Social Work, 35*(3), 309–26.

Lawston, J.M., & Meiners, E.R. (2014). Ending our expertise: Feminists, scholarship, and prison abolition. *Feminist Formations, 26*(2), 1–25. 10.1353/ff.2014.0012

Levine, J., & Meiners, E.R. (2020). *The feminist and the sex offender.* Verso Press.

Mathiesen, T. (1974). *The politics of abolition.* Halsted Press.

Miller, J.G. (1991). *Last one over the wall: The Massachusetts experiment in closing reform schools* (2nd ed.). Ohio State University Press.

Monture, P.A. (2006). Confronting power: Aboriginal women and justice reform. *Canadian Woman Studies, 25*(3/4), 25–33.

National Inquiry into Missing and Murdered Indigenous Women and Girls . (2019). *Reclaiming power and place: The final report of the national inquiry into missing and murdered indigenous women and girls.* www.mmiwg-ffada.ca/final-report/

Neve, L., & Pate, K. (2005). Challenging the criminalization of women who resist. In J. Sudbury (Ed.), *Global lockdown: Race, gender, and the prison-industrial complex* (pp. 19–33). Routledge.

Nichols, R. (2014). The colonialism of incarceration. *Radical Philosophy Review, 17*(2), 435–55.

Paiella, G. (2020, June 11). How would prison abolition actually work? GQ. www.gq.com/story/what-is-prison-abolition

Parkes, D. (2016). Women in prison: Liberty, equality, and thinking outside the bars. *Journal of Law & Equality, 12*, 123–52.

Parkes, D. (2017). Solitary confinement, prisoner litigation, and the possibility of a prison abolitionist lawyering ethic. *Canadian Journal of Law and Society, 32*(2), 165–85.

Parkes, D. (2018, September 28). Mandatory minimum sentences for murder should be abolished. The Globe and Mail. www.theglobeandmail.com/opinion/article-mandatory-minimum-sentences-for-murder-should-be-abolished/

Pate, K. (2020, February 3). Mandatory minimums are toughest on the most vulnerable. The Star. www.thestar.com/opinion/contributors/2020/02/03/mandatory-minimums- are-toughest-on-the-most-vulnerable.html

Public Works and Government Services Canada. (2019, August). Corrections and Conditional Release Statistical Overview 2018. Public Safety Canada www.publicsafety.gc.ca/cnt/rsrcs/pblctns/ccrso-2018/index-en.aspx

Richie, B. E. (2015). Reimagining the movement to end gender violence: Anti-racism, prison abolition, women of color feminisms, and other radical visions of justice. *University of Miami Race & Social Justice Law Review, 5*(2), 257–73.

Roberts, D.E. (2019). Abolition constitutionalism. *Harvard Law Review, 133*(1), 1–122.

R v. Bourque, 2014 NBQB 237, 2014 NBBR 237.

R v. Ostamas, 2016 MBQB 136, 131 W.C.B. (2d).

Shantz, J. & Ureta, E. (2020, July 23). Here's why we can abolish most of the criminal justice system now without endangering public safety. Rabble.ca. https://rabble.ca/blogs/bloggers/views-expressed/2020/07/heres-why-we-can-abolish- most-criminal-justice-system-now

Taylor, C. (2018). Anti-carceral feminism and sexual assault – a defense: A critique of the critique of the critique of carceral feminism. *Social Philosophy Today, 34,* 29–49.

The Correctional Investigator Canada. (2019, June 25). *2018–2019 Annual Report.* Office of the Correctional Investigator. www.oci-bec.gc.ca/cnt/rpt/pdf/annrpt/annrpt20182019-eng.pdf

Vetten, L. & Bhana, K. (2005). The justice for women campaign: Incarcerated domestic violence survivors in post-apartheid South Africa. In J. Sudbury (Ed.), *Global lockdown: Race, gender, and the prison-industrial complex* (pp. 255–70). Routledge.

10 Looking from northwest to southeast

Feminist carceralism, gender equality and global responses to gender-based violence

Dawn Moore and Vered Ben-David

Garland (2001) reminds us that the prison is a failed experiment now stretching out over 150 years in the global north. Steady, and in some jurisdictions, rapid expansion of the carceral enterprise through Europe and North America brings us to a fixed logic that the prison is the gold standard response to criminalized activities even as the expanding prison has no discernible positive effect on crime specifically, nor on people's quality of life, sense of safety, or economic stability more generally. On the contrary, there is plenty of evidence to suggest that the western (as defined by capitalism, colonialism, and white supremacy, not strictly geography) fixation on carcerality has the opposite effects of those stated. Far from rehabilitating "criminals", the prison guts populations of entire generations, especially of men, places an enormous economic burden on communities and states alike, is a guaranteed site of state and interpersonal violence and human rights abuses, and mandates state-based slavery (Davis, 1998; Kerr, 2015; Garland, 2001; Mauer, 2004; Sudbury, 2014).

The complete inability of the prison to deliver on its promises of safety, security and humanity is not factored into the white-western, second wave feminist insistent turn toward the state to address gender-based violence (GBV). From the 1970s to the current #metoo movement, feminist activists and scholars continue to rely on the criminal justice system (CJS) and, more importantly, its underlying carceral logics to address and ultimately eliminate GBV (Bumiller, 2008; Phipps, 2019). We want to push this observation further, noting we are forced to rely on the CJS as the *only* legitimate way to respond to GBV. This argument, if persuasive, reveals a deep dissonance in repeated promises to provide "victim centered" responses to GBV. The very fact that most people who experience GBV will not report it to authorities coupled with the reality that those who do report most often find little if any satisfaction in the outcomes of a criminal investigation suggest that, despite ongoing attempts to reform the criminal justice system, making it more "victim centered" actually does nothing to reduce or eliminate gender-based violence nor does this façade of state benevolence meaningfully address the varied needs of those who have experienced such violence. Finally, state responses to GBV are color coded. While we are using the shorthand of "white-western" in juxtaposition to the global south and west, we are doing so problematically because this framing still falls short of finding a clean way to capture the experiences of racialized peoples within the global north. BIPOC (Black, Indigenous, people of colour) folks in particular may well be geographically located in the northwest but their relationship to the state as well as their day-to-day lives arguably are much more akin to the conditions generally ascribed to the "developing" world. As such, we take the work and experience of BIPOC folks in the global north, especially their efforts to decenter the state in response to GBV, on par (but not parity) with the lived realities of folks in the global south and east. As such we want to show that white-western responses to GBV are designed primarily based on the imaginary of the white, female victim in all her documented fragility, and to the negation of women whose lived realities differ from this false standard of the "normal" victim (see Moore, Singh, Woolford & Sibley, 2019).

Despite this ongoing failure, the white-western model of carceral feminism is now a global export. The United Nations, World Bank, and the WHO are shaping global standards of "best practices" in responding to gender-based violence around carceral net widening. As a result, just like the global export of the prison itself as a model for "civilized" punishment (Pratt, 2002), the global south is increasingly handed a feminist carceral ideology that has never manifested its goals of eliminating or even decreasing GBV.

In 1989 Carol Smart cautioned that feminists have given up too much to law, a notion that inspired the small but growing anti-carceral feminist movement in the north to think more broadly about the implications of feminist carceral logics as they extend from prison to community. Around the same time that Smart was building her critique of feminist engagement with law, bell hooks (1995) offered a much needed intersectional dimension to Smart's argument. Building on the groundwork laid out by Kimberlé Crenshaw (1992) and Gayatri Spivak (1989), hooks makes the cases that victimhood is color coded in ways that are far more apparent than ever before as we watch in real time while Black, and Indigenous people are gunned down by police and we feel the rage and despair manifested in the growing Black Lives Matter movement. hooks (1995) makes the crucial argument that white and Black victims lack parity. To be Black and victimized is normal, in no need of intervention, according to hooks, whereas the mantle of victimhood, especially when donned by a white woman victimized by a Black man, can only be of service to the white, female victim. Below we challenge the later part of this claim. For now we want to work with hook's claim that victimhood strips people of agency and mandates state dependency. For hooks, the route to emancipation, especially Black women's emancipation, begins with laying down the mantle of victimhood. Smart's argument is more tempered and resigned. She surrenders to the fact that despite this dangerous submission, carceralism is so deeply embedded in collective thinking about GBV that we already, 30 years ago, were too far in to get out of criminal responses to GBV or to even think through the possibility of non-carceral, non-juridical reactions to sexual assault and domestic violence in particular.

Smart's argument, in part because of the time it was written and in part because she focused solely on the Anglo global north, failed to anticipate that a turn away from the juridical was (and remains) possible—a potentiality that hooks, Crenshaw and Davis foresaw and understood as an imperative if Black communities were ever to achieve emancipation (hooks, 1995). Indeed, global northern feminisms could break out of the juridical colonization of GBV by looking to and learning from the global south as well as the rich body of scholarship and activism coming from BIPOC communities in Europe and North America. Nations including Uganda, India, Burundi, and Ethiopia are taking anti-carceral approaches to responding to GBV with an emphasis on systemic and cultural change, mediation, and meeting victims' needs over criminal sentencing for offenders.

Logics of global governance present localized initiatives from the global south and east as "stopgap" measures for have-not nations undergoing what we might think of as a civilizing process. That is, the comparative capital inequality suffered by these nations means their judicial and penal systems are too underdeveloped and rooted in orientalized, patriarchal ideologies to be able to meet northern standards of investigation, prosecution, conviction, and incarceration. We want to make the potentially inflammatory suggestion that this capital impoverishment makes possible the ability for small groups of women, communities, and activists to explore responses to GBV outside the juridical. To be clear, we are not advocating for poverty but rather flagging that in circumstances in which a turn to the state for protection or redress is hampered by lack of systemic infrastructure, other possible responses to violence emerge. What are tacitly presented as stopgap measures on the road to civilization may well be measures that embody notions of empowerment and victim-centeredness so warmly embraced in the north and so vigorously exported to the south even as the northern model continues to fail to make good on its promises of justice and protection.

Western feminism adopts a loosely veiled orientalist lens through which to view such practices, thus foreclosing the possibility that better responses to GBV may well be found in places deemed uncivilized from a western perspective. Such colonial black-boxing relegates non-carceral responses to GBV in the global south to nothing more than quaint, localized initiatives that have little to teach us about alternative ways of addressing GBV. Underpinning this ignorance, we suggest, are strong logics of othering and civilization manifested in a white, northern supremacy reinforcing a global order in which northern responses to social problems are expected to continuously flow south, creating a hegemony of violence and its responses. This we refer to as the political economy of GBV.

#metoo serves as an instructive example and helps us to flesh out how these same worrying dynamics playing out on the world stage are mirrored in western nations. The co-opted history of #metoo is well documented. The phrase Me Too (note the absence of the hashtag) was coined by Black feminist activist Tarana Burke in 2006 as an identifier of shared experiences of GBV among urban Black women in the United States. Far from carceral logics, this initial Me Too, born in the long shadow of Anita Hill's impossible crisis of allegiance between carceral feminism and Black emancipation (Crenshaw, 1991), was intended as a sign post of empowerment, empathy and shared experience that would, in Burke's vision, give young Black women in particular an apparatus through which to move through the experience of sexual violence outside of state intervention. The now well-known story of b-list American celebrity Alyssa Milano's co-optation of Me Too in 2017 has become a cautionary tale of the co-optation by white, carceral feminists of the efforts of racialized feminists to find alternate, appropriate means of dealing with GBV that do not involve incrimination, police investigation, prosecution or state-based punishments.

Milano's #metoo, which quickly dominated social media and arguably changed the narrative of gender-based violence in the global north, focused on "call out culture," a form of public shaming targeting sexually predacious and violent men in positions of power. While many deployed the hashtag in the spirit of solidarity and empathy originally envisioned by Burke, the cases that were indelibly written onto the cultural script of the west took a decidedly punitive turn. Harvey Weinstein, Kevin Spacey, Bill Cosby, R. Kelly are all under investigation, charged, on trial or convicted of GBV related crimes. Cosby, the first to be convicted, is currently serving a six-year sentence. The uptick in turning toward the state and especially making criminal complaints in the post #metoo era is not limited to Hollywood celebrities. Statistics Canada, for example, notes regional increases in reports of GBV to police ranging from 23% to 76% in the period immediately following the massive #metoo social media campaign.

In her intersectional analysis of the "white politics" of #metoo, Phipps (2019, p. 10) concludes, "#MeToo authorizes the patriarchal, racist state through its claims to its protection … [and] legitimates the individualizing imperatives of neoliberalism as personal pain is commodified in testimonial cultures and the outrage economy of the media." Phipps' indictment of #MeToo and its imperatives of whiteness, vulnerability and personal anguish map onto emerging critiques of narratives of victimhood as prescribed not only by social media but also (and perhaps primarily) through the criminal justice system itself.

Viewing the co-optation of #MeToo through the lens of anti-carceral feminism (Kilty & Bogosavljevic, 2019; Ritchie, 2017; Lamble, 2013; Gilmour, 1990; Davis, 1998; Phipps, 2019; Bumiller, 2008) reveals the intersectional failures of the movement itself as one that now almost exclusively serves the interests of white, wealthy women who can and do conform to predetermined scripts of vulnerability as iterated through individualized, neoliberal narratives of trauma and recovery (Walklate, 2008). It also once again underscores the inability of carceral and criminal justice responses to embrace "victim centrism" as a guiding principle in establishing means through which GBV can be addressed that ultimately serve the needs of victims.

The core failing here is that carceral responses do not meet victim's needs and in many cases, often create more problems for victims than they solve. Over the past five years we have conducted interviews with 53 women who have experienced either sexual or domestic violence. In all but a handful of cases, the women we interviewed expressed a host of needs in the wake of being victimized, none of which involved punishing their perpetrators. On the contrary, victims were interested in accessing social safety nets that rarely existed and if they did, in largely inaccessible ways.

The body of evidence suggests that when the state becomes involved in cases of domestic violence typically the focus is on women, especially those with children, who are marginalized by poverty, social isolation, addiction, disability and/or minority status. The intersections of gender, class, "race" and immigration status affect the ways domestic violence victims are able to access and benefit from support (Day & Gill, 2020) as well as how willingly or even aggressively the state will step in to investigate and prosecute (Moore & Singh, 2018). Naturally this does not mean that socially advantaged people are insulated from GBV. Rather, we are pointing here to an assemblage that unevenly targets and investigates violence when it concerns socially and structurally marginalized people. The state's investigative response can be best described as regulation of victims and imposition of norms to tame the victim rather than protection of or assistance to the victim (Bumiller, 2008; Moore & Singh, 2018). While the professional literature (e.g., social work) defines domestic violence as a "social problem" and views it through an ecological model lens, the de-politicization of social and economic inequalities (the transition from a welfare to a protection system) has resulted in an individualized response to cases while ignoring or obscuring the larger context in which the problem occurs. This conceptual segregation of the victim from her social and economic environment laid the groundwork for an adversarial legal and child protection system in which a well-developed bureaucratic apparatus is focused on surveillance, investigation, assessment and data collection all under the auspices of victim centrism.

Victims who experienced state intervention, largely in the form of police investigation, detailed experiences of intimidation, threats (especially to their relationships with their children), humiliation and dismissal of their claims. For the rare few whose complaints did result in conviction, they waited in fear for their assailants to be released, anticipating retaliation and further victimization. Others, especially poor, racialized women and women with precarious immigration / asylum statuses, feared the collateral consequences of having their assailants incarcerated. For Indigenous, racialized, and poor women there was also a very legitimate fear that their communities would shame or reject them for participating in a criminal process (think again of Anita Hill). In other cases, especially those involving sexual violence, the class divide was all too apparent as women were counselled by prosecutors that they would be better served pursuing costly civil litigation over participating in a criminal prosecution.

While reporting and conviction rates are fetishized as the ultimate litmus test of a justice system's effectiveness in responding to GBV, the data from our research shows unequivocally that the promise of justice is elusive even in the rare instance of conviction. More importantly, these promises of justice are, to borrow from Lauren Berlant, cruelly optimistic. Berlant describes cruel optimism as an affect of neoliberal life. She posits that the promises of happiness, security, and prosperity made to those of us fortunate enough to live in the global north are ultimately unrealizable for almost all. The result, Berlant suggests, is a universal western disappointment and frustration as individualized attempts to follow the prescribed path to the good life result in repeated and ongoing failure to attain the unattainable. Elsewhere we have argued that the current assemblage of state-centric responses to GBV in the west is also cruelly optimistic, promising justice and safety to victims who co-operate with "the system" only for those victims to discover that cooperation is nowhere near a guarantee of justice and, more menacingly, a failure to follow the script of good victimhood often results in the criminalization and punishment of the victim herself. Despite these persistent failures of the western world to even come close to addressing, let alone reducing or eliminating GBV, global governance continues to press this failed western model of juridical redress throughout the world.

UN Women's 2013 report "Ending Violence Against Women and Girls: Program Essentials" outlines ten "main challenges" to "advances in law and policy" concerning the elimination of GBV: gender inequality, impunity, inadequate human, technical and financial investments, weak coordination and monitoring mechanisms at the national level, insufficient data and research, limited attention to neglected groups and issues, dearth of evaluations and evidence to guide programs, limited scope and coverage of services and interventions, low demand for services by survivors, fragmentation of efforts. While the report presents these challenges as global, the way they are problematized suggests that all but two of these challenges (insufficient data and low reporting) are strictly problems of economically disadvantaged nations.

There are two main points we want to draw from this. First, that the suggestion that these ten barriers are global does not appear to be in line with how UN Women actually understands, or at least talks about, GBV which suggests a clear north / south divide. Second, we want to focus on impunity as it is fetishized throughout the report (and cognate reports from the World Health Organization (WHO) and the World Bank).

UN Women names domestic and interpersonal violence, sexual violence, sexual harassment and emotional / psychological violence as the "most universally common" forms of GBV. It then goes on to list a number of forms of violence typically associated with the global south, designating them as "less documented". These include "honor" killings, femicide, prenatal sex selection, female infanticide, economic abuse, political violence, elder abuse, dowry-related violence, and acid-throwing. UN Women caps off its list noting that "particular groups of women" are more vulnerable to violence including migrants and undocumented workers, women in detention, and women in conflict or disaster zones.

Here the north / south, east / west divisions are clear: *all* women are vulnerable to *some* forms of GBV. Other forms of GBV are economically and culturally determined and thus specific to only certain parts of the world. It is crucial to note here that, for the most part, the UN and WHO see these divisions at the nation-state level and almost completely ignore grossly uneven experiences of racialized and Indigenous women in the white-western world. Following this *all* and *some* logic, the report goes on to name violence against women and girls as a "missing target" in the Millennium Development Goals (UNDP, 2005) ratified by 189 countries with a target completion date of 2015. Importantly, these goals only tangentially address GBV through its relation to economic costs and human commodification. Addressing GBV in any form was not part of the original goals set in 2000. As such, the "missing target" identified by UN Women is not GBV writ large (as the report suggests) but rather, GBV that undermines the development of human capital and this, at least according to the terms of the report, is largely a problem of the global south and east. While the report cites undefined costs of GBV in northern nations including the US, Canada, Australia and the UK, it is clear that it is inequality in the global south and east that UN Women is imagining in defining this "missing target". The north has no problem; it has the solution: the prison.

Except that the northern solutions, especially the carceral turn, are not solutions. Self-reports (more reliable than police reports) show no change in rates of GBV in Canada over a 25-year period, despite the fact that in Canada we have specialized courts to address domestic violence, specialized police squads dedicated to GBV, specialized nurses and doctors trained to respond to GBV, and the Canadian penal system is generally seen as the global leader in rehabilitative initiatives with entire prisons dedicated to treatment of sex offenders and mandatory rehabilitative programming for anyone convicted of intimate partner violence.

The north does have a problem with GBV. This problem is especially apparent when we take into account economic and social inequality within our own borders whereby Indigenous, poor and racialized women experience higher rates of violence. Canada just received the results of a fraught Inquiry into missing and murdered Indigenous women. The Inquiry reached the incendiary conclusion that rates of violence toward Indigenous women in Canada are so high as to constitute a genocide. How is it that a nation facing internally originating genocidal allegations can position itself as a world leader in responding to GBV and join other global superpowers with near identical landscapes of GBV, at least for the colonial nations, in attempting to show the global south and east how it is done?

Here we want to return to the second barrier identified by UN Women—impunity. Not only do we want to think about what makes punishment, especially harsh punishment, such a desirable goal in the quest to end GBV globally but we also want to suggest that these vengeful responses are indicative of a white supremacist political economy of violence fueled by a false narrative of the civilizing process.

Impunity is second only to gender inequality in UN Women's (2013, p. 53) list of the main challenges to implementing "effective" responses to GBV. UN women describes the challenge of impunity,

> The lack of state accountability in comprehensively addressing violence against women and girls is a significant obstacle to ending the problem. Generalized acceptance of violence against women, lack of political will, inadequate legal protections and enforcement, insufficient resource allocation and / or poor implementation of national commitments contribute to pervasive impunity. ... Ending impunity requires adequate prosecution and punishment of perpetrators; equal protection for women under the law and equal access to justice (that holds up to public scrutiny); and the elimination of attitudes that foster, justify or tolerate violence against women.
>
> (2013, p. 38)

There is no jurisdiction in the world, regardless of GDP or GINI rankings, that even comes close to meeting the requirements to correct the problem of impunity as described by UN Women. Still, this problem is clearly one framed as localized to the global south and east as indicated by the description of nations in which the problem of impunity is "particularly evident."

UN Women is not the only international organization to cite impunity or a lack of punitive response as a core problem in attempts to address GBV in the global south and east. The UN's ongoing campaign, "UNiTE to End Violence Against Women" sets its number one goal as "adoption and enforcement of national laws to address and punish all forms of violence against women and girls, in line with international human rights standards." Through a joint initiative between the UN Office on Drugs and Crime (UNODC), WHO and Stop Rape Now, an entire tool kit was developed to address the problem of impunity. Specifically, the tool kit focuses on evidence collection (both medical and legal) with a significant portion of the prescriptions dedicated to the use of rape kits, a technology of evidence collection that has also been, at best, a complete failure and at worst, a tool of state violence in the global north (Mulla, 2014; Walklate, 2014).

The deep irony here is that while each of these organizations and reports emphasizes "evidence-based practice," they concomitantly acknowledge that there is no evidence on which to base the practice. This observation alone suggests that this privileging of punishment as a preferred if not primary means of addressing GBV in the global south and east has very little to do with survivors' needs or best practices. In fact, if we look at the research on cognate practices in the north, not only are carceral responses shown to fail in the overall project of addressing GBV and "survivor centrism" but they are actually routinely held up as harmful to victims (Lemieux, 2017). Smart (1989) refers to this as the juridogenic nature of law—that legal processes often cause harms in their attempts to address harms.

If punitiveness, proven to be totally ineffective in the global north, is now enthusiastically exported to the global south and east we must ask why. We suggest that the answer lies in what we might think of a political economy of violence fueled by carceral feminism.

Alison Phipps' (2019) work on white supremacy and the #metoo movement is a helpful starting point in attempting to understand the global political economy of GBV. Phipps argues that our current framings of GBV are white-centric and rely on the deployment of white fragility as a script for what a woman should experience and perform in the wake of GBV (also discussed by Walklate), how the state ought to respond to this scripted woundedness and, more broadly, how GBV is politicized through parallel scripts of hurt and vengeance informed by a "nexus of patriarchy, capitalism and colonialism" (Phipps, 2019, p. 8). Most importantly, Phipps demands, "that we understand racism as foundational to Western public feminisms around sexual violence, rather than as one of their political effects" (p. 9). She goes on to argue,

> it is imperative to understand how race shapes the politics of sexual violence. If we do not, powerful feminist moments and movements like #metoo will continue to constitute conversations between white people about our wounds, which legitimize state and intuitional governmentalites and impede an understanding of sexual violence as produced by the intersection of patriarchal, capitalist and colonial systems.
>
> (Phipps, 2019, p. 9)

Phipps explains exactly how this imperative of white woundedness serves not only to amplify the lust for vengeance, especially when a white woman is wounded by a racialized man (a trope all too common in the global north), but also to exclude experiences of GBV of women in the global south and east because they do not conform to the rationalities of white fragility.

This too bears out in the UN and related rhetorics. Alongside calls to the carceral there is a consistent imperative to psychologize victims through euro-centric understandings of trauma and psychological pathology. PTSD (post-traumatic stress disorder), trauma syndrome, and the need for professional psychological support are all also routinely privileged in strategies, recommendations, and tool kits even if, as Phipps maintains, these logics of what is needed in the aftermath of violence are specific to white, western cultures and run antithetical to the ways in which GBV and its aftermath is understood and dealt with by non-white people even in the global north. For example, Phipps points to the tensions between resilience and resistance. Resilience is a catchphrase of contemporary, western psychology born of neoliberal doctrines of autonomy and responsibility with the promise that GBV and its ensuing scripted traumas can be "overcome" by individuals provided they have access to and use psychological supports. It involves protective factors and self-awareness and is achieved through psycho-therapeutic processes in the wake of a violent event. Resilience maintains the status quo, an observation reminiscent of the limits of the sovereign state.

Various definitions and models of resilience with regard to survivors of sexual and domestic violence and abuse share several key features: the first are market-based oriented measures that relate to the victim's ability to function well in society despite her negative experiences. This includes her ability to participate in the labor market and be a contributing member as well as the ability to function well across various social systems. Valentine and Feinauer (1993) defined resilience as "functioning well in life: employed and/or living in the community without needing state or welfare assistance, not having been institutionalized in hospitals, prisons or shelters for the homeless or battered" (p. 46). Other studies defined resilience as functioning well in life across a broad range of adult psychosocial domains (e.g., McGloin & Widom, 2001; Topitzes et al., 2013).

Resilience is constructed, conceptualized and articulated in personal, individualistic, and psychological terms and processes with no recognition of the impact of social deprivation and stressors on the lives of the victim. Resilience largely reflects the victim's capacity to reorient herself and readapt to the existing social order without interference. As long as the victim's subjective (personal pain) does not transcend to the collective and she is able to reinforce the existing power structure, she is considered resilient. Most important, the resilient victim, by virtue of keeping her suffering between her and her therapist, is depoliticized, making it possible to take the structural acts of violence (both personal and state) that are GBV and relegate them permanently and exclusively to the realm of the personal and pathological, never political.

Structuring resilience from a subjective, phenomenological perspective instead of a social, ecological one, denies the reality of women's lived experiences and precludes any social change. The mobilization of social services to support the rehabilitation of the victim as an autonomous, free, independent, and unattached subject, aims to ensure that she will (again) comply with the white, middle-class male model.

Resistance, on the other hand, targets structural power over personal pain. Phipps uses the example of Black women in the United States to illustrate how resistance is embraced vis-à-vis gender-based violence. Rather than turning toward the state (which has been and continues to be one of the main oppressors of racialized people in general and has targeted Black women in more specific, documented ways) these women accept Sojourner Truth's suggestion that they are able to "bear the lash." In contemporary terms, while their white counterparts embrace trauma as the main narrative of the violence they have endured, Black women, as Jamilal Lemieux (2017) suggests, "know that they need to tuck that shit in and keep moving." Regardless of how contemporary psychology might narrate the act of "tucking that shit in" (likely through a language of repression), this adage that racialized women must resist the narratives of trauma leading to pleas for redress from the very state that continues to wreak violence in communities reflects a deep cultural dissonance with narratives of white fragility and trauma. Rather, this invitation to resist invokes the kind of strength and community-based empowerment coupled with a willful refusal to invite the state into personal lives that were so well captured by Burke's original iteration of the #metoo movement. Pushing the argument further, LeBaron and Roberts (2010) suggest that contemporary carceral strategies born of white feminist carceralism, "…have become an increasingly central means of locking growing numbers of individuals into dependence on the capitalist market and of containing the contradictions, insecurities, and resistances generated by shifting relations of production and social reproduction" (p. 127). Musto (2019) perhaps makes the point most succinctly, observing, "…feminist attention to women's and girl's justice-involvement emerges in the same moment in which the carceral state has shapeshifted in gender-sensitized directions, raising pressing questions about how feminist ideals are used to underwrite carceral expansion" (p. 69). While Musto's work focuses on the feminization of the prison itself, the work on the false dichotomy between victim and offender, especially in the realm of GBV in which "undeserving" victims are arguably more likely to be criminalized than "saved" by the justice system, we understand the feminized prison as another arm of the political economy of GBV. The very fact that the majority of imprisoned women are also victims of violence underscores the point.

Thuma's (2019) recent study on feminism, policing and prisons in the US is even more illuminating. Thuma shows how the imperative within Black communities to resist state involvement in order to protect against becoming locked into a state of dependence on and commensurate violence at the hands of the state (Lebaron and Robert's observation) historically and contemporaneously opens Black women up to further criminalization. Thuma takes the example of the proliferation of women's self-defense classes offered as a means of protecting women from sexual and physical assault, popularized in the 1970s and 80s. She raises the dark irony that while white women were encouraged to fight back against and hurt their assailants, Black women often found themselves incarcerated for the same behaviors that found their white counterparts valorized. Rather than encouraging submissiveness, solidarity work among Black women prisoners and community supporters through organizations like Incite! served to further resistance to state involvement in their lives, even when those lives were marked by violence. On the outside, women's co-operatives such as Incite! formed defense funds for women incarcerated for self-defense, arguing that these women were doing what was necessary to protect themselves and their children in a political climate in which the state, far from protecting them, was instead a clear and constant threat to their personal, economic, and collective safety, often creating conditions to permanently lock violence into these women's lives and communities.

Alternatives to juridical redress for GBV have never been formally legitimized in the west, but that does not mean that they do not exist and in many instances that they are not sanctioned by either nation states or the UN. On the contrary, there are any number of examples of alternative, non-carceral tactics used by women and men in the global south and east to address GBV without direct state involvement.

Uganda serves as an interesting example. While the state moved to criminalize domestic violence (DV) in 2010, complainants have the option of seeking out a non-state route of reconciliation / mediation (the terms are used somewhat interchangeably) to address and hopefully stop the violence in their lives. Importantly, while the reconciliation option is overseen by a magistrate, this person's power is largely limited to assisting with mediation. Additionally, the reconciliation model in Uganda is not limited to the adversarial, western, two-party model of justice. Instead it takes the form of community justice in which family, friends, and community members supporting both people involved in the violence (victim and perpetrator) play an important role in defining what problems exist within the household that contribute to DV (including poverty) and also play a role in supporting the victim and perpetrator in their ongoing reconciliation and commitment to ending violence.

Of course this model is subject to all the same criticisms feminists have made about reconciliation in the context of GBV. The victim may well not get the protections she requires, the system still functions in a patriarchal society, part of which condones GBV and most importantly, there may be invisible forms of coercion at play that deny women's empowerment through her ability to fully express what she has experienced and what her desired outcomes might be. In her study of the model of reconciliation in Uganda, Polavarapu (2019) argues that, despite the noted drawbacks, the Ugandan model should be taken seriously the world over as an alternative to carceral responses because it offers flexibility to the victim to direct the process (and to revert to criminal justice responses if she chooses) and, as an added improvement, both male and female Ugandan activists couple reconciliation with initiatives to change cultural norms and routinized behaviors that condone GBV. Specifically, through Uganda's Centre for Domestic Violence Prevention, organizations working at the local level have developed "community mobilization intervention" in a program known as SASA! ("Now!" in Kiswahili). The initiative works by recruiting and training local men and women to become community-based, anti-GBV activists. These activists receive training on GBV and then engage at the community level with citizens as well as local authorities to create community-wide change in rationalities and practices concerning GBV. Polavarapu describes this as "reconciliation plus." recognizing that addressing GBV must include both a reactionary component (reconciliation) and a proactive component (changing norms). It is this coupling that leads Polavarapu to conclude, "…in spite of the very real drawbacks and concerns associated with such forms of justice, they can also create an opening for normative change that is not occurring when feminists rely on criminal justice and formal legal systems." She continues on to make a case for Uganda's model to be placed in the global spotlight, arguing,

> giving greater attention to and taking lessons from Uganda's approach to justice may cause internationally focussed actors to pause and consider

their assumptions. In the rule of law, development and human rights work, there has been a tendency to export Western ideas, institutions and conceptions to the rest of the world. ... Though Western ideas have historically influenced justice system reform in developing countries, it seems that at least in some cases, justice is better served when the flow of ideas is reversed.

(p. 53)

Uganda is not the only nation to have rejected the unilinear, carceral response to GBV so familiar in the west. Post-conflict, Burundi took a similar approach to Uganda. Working with NGOs, community members in five different regions were educated about the broader social, political and economic contexts of GBV and tasked with educating other community members in changing local beliefs and values with regards to women and violence. These local educators also worked with victims to help them access medical services, financial support, and secure housing, three of the main needs identified almost universally by survivors of GBV. Additionally, these same community educators worked with police, judges, and administrators to educate them on the systemic nature of GBV with an eye to prevention through changing attitudes and helping state officials like police redirect their energies from investigation and prosecution to assisting victims in accessing support.

In India, the Nari Adalat is a rural women's court made up of local women who meet on a daily basis to hear other local women's complaints of GBV. The Nari Adalat does at times revert to a criminal justice response but for the most part its work focuses on educating women on their rights, mediating conflicts, and seeking restorative justice solutions; finding needed services for women as victims (including health, housing and securing a degree of financial independence); and publicly shaming abusers as part of a broader bid to change local attitudes concerning GBV.

Other similar examples of alternative, non-carceral responses to GBV can be found in Ethiopia, Benin, Rwanda and Congo. Importantly, from the perspective of "victim-centeredness," the availability of these alternatives not only relieves victims of the "cruel optimism" of turning to the state and the ensuing trap of dependence Thuma describes, it also means that the vast sums of money that would have been directed to the single response of juridical interventions and imprisonment can be diverted to more directly addressing the needs of victims through offering financial security, stable housing, access to clean water and food, access to education and health care, all universally recognized "protective factors" that have real and lasting impacts on reducing GBV and, most importantly, are the things survivors actually want (Moore & Singh, 2015). Additionally, the low cost of implementing community-based education programs like the SASA! program in Uganda mean that prevention through social change becomes a very real possibility. Fostering attitudes that promote women's equality through micro-level norm change, at its worst, can be no less effective and is certainly far less costly than the millions spent in northern nations each year on failed prison rehabilitation programs for men who commit violence against women.

Toward an anti-carceral political economy of GBV

In her foundational (1988) essay "Under Western Eyes" Chandra Talpade Mohanty takes aim at capitalism and colonialism as the drivers for a global political order in which northern strategies to address inequality are located as the proven "best practices" to be exported to the global south and east. In 2002, Mohanty revisits her initial essay, expanding her argument to suggest that, "within a tightly integrated capitalist system, the particular standpoint of poor, Indigenous and Third World / South women provides a most inclusive viewing of systemic power" (Mohanty, 2002, p. 511).

Mohanty's call to reorient the western standpoint feminist gaze from the assumed norm of white women in the global north to poor, Indigenous (and racialized) women of the north as well as the experiences of women in the global south could be a further-reaching rallying cry than what even she imagines. Mohanty limits her analysis to economic and environmental justice. For our purposes we expand this to include other forms of injustice, especially GBV. Though it is admittedly still largely a thought experiment, viewing responses to GBV from the standpoint of economically and racially marginalized women as well as women in the global south and east by closing our white-western eyes and imagining for a moment, new ways of thinking about an anti-carceral feminism that responds to GBV become possible.

First, looking from south to north reveals that, contrary to popular narratives of human rights on the global scale, the northern practices of responding to GBV through juridical and carceral means feed crises of human rights in northern countries. The most obvious instance here is that a carceral turn in the political economy of GBV contributes not only to the mass incarceration of men but also to the rapidly expanding populations of women in prison, particularly Indigenous and racialized women. In our own research, many of the women we interviewed who had experienced GBV had themselves been incarcerated directly as a result of that violence. One woman, Mitch, an Indigenous woman in her 60s, was on parole for her second murder conviction when Kelly Struthers Montford interviewed her. Mitch's victims had both been intimate, abusive partners. When we asked Mitch why she had not sought out state support in order to address the violence she was experiencing, she explained,

> Because they do fuck all. Ain't no justice in calling the police. They just tell you to go to a shelter. No restraining order, no protection, just go to this imaginary shelter that has space for you and wait until they figure out what they want to do with you. So you do what you have to and you stay away from the cops because they're just as likely to find some reason to arrest you or to just use you to get at your man for some completely unrelated shit that has nothing to do with my broken arm or fat lip. So

I learned. I learned that you got to take care of that shit yourself. There's no other choice. You call the man nobody's going to let you crash on their couch or lend you five bucks or bail you out when then man comes for you. So I learned, yeah I learned, with the knives and stuff, I learned. And now they know, they know if you come at Mitch she's going to cut you and that's the only way I can stay alive. Though that kinda staying alive just lands you in prison but fuck it right? It's him or me and today, you're looking at me alive and him dead and if I hadn'ta done something it woulda been the other way around. I just take the ten years that comes with that because at least I'm alive.

(quoted in "Mitch" —Interview July 16, 2018)

Like so many of the women we interviewed, Mitch was in a situation where even when the law was marshalled into her life in the wake of her experiences of domestic violence, it did not make her safe. On the contrary, following Smart's assertions about the juridogenic nature of law, state involvement only made Mitch's life worse: both by making her fear the loss of community support for "calling the man," and also by criminalizing and punishing her for killing her abusers in what she considered life and death situations.

But a second advantage of looking south to north is the challenge it offers to the scripts of white fragility that dictate victim engagement with the criminal justice system. While WHO and UN Women continue to promote westernized psychological interventions like CBT (cognitive behavior therapy) as necessary "treatments" for women in the wake of violence, this amounts to what Thuma describes as the "prison / psychiatric state" (Thuma, 2014) informing a political economy of GBV in which displays of woundedness, trauma, and fragility, despite their distinct lack of cultural universality, become markers of "good and deserving" victims. In the absence of scripted white fragility, we are left with the women who can "bear the lash" and in that strength and resistance become pathological and even dangerous. Our research shows that women who fail to conform to trauma scripts are more likely to be even more deeply pathologized, criminalized, incarcerated, and also lose custody of their children.

Finally, looking south to north means taking seriously the lessons the south has to teach the north about prevention and victim-centrism. The Ugandan example shows that localized, community-specific education campaigns trump national, general campaigns targeting GBV. Except for initiatives like the Moosehide project in Canada in which Indigenous men from the Cree Nation wear a patch of moosehide on their persons to identify not only their resistance to GBV but also their commitment to educating other men and boys about violence prevention, the global north is committed to what often amounts to little more than lip service at the national level while offering no prevention initiatives at the local level, particularly in the rural communities where GBV is often most acute and localized norm change is needed.

The fluidity of the Ugandan model also emphasizes choice for victims. In the case of domestic violence, victims in North America, through the invention of "no-drop" policies, have no choice to extract themselves from the CJS once a report has been made. This lack of choice again criminalizes women, as their usual extraction attempts (failing to appear on a summons, recanting statements, committing perjury) can all be treated as criminal acts. Under the current model of carceral feminism, a battered woman's choice to stay with her abuser in a relationship is stigmatized as a deviant choice and women who make this choice are a group of "battered women who stay" (Loseke & Cahill, 1984). These women are often characterized as incompetent, weak, and lacking coping skills, which further engulfs them in the victim role and contributes to their powerlessness (Peled, Eisikovits, Enosh, & Winstok, 2000). The women's "decision to stay" is constructed as an act of coercion and entrapment rather than as an act of choice reflecting varying degrees of freedom. The lack of choice is amplified when a woman has children. Women who decide to stay with their abusers can be prosecuted for child abuse and neglect, and can and do have their children removed from their care (Moore & Hoffeler, 2019). The lack of choice for women in the north is antithetical to the entire enterprise of addressing GBV since, as Phipps points out, it replicates the patriarchal power relations that are found in every micro instance of GBV (Phipps, 2019).

Pulling the lens back, we close with a hypothesis that is specific to GBV. We understand the global export of carceral feminism as the ideological underpinning to the emerging assemblage of juridical first responses to GBV that constitute an act of colonial and white supremacist power granted to global powers by means of wealth. Wealthy nations have the resources to create an industrial complex around GBV that is state-centered and privileges carcerality and white woundedness as the primary means to understand and justify carceral responses to GBV. This state-centrism persists despite the glaring failure of this governmentality overall and especially with respect to women who are already experiencing the largely ignored inequalities and human rights abuses that are part of the everyday of the north. We suggest that wealthy states are entitled to dictate every aspect of how GBV is recognized, understood and responded to. This entitlement is an opportunity to further extend state violence into people's personal lives by dictating how the violence they experience can be resolved only through the state and with the accompanying dictate of the necessarily fragile psyche so wounded it cries for state protection because it / she lacks the ability to engage her own resiliency and ability to resist violence in all its forms. The lack of wealth in the global south (and BIPOC communities in the north) means that GBV responses must be offered on the cheap. While dictated frugality does not rule out the import of carceral feminism (which remains ignorant to the political economy of GBV), it offers up the conditions under which grassroots, localized, prevention-based and victim-centered responses are possible. The "reconciliation plus" model of Uganda, the women's courts of India, all offer geographically and culturally specific responses to GBV that present options to women experiencing violence and encourage their own empowerment and choice making. This, we suggest, is the fundament of an anti-carceral feminism that looks at GBV with southern eyes. A Venn diagram of carceralism, GBV and inequality on a global scale has the potential to offer more options to victims of GBV that would make meaningful changes in their lives by addressing the inequalities they are directly experiencing without exacerbating those inequalities through the juridogenic effects of feminist carceralism all too familiar in the global north.

This is in fact an invitation to reimagine. The call to "reimagine" the social response to GBV (as well as other systems of power such as police, child protection, etc.) is radical and challenging. It is radical because it invites us to take up Phipps' (2019) notion of resistance so as to critically rethink and reexamine fundamental assumptions and perceptions about domestic violence. It addresses domestic violence not in individualistic, atomist terms but rather from a community, social, and structural perspective that views the victim as interconnected between various eco systems in her life rather than determined by the political economy of GBV. Taking up the challenge to resist frees us from the illusive dichotomous distinction between the private and public domains. Resistance represents an abolitionist demand to engage in a dual process of acknowledging the "existent," that is, the reality of politics in the juridical and social response to GBV as well as the reality of victims' lives while, at the same time, resisting the compelling force of the "inevitability" of such an "existent" on our collective consciousness of the world. In order to resist in this way, we need to deconstruct the known and construct the unknown using abstractions that are not rooted in our daily experiences or culture.

The point is that, in order to push for a change, white westerners first need to cognitively overcome fundamental assumptions we hold as "truth" about the world. A paradigmatic shift is needed that implies structural and content variation in the way we perceive GBV and subsequent action. We go further and call for a detoxification of our perception from the influences of European-based political, legal, and economic systems. If we can free ourselves from the limitations of preexisting conceptualizations rooted in the political social order under which we operate, then we can reimagine alternatives. As Foucault presented to us in his method of "problematization," if we operate and think within the system of power of the same social and political forces that gave rise to the "problem" in the first place, we help perpetuate the problem and move away from the path to justice. The abolitionist claim made here strives to replace the ignorance discussed earlier with a reformative, transformative recognition of the lived experiences of women. In essence, reimagining GBV requires the politicization of social inequality. Despite the challenge it presents, "reimagining" as a process of social transformation opens a space for inclusion of unheard, excluded voices and consideration of factors that are not usually factored into the social response to domestic violence. The important point is that a restructured abolitionist response to GBV, as described in the southern and eastern models, takes into account the ecology of the problem and the real needs of the victims. Replacing the criminal response and policing of the "deviant/dismissed female victim" with a more comprehensive response that acknowledges the impact of social disadvantages will represent a more effective approach to GBV and help alleviate the suffering it brings to victims and their families.

References

Bumiller, K. (2008). *In an abusive state: How neoliberalism appropriated the feminist movement against sexual violence*. Duke University Press.

Crenshaw, K. (1992). Race, gender, and sexual harassment. *Southern California Law Review, 65*, 1467–76.

Davis, R.L. (1998). *Domestic violence: Facts and fallacies*. Greenwood Publishing Group.

Day, A.S. & Gill, A.K. (2020). Applying intersectionality to partnerships between women's organizations and the criminal justice system in relation to domestic violence. *The British Journal of Criminology, 60*(4), 830–50.

Garland, D. (Ed.). (2001). Mass imprisonment: Social causes and consequences. Sage.

Gilmour, K. (1990). Violence and sexual assault. In A. Amos (Ed.), *The scandal of family violence* (pp. 26–31). Uniting Church Press.

hooks, b. (1995). *Killing rage: Ending racism*. Henry Holt.

Kerr, L.C. (2015). The origins of unlawful prison policies. *Canadian Journal of Human Rights, 4*, 89.

Kilty, J.M. & Bogosavljevic, K. (2019). Emotional storytelling: Sensational media and the creation of the HIV sexual predator. *Crime, Media, Culture, 15*(2), 279–99.

Lamble, S. (2013). Queer necropolitics and the expanding carceral state: Interrogating sexual investments in punishment. *Law and Critique, 24*(3), 229–53.

LeBaron, G. & Roberts, A. (2010). Toward a feminist political economy of capitalism and carcerality. *Signs: Journal of Women in Culture and Society, 36*(1), 19–44.

Lemieux, J. (2017, January 17). Why I'm skipping the Women's March on Washington. Color Lines. www.colorlines.com/articles/why-im-skipping-womens-march-washington-op-ed

Loseke, D.R. & Cahill, S.E. (1984). The social construction of deviance: Experts on battered women. *Social Problems, 31*(3), 296–310.

Mauer, M. (2004). Thinking about prison and its impact in the twenty-first century. *Ohio State Journal of Criminal Law, 2*, 607.

McGloin, J.M. & Widom, C.S. (2001). Resilience among abused and neglected children grown up. *Development and Psychopathology, 13*, 1021–38.

Mohanty, C.T. (1988). Under Western eyes: Feminist scholarship and colonial discourses. *Feminist Review, 30*(1), 61–88.

Mohanty, C.T. (2002). Under western eyes revisited: Feminist struggles through anticapitalist solidarity. *Signs: Journal of Women in Culture and Society, 28*(2), 499–535.

Moore, D. & Hoffeler, S. (2019) 'Forty-five colour photographs': Images, emotions and the victim of domestic violence. In *Emotions and crime* (pp. 77–95). Routledge.

Moore, D. & Singh, R. (2015). Seeing crime: ANT, feminism and images of violence against women. In D. Robert and M. Dufresne (Eds.), Actor-network theory and crime studies: Explorations in science and technology (pp. 67–80). Ashgate.

Moore, D. & Singh, R. (2018). Seeing crime, feeling crime: Visual evidence, emotions, and the prosecution of domestic violence. *Theoretical Criminology, 22*(1), 116–32.

Moore, D., Singh, R., Woolford, A., & Sibley, M.A. (2019). How she appears: Demeanour, cruel optimism, and the relationship between police and victims of domestic violence. In G. Pavlich and M. P. Unger (Eds.), *Entryways to criminal justice: Accusation and criminalization in Canada* (pp. 165–91). University of Alberta.

Mulla, S. (2014). *The violence of care: Rape victims, forensic nurses, and sexual assault intervention*. New York University Press.

Musto, J. (2019). Transing critical criminology: A critical unsettling and transformative anti-carceral feminist reframing. *Critical Criminology, 27*(1), 37–54.

Peled, E., Eisikovits, Z., Enosh, G., & Winstok, Z. (2000). Choice and empowerment for battered women who stay: Toward a constructivist model. *Social Work, 45*(1), 9–25.

Phipps, A. (2019). The fight against sexual violence. *Soundings, 71*(71), 62–74.

Polavarapu, A. (2019). Global carceral feminism and domestic violence: What the west can learn from reconciliation in Uganda. *Harvard Women's Law Journal, 42*, 123.

Pratt, J. (2002). *Punishment and civilization: Penal tolerance and intolerance in modern society*. Sage.

Ritchie, A.J. (2017). *Invisible no more: Police violence against Black women and women of color*. Beacon Press.

Smart, C. (1989) Feminism and the power of law. Routledge.

Spivak, G.C. (1989). A response to 'The difference within: Feminism and critical theory'. In E.A. Meese and A. Parker (Eds.), The *difference within: Feminism* and *critical theory* (pp. 208–20). John Benjamin.

Sudbury, J. (Ed.). (2014). *Global lockdown: Race, gender, and the prison-industrial complex*. Routledge.

Thuma, E.L. (2014). Against the" Prison/Psychiatric State": Anti-violence feminisms and the politics of confinement in the 1970s. Feminist Formations, *26*(2), 26–51.

Thuma, E.L. (2019). *All our trials: Prisons, policing, and the feminist fight to end violence*. University of Illinois Press.

Topitzes, J., Mersky, J., Dezen, K., & Reynolds, A. (2013). Adult resilience among maltreated children: A prospective investigation of main effect and mediating models. *Children and Youth Services Review, 35*(6), 937–49.

UNDP. (2005). "United Nations Millennium Project, Investing in Development: A Practical Plan to Achieve the Millennium Development Goals (Main Report)." United Nations.

UN Women. (2013). "Ending violence against women and girls: Programming essentials." UN Women. www.unwomen.org/en/digital-library/publications/2013/6/annual-report-2012-2013

Valentine, L. & Feinauer, L.L. (1993). Resilience factors associated with female survivors of childhood sexual abuse. *American Journal of Family Therapy, 21*, 216–24.

Walklate, S. (2008). What is to be done about violence against women? Gender, violence, cosmopolitanism and the law. *The British Journal of Criminology, 48*(1), 39–54.

Walklate, S. (2014). Sexual violence against women: Still a controversial issue for victimology? *International Review of Victimology, 20*(1), 71–84.

11 Remembering Carol Smart

Tensions between feminism, victims' rights and abolitionism

Jennifer M. Kilty and Katarina Bogosavljevic

Anti-carceral feminism is "a movement grounded in intersectional feminist critiques, strategies, [and] actions driven to struggle against and undermine structures of oppression that give rise to violence and injustice" (Carlton, 2018, p. 285), including that which is promoted via criminalization. As such, it stands in opposition to carceral feminist calls for the criminalization and imprisonment of perpetrators of gender-based forms of violence and sexual violence (GBV). While some feminists continue to look to the law and the state to punish perpetrators of GBV, anti-carceral feminists challenge the use of incarceration and understand the state as committing additional heteropatriarchal and racist harms in its efforts to address GBV. Notably, just as they problematized the feminist movement's construction of a falsely universal "woman's voice" that reflected a more privileged white, middle class experience and the prioritization of gender-based analyses to the exclusion of considering the intersectional effects of gender, race, class, sexuality, and ability (among other possible social identity locations), Black feminist scholars have been leading the anti-carceral feminist charge (Kim, 2018; Richie, 2012).

Heiner and Tyson (2017) contend that many feminists, including both those seeking gender parity and those seeking differential treatment, have maintained an "epistemic occupation" with carceral solutions for GBV.

> As a result of this epistemic occupation, it can even seem wrong to consider non-carceral responses to violence, because dominant neoliberal logic delineates only one intelligible schema of accountability for violence—that of an individual (non-state) agent—and only one general form of legitimate response: state-centric punishment (whether confinement, execution, or other form of physical, civil, or social death). Alternative forms of community accountability and redress that break from state-centric carceral systems appear baffling, irresponsible, even monstrous. The choice seems to be confined to either ensnaring an individual with the punitive arms of the state or fomenting complete, unaccountable disorder.
>
> (Heiner & Tyson, 2017, p. 2)

Our continued reliance on carceral logic to respond to law-breaking also contributes to how we "define the social situations that structure the logic of 'criminal justice', [which] has served to express power and the work of moral entrepreneurs to define people" (Coyle, 2018, p. 329). When we center our analytic focus on the divides in the feminist movement regarding how best to respond to GBV, we are faced with a troublesome question that has plagued penal abolitionist scholars for some time, namely, as Ilea (2018) demands, "what about the sex offenders?" Men who commit acts of sexual violence are typically imagined as the stranger-rapist lurking in the bushes or as the priest or coach committing crimes against children. This rhetorical strategy is mobilized "by politicians to fuel fear and support for the expansion of the carceral state" (Ilea, 2018, p. 364). Carceral initiatives have been supported by unlikely feminist allies, who, angry after centuries of denial and failure to acknowledge GBV, demand punishment for and state recognition of the pervasive nature of sexual harassment and violence that is now colloquially described as "rape culture."

We begin this chapter by outlining the links between feminist calls for protection and responsive state interventions for GBV and the increasing power of the victims' rights movement[1] that has contributed to the emergence of a carceral feminist agenda. Building on the literature that traces the evolution of carceral feminism back to second wave feminist calls for rights, legal protections, and the professionalization of the anti-violence movement (Carlton, 2018; Carlton & Russell, 2018; Richie, 2012), we then unpack the emotions underlying feminist calls for punitive state responses to GBV. Our cultural "epistemic occupation" with the prison has "captured, confined, and inhabited our collective capacities for thinking, feeling, imagining, and acting" (Heiner & Tyson, 2017, pp. 1–2) so much so that many feminists who are critical of and/or oppose the prison industrial complex cannot be identified as penal abolitionists because they have failed to move away from law's power in their efforts to prevent and protect women from violence (Carrier & Piché, 2019). In the third section, we discuss the legacy of Carol Smart, whose work is foundational to the discipline, but has been overlooked by critical prison studies scholars. Over 30 years ago, amidst the growth in the professionalization of the anti-violence movement, Smart not only pronounced law as a gendering practice, but she also warned against relying on law to support and/or produce feminist outcomes. We conclude by outlining a feminist abolitionist response that stands outside of law's power and instead looks to community alternatives to incarceration.

Carceral feminism and the victims' rights movement

Middle class, white women have a long history of advocating for punitive forms of state intervention into social problems; for example, first wave feminists campaigned for social purity and temperance, training centres to combat juvenile delinquency, and reformatories to re-make criminalized women into "proper" ladies (Gottschalk, 2006). Second wave feminists began mobilizing in earnest about violence against women in the 1960s at which point their efforts began to dovetail with an emerging victims' rights movement. Yet critical scholars problematize the efforts of dominating (Whalley & Hackett, 2017), carceral (Bernstein, 2012), and governing feminisms (Halley, 2006) that "seek to leverage formal institutional powers—including the carceral state—vis-à-vis a white supremacist state order with the hope of securing equality between (cisgendered) men and women"[2] (Whalley & Hackett, 2017, p. 457). For example, Nagel (2015) argues that sex work prohibitionists are anti-feminist because they employ a paternalist stance aligned with "conservative anti-sex, pro-abstinence right-wing Christian 'soldiers' for *prohibitionism*" (p. 2). Public fears and anxieties about crime have increased and led to feelings of (in)security, particularly amongst white, middle class women, who are positioned as ideal victims and "sympathetic figures" so as to politically justify increased policing, surveillance, and criminalization strategies to make cities safer and to protect "proper law-abiding citizens" (Bumiller, 2008; Fattah, 1989/1992, pp. 4–5).

Together, the victims' rights and feminist movements, neoliberalism, and the punitive turn (Bernstein, 2012, 2007; Bumiller, 2008; Gottschalk, 2006; Ricordeau, 2019; Whalley & Hackett, 2017) have led to the drafting of new legislation to protect battered women through civil orders of protection and criminal remedies (Bumiller, 2008; Richie, 2012) and antitrafficking policies that increased policing and the criminalization of street-based sex work (Bernstein, 2007, 2010). Notably, the connection between the feminist and victims' rights movements resulted in state cooptation of grassroots rape crisis centres, which historically lobbied against criminalization and for peer support and self-help programs for victims of sexual assault[3] (Gottschalk, 2006; Ricordeau, 2019). Relying on carceral responses to combat GBV problematically positions victimhood "as a negative term indicating regression: healing can only come through engaging with carceral systems" (Whalley & Hackett, 2017, p. 462). Carceral feminism's reliance on the law and alignment with conservative political criminal justice agendas to remedy years of disavowal for GBV has had the detrimental consequence of casting women as always already victimized and vulnerable (Ricordeau, 2019; Smart, 1992, 1995). Building on the literature that critiques the coalitions between feminist organizations, neoliberal governance strategies, and conservative law and order politics (Bernstein, 2012; Halley, 2006; Richie, 2012; Whalley & Hackett, 2017), the next section brings an affective lens to the conversation to consider how advocacy efforts are shaped by and mobilize emotions in order to effect change.

The affective economy of punishment

To recognize victims' and women's rights through law entails a high degree of affective labor or "the putting to work of our feelings." Affective labor is similar to Hochschild's (1983/2012) notion of emotion work, which she defines as "the act of trying to change in degree or quality an emotion or feeling. To 'work on' an emotion or feeling is, […] the same as 'to manage' an emotion or to do 'deep acting'" (p. 561). While emotion work requires managing our emotions so as to produce an outward expression of the "correct" emotion in particular circumstances, we use the term affective labor to reflect the ways in which our affects, bodily experiences, and feelings are put to work *upon us* by authority figures, workplace culture, politicians, mass culture, and/or social movements. Affects, emotions, and feelings structure how we interpret our experiences (Ahmed, 2004). Affective labor shapes how we interact with others and the boundaries and borders between bodies; notably, we make objects meaningful by attaching affective value to them. Just as certain commodities increase in value over time, the growth of affective value results from the circulation of objects and signs. As objects and signs move through the "social and psychic field," affects stick to them and accumulate over time making some objects more "affective" than others, therefore creating an affective economy (Ahmed, 2004, p. 45). Punishment is an affective economy that is saturated with and structured by a variety of emotions, including anger and frustration at the continued failure to believe women who have been victimized by GBV (Heiner & Tyson, 2017; Ricordeau, 2019; Walklate, 2016), pleasure at regarding the pain of others (Carvalho & Chamberlen, 2018; Sontag, 2003) and feelings of closure for victims (Bandes, 2020).

We conceptualize the advocacy efforts of carceral feminists as affective labor. The policy changes they have secured are evidence of an affective economy of punishment: they rely upon and shore up carceral logics to remedy feelings of anger, frustration, and fear and to try to garner a sense of closure for victims (Bandes, 2020). Carceral feminists are predominantly middle class, white women who support the state's power to criminalize (Bernstein, 2012; Bumiller, 2008; Gottschalk, 2006), and whose anger at the continued cultural and political disavowal of GBV has been taken up as more legitimate than the concerns raised by Indigenous, Black and Latina/x feminists about the dangers of relying on carceral responses to address this social problem (Crenshaw, 1991; Kim, 2018; Richie, 2012; Sudbury, 2016). Indeed, we might say that "the colour of emotions is white" in that the emotional performatives of white women are often more readily accepted as legitimate (Orsini & Mussel, 2019). For example, the recent case of Felicity Huffman who was criminalized for paying an admissions consultant $15,000 to proctor and correct her daughter's SAT exam (CBC, 2019) has been juxtaposed against the case of Kelley Williams-Bolar and Tanya McDowell, two Black women convicted and imprisoned for using false addresses to register their children in better school districts. In an attempt to draw attention to the rising number of Black people imprisoned in the United States, social media commentary, memes, and news articles suggested that Huffman deserved a harsher sentence (Orsini & Mussel, 2019). This argument belies abolitionist efforts and shows how the work of radical advocacy groups is susceptible to the mainstream "law and order" agenda (Chartrand & Kilty, 2017; Sudbury, 2016).

The more we view acts of victimization as individual events, the more detached they become from the larger structural problems of racism, patriarchy, misogyny, sexism, homophobia, transphobia, and/or classism that inevitably shape them. As Spalek (2006) contends, individualizing victimhood "serves to disempower victims since they are encouraged to think about themselves as individuals with needs that are linked to criminal justice process, which then becomes part of their process of feeling" (p. 13). The victims' rights and carceral feminist movements represent one arm of the socio-political and cultural systems that individualize victimhood and their efforts work on our affects, feelings, and emotions in ways that constitute divisive distinctions between victim and offender and ideal and non-ideal victims and offenders. As such, we maintain that the affective labor engaged in by carceral feminists (re)establishes punishment and its associated "masculinist institutions of big business, the state, [...] the police," and law as "allies and saviors" (Bernstein, 2012). It is with this critique in mind that we turn more closely to the legacy of Carol Smart, who warned feminists long ago about turning to law to fight GBV and whose work parallels penal abolitionist calls for dismantling masculinist institutions.

Carol Smart's feminist legacy and the pursuit of a more complex affective orientation

Carol Smart is one of the most important foremothers of contemporary feminist criminology, yet penal abolitionist scholars have consistently failed to mobilize her work. This is likely due to the fact that Smart focuses her analytic attention on the power of law, rather than the penal system.[4] However, just as penal abolitionist scholars question the continued positioning of "crime" and "the offender" as criminology's primary objects of inquiry (Brown & Schept, 2017; Coyle, 2018; Coyle & Schept, 2017, 2018; Mathiesen, 1974), Smart posited that we need to question what criminology has to offer feminism rather than the typical query of what feminism can offer criminology. Similarly, her call to look outside law for remedies to social problems parallels the abolitionist goal of dismantling racist and misogynist social institutions. In contradistinction to the carceral feminist turn that belies the abolitionist ethos of building community and rejecting carcerality, Smart's pioneering work problematizes turning to law and the criminal justice system for gender and racial justice.

Smart describes law as a gendering practice because "law does not stand outside gender relations and adjudicate upon them. Law is part of these relations, and is always already gendered in its principles and practices" (Smart, 1995, p. 43). In that sense, law is "an important signifier of masculine power" that "disqualifies women's experience/knowledge" (Smart, 1989, p. 2; 1995). Smart (1989) also problematizes the notion that we can achieve an effective form of feminist jurisprudence, which she claims is at risk of "a double trap—that of the 'androcentric standard' and that of continuing to fetishize law" (p. 68). Since legal and criminal justice reform requires accepting and working within law's terms of reference, Smart (1989, 1995) contends that we must work outside law so as not to be subject to law's power to determine truth. Given that women's claims of GBV have historically been denied, disregarded or dismissed, evidenced by the low rates of conviction in the small number of sexual assault cases that actually make it to trial (Johnson, 2012), Smart (1989, 1995) advocates seeking non-legal strategies to address social problems. Feminist legal victories, including rape shield laws, the battered woman's syndrome legal defense, specialized domestic violence courts, and mandatory arrest policies, do not challenge the "fundamental problem of phallocentrism which disqualifies women's experience of sexual abuse" (Smart, 1989, p. 49).

With respect to GBV, Smart (1989, 1995) contends that "technological developments have refracted law's power by making different elements and functions of the body 'subject to legal regulation'" (1995, p. 97). Given that both law and carceral logic work to regulate women's bodies and reproduce them as signifiers of madness and badness via criminalization and medicalization (Carlton, 2018; Carlton & Russell, 2018; Chartrand & Kilty, 2017; Ricordeau, 2019), they position women's bodies as "a point of entry for social values and norms" (Smart, 1989, p. 113) that are historically and culturally situated. In this way, law (and by extension the penal system) is not easily cast as a "tool of liberation or of oppression"; instead, it is "a kind of institutionalized and formalized site of power struggles" (Smart, 1989, p. 138). Just as abolitionists warn us to think outside of carceral logics (Chartrand & Kilty, 2017; Coyle, 2018; Coyle & Schept, 2017, 2018; Ricordeau, 2019), Smart (1989) cautions that law's power restricts us to using its language, methods and procedures, which reinforces law's significance. She argues that there is a juridogenic effect to using law in that it purports to give remedy to, but instead creates further forms of harm, such as how rights-based claims have led to technologies of knowledge production that disregard and/or disqualify alternative and subjugated knowledges (Smart, 1989). This point is evidenced by the professionalization of criminal justice services, including those for victims of GBV (Richie, 2012; Spalek, 2006), and the growth of retributive punishment strategies that have increased rates of incarceration and created "more repressive conditions for women" and men (Heiner & Tyson, 2017, p. 4). As Richie (2012) maintains, if our goal shifts away "from structural transformation to accessing resources, establishing bureaucracy, or policy reform, the potential for lasting change is threatened" (p. 76). This leads us to our final point—that feminist criminologists need to adopt a penal abolitionist (dis)epistemology and ethic (Ben-Moshe, 2018) in order to prevent and pursue justice for GBV.

Abolitionist lessons for and from the feminist killjoy

Abolitionist work requires an intersectional approach that resists engaging in criminal justice reform that reinforces existing structures and appropriates feminist and anti-oppression language (Chartrand & Kilty, 2017; Ricordeau, 2019). Feminists need to recenter the key abolitionist principles of dismantling oppressive social institutions, changing our responses to criminalized harms, and building community capacity. For some feminists, however, it can be especially difficult to understand carceral responses to GBV as largely inappropriate and as failing to counter the material conditions that underlie criminality, including toxic masculinity, rape culture, housing injustice, lack of affordable education, and lack of access to affordable health and mental health care (among others) that are continually (re)produced by the structuring forces of patriarchy, misogyny, racism, colonization, and capitalist class arrangements (Coyle & Schept, 2017, 2018; Davis, 2003; Kim, 2018; Pelot-Hobbes, 2018; Richie, 2012).

Ben-Moshe (2018) positions abolition as a dis-epistemology and ethical demand for a non-carceral future and refers to de Haan's description of penal abolitionism's three domains, namely that it is: "a social movement aimed at abolishing current punitive penal structures; a theoretical perspective reconceptualizing oppression within carceral and criminal (in)justice spaces and their resistance; and a strategy that promotes the creation of a more equitable, safe and just society" (p. 341). She also contends that this is the work of the feminist killjoy, Sara Ahmed's (2010) term for feminists (and by extension abolitionists) as "affect aliens" who destabilize and destroy cultural practices, views, and language that others perceive as leading to happiness. Given our socio-political, cultural, and deeply affective investments in punishment (Dilts, this volume), emotions can lead us to focus on the individual harms produced by singular cases and events to the exclusion of considering the socio-structural conditions that are at the root of criminal harms, which can seem too big for any one person, group, or even movement to attend to. As Dilts (this volume) contends, culturally we "receive identifiable material, psychic, and symbolic benefits and privileges from mass incarceration and its direct relation to heteropatriarchal white supremacy," which he refers to as "carceral enjoyments." His point is that we experience a sense of enjoyment from punishing wrongdoers in an environment where incarceration creates social death. In this sense, our social life is inextricably tied to, even parasitic upon, the social death of others. It is the work of the feminist killjoy to dispel her sisters of the notion that legal and carceral reforms and further investments in punishment will lead to happiness and recovery from the trauma of victimization—just as Carol Smart called for us to do over 30 years ago. Unfortunately, it is difficult to inspire an affective reorientation that supports penal abolition when we derive pleasure and closure from punishment (Bandes, 2020; Carvalho & Chamberlen, 2018; Dilts, this volume; Sontag, 2003).

Rather than relying on the penal system to create a safe society, we must imagine a world without human cages, a society that does not rely on a monolithic institutional response to harms and victimization, and communities that experience a more equitable distribution of wealth and resources and that participate in the governance of and response to social and criminal harms. To create this social landscape, we must abandon carceral logics as our preeminent method of interpreting and responding to these harms, and remember that "abolition is not just an agenda for demolishing but also for building" (Ben-Moshe, 2018, 353; Coyle, 2018; Davis, 2003; Mathiesen, 1974; Ricordeau, 2019). We conclude by suggesting a multipronged approach for doing this "building work," which begins by creating a transformative agenda and entails an educational strategy, alternatives to criminalization and punishment, and strategies for strengthening community-based welfare and social supports.

A transformative agenda requires a logic rooted in Mathiesen's (1974) notion of the unfinished and the ongoing struggle to improve, revise, and move toward a decolonial, anti-racist and anti-oppressive society—an abolition democracy (Davis and Mendieta, 2005). Where reformist strategies further entrench carceral logic and practice, abolitionist strategies must remain in flux to avoid cooptation—a true social movement grounded in "trial and error, and in understanding disorientation as generative" that requires we "abandon our attachment to knowing and especially to knowing all(s)" (Ben-Moshe, 2018, p. 348). The unfinished, therefore, not only signals rejecting carceral logics, it "involves complex affect" that is likely "infused with fear and anxiety in the face of the unknown" (Heiner & Tyson, 2017, p. 22). This requires moving toward an affective orientation that prioritizes life-affirming interventions, and thus a radical compassion that challenges the "enforce[ment of] normative projects of orderliness or truth" and that makes us uncomfortable enough to orientate our "humanizing emotions" towards both victims and perpetrators of harm (Berlant, 2004, p. 5). Radical compassion acknowledges that "it is hurt people who hurt other people. Understanding that harm originates from situations dominated by stress, scarcity, and oppression, [therefore] one way to prevent violence is to make sure that people have support to get the things they need" (Hayes & Kaba, 2018, n.p.). For this to occur, we require widespread social and cultural education. While resistance and protest can have a powerful educative component (Carlton, 2018, p. 301), we should also endeavor to improve our public education systems so that they address systemic social oppressions like structural racism, colonization, patriarchy, misogyny, and consent in sexual encounters, which can be a difficult political proposal to garner support for.[5] Abolition requires that we let go of our "attachments to forms of knowledge that rely on certainty" (Ben-Moshe, 2018, p. 247), which is a particularly stressful and anxiety-provoking approach—especially when it comes to sexual education and accepting alternatives to criminalization and punishment for GBV.

Notably, these alternatives do not have to be new ideas—we have many of them in place already—and they should be mobilized in conjunction with a moratorium on the construction of any new prison spaces (Davis, 2003; Mathiesen, 1974; Ricordeau, 2019). Eliminating mandatory arrest policies[6] and mandatory minimum sentences, scaling up community accountability and thus involvement in governance and oversight, decriminalization and regulation of sex work and drugs so as to prioritize harm reduction are but a few possibilities. The goal here is to forego "the desire to discover one single alternative system of punishment that would occupy the same footprint as the prison system" (Davis, 2003, p. 108). For example, Taylor (2018) cites two U.S. organizations, Communities Against Rape and Abuse (CARA) and GenerationFIVE, that are transformative in that they are victim-centered and aim to "hold perpetrators of violence accountable without pathologizing them or ostracizing them in the counterproductive ways that characterize the criminal punishment system" (p. 42).

At first glance, an abolitionist framework might not appear concrete enough, but work that questions the structural relationships and networks of power between intimate violence, police violence, and the violence of incarceration can disrupt carceral logics and develop community accountability (CA) and involvement. Heiner and Tyson (2017) contend that the "affective experience of CA as a decolonial praxis can be so profound" that it can lead to "a kind of existential death, risking parts of the self/selves that are the product of oppressive systems, but to which an individual or community has become attached" (p. 23). This kind of affective reorientation is required in order to generate community involvement in a transformative agenda. To conclude, we suggest that feminists and their allies wear their identity as a feminist killjoy proudly and reveal the fantasy that carceral logics adequately nurture our emotional state and keep us safe. Redirecting emotions that underpin calls for carceral punishment toward an abolitionist ethos can be liberating and mobilizing for social justice praxis (Gould, 2009). To quote Carol Smart (1995): "Law is never a stable ally, indeed it is hardly an ally at all. If feminism identifies harms in the domain of sexuality I suggest that we should recognize that law is more a part of the problem (in the way that it genders, sexes and sexualizes the female and male body) than part of the solution" (p. 52).

Notes

1 We focus our argument on the part of the victims' rights movement that is aligned with the conservative law and order agenda that relies on carceral responses to law-breaking (Fattah, 1989/1992). These groups are distinct from the "unofficial victims' movement" that privileges alternatives to confinement like restorative justice and "whose activities are aimed at achieving common political and social goals" (Spalek, 2006, p. 5).

2 We use the more commonly accepted term carceral feminism throughout this chapter.

3 For example, rape crisis centres funded by the U.S. Department of Justice's Law Enforcement Assistance Administration encourage victims to report sexual assault to the police and in some cases refuse service to those who fail to do so (Gottschalk, 2006; Taylor, 2019).

4 Following Carrier & Piché (2015, n.p.) we use the term penal system rather than the prison industrial complex (PIC), which they argue does "not enact a problematization of incarceration and punishment *in toto.*"

5 For but one example, in 2018, the newly elected Conservative provincial government in Ontario, Canada, led by Premier Doug Ford, rolled back the updated sexual education curriculum that addressed diverse families, same sex relationships, gender identity and consent in sexual relationships to return it to the dated 1998 curriculum that did not address any of these issues (Alphonso, 2018).

6 Richie (2012) argues that because "there are differential impacts of arrest on marginalized communities, some women who experience male violence may not call upon the police if they know they can expect an enhanced response from law enforcement and the judicial system" (p. 83).

References

Ahmed, S. (2004). *The cultural politics of emotion*. Edinburgh University Press Ltd.

Ahmed, S. (2010). *The promise of happiness*. Duke University Press.

Alphonso, C. (2018) Ford government scraps controversial Ontario sex-ed curriculum. The Globe and Mail. Retrieved October 17, 2019 www.theglobeandmail. com/canada/article-doug-ford-government-scraps-controversial-ontario-sex-ed-curriculum/

Bandes, S. (2020). Closure in the criminal courtroom. In S. Bandes, J. Madeira, Temple and White (Eds.), *Research handbook on law and emotion* (pp.1–30). Edward Elgar Publishing.

Berlant, L. (2004). Introduction: Compassion and (withholding). In L. Berlant, (ed.) *Compassion: The culture and politics of an emotion* (pp. 1–13). Routledge.

Ben-Moshe, L. (2018). Dis-epistemologies of abolition. *Critical Criminology, 26,* 341–55. doi.10.1007/s10612-018-9403-1.

Bernstein, E. (2007). The sexual politics of the "new abolitionism". *A Journal of Feminist Cultural Studies, 18*(3), 128–51.

Bernstein, E. (2010). Militarized humanitarianism meets carceral feminism: The politics of sex, rights, and freedom in contemporary antitrafficking campaigns. *Signs, 36*(1), 45–71.

Bernstein, E. (2012). Carceral politics as gender justice? The "traffic in women" and neoliberal circuits of crime, sex, and rights. *Theoretical Sociology, 41,* 233–59.

Brown, M. & Schept, J. (2017). New abolition, criminology and a critical carceral studies. *Punishment & Society, 19*(4), 440–62. doi.10.1177/1462474516666281

Bumiller, K. (2008). *In an abusive state: How neoliberalism appropriated the feminist movement against sexual violence*. Duke University Press.

Carlton, B. (2018). Penal reform, anti-carceral feminist campaigns and the politics of change in women's prisons, Victoria, Australia. *Punishment & Society, 20*(3), 283–307. doi:10.1177/1462474516680205

Carlton, B. & Russell, E.K. (2018). Entrenching women's imprisonment: An anti-carceral critique of rights-based advocacy and reform. In E. Stanley (Ed.), *Human rights and incarceration* (pp. 181–205). Palgrave.

Carrier, N. & Piché, J. (2015). Blind spots of abolitionist thought in academia: On longstanding and emerging challenges. *Champ Pénal/Penal Field, XII.* Retrieved from http://journals.openedition.org/champpenal/9162.

Carrier, N. & Piché, J. (2019). On (In)justice: Undisciplined abolitionism in Canada. *Social Justice, 45*(4).

Carvalho, H., & Chamberlen, A. (2018). Why punishment pleases: Punitive feelings in a world of hostile solidarity. *Punishment & Society, 20*(2), 217–34.

CBC (2019, October 25). Felicity Huffman released early from prison over college admissions scandal. CBC. Retrieved from www.cbc.ca/news/entertainment/huffman-prison-early-release-1.5335452.

Chartrand, V. & Kilty, J.M. (2017). Corston principles in Canada: Creating the correctional woman and moving beyond the prison. In L. Moore, P. Scraton & A. Wahidin (Eds.), *Women's imprisonment and the case for abolition: Critical reflections on Corston ten years on* (pp. 109–28). Routledge.

Coyle, M. J. (2018). Transgression and standard theories: Contributions toward penal abolition. *Critical Criminology, 26,* 325–39. doi.10.1007/s10612-018-9404-0

Coyle, M. J. & Schept, J. (2017). Penal abolition and the state: colonial, racial and gender violence. *Contemporary Justice Review, 20*(4), 399–403. doi.10.1080/10282580.2017.1386065.

Coyle, M. J. & Schept, J. (2018). Penal abolition praxis. *Critical Criminology, 26*, 319–23. doi.10.1007/s10612-018-9407-x

Crenshaw, K. (1991). Mapping the margins: Intersectionality, identity politics, and violence against women of color. *Stanford Law Review, 43*(6), 1241–99.

Davis, A.Y. (2003). *Are prisons obsolete?* Seven Stories Press.

Davis, AY. & Mendieta, E. (2005). *Abolition democracy: Beyond empire, prisons, and torture.* Seven Stories Press.

Dilts, A. (2021). Carceral enjoyments & killjoying the social life of social death. [this volume, pp. –]

Fattah, E.A. (1989/1992). Victims and victimology: The facts and the rhetoric. In E.A. Fattah (Ed.), *Towards a critical victimology* (pp. 29–56). The Macmillan Press Ltd.

Gottschalk, M. (2006). *The prison and the gallows: The politics of mass incarceration.* Cambridge University Press.

Gottschalk, M. (2015). *Caught: The prison state and the lockdown of American politics.* Princeton University Press.

Gould, D.B. (2009). *Moving politics: Emotion and ACT UP's fight against AIDS.* The University of Chicago Press.

Halley, J. (2006). *Split decisions: How and why to take a break from feminism.* Princeton University Press.

Hayes, K. & Kaba, M. (2018). The sentencing of Larry Nassar was not 'transformative justice'. Here's why. The Appeal. https://theappeal.org/the-sentencing-of-larry-nassar-was-not-transformative-justice-here-s-why-a2ea323a6645/ Last accessed March 26, 2021.

Heiner, B.T. & Tyson, S.K. (2017). Feminism and the carceral state: Gender responsive justice, community accountability, and the epistemology of antiviolence. *Feminist Philosophy Quarterly, 3*(1), 1–37. doi.10.5206/fpq/2016.3.3

Hochschild, A.R. (1983/2012). *The managed heart: Commercialization of human feeling* (3rd ed.). University of California Press.

Ilea, A. (2018). What about 'the sex offenders'? Addressing sexual harm from an abolitionist perspective. *Critical Criminology, 26*, 357–72. doi.10.1007/s10612-018-9406-y.

Johnson, H. (2012). Limits of a criminal justice response: Trends in police and court processing of sexual assault. In E.A. Sheehy (Ed.), *Sexual assault in Canada: Law, legal practice, and women's activism* (pp. 631–33). University of Ottawa Press.

Kim, M.E. (2018). From carceral feminism to transformative justice: Women-of-color feminism and alternatives to incarceration. *Journal of Ethnic & Cultural Diversity in Social Work, 27*(3), 219–33.

Mathiesen, T. (1974). *The politics of abolition.* Wiley.

Nagel. M. (2015). Trafficking with abolitionism: An examination of anti-slavery discourses. *Champ Pénal/Penal Field, 12*, 1–17.

Orsini, M. & Mussel, L. (2019). Felicity Huffman: White is the colour of remorse. The Conversation. https://theconversation.com/felicity-huffman-white-is-the-colour-of-remorse-123647 Retrieved, November 29, 2019.

Pelot-Hobbes, L. (2018). Scaling up or scaling back? The pitfalls and possibilities of leveraging federal interventions for abolition. *Critical Criminology, 26*, 423–41. doi.10.1007/s10612-018-9401-3

Richie, B.E. (2012). *Arrested injustice: Black women, violence and America's prison nation.* New York University Press.

Ricordeau, G. (2019). *Pour elles toutes: Femmes contre la prison.* Lux Editeur.

Smart, C. (1989). *Feminism and the power of law.* Routledge.

Smart, C. (1992). Disruptive bodies and unruly sex: The regulation of reproduction and sexuality in the nineteenth century. In C. Smart (Ed.), *Regulating womanhood* (pp. 7–32). Routledge.

Smart, C. (1995). *Law, crime and sexuality.* Sage Publications.

Sontag, S. (2003). *Regarding the pain of others.* Picador/Farrar, Straus & Giroux.

Spalek, B. (2006). *Crime victims: Theory, policy and practice,* Palgrave MacMillan.

Sudbury, J. (2016). Rethinking antiviolence strategies: Lessons from the Black Women's Movement in Britain. In INCITE! Women of Color Against Violence (Eds.), *Color of violence: The INCITE! anthology* (pp. 13–24). Duke University Press.

Taylor, C. (2018). Anti-carceral feminism and sexual assault—A defense. *Social Philosophy Today, 34,* 29–49.

Walklate, S. (2016). The metamorphosis of the victim of crime: From crime to culture and the implications for justice. *International Journal for Crime, Justice and Social Democracy, 5*(4), 4–16.

Whalley, E. & Hackett, C. (2017). Carceral feminisms: the abolitionist project and undoing dominant feminisms. *Contemporary Justice Review, 20*(4), 456–73. doi.10.1080/10282580.2017.1383762.

12 Carceral enjoyments and killjoying the social life of social death

Andrew Dilts

Introduction: "No prison is safe for no one"

During the summer of 2012, CeCe McDonald, a transwoman of color, survived a racist and transphobic attack by a white supremacist in Minneapolis, MN. Like many survivors of such gendered violence, McDonald was criminalized and subsequently convicted of second-degree manslaughter for defending herself (Richie, 1996; Richie, 2012). And like nearly all incarcerated transwomen in the United States, she was sentenced to serve her imprisonment in a men's prison, despite her gender identification as a woman (Pearce, 2012). Her incarceration galvanized supporters both inside and outside prison who organized alongside McDonald, eventually securing her release in 2014, after she accepted a plea agreement. McDonald's experience of being violently attacked, of being criminalized by the state for defending her life, of fighting for her freedom, and her life since her release is also now the subject of a documentary film made by the filmmaker Jac Gares, *Free CeCe*. In that film, in press interviews, public lectures, her letters from prison, and in other writings, McDonald has become a powerful critic of the criminal punishment system in the United States, and in particular, how that system targets queer, trans★, trans-femme, and transwomen of color already subjected to state and interpersonal violence for merely appearing in public (McDonald, 2015, 2017).

While McDonald was incarcerated in Minneapolis, she was held for long durations in so-called "protective custody," ostensibly for her own safety from sexual assault by other incarcerated people. Protective custody is at best a euphemism for solitary confinement, and more precisely a form of punitive isolation and torture (Zurn, 2019). Speaking at a conference in 2014, she was asked how she felt about how her case has been used to spotlight the conditions of transwomen incarcerated in men's facilities. She answered:

> I know people kind of want to sensationalize the fact that I was a transwoman in a men's prison … I just want to say that all prisons are fucked up. It wouldn't matter if I went to a women's prison … you know, they're talking about building a new trans prison in California? It's like, no prison is safe for no one. You want to capitalize off of me through a fucked

up system? And I'm not having it. ... I would rather die than go to any prison. ... There is no way that you can convince me that being in a men's prison or being in a women's prison, or being in a trans prison, being in a fucking unicorn prison, I don't care. It's not beneficial to anyone. It's not beneficial me, it's not beneficial to you, it's not beneficial to our community. And that's where the truth lies. ... But think about all the other people who are in prison. ... Let's remind ourselves, there are still people in there who are struggling, and we have to be in solidarity with them.

(McDonald, 2014a)

McDonald's answer reflects the long, but often unacknowledged, tradition of radical queer, trans, and women of color critique of the state that has been a central part of liberation struggles since at least the late 1960s in the United States, in response to pervasive state and non-state violence against them (Hobson, 2016).[1] Quite simply, the critique holds that the modern state is a primary source of normalizing violence, that this is not a failure but rather its essence, and as such, the inclusion of "difference" into that system on its terms continues and maintains that violence. Elsewhere, I have argued that McDonald's analysis of her own experience and the overlapping carceral systems in which she is captured can be understood within the tradition of critical genealogy, and as an exemplary instance of what I term abolitionist genealogy. In giving a critical redescription of her own experiences of criminalization, incarceration, and survival, McDonald critically re-describes the dominant description of her own incarceration—disrupting violent understandings of terms such as "safety"—demonstrating the simultaneous subject and object positions she inhabits.[2]

In this essay, however, I return to McDonald's analysis to foreground its particular *affect* in responding to a question about how she experienced being "out of compliance" with the violent gender binary imposed on her by the state (Girshick, 2011).[3] I argue that both the *content* and *manner* of her response models an abolitionist response to what might be thought of as a contemporary articulation of W.E.B. Du Bois' 1901 formulation of the "ever unasked question": "How does it *feel* to be a problem?" (Du Bois, 1997) It is an intentionally and powerfully disruptive response not merely to the facts of incarceration, but to affective attachments held by those who continue to believe that incarceration can be reformed. In response, and in her wider commentary and writing, McDonald confronts the simultaneous material politics of incarceration in the United States and a part of its key affective scripts: *the powerful desire for prison reform*, especially in its most progressive forms, to address the suffering of incarcerated people without questioning the prison itself.

One of the (many) problems faced by prison abolitionists, police abolitionists, and anti-carceral theorists and activists is *enjoyment*. There is a persistent problem that putatively "innocent" members of society receive identifiable material, psychic, and symbolic benefits and privileges from mass incarceration and its direct relation to hetero-patriarchal white supremacy in the United States. They (read: "we" persons that are less subjected to confinement and state supervision) also *enjoy* these benefits and privileges. They/We enjoy specific material and affective enjoyments from the confinement, torture, exile, disenfranchisement, and generalized forms of social and civil death visited upon others throughout the carceral archipelago in the United States. Those committed to the abolition of such a system must confront such enjoyments, not because they are deserving of respect (they are not), but because they represent a serious obstacle to abolitionist and decolonial projects.

McDonald's analysis is an identifiable *kind* of political-epistemological work that is a necessary (yet insufficient) part of the work of building the "abolition-democracy." The term, "abolition-democracy" comes from W.E.B. Du Bois, and it has been taken up subsequently by theorists such as Angela Davis, George Lipsitz, and the late Joel Olson as a project of world building, in which Black liberation would be positively assured beyond the "negative" freedom of 19th century emancipation (Davis, 2005; Du Bois, 1995; Lipsitz, 2004; Olson, 2004).[4] It is my claim that a part of this project requires the disruption of pleasures and enjoyments that depend on the continued functioning of the prison as a site of moral and political differentiation. And moreover, that such a disruption must also target the very *desire* to save, perfect, and protect the prison with reformist programs and well-intentioned progressive models of inclusion that continue to accept the premise that prison can be made safe for anyone.

Specifically, I trace a series of claims that together insist on the necessity of identifying, confronting, and disrupting what I will call "carceral enjoyments." Such enjoyments are produced as parasitic forms of social life, "purchased" through the racialized social death of others, effected in our contemporary moment by the practice of incarceration. If we want to disrupt the functioning of the white supremacist, hetero-patriarchal, and settler-colonial state formation in which we find ourselves, we need to be attendant to the specific pleasures or enjoyments of carcerality—the parasitic social life produced by the social death of confinement—and actively develop strategies to disrupt those pleasures and enjoyments. Recognizing both our material and affective attachments to such carceral enjoyments lets us cultivate and redistribute certain kinds of "bad feeling," and embrace certain ways of "killing joy." Becoming an abolitionist killjoy, I will argue, is a necessary (but insufficient) part of abolitionist projects and ought to be embraced rather than avoided. This means supporting killjoys, becoming killjoys ourselves, and above all, ceding the floor to those best situated and able to disrupt the flow of the "good feelings" of carcerality, *including the good feeling of "reform."*

To make this case I explicate three conceptual claims and offer a normative model of abolitionist practice.[5] First, as claimed by critical carceral studies scholars, I describe how incarceration in the U.S. is diagnosed as an institution of social death. Incarceration unites civil and social death through the ethno-racial prison as a site of social death-making, marking the U.S. social order as governed by white supremacy. As a result, these scholars argue that the paradigmatic socially dead figure is less "the slave" than "the prisoner." Second, by linking this model of social death in the U.S. to scholarship demonstrating how the defense of "property" itself is a function of building and maintaining whiteness as property (through its protection by the police), I show how the social death of incarceration is white supremacist in essence. Racial capitalism defines the United States and abolitionist projects must reflect this reality. Third, I argue that there is another "side" of social death: namely social life produced through social death, and in the U.S. one form of this is parasitic specifically on the social death of incarceration and confinement. This parasitic social life I will mark as "carceral enjoyments." A key part of how these "enjoyments of property" operate is through an epistemological block, or what philosophers of race and gender refer to as an epistemology of ignorance. Lastly, I identify one possible resource for frustrating the social life of social death: to disrupt carceral enjoyments and frustrate the flows of affective pleasures which are attached to them through a political epistemological project of supporting and becoming "killjoys." Borrowing form Sara Ahmed's figure of the feminist killjoy, I re-read McDonald (and her answer to the question of how it feels to be a problem) as a powerful abolitionist killjoy, and think toward what a practice of abolitionist kill-joying might look like as part of a broader project of building abolition-democracy.

From civil to social death/from slavery to incarceration

As Orlando Patterson describes it, slavery is the paradigmatic form of social death: the internal exclusion of persons from sociality through natal alienation (Patterson, 1982). This is a stripping of not simply one's legal rights but also the destruction of inter-generational social relations that would otherwise be grounded by birth and an understanding of *kinship* that produces a lineage itself across time. To be a slave, Patterson writes, was to be "truly a genealogical isolate" and be removed not simply from society, but from any meaningful relation to a social past or collective future (Patterson, 1982, p. 5).[6] As Perry Zurn describes it, social death is always "out of sync with physical death" and "may belong to whoever—or indeed whatever—lives and dies in a network of relation" (Zurn, 2020). Social death is, therefore, an abjected position *within* social relations and which is co-constitutive of those relations as domination.[7]

But to diagnose the practice of *incarceration*—i.e. the forced confinement and isolation of stigmatized persons from their existing kinship and social relations—as producing *social* death requires an expansion or reworking of Patterson's analysis. Specifically, it moves beyond the more common legalistic framework typically employed in critical prison studies of what Colin Dayan calls the "legal fiction" of "civil" or "civic" death (Dayan, 2005).[8] The framework of civil death has long been used as a framework to describe the stripping of *political* rights as part of state-based punishment. This legal fiction occurs *directly* as a fact of incarceration in that political rights—such as those of assembly, speech, public appearance—are immediately disrupted by forced confinement. And it occurs indirectly, marking so-called "collateral consequences" of conviction and incarceration. In the United States the paradigmatic form of civic death is the stripping of definitive "democratic" rights of self-governance such as suffrage, jury service, and eligibility to hold public office (Chin, 2012; Dilts, 2014; Ewald, 2002, 2012; Grady, 2012; Holloway, 2014; Karlan, 2004; Manza et al., 2004). These exclusions presume, of course, that the civically dead person was already a full member of civil society.

What has emerged in the critical scholarship on incarceration and collateral consequences, however, are repeated arguments linking *civic* death in relation to Patterson's theory of *social* death, tying the legal fiction of civic death to the natal alienation of social death. Roughly, we can see separate these arguments into two broad camps. The first camp takes the two forms of death (civic and social) to be conceptually distinct but related in some specific way, while the second camp insists that any conceptual distinction between them has been collapsed through specific legal transformation. At stake here is (1) the relationship between law and natal alienation (i.e. are the legal processes of rights restrictions thought to be distinct from social processes of natal alienation?), and (2) the role that race plays in these accounts (i.e. at what level of social process is race formed and maintained in relation to the law?).

Within the first camp, civil and social death are connected through the practice of incarceration in a variety of forms. Three kinds of connections stand out: as analogical, as counterparts, and as symptom. For paradigmatic examples of each, we can briefly look at three accounts produced by critical prison scholars in the last 20 years. First, Loïc Wacquant argues that incarceration produces *civic* death analogously to slavery's production of *social* death: "Just as bondage effected the 'social death' of imported African captives and their descendants on American soil *mass incarceration also induces the civic death* of those it ensnares by extruding them from the social compact" (Wacquant, 2001, p. 119) For Wacquant, the formation of a series of "peculiar" institutions operates as a structural homology for the management of labor extraction and political rule. As such, a "redundant population" is produced and then socially isolated from the formal economy, managed through a series of successive institutions: chattel slavery, Jim Crow, the ghetto, and now, the prison/hyper-ghetto.

Second, Caleb Smith argues that the civic death of the prisoner is the "counterpart" to the social death of the slave, and the two function *together* in the antebellum south as "intrusive" (bringing the slave *in*) and "extrusive" (forcing the convict *out*) representations of social death, thus modifying Patterson's own account of the two ways in social death could be represented (as intrusive and extrusive) (Smith, 2009, p. 44).[9] Third, Joshua Price argues that whereas civil death is restricted to the legal realm, social death "goes beyond" civil death and "includes the suspension of those [legal] rights" (Price, 2015, p. 19). Civil death is, according to Price's extensive interview-based study of prison and jail conditions in the United States, a symptom of social death.

As each of these approaches implies but does not always state expressly, the peculiar connection between civil and social death, however, cannot be read in isolation from the legal history of chattel slavery and its "abolition" in the mid-19th century. Each approach notes deep connections between the legal fiction of civil death and social death, yet at the same time these approaches all insist that the two categories remain conceptually distinct, if nevertheless related. If we *foreground* the historical, material, and legal connection, as Joy James argues, then any conceptual distinction in the postbellum United States between social and civic death becomes untenable (James, 2005). The express authorization of involuntary servitude as punishment for a crime in the 13th Amendment to the U.S. Constitution draws civic and social death together through the ongoing connection between abjected blackness and criminality, even as it operates under a mask of racial neutrality under the law. In contrast to the aforementioned relationships (as analogical, as counter-parts, or as symptom), James' reading emphasizes the relationship between civil and social death as a *transformation* through which racialized bodies are targeted by colorblind social policy through racialized enforcement and exploitation.

A weak form of this argument drives what has become the popular center-left understanding of the Prison Industrial Complex as a reconfiguration of slavery under a new form (or as a "new Jim Crow"). But James' reading of the transformation effected by the 13th Amendment is stronger: this loophole does not merely *allow* for racially discriminatory practice to continue under different terms, but rather, that the social death of slavery is written into the civil death of incarceration, *transforming social death into a permanent legal category* and signifying both criminality and blackness as inseparable. James writes:

> Congress resurrected social death as a permanent legal category in U.S. life, yet no longer registered the socially dead with the traditional racial markings. Breaking with a two-hundred-year-old tradition, the government ostensibly permitted the enslavement of nonblacks. Now not the ontological status of "n*****" [redacted] but the ontological status of "criminal" renders one a slave. Yet, as became apparent in the convict prison lease system, blackness remained the signifier of social death, although now all those relegated to prisons would be imbued with that pariah race status.
> (James, 2005, pp. xxviii–xxix)

At this point in history, the prison thus reflects both (1) existing ethno–racial divisions, and (2) also (re)produces ethno–racial distinctions under the sign of "criminal justice," produced through an ontological and semiotic exchange produced by the exception in the 13th Amendment.[10] As Brady Heiner argues, the prison produces social death as the "postbellum sedimentation of the institution of slavery" (Heiner, 2007, p. 219), through the "semiotic transfer of social death across contexts from the postbellum period to the present practices of mass incarceration, which predominantly and disproportionately target black and other people of color" (Heiner, 2015, p. 38).[11]

These stronger readings of the relationship between civic and social death are helpful because they reflect *how* racial categories themselves were made and re-made through natal alienation in the U.S., pushing past models that rely on relatively static understandings of civil and legal processes as "applied" to persons rather than as "making" persons. That is, one of the things which distinguishes the second set of approaches is how their accounts follow a conception of race and race-making that acknowledges how race is a social *and* legal construction: various markers of difference are given political and social meaning and then used to justify and create differential outcomes along those markers of difference. The "fiction" of race does not make it unreal, but rather it is a fiction that is enforced through violence, especially in state-based forms of criminalization and incarceration.[12]

As such, incarceration is read by scholars as already an institution of racialized domination and always already an institution of *simultaneous* social and civic death. Moreover, by taking up this view on the production of social death—overlapping and coincident with civic death through the re-inscription of natal alienation onto the "post" slavery category of "the criminal"—this approach opens a more specific account of social death in the United States than Patterson provides, and lets us trace the interconnected conceptual, historical, and practical links between the legal production of racialized difference, practices of state punishment, and democratic legitimacy with the production of social death. As Lisa Cacho puts it in her study of the criminalization of migrant populations in the United States, social death marks being, "*ineligible for personhood*—as populations subjected to laws but refused the legal means to contest those laws as well as denied both the political legitimacy and moral credibility necessary to question them" (Cacho, 2012, p. 6; original emphasis). Such an approach helps us to identify the forms of social and legal "life" which the racialized social death of incarceration produces. This is a more flexible and capacious understanding of social death, and more able to address instances of social death outside of Patterson's original object of study (and hopefully in a way that is more materially based on the experiences of incarcerated persons).

The whiteness of police/the whiteness of property

I want to make a stronger and more specific claim: under the specific legal structure produced in the postbellum United States, social death becomes intimately tied to the production of *whiteness* as property (following Cheryl Harris), to the political system of *white supremacy* (following Charles Mills), and to the enforcement of law as the enforcement of ethno-racial distinctions (following Nikhil Singh) (Harris, 1993; Mills, 1997; Singh, 2014). To try and render a person as socially and civically dead in the United States is to try and strip them of (or bar them from) the property of *whiteness*.[13] A key root of *political authority* itself in this context derives its legitimacy from a Lockean conception of property as an extension of self-ownership.[14] But such self-ownership, as Carole Pateman has demonstrated, was already restricted to male-masculine persons in theory as well as practice, and as Charles Mills has likewise shown, partially productive of Whiteness itself (Pateman, 1988). As Ashon Crawley puts it, "Whiteness is a capacity for possession as the grounds for identity, and we learn from indigenous and settler colonial studies that the settler state stakes its claim on the acceptance of violence, the claim of property that produces a displacement from land, a violent encounter with people" (Crawley, 2017, p. 6). The settler state's legitimacy is contingent on its ability to deploy *punitive* power for the protection of such property. To defend property with the force of law (i.e. punishment) is to defend it against property-less "thieves," "savages," and "idiots" who do not abide "reason." The differential work of identifying non-propertied others is, in Lockean terms, already a process of criminalizing and policing non-white persons on gendered, ablest, and patriarchal terms (Cacho, 2012, pp. 24–25; Clifford, 2014; Dilts, 2012b; Pateman, 1988).

State racism ought to be understood therefore, not simply as discriminatory conduct, mere exclusion from the polity, or an affective grounds of dislike or abjection, but rather what Cacho calls, "a killing abstraction" that prescribes specific actions and corresponding affective scripts (Cacho, 2012, p. 7).[15] The defense of property, with the force of biological and social death under such terms, becomes a defense of whiteness itself (or at the very least an attempt to *become* white or *appeal* to whiteness' authority). This is the heart of what it means to assume deputization to enforce and to protect such property: to become the *police*.[16] To be deputized into such a system (by choice or assumption) is to align with whiteness and claim protection *as* white. As Frank Wilderson puts it: "Whiteness, then, and by extension civil society ... must first be understood as a social formation of contemporaries who do not magnetize bullets ... In short, white people are not simply 'protected' by the police, they are—*in their very corporeality*—the police" (Wilderson, 2003, p. 20; original emphasis).

Nikhil Singh offers a sustained reading of this linkage (between whiteness and police), arguing that in the United States:

> Police action ... developed along the continuum of racial management that moved from biopolitical inclusion (an ever-graduating whiteness) to necropolitical destruction of entire communities (genocide). It is important here to understand the production of whiteness as an active and ongoing social process—one built on a prior history of racial differentiation, but one that also worked by generating new distinctions.
>
> (Singh, 2014, p. 1093)

For Singh, the specific historical trajectory out of which U.S. police forces developed out of slave patrols and citizen militia is simultaneously a project of the redistribution of violence from the public to the state as well as an epistemological project of repressing the history of settler-colonial white violence (Singh, 2014, p. 1093). Singh extends key claims of critical race theory (again drawing on the work of Harris and Mills) to read whiteness as a property relation that is integral to the formation and maintenance of white supremacy as a political system which differentially assigns rights and privileges both according to a color-line which is always also a project of reproducing (and redrawing) that color-line. Centrally, the (re)production of racial difference in and through *private* property relations (and the accumulation and circulation of capital predicated on the alienation of labor) lets us recognize this as a part of what Cedric Robinson terms, "racial capitalism" (Kelley, 2017; Melamed, 2015; C.J. Robinson, 2000).[17] As Robinson explains, there is both a longer history of the political technology of race shaping capitalism, and also a deeper connection between race and class than typically acknowledged by scholars (especially Marxists in the United States). The Black radical tradition, Robinson shows, offers a powerful corrective to this mistake. Attending to the particular ways that the state enforces property law—in and through punitive systems that are raced and gendered—sheds light on *how* this works in the United States historically.[18]

As Singh explains, the production of a racial binary, and the political assignment of persons to political positions within that binary, is itself the work of the Anglo-American racial capitalism project:

> Neither blackness nor whiteness is ... strictly reducible to specific white people or black people. Rather, whiteness and blackness as well as other modern racial forms emerge as subject positions, habits of perception, and modes of embodiment that develop from the ongoing risk management of settler and slave capitalism, and more generally racial capitalism (i.e., capitalism). ... [A] sharply dualist conception of blackness and whiteness accrues special force within the Anglo-American variant of capitalism that attains global reach in the nineteenth and twentieth centuries.
>
> (Singh, 2014, p. 1096)

There are two key moves here: first Singh argues that whiteness functions as a system that is deeply intertwined with specific practices of governance (risk management, settler colonialism, state/slave capitalism, etc.). This is a more general claim, and one which could be used as an analytic device to think about various manifestations of "whiteness" in different historical and geographical contexts. Second, Singh argues that this *particular* manifestation as *the* system of racial domination in the Anglo-American context takes its specific form as blackness and whiteness (where the political structure of authority maps to existing markers of difference to define those subject positions in concrete ways, e.g. de facto and de jure segregation, practices of chattel slavery and the rise of state-organized police forces in the post bellum period in the U.S.). Singh's analysis demonstrates how there is an inseparable genealogical and conceptual connection between whiteness and policing itself that, as suggested by Wilderson, cannot be undone merely through the inclusion of otherwise "non-white" persons into police forces or offices of the state under racial capitalism.

This stronger reading acknowledges that whiteness is at the core of the liberal rule-of-law tradition in the United States. Moreover this reading indicates that social and civil death have become co-constitutive with social order and civil society more generally, and are enacted through the violence of policing and natal alienation of punitive confinement.[19] As Dylan Rodríguez argues, the "well-functioning white-multicultural civil society" functions *through* the prison as a "focused site of massive black/brown disappearance and disintegration" (Rodríguez, 2004, pp. 201–2). That is, the hegemonic form of civil society functions *not in spite of* racialized social death, but *through it.* The ethnoracial prison has become part-and-parcel with liberal and progressive visions of multicultural civil society in a foundational way.[20] This means that proposals which appeal to such visions of liberal and multicultural society (or which refer to some idyllic period before "mass incarceration" took hold) do so as ways to ultimately avoid addressing the underlying connections between the social death of incarceration itself and the production of that meaning.

These linkages—of whiteness to property to civil society to the force of law and to the production of racialized social death—are an historical and material contingency: a *political* ontology. That which "is" should be understood as "has become" (Beauvoir, 2011, p. 12). And in contrast to Patterson's general accounting of social death, which is not tied in such specific ways, social death *in the Anglo-American* context is such that anti-Black racism, patriarchal authority, and settler-colonial genocide are rightly a part of the tradition of "American" liberalism and not merely an aberration to it. This is what should allow us to understand the ease with which "blackness" and "criminality" could be so easily linked throughout U.S. history, because *criminality* has been deployable as a "stable" marker of social, political, and moral difference that could in turn shore up encroachments against white supremacy (Dilts, 2012a; Holloway, 2014; Muhammad, 2010; Murakawa, 2014).

Just as the antebellum United States was a *slave society,* multicultural civil society in the United States today *has become a prison society,* and U.S. democracy functions as a "penal democracy" (James, 2005, p. xxi) or a "prison nation" (Richie, 2012). This social and political order functions under white supremacy as a political system that relies on the policing of property relations, articulated through its criminal punishment system even if this functioning is masked by the rhetoric of liberal inclusion and color-blind "justice." This implies that most prison "reform" agendas—those that seek to address only the most egregious practices of the prison-industrial-complex, those that focus only on the "innocent" or "non-violent" offenders, or those that aim at some "correct" level of incarceration—operate through the disavowal of the prison itself as an instrument of racialized social death (Gilmore, 2015; Wilderson, 2003). Thus, we can provisionally assert that contemporary forms of social death thus function *narrowly* through the practice of confinement itself, *broadly* through the criminalization of non-white persons, and *extensively* through the law itself and its models of legal change via "reform" (Petersen, 2020).

"The other side of social death"[21]/carceral enjoyments

To date, the single best critical-theoretical account of the social death effected by incarceration is Lisa Guenther's study of solitary confinement in the United States (Guenther, 2013). Guenther shows how extreme isolation and solitary confinement of persons destroys the conditions of inter-subjective relationality and, in turn, meaningful subjectivity. Isolation itself is generative of a "forced self-betrayal," properly described by those who have been forced to experience it, as the nightmare of *living death* (Guenther, 2013, p. 214). As such, for Guenther social death occurs with the confinement of corporal beings (including non-human animals). Such attention to the lived experience of social death is a vital contribution to our understanding, reminding readers that the nightmare of social death must never be reduced to a mere "theoretical abstraction" (Brown, 2009, p. 1233).[22]

Guenther, through giving the floor to people subjected to the violence of isolation and confinement in its extreme forms, shows how the boundary between life and death is marked by an aporia. As the incarcerated philosopher Spoon Jackson puts it, "Like Socrates, I was sentenced to death. Not at the height of my wisdom and awareness, but at the age of twenty. I was tried for the death penalty thirty-five years ago and given the other death penalty of life without parole. A slower death, more hideous, because I do suffer death, sometimes daily, and it is a living death" (Jackson, 2014).[23] Yet, this *living death* of solitary confinement is itself full of life: that is its punishment. And it is to Guenther's credit that her account of social death also carries with it an account of resistance. She maps specific ways that some individuals placed under these conditions do in fact *live* despite their torture. They are often able to stave off the complete destruction of self that is typical of solitary confinement. Social life, as a mode of resistance can thus become a counter-movement to social death, even in diminished forms as "coping mechanisms" (Guenther, 2013, pp. 214–20, 220). People held in solitary confinement create art and literature for themselves and others, they speak, and in their most powerful refusals of their condition—as seen in the widespread hunger-strikes throughout 2013 across California organized entirely by incarcerated people under the most restrictive of conditions—they engage in political action in arguably paradigmatically Arendtian terms (Guenther, 2015). There is an incredibly powerful social *life* of those positioned as socially *dead*.

But what Guenther does not explore at length, and which is largely (but not completely) absent in the critical literature linking incarceration to social death and natal alienation, is another side of the social life produced by social death. Namely, the ways that incarceration, criminalization, civic death, and broader practices of carcerally produced social death produce the social life, political membership, and the freedom of non-incarcerated and so-called "innocent" persons. In distinction from the resistant forms of social life enacted by incarcerated persons, this other production of social life is *parasitic*: purchased by those who are "free" through the suffering of the socially dead through specific material practices of de-humanization and de-animalization. Or, as Guenther does put it provocatively at one point, "The social death of prisoners sticks to the social life of those who have not ever set foot in a prison and could not possibly know what it is like" (Guenther, 2013, p. 255).

Guenther is not the first to note this production, of course. As Stephen Dillon puts it, drawing on Assata Shakur's account of her incarceration, "The spaces of the prison, ghetto, and home … collude with each other, composing an expansive grid of captivity that immobilizes and disposes of racialized and gendered populations. If Shakur's jail captures some, it also immunizes other bodies from such routine abjection and social death, thus securing capital, whiteness, and white life" (Dillon, 2018, p. 117). This logic of immunization rests on the idea that a body can be made stronger and healthier through the controlled presence of some acceptable level of a weakened pathogen. The life of the immunized body is strengthened naturally by the production of "anti-bodies" that are resilient to the pathogen. The "pathogen" remains *within* the body, but always in a controlled condition for the sake of producing immunity for the body. Seeing the jail and its practices of racialized and gendered capture, abjection, and social death shows how it becomes seen as *necessary* to the maintenance of the otherwise fragile bodies of capital, whiteness, and white life.

To acknowledge how social death "sticks" to social life in this way, attempting (yet possibly always already failing) to immunize some through the capture and domination of others, illustrates two important forms of social life: a resistant form (produced under the conditions of social death, reflecting the agency of the oppressed, the enslaved, and the captive) and a parasitic form (produced *by* social death, "purchased" at the expense of the socially dead).[24] As Patterson describes it, human parasitism is the attempt to *live off* another's social life through the killing abstraction of social death. This involves decidedly non-abstract practices of domination, alienation, and subordination, both violent and quotidian. A parasite's life thus becomes dependent on the host, but often in ways that are camouflaged, supporting the life of the parasite under that cover.[25] Such camouflage may account for the way, as Guenther notes, individuals live in a prison society, *even if they do not realize it,* living off of practices of solitary confinement and natal alienation: turning selves against selves.

If this is the case—that the prison itself functions today as an instrument of social death that parasitically produces social life under the terms of white supremacy—then this forces us to ask new questions: what does it mean to be attached to forms of social life produced by practices of social death? What does it mean to be attached to the enjoyment of such a life? What does it mean to be unable to confront such enjoyments because they not only are difficult to know, but to acknowledge them would implicate the enjoyment of one's own life in the reproduction of social death and maintenance of suffering? What if the problem we face is not simply that social death is produced and maintained through incarceration, but also that *enjoyable forms of freedom and social life* are produced which are dependent on the social and civic death of others.[26]

The social life produced by social death is an instance of what Saidiya Hartman calls a, "property of enjoyment" (Hartman, 1997; Hartman & Wilderson, 2003). Suffering, Hartman argues, is "enjoyed" both consciously and unconsciously by people in positions of authority and privilege. They build deep investments in the social world that is produced by that suffering and which cannot simply be abolished without disrupting those forms of privilege directly. Privileges cannot be merely redistributed or formerly subordinated persons included into authority to undue these investments. Rather, as her analysis of chattel slavery in the 19th century shows, the legal status of the slave as a thing, as a property, indelibly links the "use" of that property to its "enjoyment." The fungibility of the slave as an interchangeable commodity was the basis of the "joy" experienced by the master's ability to project their "feelings, ideas, desires, and values" onto the body of another (Hartman, 1997, p. 21). This enjoyment—this joy in "use"—is both affective (it provides concrete instances of pleasurable "enjoyment" through the bodily suffering of the slave) and conceptual (in that the meanings of very terms of the civil society are formed in and through the abjection of the slave). "The slave," Hartman states, "is the object or the ground that makes possible the existence of the bourgeois subject and, by negation or contradistinction, defines liberty, citizenship, and the enclosures of the social body" (Hartman, 1997, p. 62). As such, to abolish slavery it is also necessary abolish these specific enjoyments: white liberty, white citizenship, and the white social body.

But if it is through the enjoyment (or restriction) of these conceptual properties that the contemporary prison functions, we then ought to extend Hartman's analysis of the economy of pleasure in the enjoyment of property under a slave society to enjoyment of social life in a prison society. This is the connection between the descriptive analysis given above with the interpretive claim offered here. Specifically, the social death effected by the prison in the current moment has a three-fold connection back in time and space to its paradigmatic 18th and 19th century form: (1) genealogical (through the authorization of social death as punishment for crime in the 13th Amendment), (2) structural (in the homological relation between slavery and the prison), and (3) conceptual (in that the contemporary terms of liberal freedom, political membership, and individual autonomy are defined in contradistinction to the criminalized other).

In the contemporary period, the figures of the "prisoner," the "inmate," the "convict," or the "felon," have become relatively unthinkable as political *subjects*, and yet also knowable as *objects* to be "enjoyed," both indirectly and directly (from the perspective of the enjoying agent). Directly, for example, they are used and enjoyed as objects of cultural consumption (across the political spectrum from *Orange is the New Black* or *The Wire* to *COPS* or National Geographic's *Lockdown*) or academic consumption. But more perniciously they are enjoyed indirectly: used as fungible sources of labor (in industries as diverse as customer service, manufacturing, and fire-fighting), as bodies to boost census counts and therefore redistribute political power (through prison-based gerrymandering and felon disenfranchisement), or conceptually giving normative value and descriptive meaning to the categories of "free," "white," "male," or "citizen."

A "carceral enjoyment," following Hartman, is the use of "the prisoner," "the inmate," "the convict," or "the felon" as the ground through which "free" feelings, ideas, desires, and values are projected, and take shape. Perhaps it is the case that the enjoyment of the seemingly "free" person in a prison society is *directly* experienced through the watching of suffering itself. In this way, it might directly mirror what Hartman identifies as visceral pleasures experienced by the slave master when directing the *use* of their property. Yet even in the absence of such overt scenes, the social death of the prison itself and its attendant production of social life is dependent on, parasitic on, and fabricated by said deaths in both abstract and specific material forms of *unfreedom*. As Jared Sexton notes, "social death might be thought of as another name for slavery and an attempt to think about what it comprises, and social life, then, another name for freedom and an attempt to think about what it entails" (Sexton, 2011, p. 17). That is to say, in using the language of "enjoyments" it is possible to distinguish between the "pleasures" one might experience at the level of affect (such as the patriotic pleasure of voting even while also living under the conditions of felon disenfranchisement, or when one consumes media about the prison) which always functions on the level of "joy" or "jouissance," from the particular affective *attachment* produced by their enjoyment (their use), whether conscious or otherwise.

In the absence of overt scenes of subjection and domination, there remains the deeper epistemological problem: many carceral enjoyments appear as "unknown" to those who are not targeted directly by the criminal punishment system or to those who escape its grasp. Incarceration is often "out of sight" and "out of mind" for many people in the United States. This lack of "knowledge" is not simply a matter of convenience, but more properly operates through an epistemology of ignorance that structures this "not knowing" (Alcoff, 2007; Mills, 1997; Sullivan & Tuana, 2007) or alternately under the epistemological block of "constitutive exclusion," (Kramer, 2017) supporting a *polity* that is hetero-patriarchal, settler-colonial, and white supremacist but which operates under the "camouflage" of "criminal justice." As Paula Ioanide explains:

These epistemologies encourage everyone to know how to ignore knowledge, information, and testimonies about the histories of advantage and disadvantage predicated on racial, gender, sexual, national, citizenship, and religious classification. They produce the failure to see how the fates of different people are ultimately linked. The epistemologies of white ignorance produce the failure to experience any ethical upheaval about violence and discrimination—or worse, *the tendency to morally justify these acts.*
(Ioanide, 2015, p. 12, emphasis added)

We are, interestingly, at a moment in which *knowledge* of the criminal punishment system is more widespread than perhaps ever before, and in particular, that it is an instrument of white supremacy and violence. Beyond best-sellers that name mass incarceration as the "New Jim Crow," we have widely seen documentaries such as *13* and *The House I Live In*, professional athletes (including N.F.L. quarterbacks, U.S. Open Champions, and entire professional basketball teams in the W.N.B.A. and N.B.A.) speak openly about white supremacy and have engaged in wildcat strikes. And (most importantly) we continue to see the largest social movement and mass uprising in at least 50 years lead by queer youth of color, many of whom operate from an expressly police- and prison-abolitionist perspective. Yet at the same time, even with this increasing dissemination of "knowledge" about mass incarceration, it frequently operates by marking the *dysfunction and failure* of an otherwise "benign" practice of incarceration, focusing on the injustices within the criminal punishment system rather than the injustice of the criminal punishment system, focusing on police violence rather than the violence of policing, and often preempting the deeper analysis of incarceration's racialized and colonial history.[27] In this way, "reform" itself becomes a property of enjoyment, part of the social life of social death produced by the prison.[28] In addition to the narrow and broad productions of social life produced by the social death of confinement and criminalization of non-white persons, there is the extensive production of social life produced by the social death of settler-colonial law: reform. Reform can thus be seen as an attempt to ameliorate social death by keeping the host alive, so that the parasite continues to survive.

Abolitionist killjoys

To recap the argument so far as a series of hypotheticals: First, if it is the case that there is a connection between the social death of slavery and the social death of incarceration, then second, we ought to recognize that the social death of incarceration is fundamentally linked to the whiteness of policing (as part of the system of racial capitalism under which we live, and the (re)production of whiteness itself), and third, that wherever there is social death there is a constitutive parasitic social life produced to which we are affectively and epistemologically attached. As such, we arrive at this question: If the social life produced by the social death in the prison is a *property of enjoyment*, producing something like civic and social forms of carceral pleasures or enjoyments, then how can the affective attachments be disrupted such that a reconfiguration—a rebuilding—of the world is possible?

By extending Sara Ahmed's figuration of the "feminist killjoy," I argue that we might disrupt carceral enjoyments *and* our attachments to them by directly obstructing them, because this figuration and practice is focused on the affective and epistemological registers of such enjoyments. At a minimum, we must insist on the presence of incarcerated and formerly incarcerated persons at the "table" as a reconfiguration of social and civic life around those who resist social death. The production of social life attendant to this epistemological block can only be addressed by dramatically changing whose voices are heard, acknowledged, and centered in practices of collective freedom that are anti-carceral and abolitionist. Mere descriptive presence, however, is nevertheless insufficient as well, and an ongoing practice of refusal and critique remains necessary to abolitionist praxis. That is to say: We need more killjoys at the table, and we need to be willing to constantly up-end the table as we continue, shifting reformist attachments to abolitionist ones. This would be, to follow Crawley, to embrace Black social life: "Black social life has been the constant emergence of abolition as the grounding of its existence, the refusal of violence and violation as a way of life, as quotidian. Black social life … is an abolitionist politic, it is the ongoing 'no,' a black disbelief in the conditions under which we are told we must endure" (Crawley, 2017, p. 6).

Ahmed introduces the figure of the killjoy by narrating the experience of *becoming* a feminist. As she puts it in her 2010 article "Feminist killjoys (and other willful subjects)," becoming a feminist is also an experience of becoming "the problem" (Ahmed, 2010a).[29] It can be, she writes, "an alienation from happiness," by becoming out of alignment with those things one believes (or has come to believe) are "right things." This experience of unhappiness, however, is a productive force. Grounded in a phenomenology of feminist and anti-racist consciousness, Ahmed argues that becoming aware of this alienation from what one expects to make one's self happy is a resource for imagining other worlds, other ways of being. Reclaiming this particular form of unhappiness, this disconnection from expected desires, is to claim the identity of the killjoy: "the one who gets in the way of other people's happiness. Or just the one who is in the way—you can be in the way of *whatever*, if you are already perceived as being in the way" (Ahmed, 2010a). The killjoy contrasts with and disrupts the expected affective scripts imposed on persons by virtue of oppressive social and political orders.

The recognition that there *is* a gap between how one might feel and how one "ought" to feel, Ahmed insists, reveals that that another world is possible. As Ahmed puts it succinctly on her own website: "Killing joy is a World Making Project" (Ahmed, n.d.) This project begins for the killjoy by creating "bad feeling" for those around her both through simple presence and through actions (disruption, willfulness). Importantly, the killjoy appears as such not simply because of willfulness, but by appearing to be willful simply for drawing attention to conditions that are otherwise ignored, suppressed, or disavowed. It is *not* the case that the killjoy is the source of bad feeling, but rather the killjoy "creates" bad feeling by drawing attention to the already existing bad feeling for *some* at the table that is the condition of possibility for the *good* feeling experienced by others. That they (the killjoy) are blamed for the bad feeling is because they take up their already abjected position as a resource, redirecting it toward others. As Ahmed notes, those who point out racism or sexism are very familiar with this phenomenon: *they* are often accused of being racist or sexist in response. The work of the killjoy is about *knowledge* and *knowing* in that it "shows how the familiar is not revealed to those who can inhabit it. For queers and other others the familiar is revealed to you, because you do not inhabit it. To be 'estranged from' can be what enables a 'consciousness of.' This is why being a killjoy can be a knowledge project, a world-making project" (Ahmed, 2010a).

In this way—working and feeling in the gaps between affective attachments we are "supposed" to have and the bad feeling generated by questioning or rejecting those attachments—the world-making project of being (and becoming) a killjoy is to embrace the worldly (and "sweaty") work of conceptualization. Ahmed argues that feminist ideas are, "What we come up with to make sense of what persists" (Ahmed, 2017, p. 12). The ideas that are generated in this way are what she calls "sweaty concepts"—those that resist full abstraction from a particular material situation and refuse to be seen as something "outside" the world which they seek to describe. Sweaty concepts are those that are "worldly" and which are "also a reorientation to a world, a way of turning things around, a different slant on the same thing. ... one that comes out of a description of a body that is not at home in the world" (Ahmed, 2017, p. 13).

Because killjoys, as instances of what Ahmad calls "affect aliens," feel this conceptual separation through their affective distance from "good feelings," they are especially suited to disrupt epistemologies of ignorance. By working within the archives of subjugated knowledges and insisting upon their relevance, they can bridge what might otherwise be distinct academic and political projects. Importantly, because epistemologies of ignorance are forms of *willful* not knowing (rather than a traditional ignorance of facts), then the willfulness of the killjoy is an essential aspect of their force. "Willfulness could be rethought as style of politics," Ahmed writes, "*a refusal to look away from what has already been looked over.* The ones who point out that racism, sexism, and heterosexism are actual are charged with willfulness; they refuse to allow these realities to be passed over" (Ahmed, 2010a; original emphasis). Being a feminist, she argues, "involves political consciousness of what women are asked to give up for happiness" (Ahmed, 2010a). As Liat Ben-Moshe notes, this is the work of "dis-epistemology"—of "letting go of attachment to certain ways of knowing" (Ben-Moshe, 2020, p. 126).[30] By extension, being a prison abolitionist killjoy would involve raising the political consciousness of what people of color are *forced* to do for the production of white happiness, white freedom, and white citizenship, of marking the carceral enjoyments, and in particular, of marking their racial and sexual genealogies.

Beyond this specific epistemological disruption, bringing to light the parasitic forms of happiness produced through social death, the killjoy works to directly obstruct the happiness of the prevailing social and political order. As Ahmed puts it, the willfulness of the feminist killjoy is a "willing to cause its [the flow of happiness'] obstruction." What would it mean to "get in the way" of carceral mentalities, carceral practices, and carceral enjoyments? Ahmed provides us with material models: the purest form of willfulness, she notes, of such an obstruction, is the hunger strike: "a body whose agency is expressed by being reduced to obstruction, where the obstruction to others is self-obstruction, the obstruction of the passage into the body" (Ahmed, 2010a). The central imperative of the hunger strike is to disrupt the normal operations of the carceral system as such, by focusing on the most "normal" of operations for creaturely persons: the daily process of feeding large numbers of incarcerated persons.[31] Moreover, such theoretical resources have already been theorized and practiced by incarcerated persons themselves.[32]

But even without being at its must openly resistant and defiant, the range of options for the political, epistemological, and affective disruption provided by the killjoy is wide. And perhaps most importantly, served merely by the presence of those who do not belong at "the table" (the metaphor that Ahmed deploys throughout her work). As Ahmed notes, most of the work of the killjoy is done merely by being present "at the table" *as a willful problem,* such that the "seats" at the table would necessarily be remade: "To be unseated by the table of happiness might be to threaten not simply that table, but what gathers around it, what gathers on it" (Ahmed, 2010a). What bodies would accomplish this simply by being present? And what would it mean to remake the "table" not around the properties of enjoyment that are part and parcel with the social life of social death, but rather by raking up the accusation of being a killjoy and embracing its willfulness, stickiness, and tension?

Conclusion: "Keep it, spread it, or do what you want with it..."

Merely being at the table, however, is not enough. As Ahmed notes, the work of the killjoy is in concert with others, part of a broader project of killing the social life that has been organized around knowledges and enjoyments of the suffering of others. Ahmed calls for a "killjoy movement," in the company of other killjoys: transfeminist killjoys, ethnic killjoys, crip killjoys, indigenous feminist killjoys (Ahmed, 2017, p. 267). The abolitionist killjoy would join in this coalitional project, and travels under an umbrella of abolitionist politics (predicated on, and without giving up a commitment to, Black politics, queer politics, feminist politics, decolonial politics, etc.).

I suggested at the beginning of this essay that McDonald is a model abolitionist killjoy—someone whose presence and analysis can disrupt the "good feelings" that we have about the prison and prison reform, and who inculcates a productive set of negative affects toward the current state of affairs. McDonald rejects the possibilities of carceral reforms not merely by stating the facts of the matter (that prison cannot be made "safe" for anyone) but she also disrupts the affective attachments we may hold for "progressive" prison reform proposals (such as a "trans prison").

First, McDonald does the epistemological work of the killjoy, making the implied premise of the question clear: that we believe that there is even such a thing as a "safe" prison environment. And she disrupts that premise by marking it as a *fantasy*: as a unicorn. And she does this by also rejecting the terms of analysis as they have been offered: that safety is a feature of prisons and that protection can be provided through isolation and segregation. Speaking elsewhere, McDonald drives home this epistemological killjoying project, refusing to allow others to continue to live in structured ignorance of the functioning of mass incarceration in the United States, and the role that incarcerated persons have in disrupting that regime of knowledge:

> I think it's time that people know these things, now. Any time that you're being attacked in your community, and you ask the police to help you and they say no, I think people should know about that ... because somebody's

going hear about this and they're going to spread the word, and then they're going to spread the word. For me now … this is my healing process. This is a part of me getting every little thing off my mind and off my chest, and … let the world know… this is how I was treated, this how my family was treated, this is how my friends was treated, this is how strangers are treated, this is how everyone is treated. … Literally, I'm almost to the point of where I'm just gonna stop a person on the street and just give them like a ten-minute briefing and just walk off. I don't want nobody, I don't want nothing, just listen to this for five minutes, keep it, spread it, or do what you want with it, and walk off.

(McDonald, 2014b)

McDonald explains how a lack of knowledge about the routine violence visited upon trans★ persons is because of a lack of venues where gender non-conforming individuals can (and must) be encountered. Speaking forcefully from this position and experience is necessarily disruptive both to the current state of affairs ("this is how everyone is treated") and the expectations of "successful" discourse ("do what you want with it"). If a part of the problem we face in understanding the reach and effects of mass incarceration is epistemological—the structured silencing of some voices and a production of non-knowledge—then to have hegemonic understandings of the world disrupted by those for whom mass incarceration and its effects are known all too well is philosophically and politically important.

Second, McDonald engages in a paradigmatically critical account of incarceration that disrupts the reformist fantasies of finding "alternatives" to the prison.[33] She offers a direct refusal of the given terms of analysis and practice that support the current state of affairs, bringing to the foreground a core prison abolitionist claim: the prison cannot be made "safe" for anyone, and in particular, that making it "gender responsive" for women (the fastest growing group of incarcerated persons in the U.S.) and for trans★ persons is not the goal. This disruption builds on a wide body of critical literature refusing the language of "safety" and reformist "success" that has driven a prison-building boom under the rubric of "gender responsiveness" (CURB, 2007; Heiner & Tyson, 2017; Lawston & Meiners, 2014; Shaylor, 2008).[34] More generally, McDonald obstructs the reformist hopes of "getting the prison right" and calls out those who might seek to reconcile the prison with the prevailing form of multicultural civil and political society. They are already reconciled as such. McDonald refuses both the notion that her own incarceration was justifiable on the basis of her personal "safety" and the more generally held belief that prisons themselves can ever be made anything other than locations that produce social death for the sake of others.

And lastly, she offers a call for solidarity and support for those who continue to live outside the demos and behind bars. Note the *affect* of this call and the response it receives from audience. Lest anyone think that the killjoy is joyless, that the cultivation of bad feelings against the "good" feelings of parasitic social life is joyless, here is evidence that it is anything but that. It is, in classic critical formulation, the re-evaluation of "good" and "bad" in relation to the sticky objects in the world. It is sweaty concept formation, based in a willful subjectivity. It is this kind of refusal of carceral enjoyment—specifically of the reformist desire to fix the prison for TGNCI folks—which ought to be at the center of anti-carceral theory and practice.

For Ahmed, the account of the feminist killjoy does not imply that all women necessarily disrupt the feelings of patriarchal happiness, but rather, in *becoming* a feminist, a new relation between the "good feelings" of the social life produced by forms of social death becomes possible. In McDonald's case, her descriptive representation as a formerly incarcerated transwoman of color does necessary disruptive work, but the killjoying comes as well from her abolitionist analysis and embrace of being out of step with reformism. She disrupts the affective and normative scripts of "reintegration" or "re-entry" (which are fully captured by the carceral state). As an abolitionist killjoy, she argues for world-making. She holds open the possibility for other others to join in the movement (through solidarity) to become killjoys as well.

As Joel Olson argues in the closing pages of *The Abolition of White Democracy*, "[N]o privilege held can compare to a world in which privilege does not exist" (Olson, 2004, p. 145). In a similar vein, McDonald argues that there is no form of prison that can ameliorate the suffering of those inside prison better than a world without prisons. And neither is there a form of prison that can soothe the suffering of those who have been victims of violence, harm, and aggression, better than working to create a world without prisons. That prison may seem to soothe now is only because of the carceral enjoyments of the social death of the criminalized other, the suffering of the marginalized other, and the bad faith of parasitic social life. And to build a world without prisons, to attack the conditions of social death that are effected by and through the prison, would be felt as costly to those whose social lives currently depend on the productive labor of the incarcerated worker, the civic labor of the disenfranchised felon, and the moral labor of the "guilty" convict. But to understand those costs as *losses* would be to misunderstand the enjoyment of these privileges, these properties, as deserved rather than the parasitic enjoyments that they are.

Notes

1 On the philosophical importance of this tradition to critical prison studies, see Guenther & Taylor (2016).
2 I take this wonderful and concise definition of genealogy as the "critical redescription of a domination description" from Ladelle McWhorter (1999, p. 43).
3 Moreover, as has been well documented by critical carceral studies scholars, historians of the prison, and especially incarcerated people, a primary "organizational" principle of the prison is sex-assigned-at-birth segregation. This means not only is gender-violence an *essential* characteristic of the practice of incarceration, but also that TGNCI (trans, gender-non-conforming, and intersex) persons are

always "out of compliance" when incarcerated (Kunzel, 2010; Levi & Waldman, 2011; R.K. Robinson, 2011; Spade, 2011; Sylvia Rivera Law Project, 2007).

4 I take up the idea of Abolition Democracy as a *framework* for critical analysis in Dilts (2019).

5 There is a logical order to these claims, yet I also think that they are importantly interdependent, better thought of as abstracted points in a broader constellation of concepts that can work together as a model for how to understand our present through a materialist historical method. By constellation, I am thinking of Adorno's formulation of the term in which "history is a *constellation* that can really be grasped only with the help of an elaborate philosophical theory, and not by reducing it to individual concepts or pairs of concepts" (Adorno, 2006, p. 87). Adorno describes the constellation as made up of "individual phenomena" that are also illuminated by the constellation of which they are a part:

> If what is at stake is a type of thought that does not follow the procedures of identity philosophy and that defines the concepts it employs only by virtue of the *constellation* in which they obtain a specific value, then it follows necessarily that dialectical thinking will not just apply to the phenomenon it scrutinizes but will also point beyond it. Just as the constellation always consists of individual phenomena, so too light can fall on individual phenomena only from the constellation. Moreover, I should like to add that the illuminating force of such models and model concepts is all the greater, the more intensively you immerse yourselves in the details of individual phenomena. ... This suggests that there is a kind of reciprocal interaction between the constellations, on the one hand, and events on the micrological plane, on the other.
> (Adorno, 2006, pp. 184–5)

This approach is helpful for abolitionist theorizing because abolitionist praxis reaches dialectically beyond the current capacity of concepts to capture the present moment.

6 In particular, see pp. 5–8 of Patterson for his account of how natal alienation functions by cutting off the slave's birth ties from a past and a future traceable through lineage. Thank you to Lisa Guenther for reminding me of the importance of this important temporal isolation at the heart of social death.

7 As Zurn notes in his excellent overview of the *concept* of social death, not only is the term contested in its philosophical and social scientific uses, it is also closely related to other terms such as Lauren Berlant's idea of "slow death." Its contestation often hinges on questions of agency (see, for instance Neil Robert's critique of Patterson) while its fellow travelers draw attention to its open-ended temporality. In both cases, what is often revealed by following these lines of analysis, and which Zurn notes succinctly, is that the concept of "death" itself is less definitive and precise than typically assumed (Berlant, 2007; Roberts, 2015; Zurn, 2020). See also Stanley (2011; 2013).

8 I use the terms "civic death" and "civil death" interchangeably in this essay.

9 See also pp. 38–45 of Patterson (1982) for his account of these two conceptions of social death.

10 See also Eduardo Mendieta's formulation: "The ethnoracial prison, as extension of the ghetto, continues this form of natal alienation and social death through its policies of cultural, social, and political exclusion" (Mendieta, 2004, p. 54).

11 See also Heiner (2003).

12 I argue that these stronger approaches are genealogical in their method (Dilts, 2017).

13 It is important to not conflate *attempts* to render someone as social dead with one being rendered socially dead. As Ashon Crawley brilliantly reminds us, both the quotidian and extraordinary violence of white supremacy is often driven by the failure to have "successfully" reduced someone to a position of social death. Reflecting on the white supremacist murder of members of EAME Church, Crawley writes,

> White supremacy, its rapacious and incessant antiblackness, is the constant emergence of fear, the fear of being engulfed, and changed, by this radical abundance. Dylan Roof murdering the members of Emmanuel African Methodist Episcopal Church in Charleston, SC, illustrates the ways his was not the violence of someone who believed that social death—the state of total powerless—was achievable but was the violence of one terrified by its impossibility.
> (Crawley, 2017, pp. 22–3)

14 This is a simplification of the roots of the liberal tradition and its influence on U.S. political ideology, but one that I have taken up in more complexity elsewhere, with specific reference to the influential role of John Locke on American political development and the philosophies and jurisprudence of punishment. See, in particular, chapters 4 and 5 of Dilts (2014).

15 Cacho draws on Ruth Wilson Gilmore's definition of racism as "the state-sanctioned or extralegal production and exploitation of group-differentiated vulnerability to premature death" (Gilmore, 2007, p. 28). See also Ladelle McWhorter's work for a Foucauldian account of how the distinction between those who may live and those who must die is drawn through the appearance of modern racism (McWhorter, 2009).

16 On this parenthetical point see Joel Olson's gloss on the specific role police forces played in assimilating migrants into whiteness as a political system, drawing on the historical work of Noel Ignatiev, Henry Allen, and David Roediger (Olson, 2004, p. 45).

17 The particular colonial structure of race, capitalism, and accumulation likewise goes deeper (Nichols, 2020; Park, 2016).

18 See, in particular, Haley (2016). For an overview of scholarship making explicit connections between race and *gender* under theories of racial capitalism, see also Sweeney (2020).

19 As scholar and activist Erica Meiners has noted, it important to emphasize the violence *of* policing, rather than reify the idea implied by the more typical turn of phrase, "police violence," that there is a mode of policing which is ever not violent in a meaningful sense.

20 This is, arguably, another way of invoking the careful historical work done by scholars such as Naomi Murakawa and Elizabeth Hinton, who show that the U.S. prison buildup was constructed over a nearly 50-year project of liberal governance from Kennedy and Johnson right through to Clinton and Obama (Hinton, 2015; Murakawa, 2014). From a longer historical perspective, this is also to note that early modern liberal thought (Locke, most paradigmatically) is grounded on racializing, gendering, and normalizing assumptions of subjectivity and punitive practices that make this historical contingency materially "sticky."

21 I take this sub-heading from Ioanide (2015).

22 Brown argues that a danger in work on social death is that Patterson's account of it has become little more than a concept or abstraction, ignoring how Patterson's own work actually resists such a reduction.

23 I explore this aporia between life and death under the terms of incarceration in Dilts (2015).

24 These two forms are neither exhaustive, nor even necessarily distinct, as it is possible (if not common) for forms of resistant social life to also be parasitic on the social death of others. Thank you to Sarah Tyson for reminding me of the importance of this point. Additionally, the economic metaphor of "purchase" here is not meant to imply that social life is in fact a scarce or finite resource, but rather that it is treated as such under the logic of parasitism.

25 Resistant social life may, of course, also operate under various forms of "cover" (Cohen, 2004; Kelley, 1994; Scott, 1992).

26 I am indebted to the work of Elisabeth Anker in helping me formulate these questions (Anker, 2020).

27 As Robert Nichols (2014) has noted, many anti-prison scholars foreground accounts of mass incarceration under such rubrics, reifying the notion of "acceptable" levels of incarceration. Doing so suppresses Indigenous critiques of settler colonialism that identify the legal system itself as dominating and oppressive. This might be read as an instance of what Kristie Dotson (2011) categorizes as "epistemic silencing."

28 As readers of Foucault will no doubt recognize, this is not a new relationship between the prison and its reform (Foucault, 1995, p. 265).

29 Ahmed gives an extended account of this figure (and its specific relations to "happiness" in Ahmed (2010b) She returns to the figure extensively (and offers a "killjoy manifesto") in Ahmed (2017). Portions of my own account of the abolitionist killjoy appear in an abbreviated form in Dilts (forthcoming).

30 Ben-Moshe describes this dis-epistemological work of abolition to be the same kind of work done by Ahmed's killjoy figure (Ben-Moshe, 2020, p. 128).

31 I take the term "creaturely" from Guenther (2016).

32 See Banu Bargu's *Starve and Immolate* for analysis of how hunger strikes and organized death fasts by prisoners in Turkey can be conceptualized as a politics of human weapons. In the United States, it is worth noting the specific demands made by participants in 2013 renewal of hunger strikes throughout the California prison system (Ashker et al., 2014; Bargu, 2014).

33 On the basic problem of the notion of "alternatives" see (Conrad, 2012; Davis, 2003; Foucault, 2000, 2009).

34 On the importance of rethinking the category of "safety" itself from a radical perspective with an emphasis of community accountability, see Tyson (2014).

References

Adorno, T.W. (2006). *History and freedom: Lectures 1964–1965* (R. Tiedemann, Ed.; R. Livingstone, Trans.). Polity Press.

Ahmed, S. (n.d.). Feministkilljoys. https://feministkilljoys.com/

Ahmed, S. (2010a). Feminist killjoys (and other willful subjects). *The scholar and feminist online, 8*(3).

Ahmed, S. (2010b). *The promise of happiness*. Duke University Press.

Ahmed, S. (2017). *Living a feminist life*. Duke University Press Books.

Alcoff, L.M. (2007). Epistemologies of ignorance: Three types. In S. Sullivan & N. Tuana (Eds.), *Race and epistemologies of ignorance* (pp. 39–57). SUNY Press.

Anker, E.R. (2020). "White and deadly": Sugar, slavery, and the sweet taste of freedom. *Theory & Event, 23*(1), 169–206.

Ashker, T., Castellanos, A., Jamaa, S.N., Franco, G., Guillen, A., Powell, L., Redd, P., Sandoval, A., Troxell, D., Williamson, J., & Yandell, R. (2011). *Prisoners' Demands.* https://prisonerhungerstrikesolidarity.wordpress.com/the-prisoners-demands-2/

Bargu, B. (2014). *Starve and immolate: The politics of human weapons.* Columbia University Press.

Beauvoir, S. de. (2011). *The second sex* (C. Borde, Trans.). Vintage.

Ben-Moshe, L. (2020). *Decarcerating disability: Deinstitutionalization and prison abolition.* University of Minnesota Press.

Berlant, L. (2007). Slow death (sovereignty, obesity, lateral agency). *Critical Inquiry, 33*(4), 754–80. https://doi.org/10.1086/521568

Brown, V. (2009). Social death and political life in the study of slavery. *The American Historical Review, 114*(5), 1231–49.

Cacho, L.M. (2012). *Social death: Racialized rightlessness and the criminalization of the unprotected.* New York University Press.

Chin, G.J. (2012). The new civil death: Rethinking punishment in the era of mass conviction. *University of Pennsylvania Law Review, 160,* 1789–1833.

Clifford, S. (2014). The capacity contract: Locke, disability, and the political exclusion of "idiots." *Politics, Groups, and Identities, 2*(1), 90–103.

Cohen, C.J. (2004). Deviance as resistance: A new research agenda for the study of Black politics. *Du Bois Review: Social Science Research on Race, 1*(1), 27–45.

Conrad, R. (Ed.). (2012). *Prisons will not protect you.* Against Equality Publishing Collective.

Crawley, A.T. (2017). *Blackpentecostal breath: The aesthetics of possibility.* Fordham University Press.

CURB. (2007). *How "gender responsive prisons" harm women, children, and families.* CURB: Californians United for a Responsible Budget.

Davis, A. (2003). Racialized punishment and prison abolition. In T. Lott & J. Pittman (Eds.), *A companion to African-American philosophy* (pp. 360–9). Blackwell Publishing.

Davis, A. (2005). *Abolition democracy: Beyond empire, prisons, and torture.* Seven Stories Press.

Dayan, C. (2005). Legal Terrors. *Representations, 92*(1), 42–80. https://doi.org/10.1525/rep.2005.92.1.42

Dillon, S. (2018). *Fugitive life: The queer politics of the prison state.* Duke University Press.

Dilts, A. (2012a). Incurable blackness: Criminal disenfranchisement, mental disability, and the white citizen. *Disability Studies Quarterly, 32*(3). https://dsq-sds.org/article/view/3268/3101

Dilts, A. (2012b). To kill a thief: Punishment, proportionality, and criminal subjectivity in Locke's Second Treatise. *Political Theory, 40*(1), 58–83. https://doi.org/10.1177/0090591711427000

Dilts, A. (2014). *Punishment and inclusion: Race, membership, and the limits of American Liberalism.* Fordham University Press.

Dilts, A. (2015). Death penalty "abolition" in neoliberal times: The SAFE California Act and the nexus of savings and security. In G. Adelsberg, L. Guenther, & S. Zeman (Eds.), *Death and other penalties: Philosophy in a time of mass incarceration* (pp. 106–29). Fordham University Press.

Dilts, A. (2017). Toward abolitionist genealogy. *The Southern Journal of Philosophy, 55,* 51–77. https://doi.org/10.1111/sjp.12237

Dilts, A. (2019). Crisis, critique, and abolition. In D. Fassin & B.E. Harcourt (Eds.), *A time for critique* (pp. 230–51). Columbia University Press.

Dilts, A. (forthcoming). How does it feel to be(come) a problem? Active intolerance and the abolitionist killjoy. *Theory & Event*.

Dotson, K. (2011). Tracking epistemic violence, tracking practices of silencing. *Hypatia*, *26*(2), 236–57. https://doi.org/10.1111/j.1527-2001.2011.01177.x

Du Bois, W.E.B. (1995). *Black reconstruction in America*. Simon & Schuster.

Du Bois, W.E.B. (1997). *The souls of Black folk*. Bedford Books.

Ewald, A.C. (2002). "Civil death": The ideological paradox of criminal disenfranchisement law in the United States. *Wisconsin Law Review*, *2002*(5), 1045–38.

Ewald, A.C. (2012). Collateral consequences in the American states. *Social Science Quarterly*, *93*(1), 211–47.

Foucault, M. (1995). *Discipline and punish: The birth of the prison* (A. Sheridan, Trans.). Vintage Books.

Foucault, M. (2000). Pompidou's two deaths. In J. Faubion (Ed.), *Power* (pp. 418–22). The New Press.

Foucault, M. (2009). Alternatives to the prison: Dissemination or decline of social control? *Theory, Culture & Society*, *26*(6), 12–24.

Gilmore, R.W. (2007). *Golden gulag: Prisons, surplus, crisis, and opposition in globalizing California*. University of California Press.

Gilmore, R.W. (2015, February 23). The worrying state of the anti-prison movement | Social Justice. *Social Justice*. www.socialjusticejournal.org/the-worrying-state-of-the-anti-prison-movement/

Girshick, L. (2011). Out of compliance: Masculine-identified people in women's prisons. In E.A. Stanley & N. Smith (Eds.), *Captive genders: Trans embodiment and the prison industrial complex* (pp. 189–208). AK Press.

Grady, S.C. (2012). Civil death is different: An examination of a post-Graham challenge to felon disenfranchisement under the Eighth Amendment. *Journal of Criminal Law & Criminology*, *102*(2), 441–70.

Guenther, L. (2013). *Solitary confinement: Social death and its afterlives*. University of Minnesota Press.

Guenther, L. (2015). Political action at the end of the world: Hannah Arendt and the California prison hunger strikes. *Canadian Journal of Human Rights.*, *4*, 33.

Guenther, L. (2016). Beyond guilt and innocence: The creaturely politics of prisoner resistance movements. In P. Zurn & A. Dilts (Eds.), *Active intolerance: Michel Foucault, the Prisons Information Group, and the future of abolition* (pp. 225–40). Palgrave Macmillan.

Guenther, L. & Taylor, C. (2016). Introduction: Queer, trans, and feminist responses to the prison nation. *PhiloSOPHIA*, *6*(1), 1–8. https://doi.org/10.1353/phi.2016.0002

Haley, S. (2016). *No mercy here: Gender, punishment, and the making of Jim Crow modernity*. The University of North Carolina Press.

Harris, C.I. (1993). Whiteness as property. *Harvard Law Review*, 1707–91.

Hartman, S. (1997). *Scenes of subjection: Terror, slavery, and self-making in nineteenth-century America*. Oxford University Press.

Hartman, S. & Wilderson, F.B., III. (2003). The position of the unthought. *Qui Parle*, *13*(2), 183–201.

Heiner, B. (2003). Commentary: Social death and the relationship between abolition and reform. *Social Justice*, *30*(2), 98–101.

Heiner, B. (2007). "From the prison of slavery to the slavery of prison": Angela Y. Davis's abolition democracy. *Radical Philosophy Today*, *5*, 219–27.

Heiner, B. (2015). Excavating the sedimentations of slavery: The unfinished project of American abolition. In G. Adelsberg, L. Guenther, & S. Zeman (Eds.), *Death and other penalties: Philosophy in a time of mass incarceration* (pp. 13–41). Fordham University Press.

Heiner, B. & Tyson, S. (2017). Feminism and the carceral state: Gender-responsive justice, community accountability, and the epistemology of antiviolence. *Feminist Philosophy Quarterly, 3*(1). http://ir.lib.uwo.ca/fpq/vol3/iss1/3

Hinton, E. (2015). "A War within our own boundaries": Lyndon Johnson's Great Society and the rise of the carceral state. *Journal of American History, 102*(1), 100–12. https://doi.org/10.1093/jahist/jav328

Hobson, E.K. (2016). *Lavender and red: Liberation and solidarity in the gay and lesbian left* (1st ed.). University of California Press. www.jstor.org/stable/10.1525/j.ctt1f5g4xf

Holloway, P. (2014). *Living in infamy: Felon disenfranchisement and the history of American citizenship.* Oxford University Press.

Ioanide, P. (2015). *The emotional politics of racism: How feelings trump facts in an era of colorblindness.* Stanford University Press.

Jackson, S. (2014). One foot in darkness. In S. Tyson & J. Hall (Eds.), *Philosophy imprisoned: The love of wisdom in the age of mass incarceration* (pp. 125–26). Lexington Books.

James, J. (2005). *The New abolitionists: (Neo)slave narratives and contemporary prison writings.* SUNY Press.

Karlan, P. (2004). Convictions and doubts: Retribution, representation, and the debate over felon disenfranchisement. *Stanford Law Review, 56*(5), 1147–70.

Kelley, R.D.G. (1994). *Race rebels: Culture, politics, and the black working class.* Free Press.

Kelley, R.D.G. (2017, January 12). *What did Cedric Robinson mean by racial capitalism?* Boston Review. https://bostonreview.net/race/robin-d-g-kelley-what-did-cedric-robinson-mean-racial-capitalism

Kramer, S. (2017). *Excluded within: The (un)intelligibility of radical political actors.* Oxford University Press.

Kunzel, R. (2010). *Criminal intimacy: Prison and the uneven history of modern American sexuality.* University Of Chicago Press.

Lawston, J. & Meiners, E. (2014). Ending our expertise: Feminists, scholarship, and prison abolition. *Feminist Formations, 26*(2), 1–25.

Levi, R. & Waldman, A. (Eds.). (2011). *Inside this place, not of it: Narratives from women's prisons.* McSweeney's Books.

Lipsitz, G. (2004). Abolition democracy and global justice. *Comparative American Studies An International Journal, 2*(3), 271–86. https://doi.org/10.1177/1477570004047906

Manza, J., Brooks, C., & Uggen, C. (2004). "Civil death" or civil rights? Public attitudes towards felon disenfranchisement in the United States. *Public Opinion Quarterly, 68*(2), 276–87.

McDonald, C. (2014a). *The Struggle for Trans Liberation: A conversation with CeCe McDonald.* http://youtu.be/emx5iHwbPOg

McDonald, C. (2014b, September 4). *"I Use My Love to Guide Me" —Surviving and Thriving in the Face of Impossible Situations.* www.youtube.com/watch?v=AorudSjIhEk

McDonald, C. (2015). Foreword. In E.A. Stanley & N. Smith (Eds.), *Captive genders: Trans embodiment and the prison industrial complex* (2nd ed.).

McDonald, C. (2017). "Go beyond Our Natural Selves" The Prison Letters of CeCe McDonald. *TSQ: Transgender Studies Quarterly, 4*(2), 243–65. https://doi.org/10.1215/23289252-3815045

McWhorter, L. (1999). *Bodies and pleasures: Foucault and the politics of sexual normalization.* Indiana University Press.

McWhorter, L. (2009). *Racism and sexual oppression in Anglo-America: A genealogy*. Indiana University Press.

Melamed, J. (2015). Racial capitalism. *Critical Ethnic Studies*, *1*(1), 76–85. https://doi.org/10.5749/jcritethnstud.1.1.0076

Mendieta, E. (2004). Plantations, ghettos, prisons: US racial geographies. *Philosophy & Geography*, *7*(1), 43–59.

Mills, C.W. (1997). *The racial contract*. Cornell University Press.

Muhammad, K.G. (2010). *The condemnation of blackness: Race, crime, and the making of modern urban America*. Harvard University Press.

Murakawa, N. (2014). *The first civil right: How liberals built prison America*. Oxford University Press.

Nichols, R. (2014). The colonialism of incarceration. *Radical Philosophy Review*, *17*(2).

Nichols, R. (2020). *Theft is property! Dispossession and critical theory*. Duke University Press.

Olson, J. (2004). *The abolition of white democracy*. University of Minnesota Press.

Park, K.-S. (2016). Money, Mortgages, and the Conquest of America. *Law & Social Inquiry*, *41*(4), 1006–35. https://doi.org/10.1111/lsi.12222

Pateman, C. (1988). *The sexual contract*. Stanford University Press.

Patterson, O. (1982). *Slavery and social death: A comparative study*. Harvard University Press.

Pearce, M. (2012, June 18). Transgender woman sentenced to men's prison in Minnesota killing. *Los Angeles Times*. http://articles.latimes.com/2012/jun/18/nation/la-na-nn-transgender-woman-sentenced-to-mens-prison-20120618

Petersen, A.M. (2020). *Anti-blackness and the possibility of legal change: An abolitionist analysis of the post-1992-uprising reform of the L.A.P.D.* [Ph.D. diss., University of California, Irvine].

Price, J.M. (2015). *Prison and social death*. Rutgers University Press.

Richie, B.E. (1996). *Compelled to crime: The gender entrapment of battered Black women*. Routledge.

Richie, B.E. (2012). *Arrested justice: Black women, violence, and America's prison nation*. NYU Press.

Roberts, N. (2015). *Freedom as marronage*. The University of Chicago Press.

Robinson, C.J. (2000). *Black marxism: The making of the Black radical tradition*. University of North Carolina Press.

Robinson, R.K. (2011). Masculinity as prison: Sexual identity, race, and incarceration. *California Law Review*, 1309–1408.

Rodríguez, D. (2004). *Forced passages: Imprisoned radical intellectuals and the U.S. prison regime*. University of Minnesota Press.

Scott, J. (1992). *Domination and the arts of resistance: Hidden transcripts*. Yale University Press.

Sexton, J. (2011). The social life of social death: On Afro-pessimism and Black optimism. *In Tensions Journal*, *5*, 1–47.

Shaylor, C. (2008). Neither kind nor gentle: The perils of "gender responsive justice." In P. Scraton & J. McCulloch (Eds.), *The violence of incarceration* (pp. 145–63). Routledge.

Singh, N.P. (2014). The whiteness of police. *American Quarterly*, *66*(4), 1091–99. https://doi.org/10.1353/aq.2014.0060

Smith, C. (2009). *The prison and the American imagination*. Yale University Press.

Spade, D. (2011). *Normal life: Administrative violence, critical trans politics and the limits of law*. South End Press.

Stanley, E. (2011). Near life, queer death: Overkill and ontological capture. *Social Text*, *29*(2 (107)), 1–19. https://doi.org/10.1215/01642472-1259461

Stanley, E.A. (2013). *Queer remains: Insurgent feelings and the aesthetics of violence* [Ph.D. diss., University of California, *Santa Cruz*].

Sullivan, S., & Tuana, N. (Eds.). (2007). *Race and epistemologies of ignorance.* State University of New York Press.

Sweeney, S.J. (2020). Black women in slavery and freedom: Gendering the history of racial capitalism. *American Quarterly, 72*(1), 277–89. https://doi.org/10.1353/aq.2020.0014

Sylvia Rivera Law Project. (2007). *"It's war in here": A report on the treatment of transgender and intersex people in New York State men's prisons.* The Sylvia Rivera Law Project. https://srlp.org/its-war-in-here/

Tyson, S. (2014). Experiments in responsibility: Pocket Parks, radical anti-violence work, and the social ontology of safety. *Radical Philosophy Review, 17*(2), 421–34. https://doi.org/10.5840/radphilrev201471820

Wacquant, L. (2001). Deadly symbiosis: When ghetto and prison meet and mesh. *Punishment & Society, 3*(1), 95–134.

Wilderson, F.B., III. (2003). The prison slave as hegemony's (silent) scandal. *Social Justice, 30*(2), 18–27.

Zurn, P. (2019). Waste culture and isolation: Prisons, toilets, and gender segregation. *Hypatia, 34*(4), 668–89. https://doi.org/10.1111/hypa.12498

Zurn, P. (2020). Social Death. In G. Weiss, A.V. Murphy, & G. Salamon (Eds.), *50 Concepts for a Critical Phenomenology* (pp. 309–14). Northwestern University Press.

Part IV

Multispecies carceralities

13 The "carceral enjoyments" of animal protection

Kelly Struthers Montford and Eva Kasprzycka

Since the 1980s, animal protection organizations in the United States have increasingly called on criminal law to advance animal interests. Justin Marceau (2019) shows there are multiple competing explanations for this. For instance, nonhuman animal advocates are constrained by the limited avenues for legal remedies. Those seeking to improve the material lives of nonhuman others have found themselves funneled into the realm of criminal law. Animal criminal law's growingly tough-on-crime approach makes for good fundraising and, thus, contributes to the viability of these organizations. If the punishment is 'too lenient,' protectionists often engage in media campaigns asking for financial support to ensure this does not happen again. If the organization is satisfied with the outcomes—which have ranged from prison sentences sometimes followed by deportation—they can use this as an example of their 'effectiveness' in advocating on behalf of animals and public safety. The protection movement does so in a context in which the prison remains an institution in which the caging of an animalized other is justified for the benefit of the public. We suggest that the animal protection movement in the U.S. is endemically rooted in the carceral enjoyments (see Dilts, this volume) stemming from the criminalization of racialized others using animal cruelty laws. Given that the animal remains constituted in proximity to blackness and the sub-human (Kim, 2017, 2018), we argue that carceral animal law attempts to elevate the animal through the continued subjugation of blackness—now enacted by the prison system rather than the institution of slavery.[1]

In this chapter, we build on the work of Andrew Dilts (this volume) who argues that our attachment to and preference for criminal punishment and incarceration is the ongoing result of willfully ignoring the empirical evidence showing the prison's failure to rehabilitate or protect outside communities. The refusal to recognize the prison system's gross inability to rehabilitate and protect is due to an affective attachment to the prison's material and ideological enjoyments, including its contribution to white supremacy and racial subjugation. Dilts' insights will be used to scrutinize recent developments in animal cruelty law to show how the carceral animal protection movement engages in both of these maneuvers to normalize injustices inherent in the industrial prison and meat complexes. Using empirical evidence showing the failure of the prison, others have critiqued the animal protection movement's reliance on the carceral system. We suggest that this critique is incomplete and should be supplemented by grappling with our emotional response to harms against nonhuman animals and the deconstruction of our affective commitment to criminal punishment. Using Sara Ahmed's contributions to affect theory, Dilts suggests that part of the prison abolitionist project is the killjoying of the enjoyments flowing from the prison—that is, the constitution of bad feelings towards the prison and its attendant benefits and privileges. We suggest that an effective strategy for changing animal protectionists' and public support of the criminalization of animal abuse—and, therefore, the punishment system—also requires the avowal of emotions such as sadness, rage, and fear, that mobilize punitive responses and feed the carceral appetite. Such an approach facilitates the constitution of an alternative 'other' who is not 'the criminal' (to be targeted and incapacitated), but allows us to organize against 'alternative others' such as structures and institutions that cause overwhelming amounts of social harm. We then suggest that a redirection away from the criminal other and toward "alternative," structural others to more resolutely address systemic and institutional abuses against nonhuman animals.

Claire Jean Kim suggests that part of the ongoing abolitionist work responding to slavery and animal oppression is to wage a "war against the human." (2018, p. 29). This requires thinking together and carefully about Black and animal liberation because of their respective subjugations in service to the human (Kim, 2017, 2018; Ko, 2019). It is not the case that those concerned about animals can afford to engage in projects of epistemic or racial innocence, nor can those advancing racial justice ignore the symbolic and material treatment of nonhumans. Instead, "the war against the 'human' is most effectively, and perhaps necessarily waged on these two fronts at once, from both sites of ontological opposition" (Kim, 2018, p. 30). To engage in the inseparable projects of prison abolition and animal liberation is, then, to affirm our shared "creaturely existence" and at once a call for "new possibilities of intercorporeal life" (Guenther, 2016).

Carceral animal protection

Law remains representative and constitutive of our social values. Justin Marceau's *Beyond Cages: Animal Law and Criminal Punishment* (2019) provides a comprehensive account and critique of the U.S. animal protection movement's increasing alliance with state punishment systems, including prosecutors, law enforcement, and immigration officials. Marceau labels this a "tough-on-crime" movement whose actions are antithetical to civil rights and social justice objectives. While the movement is somewhat diverse, the motto of a leading organization is "Abuse an animal—go to jail!"—a tagline, Marceau claims, that is largely representative of the movement itself (Marceau, 2019, p. 2). It is clear that many animal protectionists are ratcheting up the range of carceral responses to animal harm. For example, the punitive demands of carceral animal protection are wide-ranging:

If a jurisdiction adopted all of the reforms advocated for by the carceral animal law movement, a person who became ill and neglected his dog could face mandatory arrest, would be charged by a movement-funded prosecutor, would face felony liability, would be sentenced to an increasingly long maximum term of imprisonment, and would have to be listed on a publicly available abuse registry. The sum is greater than the component parts of this carceral project.

(Marceau, 2019, p. 274)

This tough-on-crime agenda also advocates for trying juveniles as adults (p. 151). These are demands made in a context where animal cruelty legislation exists in each of the 50 U.S. states, many of which include felony provisions. The category of felony is not consistently applied across states, but, generally includes sentences in excess of 12 months to be served at either state or federal institutions.

Under the Trump administration and as a result of lobbying efforts of animal protection organizations, the *Preventing Animal Cruelty and Torture Act [PACT]* was enacted on November 25th, 2019. This bi-partisan bill was largely drafted by the Animal Legal Defense Fund (ALDF) and received unanimous support from the Senate and the House of Representatives. Representatives of animal protection organizations interviewed by *The New York Times* have lauded this as reflective of "American values" that will "truly bring justice for the animals…by ensur[ing] some of the most horrific acts of animal cruelty are prosecuted to the fullest extent of the law" (Schindler as quoted in Zaveri, 2019). PACT, a legal reform bolstered by a nationalist rhetoric of "civilized society" and "American values," represents a Western trend of prioritizing the strengthening of criminal cases against individual perpetrators at the expense of saving the vast majority of animals from violent abuse. PACT establishes federal jurisdiction in cases where extant state law would not apply, provides for increased policing and investigatory powers, and denotes maximum prison sentences. Prior to PACT's enactment, the U.S. did not have a *federal* felony law specific to animal cruelty.[2]

Although, the celebratory tone of politicians and many animal advocacy organizations, PACT effectively applies to a very small minority of animals with whom we are in relation. Excluded from PACT are nonhuman animals subject to scientific experimentation, those who jeopardize human life or threaten property, those in veterinary settings, and it does "not apply to people who slaughter animals for food or to those who hunt, trap and fish" (Zaveri, 2019; Johnson 2019). What PACT makes a federal crime is the "crushing, burning, drowning, suffocating, impaling or sexual exploitation" of nonhuman animals not included under state law (ALDF, n.d., "Laws that protect animals"). Despite its narrow and reductionary scope, this legislation expands the purview of the criminal punishment system. Previous federal legislation, for example, only prohibited the sale of "crush videos" and not the actions of those harming animals in said videos. The fact that PACT establishes federal felony law coincides with a long history of legal exclusion and social death—a topic examined in sections below.

Animal cruelty laws have existed in many U.S. states for more than 200 years, yet have had seemingly little positive material impact for the animals they are meant to protect. The number of nonhuman animals mutilated, confined and subject to nightmarish conditions has never been higher than at this present moment. Marceau (2019) showcases how such a record of failure demonstrates the inability of these laws to shift our speciesist practices and norms, and, instead, might "be blamed in part for entrenching such norms" (p. 23). Carceral animal law initiatives prioritize the advancement of punitive responses to sensational accounts of individual abuse against companion animals. In pursuing felony cruelty laws that cannot be applied to animals in industrial agriculture, the animal protection movement affirms popular opinions that assert 'farm' animals are less morally relevant than companion animals. Considering the way animal cruelty laws have fallen short in protecting the vast majority of nonhuman animals while normalizing systemic abuses and the mass-violence experienced by 'farm' animals, why do organizations committed to nonhuman animals continue to advocate for increasingly punitive responses? Marceau suggests that this is a matter of mattering; for the movement, "these prosecutions demonstrate that animal suffering matters" (2019, p. 22). What does it mean, then, to engage in a project of symbolically improving the status of certain nonhuman others while supporting and seeking to expand incarceration, which is both symbolically and materially detrimental for prisoners, their communities, and nonhuman animals?

Animal protection's propensity for social killing

On its face, animal cruelty laws might not seem to be tactics of racial oppression. In some jurisdictions, nascent statistical data shows that in some jurisdictions Black individuals are overrepresented, whereas in others such as Ohio, arrests and prosecutions for animal cruelty are consistent with the population's demographics.[3] A focus on demographics and a language of overrepresentation belies the settler colonial and anti-Black racism foundational to the U.S., and perpetuates a myth of racial neutrality (see Murawaka & Beckett, 2010; Murakawa, 2019; see also Nichols, 2014). Demographic parity does not mean that animal cruelty laws are not racist in their origin or function. First, there is no outside of race, and "race is never irrelevant when it comes to justice system reforms" (Marceau, 2019, p. 151). Second, critical prison and Black studies scholars convincingly argue that the prison is a legal institution of civil and social death that unmakes humanity and makes race via the status of the convict. This is because the prison's function continues the project of racial slavery, with 'the convict' now legally and symbolically tied to blackness (Dilts, this volume).

Whereas civil death is to become 'legally dead'—in the sense of being stripped of civil rights, as is often the result when convicted of a felony—social death is a condition "in which one is denied kinship entirely by the force of law, [and] is reserved for the 'natal alienation' and 'genealogical isolation' characterizing slavery" (Sexton, 2010, p. 41). The past 20 years of scholarship on civic and social death have parsed and compared how these forms of oppression differ and overlap. Dilts, however, argues that incarceration in the U.S. makes these inextricable. Drawing from Joy James, Dilts posits that it is not the case that the 13th Amendment "merely *allows* for racially discriminat[ory] practice to continue under different terms, but rather, that the social death of slavery is written into the civil death of incarceration, *transforming social death into a permanent legal category* and signifying both criminality and blackness as inseparable" (Dilts, this volume, p. 201). Because Blackness is constituted through its distancing from whiteness and propinquity to the animal, this also signifies animality as commensurate with criminality and Blackness. For Dilts, legal categories are transformed by the prison, and so too is "the paradigmatic socially dead figure ... less 'the slave' than 'the prisoner'" (this volume, p. 198). Race-neutral criminal law and social policies are then anything but. Because the 13th Amendment maintains "involuntary servitude as punishment for crime…[there is an] ongoing connection between abjected blackness and criminality, even as it operates under a mask of racial neutrality under the law" (Dilts, p. 201). The prison is deployed to support white supremacy and its attendant norms— especially the ownership of private property, which will be explored below.

Understanding racialization as a contingent political project, Dilts argues that paradigms of whiteness and Blackness are not necessarily derived by how individuals choose to identify, but are subject positions and modes of embodiment that can be made— and remade— through law[4] and incarceration. To better illustrate, he cites the following from James:

> Breaking with a two-hundred-year-old tradition, the government ostensibly permitted the enslavement of nonblacks. Now not the ontological status of "n*****[redacted]" but the ontological status of *"criminal"* renders one a slave. Yet, as became apparent in the convict prison lease system, blackness remained the signifier of social death, *although now all those relegated to prisons would be imbued with that pariah race status.*
>
> (Emphasis added, as cited in Dilts, this volume, p. 201)

As such, any support of the criminal punishment system in the U.S. is expressly implicated in the "racialized social death" of those subject to these institutions.

The increased criminalization of animal cruelty cannot be divorced from the prison's enactment of social and civil death. Rather, it represents the animal protection movement's willingness to intensify the prison system's literal and symbolic power in imbuing "that pariah race status." In doing so, animal cruelty law encourages the carceral enjoyments reaped from the social killing of racialized populations. Initiatives like PACT encourage white violence by supporting the social killing of minorities, while, also, dismissing the mass violence and suffering caused by animal agriculture. While PACT might seem anomalous and tied to the U.S.'s increasing punitive appetite, animal protection's use of criminal law and its implication in racial injustice is not a recent development. Rather, it is foundational to the history and progress of nonhuman animal protection in the West.

Paula Tarankow's research on the use of animal cruelty provisions in the District of Columbia from 1880 to 1920 is instructive in understanding the movement's historical approach to race and animal protection. Marceau concludes that this research "supports a hypothesis that the very origin story of animal cruelty prosecutions is one of profound racism" (2019, p. 169). Tarankow's analysis of the archives of the Humane Society shows that soon after emancipation, the movement understood its role as protecting animals from those who had formerly been enslaved, citing that slavery had uncivilized enslaved subjects who were, therefore, likely to cause harm to animals. In light of this strategic narrative, it appears the movement's "initial motivations for criminalizing abuse were not lacking in racist underpinnings" (Marceau, 2019, p. 167).

Labor market conditions and the racist stereotyping of formerly enslaved persons also coalesced to produce a context in which increased criminalization occurred. These individuals were impoverished and relied on unhealthy animals—often the only ones they could afford to purchase—to earn a living. This context led to Black individuals being disproportionately targeted and punished for animal cruelty before the dawn of the 20th century. The protection movement imagined the injustices of chattel slavery to be resolved, and labelled Black persons "the new 'slave drivers'" of the nonhuman animals upon whom they relied for their economic survival (Marceau, 2019, p. 168). Essentially, early animal cruelty laws pitted Black persons against animals; and, in heralding such laws as moralizing and civilizing, such reforms gained political traction and social support. During this time, animal protectionists were also explicitly critical of state officials and judges who showed leniency by taking poverty and marginalization into account when punishing individuals under animal cruelty provisions (Marceau, 2019, p. 169). These discourses—that violence committed by Black men was the main form of animal abuse, and punishment the appropriate solution—occurred within a context devoid of empirical support for such claims (Marceau, 2019, p. 169).

Symbolic "justice" and racial control

Recent cases continue to show that the criminalization of animal abuse—like criminal punishment writ large—are mechanisms of racialized control occurring within social contexts shaped by overlapping forms of discrimination, inequality, and marginalization. Recently, two Black men have been the subject of public scorn and sentenced to incarceration for the abuse of dogs. Perhaps, most well-known is the 2007 prosecution of Michael Vick, former National Football League star, who served 23 months under federal sentence for financing and running an interstate dogfighting operation, which included the abuse and execution of dogs used for fighting. Marceau (2019) shows that this was a case of exceptional prosecution, in which federal prosecutors tried the case against Vick—despite him having committed what would typically be tried as a state offense. Concerned that using state law would be too lenient, prosecutors tried him under the Travel Act, which prohibits interstate travel for the purposes of illicit gambling operations. Following his conviction in federal court, Vick was also tried by the State of Virginia. The accused faced zealous targeting by federal and state prosecutors, and his sentence far exceeded sentencing guidelines which recommended against incarceration for a conviction such as his (Marceau 2019, p. 173). Looking at the same case, Claire Jean Kim (2015) suggests that the criminal punishment system and the public's response to Vick demonstrates the appetite for 'putting' successful Black individuals 'back in their place.' Having grown up in abject poverty, Vick's success in a sports organization largely controlled by wealthy white persons whose elitism is built on the labor of young Black men was seen as exceptional and tenuous. Following his arrest and charging, his actions were read by the public as another example of the recalcitrance of Black men who are 'predisposed' to criminality (Kim 2015).

Marceau underscores that prior to the enactment of PACT, federal law only criminalized one form of animal cruelty—dogfighting and cockfighting: "the practices with the greatest connections to people of colour" (2019, p. 185). Following the Vick case, there was a marked increase in the arrest of Black men for dogfighting:

> In the five years following the Vick case, blacks accounted for 74 percent of all arrests for dogfighting, a nineteen-percent increase over the five years prior. The actual number of blacks arrested for dogfighting tripled from 64 to 306 within this same time period, and out of all the racial groups, blacks were the only group to have experienced an increase in dogfighting arrests in the five years following Vick's conviction.
>
> (Marceau, 2019, p. 186)

Vick's punishment and its influence on future convictions make apparent that any illusion of legal sentencing being objective or objectively race-neutral is difficult to maintain. Because "Vick's involvement and the victimization and killing of dogs represented an aggravating circumstance," the court was able to justify an upward departure on sentencing guidelines (Piquero et al., 2011, p. 539). Upward departures are made possible for defendants with prior convictions, a history of violent offenses or if a high risk of recidivism is clearly established to be a danger to society (US Sentencing Commission, 2010). At the outset, the pertinent Guidelines indicate that "aggravating circumstances… will occur rarely and only in exceptional cases." (US Sentencing Commission, 2010).[5] In Vick's case, the upward departure was justified on the grounds of the "heinous, cruel and inhumane" killing of pit bulls. The grievous language used in the Department of Justice News Release reads like alleged aggravated circumstances surrounding a death penalty case—"[s]erial killers and axe murderers rarely make such a concession" (Kurland, 2010, p. 488). The symbolic and sensational hues surrounding Vick's crime colored the court's decision and permeate into cases beyond his own.

The judicial system's practice of upping criminal sentencing in cases involving Black persons and companion animals is not limited to dogfighting or gambling. In 2014, Black Baltimore police officer Alec Taylor was sentenced to one year in prison for killing his girlfriend's puppy, Rocko, after he urinated indoors. State Attorney, John McCarthy said "I think it's important that he was held responsible. I think it's important he is going to jail" (CBS Baltimore, 2014). One cannot be certain if the journalist quoting McCarthy chose to shorten his remarks, but readers are not provided reasons that divulge exactly why McCarthy thinks the jailing of Taylor is "important." One may interpret that it is important to the State Attorney because of what Taylor's harsh sentence means for animal protection; but, the unsaid tenors take on racial reverberations. It seems important that people like Taylor go to jail because of reasons outside of the suffering experienced by Rocko (legal property) and his "owner" (as stipulated by law). In McCarthy's statement, the victims in this crime are absent in lieu of the penalization of white property's effacement. White supremacy is maintained through both what is uttered and unsaid—the State Attorney's silence regarding nonhuman victims is a configuration pregnant with racial control.

In the same year as Taylor's offence, a young Black man, Andre Robinson, was seen on video luring and then kicking a stray cat. Both Robinson's lawyers and legal aid attorneys acknowledged the severity of the incident, yet were surprised by the extent to which—mainly white—animal protectionists called not only for his incarceration, but for him to receive the maximum penalty despite this being his first offense. That agents within institutionalized white supremacy, such as Robinson's lawyers and attorneys, were taken aback by the extent of white rage demonstrated by animal protectionists illustrates the kind of fervor steering the movement's direction.

The prosecution and incarceration of Black men for their abuse of companion animals has been derided by commentators as both racist and as evidence that state representatives and animal protectionists are more concerned with harms against nonhumans than Black individuals (see for example Kim, 2015; Marceau, 2019). Worse yet, this concern is made apparent through the severity of prison sentences. For example, in an editorial published by *The Guardian*, academic Jason Nichols argues that how we gauge "mattering" is evident through punishment (2015). Looking at Alec Taylor's year-long sentence for killing a dog, Nichols observes that such a punishment "might not seem like much, but it is longer than the sentences given to the killers of Michael Brown, Eric Garner, Trayvon Martin, Rekia Boyd or 7-year-old Aiyana Stanley-Jones" (2015). Because of this discrepancy in the administration of punishment, Nichols argues that while calling Black individuals "animals" is the latest epithet for African Americans, this is inaccurate because "we punish people for killing animals" (2015). What unites these seemingly discrepant movements is that the carceral state is asked to punish in order to recognize and/or elevate the status of those who are often noncriminally killed.

The way carceral animal law chooses to make nonhuman animal abuse "matter" becomes another tool for racial subjugation, much the way the war on drugs serves as justification for draconian sentencing that produces profoundly unequal outcomes for nonwhite communities. The animal protection movement's appetite for racial control stretches beyond the exacerbation of racial disparities in the criminal justice system and into xenophobic attitudes and practices of expulsion and deportation. Recently, anti-immigration sentiments have been especially strong in the animal protection movement's work on animal agriculture. In 2017, anti-immigration campaigners, environmental activists, and animal protectionists from Nebraska worked together to prevent the establishment of an industrial poultry farm. Agricultural workers in the U.S. are largely non-white, with Latinx individuals constituting 75% in this employment sector that is "one of the most dangerous workplaces in America" (Marceau, 2019, p. 188). Characterized by egregious working conditions where workers must perform repetitive and violent work with ever increasing quotas that are impossible to achieve in a "humane" manner, workers become desensitized to violence, and have been shown to suffer from workplace-related traumatic stress disorders, then take this violence into their home and community settings (Fitzgerald et al., 2009; Marceau, 2019; Muller, 2018). While matters of citizenship and labor injustice provide salient reasons for being opposed to animal agriculture, this is not the approach taken by animal welfarist organizers. Instead, animal and environmental protectionists partnered with those who did not want immigrant labor moving into "their" communities—these sentiments were especially pronounced against those of Somali origin, seemingly because of their Muslim faith. The involved animal activists were not ignorant of the fact that these local campaigners had previously organized to prevent "illegals" from renting apartments, purchasing homes, and garnering employment in the neighboring community. In effect, "the activists' work with avowed (and effective) xenophobes branded them and the movement more generally as racists opposed to immigration" (Marceau, 2019, p. 158).

While prosecutions are especially rare relative to the scale of violence occurring in sites of factory-farming and slaughter, those that do proceed are overwhelmingly racist and classist. Unlike their low-level workers, owners and management of agricultural corporations and slaughterhouses are typically white (Marceau, 2019; Pachirat 2011). When evidence of abuse arises, Marceau argues that they exhibit a familiar pattern of "purported shock and disavowal by the executives, and prosecution of the low-level employees who are oftentimes recent immigrants, or people of colour" (p. 190). In a case about the abuse of animals at Bettencourt dairy farm in Idaho, executives not only publicly denounced the three low-level staff being investigated—Jesus Garza, Jose Acensio, and Javier Victor Rojas Loayza—but worked with local law enforcement to have them prosecuted and deported. State officials characterized these executives as "heroes" for their cooperation and publicly condemned the negative attention the farm continued to receive after the workers were convicted (Marceau, 2019). In effect, prominent state officials sought to assure the public that the problem had been resolved through these convictions, and that the corporation was deserving of patronage.

In a 2008 case about the Hallmark Meat Company, two low-level employees, Daniel Ugarte Navarro and Rafael Sanchez Herrera, pled guilty to charges of animal abuse following the release of undercover footage. Navarro received a prison sentence of nine months, and Herrera was sentenced to six months of incarceration followed by deportation. Herrera is the father of two American-born children. Brought forth by the Humane Society of the United States and the Department of Justice, Marceau describes this Hallmark case as extraordinary because it also involved a civil suit that sparked the "largest-ever meat recall…and largest-ever judgement for an animal abuse case"—a $500 million settlement under the False Claims Act (Bottemiller, 2012). This Act is meant to prosecute government contractors who commit state fraud. Hallmark had a contract with the U.S. Department of Agriculture to supply beef for the National School Lunch Program, and video footage showed them abusing and slaughtering 'downer' cows who are prohibited from entering the food supply for public safety reasons. The company would pay very little of the settlement amount, with the Humane Society of the United States stating that, despite this, the judgement maintains symbolic value "and is intended to deter future animal cruelty in the nation's slaughterhouses" (as cited in Bottemiller, 2012). Here animal protectionists communicate to the public that it is possible for slaughterhouses to be cruelty-free and legitimize animal agriculture as a socially-acceptable institution should extant laws be followed. It is likely that this settlement has had no material benefit for the victims, i.e. 'farmed' animals. Logic such as this, as we will discuss below, contributes to a broader epistemology of ignorance that permits our continued consumption of animal products—a carceral enjoyment in and of itself. The carceral animal protection movement, as we next discuss, demonstrates a commitment to epistemological ignorance and its concomitant carceral enjoyments.

The epistemological ignorance of carceral enjoyments

Building on the scholarship of philosophers of race and gender, Dilts argues that "epistemologies of ignorance are forms of *willful* not knowing (rather than a traditional ignorance of facts)" (2018, p. 20). This willful ignorance prevents acknowledging one's implication in and benefits stemming from the systems and practices that remain unaddressed in any meaningful manner. This ignorance, in the context of the criminal punishment system (CPS), takes its form in critiquing how the criminal punishment system is *applied* in a discriminatory manner that violates rights, rather than a wholesale interrogation of the system's function, its impacts, and its colonial and racial history. An epistemology of ignorance begets reform efforts rather than abolition. More so, it informs the animal protection movement's approach to criminalization and incarceration.

In its position statement on "Sentencing for Animal Cruelty Cases," the Animal Legal Defense Fund acknowledges issues in how the CPS is *applied,* but defends its position as a social institution:

> The Animal Legal Defense Fund recognizes that the United States is facing a crisis of mass-incarceration which is supported by—and contributes to—institutional biases based on race, socioeconomic status, and other factors. We also recognize that *incarceration has a valid place* as one of several justice system tools for addressing animal cruelty.
>
> (ALDF, n.d., position statement, p. 3; emphasis added)

The ALDF elaborates that incarceration serves multiple purposes:

> First and foremost, incarceration serves a community safety purpose—it removes offenders from society for a period of time during which they are prevented from harming others, including animals, which can be especially important in cases of known recidivism. Second, incarceration may act as a deterrent, dissuading would-be offenders from committing crimes. Third, incarceration can serve as an opportunity to provide convicted offenders access to resources for rehabilitation to minimize risk of recidivism.
>
> (ALDF, n.d., position statement, p. 3)

While incapacitation, rehabilitation, and deterrence are common tropes mobilized to support incarceration, the inability of the prison to achieve these measures is also commonly documented (and therefore not unknowable).

Placing those who abuse nonhuman animals in prisons fails to *prevent* the harming of them—one of ALDF's chief rationales for endorsing carceral punishment. The prison instead places prisoners in specific relationships with nonhumans under the guise of rehabilitation, such as dog and horse training programs, factory-farming, and slaughterhouse labor (see Furst, 2006; Struthers Montford, 2019). Factory-farming and slaughterhouse prison training programs are antithetical to any form of rehabilitation and require violence against animals (Fitzgerald, 2012; Struthers Montford, 2019). Even in the event that those convicted of animal cruelty are not assigned to animal training or animal agriculture, the prison's infrastructure is extremely resource-intensive to run, often polluting surrounding bodies of water and killing aquatic life and others reliant upon it (Moran, 2015; FTP, 2018). Some prisons have been built in locations that are critical habitats for free-living animals and, as a result, their survival is impossible (Corporate Watch, 2018). Regardless of whether or not those convicted of animal cruelty are put in direct contact with nonhuman animals while inside, prisons are institutions that operate on violent subjugations between humans, nonhuman animals and the environment. At most, a prison sentence will briefly incapacitate those convicted before sending them back into communities with a violence vivified by the experience of incarceration. Incarcerating such people does more harm than good and fails to make non-human animals (and humans) safer. Given that prison jurisdictions often publicly promote their animal training and agricultural programs (see, for example, Colorado Correctional Industries, n.d., "Farming"), and because the failure of the prison is widely known, we suggest that statements such as those made by the ALDF are the result of a concerted effort to *not fulsomely know* or to *not grapple with* the realities of a system in which one works and, ultimately, seeks to strengthen. The ALDF simultaneously recognizes and negates the "parasitic life" (Dilts, this volume) produced by the criminal punishment system.

Companion animals as white property

Cheryl Harris' contributions to critical race theory fillets the power dynamics and social construction of whiteness to showcase how its invisibility reinforces white supremacy. Harris' analysis of "whiteness as property" elicits symbolic and literal meanings that defuse the presumed normative and superior status of whiteness (1993). Her precise attention to "property," its complicated relationship to the law and its tangible and figurative value, exposes some of the psychological underpinnings that upholster racial embodiment. "Whiteness," explains Harris, "has functioned as self-identity in the domain of the intrinsic, personal, and psychological; as reputation in the interstices between internal and external identity; and, as property in the extrinsic public, and legal realms" (Harris, 1993, p. 1725). The perpetuation of racial discrimination is founded on a belief that racial hierarchies are a result of biology and not abjective ideology. The property of whiteness is symbolic; but, its exchange in socio-political economies has profound material effects. As a figurative possession with literal consequences, this form of property is capriciously reactive because (a) the bio-pseudoscience supporting racial hierarchies is blatantly and empirically untrue and (b) "whiteness is given a value when it does not inherently have any meaning, much less value" (Gaffney, 2015, p. 13). The principles upon which white supremacy thrusts itself are erroneous—to put it lightly—and, therefore, require fervid persistence to be sustained, producing what Harris calls a "highly volatile and unstable form of property" (Harris, 1993, p. 1720). This volatility reacts to anything near and in this context of advocating for prisons to defend victims, anti-Black and colonial ideologies collide to fix the parameters of victimhood to surround the property of whiteness.

As noted by Dilts, "under the specific legal structure produced in the post-bellum United States, social death becomes intimately tied to the production of *whiteness* as property" (this volume, p. 199). Dilts, also aptly surmises that "[a] key root of political authority itself in this context derives its legitimacy from a Lockean conception of property as an extension of self-ownership" (this volume, p. 202). Nonhuman animals are—from the law's perspective—property. The ALDF's initiative may stem from a belief that nonhuman animals should not be considered mere property; but, the type of "property" ALDF defends through PACT's enactment, is, customarily and effectively, a property of whiteness. Considering the general importance of Lockean liberalism "on American political development and philosophies and jurisprudence of punishment," the animals we choose to protect are threads woven into the property of whiteness (Dilts, this volume, p. 217).

Traditionally, companion animals in the West are property to white communities. During the 16th and 17th centuries, during which Europeans came to the Americas to settle, increase their wealth, and broaden their influence over global affairs, the relationship between humans and companion animals was being rewritten ideologically and substantially. Domesticated animals—largely, but not exclusively dogs and cats—became pets in English households no longer for the sole purpose of providing protection or 'pest' control, but for the novel enjoyment of their company. For the first time, nonhuman animals were given human names and rewarded for exhibiting human qualities; ergo the thought of their slaughter for purposes of consumption evoked disgust (Thomas, 1996). It is also worth noting that during the era in which Canadian and American sovereignties were inaugurated, so, too, were the first animal protection organizations. Pet ownership, historically, was a pastime of the rich and affluent that has since "filter[ed] down to the middle class" and not much has changed since (Herzog, 2017). Of course, persons from all ethnicities and races have welcomed pets into their homes; but, "[t]he biggest differences among groups in pet ownership" in the U.S. today are "associated with race and ethnicity… white Americans are the most likely to own pets and African Americans least likely" (Herzog, 2017). Using data gathered from the American Veterinary Medical Association, Sarah Mayorga-Gallo reports that white Americans are more than twice as likely to own pets than African Americans (Mayorga-Gallo, 2018, p. 505). Likely due to the demographics they belong to, pets are flourishing at an unprecedented rate (Horspool, 2013)—as are the mainstream carceral responses invoked to "protect" them.

Companion animals furnish the white affective community (Fox & Gee, 2017; Crossman & Kazdin, 2017; Cepeda-Gallo & Taylor, this volume) not only because their value in social economies has been largely imputed by white Americans. There is ample scholarship recording the co-option of domestic canines to hunt, maim, constrain and/or kill enslaved Africans (see Cepada-Gallo & Taylor, this volume). The racial animus in using pets to control Black people did not dissolve with slavery's "abolishment"—it has only become modernized through policing. This transition's imprint on the collective memory and imagination is, also, well documented by academics. In the social unrest fronted by the Black Lives Matter movement, dogs co-opted into police brutality are weaponized against racialized bodies who protest against racial violence enacted by police forces. The utilization of dogs for the purpose of protecting white hegemony and property is as relevant as ever; one only needs to skim through titles of popular news media—like *The Washington Post*, for example: "Trump's warning that 'vicious dogs' would attack protesters conjured centuries of racial terror" (Trent, 2020). The extension of white property and its effacement become emotionally laden because pets are part of the white affective economy. Nonhuman animals have always been and continue to be a part of white violence.

Parasitic life and killjoying's redirection of emotions

Dilts understands parasitic life to be the flip side of social death, in which "putatively 'innocent' members of society receive identifiable material, psychic, and symbolic benefits and privileges from mass incarceration and its direct relation to hetero-patriarchal white supremacy in the United States" (this volume, p. 198). Our enjoyments are affective and conceptual, with these enjoyments meted out through the subjugation and "'use' of the slave." The self-conceptual and ideological contours of civil society are made in relation to the abjected slave (i.e., through which the prison attached "the pariah race status" to the convict). It is against the slave that dominant forms of subjectivity and social norms are constituted—a totalizing sign and fantasy that upholds and procures hegemonic authority and a subjecthood recognizable by the state. The master/slave schema is modernized to confer privileges gained from social inclusion such as citizenship rights. Carceral enjoyments leeched from this symbolic economy include material benefits like the ability to vote, access to social housing, freedom to move across borders, etc. There are two ways in which epistemologies of ignorance are related to carceral enjoyments: first, the fact that our dominant ways of life produced by this form of life and death cannot be acknowledged; and second, that even when confronted with knowledge of the racial oppression constituted by the CPS, parasitic life entails clinging to the material and symbolic privileges "purchased through the racialized social death of others" (Dilts, this volume, p. 198). It is within such a frame that the ALDF can both gesture to the race-based issues inherent in the prison system while at the same time affirming its use as a social institution.

PACT, like other animal cruelty laws, offers citizens a quasi-therapeutic consolidation of their inhumane treatment towards production animals by championing the protection of animals brushed in white strokes. Meanwhile, the 8.38 billion land animals in the U.S., who share the capacities we take to be relevant to the ethical standing of companion animals, are subject to intensive cruelty, dramatically shortened lives, and high-efficiency killing (U.S Animal Kill Clock, 2018). As mentioned, PACT does "not apply to people who slaughter animals for food" (Zavier, 2019; Johnson, 2019). Reformist initiatives pursued by animal protection groups are part of a Western legislative trend that boasts compassionate progress in human-animal relations while discursively pushing the most vulnerable animals out of consideration. According to ALDF, it would appear that pets—as an extension of owner's whiteness—are worthy of our protection. Animals who experience cruelty every single day of their unnaturally shortened lives are ushered beyond the peripheries of public attention. In the same gesture that PACT uses to calcify Black persons into communities of the socially dead, 'farm' animals are distanced further and further away from the "community of the living" (Wolfe, 2012, p. 105).

What do citizens become when they can assure themselves of their kindness by increasing the penalization of abuse against animals we keep in our homes while excluding comparisons with the animal abuse and suffering in factory farms and the animal bodies we keep in our refrigerators and serve up on plates? There is ample research on the cognitive dissonance permeating attitudes towards animals intended for companionship and consumption; but, the racial implications of stratifying the moral value assigned to other animals has missed adequate scrutiny. In light of PACT's recent implementation, this oversight requires addressing. Two distinct proliferations of cognitive dissonance compound into a political agenda that oppresses two very different types of beings in the passing of one legal act: first, an ethical and legal discordance which determines that the animals we choose to eat carry less moral merit than the animals we choose to care for; second, the ALDF's admission that "mass-incarceration…is supported by—and contributes to—institutional biases based on race" while insisting "that incarceration has a valid place" in addressing animal cruelty (ALDF, n.d., position statement). Legal reforms like PACT manifest from intersections between speciesist and racist belief systems to license the forced subordination of those deemed less-than-human. At the precise juncture where these two forms of cognitive dissonance meet and amalgamate, they produce a "philosophico-juridical space" that legitimizes the social killing of Black persons while engendering the "techno-scientific mass-slaughtering and exploitation of nonhuman animals" (Derrida, 2004, p. 74, 65). Prison abolition and animal liberation remain inextricably bound together.

Abolitionist efforts, as proposed by Dilts, require that we "confront such enjoyments not because they are deserving of respect (they are not), but because they represent a serious obstacle to abolitionist and decolonial projects" (this volume, p. 198). For both Dilts and for Michael Mopas and Dawn Moore (2012), this confrontation will be at the level of affect. Specific to affect, Dilts suggests that, at some level, 'we' enjoy the suffering produced by the CPS. Perhaps, it is then the case that animal protectionists—working within a frame of whiteness under a masquerade of supposed racial-neutrality—'enjoy' the suffering of the individual convicted of animal abuse, who is caged in an institution that treats its captives 'like' animals (see Struthers Montford, 2016).

Seeking to elevate certain animals above the convict/slave continues the same logic in which scientists in the 18th and 19th centuries taxonomized whites as superior, by placing them above and against 'the animal' and 'the slave' (Kim, 2017, 2018). Kim argues that "the Slave performed a vital function in the symbolic and libidinal economies of the Human…the counterpoint against which the Human could gain self-knowledge and coherence" (Kim, 2018). The counterpoint of the slave, however, exists in relation to the animal. Drawing on the U.S.'s history of racial slavery, Kim surmises that "the Black person's humanity was a technicality to be ritually counteracted through myriad practices of slave-animal conflation, including branding slaves, selling slaves at auction, and feeding slaves at the trough with pigs" (2018, pp. 28–29). The "human," then, "is produced through the *simultaneous abjection of slaveness/*

blackness and animality. 'Slave' and 'animal,' in other words, serve as dual onto-logical counterpoints to the 'human.' At the same time, 'slave' and 'animal' are also defined in relation to each other, completing the triangular dynamic" (Kim, 2018, p. 29). Kim states that neither animal ethics nor Black liberation can advance without the "bringing together of [these] two ethical issues, a *putting into relation*" (2018, p. 29). In so doing, Kim argues that "animal abolition" is, then, *abolition* writ large, if this is "understood as the historic effort to dismantle the antiblack racial order and secure meaningful freedom for Black people for the first time" (p. 29). Prison abolition in the context of the United States, we insist, is also a social justice movement that ought to orient itself to the same foundational goal.

The killjoying of the carceral enjoyments of animal protection is necessarily a project of species and racial justice. By appropriating Ahmed's feminist cri-tique of happiness, Dilts urges that prison abolition requires engagement with killjoying—the creation of "bad feelings" against the "good feelings" of parastic social enjoyment produced by the carceral (this volume, p. 199). Because policy makers and experts fail to engage and take seriously the role of emotion, Mopas and Moore (2012) claim that public policy continues to be informed by tough-on-crime and fear-based approaches—rather than empirical evidence. It is their argument that critical scholars, especially those seeking to reframe how we respond to offending, "must start to accept people's fear and anger as legitimate reactions to crime and redirect these emotions toward more productive ends" (2012, p. 185). This requires accepting that "what one *knows* does not neces-sarily determine how one *feels*" (Mopas & Moore, 2012, p. 194). For Mopas and Moore, the role of the public criminologist is, then, not to continually communicate to the public and policy makers that people's fears are irrational, but, to instead "establish—through emotions—the *relationship* between them-selves and the imagined criminal other" (Mopas & Moore, 2012, p. 184). This is because the "criminal other" shores up boundaries around a community that shares a sense of victimization relative to this other. By directly addressing emotions, Mopas and Moore have found it easier to redirect and reconsti-tute links between the "we" of a community and "the other" in its fringes. Rather than an individualized and decontextualized account of offending and social harm, they argue that through community organizing and empower-ment, an "alternative other" emerges against which to resist and/or demand change. Such "alternative others" are namely police forces, media, and other components of the criminal punishment system which endanger communities far more than they contribute to safety. For Mopas and Moore, emotions are the hinge through which radical action and education can occur.

Companion animals hold a prominent place in our social and familial fabrics. Because of their emotional value, resisting carceral animal protection will require engaging with the deep emotional ties we hold with them. Presenting "the facts" and realities of the criminal prison system to animal protection organizations will likely fail because of their emotionally laden perspectives on animal abuse. Advocates and donors are often fiercely passionate about bettering the lives of other animals, not least because they engage with harms against animals on a regular basis. Abolitionists seeking to build safer and more ethical communities will need to respond to emotions such as anger and fear elicited by animal abuse, as well as the satisfaction and pleasure evoked when abusers are imprisoned or deported. Further, animal liberationists must supplant these emotional reactions with owning up to a parasitic freedom that is constituted through the social death of the slave/convict—a subject position comprised by a relation to the animal.

Animal protectionists are rightly angry about how nonhuman animals are treated, as should be the broader "we"; but, this anger and organizing ought to be directed at structures, institutions, and ideologies founded and constituted through the subjugation of nonhuman animals. Bad feelings could be effectively channeled towards colonial property regimes, racial capitalism, the animal agriculture industries that are leading drivers of climate change, the ubiquitous animal cruelty that structures our cultures, immigration policies that subjugate precarious workers, and a myriad of other culprits tangential to carcerality. Incarcerating and deporting already very marginalized individuals might satiate a carceral appetite; however, this "enjoyment" is short-lived while its contribution to the reproduction of hierarchal categorizations is not. Suggesting the penal system is a solution to animal cruelty sustains the oppressive logics that license our violent domain over other animals, in that it upholds long-standing structures of racial capitalism, settler colonialism, and anti-Black social orders that require the subjugation of animals and animality.

Conclusions: Toward a creaturely politics of abolition

Likely due to the demographics they belong to, pets are flourishing at an unprecedented rate (Mayorga-Gallo, 2018)—as are the mainstream carceral responses invoked to "protect" them. Data regarding animal cruelty punishment's disproportionate penalization of Black persons is lacking and its collection is ongoing. Although the investigation of such data is important, it is not crucial to this chapter's position. PACT's capacity to target racialized bodies in the U.S.'s agenda of mass-incarceration is significant, and symptomatic of the larger issue this chapter aims to address. PACT's unanimous passing represents a growing trend of animal protection's willingness to intensify the prison system's literal and symbolic power in conferring "that pariah race status." (James as cited in Dilts, this volume, p. 201).

As we have argued throughout this chapter, the mainstream animal protection movement's shoring-up of criminal law is not a matter of ignorance of the extensively researched and documented inability of the prison to deter, rehabilitate, or enhance public safety. Instead, this is perhaps better understood as a carceral enjoyment (Dilts, this volume), whereby, despite awareness of the overwhelming problems with criminalization and incarceration, those who benefit from this system of racial oppression continue to advocate for its use. Calls for increased and harsher punishment feed our broader appetite for racial control, while only symbolically elevating the status of specific non-human animals with little to no material improvements. In so doing, Blackness is then placed below the status of the protected animal, and rendered once again symbolically and materially—through the social death enacted by these punitive systems—as subhuman. The prison is at once materially and symbolically enmeshed in the (re)making of race and species. Part of fashioning public opinion with dissonant attitudes towards other animals is amplified by racial ascriptions to specific nonhuman animal species. The presence nonhuman animals have in North American cultural history and their monetary and emotional value cannot be interpreted in isolation from the legal history of chattel slavery. On the other side of the dialectic coin, white supremacy's presence in the history of nonhuman animals makes it impossible to dismantle anthropocentric indexes that determine determining which animals are worthy of our sympathetic consideration.

If we understand abolition to be a project of racial and species liberation, then prison abolition is foundational to what afro-pessimists call for: the "end of the world" structured by the ontological schema of racial slavery. For Guenther, "the genocidal logic" of carceral power is exercised on the borderlands of humanity, race, and animality: "It is precisely by attacking and undermining the creaturely existence of detainees that 'equitable' or 'honourable' justice is denied to them" (2016, p. 234). The harms of caging are exercised through intensive confinement in which meaningful embodied relations of one's choosing are denied. Guenther's approach to abolition is embodied and creaturely—it thwarts "the liberal assumption that, in order to be a political animal, one must rise above 'mere' animality" (2016, p. 227). Rather, Guenther, like others in this volume,[6] urges us to move beyond "the moral-legal categories of guilt and innocence. This calls for both a rejection of moral discourses on 'compassion,' 'empathy,' and 'tolerance,' and an affirmation of the creaturely politics of active intolerance and intercorporeal subjectivity" (Guenther 2016, p. 226). The forms of civil life which abolitionist efforts seek to constitute do not parasitically rely on the social death of abjected subhuman and nonhuman others.

Instead, efforts to build abolition envision new forms of civic life as its goal, a social fabric that weaves an "elaborated form of embodied, creaturely life…this creaturely life of radical decarceration moves beyond good and evil but—precisely as such—it affirms the ethical and political potential of intercorporeal solidarity" (Guenther, 2016, p. 236). This is because parsing good/evil, innocent/guilty will always shore up the punishable and cageable other against whose detention our parasitic freedom is produced. Animal liberation is intimately related and bilaterally tied to broader projects of slavery and prison abolition; projects of racial justice also cannot ignore the symbolic and material treatment of nonhumans. Abolition efforts then ought to advocate for forms of political subjectivity that are creaturely, thereby rendering schemas of life that uphold the human-subhuman-animal triad inarticulable (Kim 2017, 2018).

Notes

1   Recent socio-legal scholarship has compiled a robust literature that elaborates how the prison system has replaced the institution of slavery through its historical connection to plantation slavery because of the mass-incarceration of Black persons, the type of systemic violence they experience during and after incarceration and, not least, due to the legal requisite of the U.S.'s Constitution's 13th Amendment, which abolished slavery and "involuntary servitude, except as a punishment for crime."

2   Prior to PACT, federal law did criminalize dogfighting and cockfighting, practices that Marceau writes are heavily tied to Black and brown persons, according to the white imagination (Marceau, 2019, p. 184).

3   Nascent statistics on arrest, charging, and prosecution for animal cruelty in the U.S. show that white persons are underrepresented while Black persons are overrepresented for those arrested and/or charged with animal cruelty (Marceau, 2019, p. 169). Animal cruelty charges in Ohio, however, are representative of the demographic distributions.

4   Law has also intervened to define Indigenous identity; through marriage, white women became (legally) Indigenous and Indigenous women became (legally) white as a means to exclude them from band memberships and property claims to land and/or inheritance (Lawrence, 2003).

5   www.ussc.gov/guidelines/archive/2010-federal-sentencing-guidelines-manual.

6   See Parkes (Chapter 9) and Meiners et al. (Chapter 4), this volume.

References

Animal Legal Defense Fund. (n.d.). *Animal Legal Defense Fund position statement on sentencing for animal cruelty crimes.* 1–10. [Internal document, shared with Kelly Struthers Montford].

Animal Legal Defense Fund. (n.d.). Laws that protect animals. Accessed September 25, 2020. https://aldf.org/article/laws-that-protect-animals/

Bottemiller, H. (2012, July 30). Landmark settlement reached in Westland-Hallmark meat case. Retrieved September 25, 2020, from www.foodsafetynews.com/2012/11/landmark-settlement-reached-in-westlandhallmark-meat-case/

CBS Baltimore. (2014, October 08). Former Baltimore City Officer Sentenced 1 Year For Puppy's Choking Death. Retrieved September 25, 2020, from https://baltimore.cbslocal.com/2014/10/08/former-baltimore-city-officer-to-be-sentenced-in-puppy-choking-death/

Crossman, M. K., & Kazdin, A. E. (2017). Perceptions of animal-assisted interventions: The influence of attitudes toward companion animals. *Journal of Clinical Psychology, 74*(4), 566–78. doi:10.1002/jclp.22548

Colorado Correctional Industries. (n.d.). Farming. Retrieved September 25, 2020, fro www.coloradoci.com/manufacturers/agriculture/farming.html?intro

Corporate Watch (2018, August 15). *Prison island: A new report on prison expansion in England, Wales, and Scotland.* Corporate Watch. https://corporatewatch.org/prisonisland/

Derrida, J., Roudinesco, É, & Fort, J. (Trans.). (2004). *For What Tomorrow: A Dialogue.* Stanford University Press.

Dilts, A. (this volume). Carceral enjoyments and killjoying the social life of social death, pp. xx–xx

Fight Toxic Prisons. (2018, February 12). Horrific conditions for live-stock animals in Texas prisons exposed and other updates from Malik Washington. Retrieved September 25, 2020, from https://fight-toxic-prisons.org/2018/02/12/horrific-conditions-for-live-stock-animals-in-texas-prisons-exposed-and-other-updates-from-malik-washington/.

Fitzgerald, A.J., Kalof, L., & Dietz, T. (2009). Slaughterhouses and increased crime rates: An empirical analysis of the spillover from "The Jungle" into the surrounding community. *Organization & Environment, 22*(2), 158–84.

Fitzgerald, A. (2012). Doing time in slaughterhouses: A Green criminological commentary on slaughterhouse work programmes for prison inmates. *Journal for Critical Animal Studies, 10*(2), 12–46.

Fox, R. & Gee, N.R. (2017). Great expectations: Changing social, spatial and emotional understandings of the companion animal–human relationship. *Social & Cultural Geography, 20*(1), 43–63. doi:10.1080/14649365.2017.1347954

Furst, G. (2006). Prison-based animal programs: A national survey. *The Prison Journal, 86*(4), 407–30.

Gaffney, K. (2015). Whiteness as cursed property: An interdisciplinary intervention with Joyce Carol Oates's Bellefleur and Cheryl Harris's "Whiteness as Property". *Bearing Witness: Joyce Carol Oates Studies, 2*(1), 3.

Guenther, L. (2016). Beyond guilt and innocence: The creaturely politics of prisoner resistance movements. *Active Intolerance*, pp. 225–40. doi:10.1057/9781137510679_16

Harris, C.I. (1993). Whiteness as property. *Harvard Law Review, 106*(8), 1709.

Horspool, L. (2013). Animal health markets and opportunities: Companion animal landscape. In *Long-acting animal health drug products*, pp.14–45. doi:10.1007/978-1-4614-4439-8_2

Herzog, H. (2017, July 3) Large study finds pet owners are different. Psychology Today. www.psychologytoday.com/ca/blog/animals-and-us/201707/large-study-finds-pet-owners-are-different

Johnson, T. (2019). House and senate pass bill making animal cruelty a federal offense. *Journal of Law and Social Policy*. Accessed September 25, 2020 http://jlsp.law.columbia.edu/2019/11/20/house-unanimously-passes-bill-making-animal-cruelty-a-federal-offense/

Kim, C.J. (2015). *Dangerous crossings: Race, species, and nature in a multicultural age.* Cambridge University Press.

Kim, C.J. (2018). Abolition. In L. Gruen (Ed.), *Critical terms for animal studies* (pp. 15–33). University of Chicago Press.

Kim, C. (2017). Murder and mattering in Harambe's house. *Politics and animals, 3.*

Ko, A. (2019). *Racism as zoological witchcraft: A guide for getting out.* Lantern Books.

Kurland, A. H. (2010). The prosecution of Michael Vick: Of dogfighting, depravity, dual sovereignty, and "A Clockwork Orange". *Marquette Sports Law Review, 21,* 465.

Lawrence, B. (2003). Gender, race, and the regulation of Native identity in Canada and the United States: An overview. *Hypatia, 18*(2), 3–31.

Marceau, J., & Cambridge Core EBA eBooks Complete Collection. (2019). *Beyond cages: Animal law and criminal punishment.* Cambridge University Press. doi:10.1017/9781108277877

Mayorga-Gallo, S. (2018). Whose best friend? Dogs and racial boundary maintenance in a multiracial neighborhood. *Sociological Forum. 33*(2), 505–28. doi:10.1111/socf.12425

Mopas, M. & Moore, D. (2012). Talking heads and bleeding hearts: Newsmaking, emotion and public criminology in the wake of a sexual assault. *Critical Criminology, 20*(2), 183–96. doi:10.1007/s10612-011-9134-z

Moran, D. (2015). Budgie smuggling or doing bird? Human-animal interactions in carceral space: Prison(Er) animals as abject and subject. *Social & Cultural Geography, 16*(6), 634–53. doi:10.1080/14649365.2014.1001429

Muller, S.M. (2018). Zombification, social death, and the slaughterhouse: U.S. industrial practices of livestock slaughter. *American Studies, 57*(3), 81–101.

Murakawa, N. (2019). Racial innocence: Law, social science, and the unknowing of racism in the U.S. carceral state. *Annual Review of Law and Social Science, 15*(1), 473–93. doi:10.1146/annurev-lawsocsci-101518-042649

Murakawa, N., & Beckett, K. (2010). The penology of racial innocence: The erasure of racism in the study and practice of punishment. *Law & Society Review, 44*(3/4), 695–730. doi:10.1111/j.1540-5893.2010.00420.x

Nichols, R. (2014). The colonialism of incarceration. *Radical Philosophy Review, 17*(2), 435–55.

Nichols, J. (2015, April 28). Black Baltimore residents aren't 'animals'. We punish people for killing animals. *The Guardian*. Retrieved September 25, 2020, from www.theguardian.com/commentisfree/2015/apr/28/black-baltimore-residents-arent-animals-we-punish-people-for-killing-animals

Pachirat, T. (2011). *Every twelve seconds: Industrialized slaughter and the politics of sight.* Yale University Press.

Piquero, A., Piquero, N., Gertz, M., Baker, T., Batton, J., & Barnes, J. (2011). Race, punishment, and the Michael Vick experience. *Social Science Quarterly, 92*(2), 535–51. Retrieved September 25, 2020, from www.jstor.org/stable/42956499

Sexton, J. (2010). People-of-color-blindness: Notes on the afterlife of slavery. *Social Text, 28*(2), 31–56. doi:10.1215/01642472-2009-066

Struthers Montford, K. (2016). Dehumanized denizens, displayed animals: Prison tourism and the discourse of the zoo. *PhiloSOPHIA, 6*(1), 73–91.

Struthers Montford, K., & Philosophy Documentation Center. (2019). Land, agriculture, and the carceral: The territorializing function of penitentiary farms. *Radical Philosophy Review, 22*(1), 113–41. doi:10.5840/radphilrev2019249

Thomas, K. (1996). *Man and the natural world: Changing attitudes in England 1500–1800.* Oxford University Press.

Trent, S. (2020, 1 June) Trump's warning that 'vicious dogs' would attack protesters conjured centuries of racial terror. *The Washington Post.* Accessed September 25, 2020. www.washingtonpost.com/history/2020/06/01/trump-vicious-dogs-protesters-civil-rights-slavery/

U.S. Animal Kill Clock. (2018). 2018 U.S. Animal Kill Clock. Retrieved September 25, 2020, from https://animalclock.org/

U.S. Sentencing Commission. (2010, November 1). *2010 Federal Sentencing Guidelines Manual.* Retrieved September 25, 2020, from www.ussc.gov/sites/default/files/pdf/guidelines-manual/2010/manual-pdf/2010_Guidelines_Manual_Full.pdf

Wolfe, C. (2012). *Before the law: Humans and other animals in a biopolitical frame.* University of Chicago Press.

Zaveri, M. (2019, November 25). President Trump signs federal animal cruelty bill into law. *The New York Times*. Retrieved September 25, 2020, from www.nytimes.com/2019/11/25/us/politics/trump-animal-cruelty-bill.html

14 Carceral canines

Racial terror and animal abuse from slave hounds to police dogs

Paula Cepeda Gallo and Chloë Taylor

The genealogical links between slavery, settler colonialism, and the contemporary institutions of police forces and prisons in North America are
well established. In the United States and Canada, police forces were initially established to patrol for and capture escaped slaves and as paramilitary
organizations to quell Indigenous resistance (Mogul et al., 2012, p. 51; Nichols,
2014, p. 446). Mogul, Ritchie, and Whitlock write that "While many police
forces have evolved into sophisticated, professionalized institutions, in some
ways, their purpose, targets, and tactics have remained much the same" (Mogul
et al., 2012, p. 51). Similarly, early in their history prisons in North America
took on the roles of perpetuating slavery through convict leasing (Davis, 2003),
maintaining Jim Crow laws through lawful discrimination against disproportionately racialized "convicts" (Alexander, 2011), sustaining the racialized
American ghetto through parole restrictions and the infliction of poverty
(Wacquant, 2009), and extending racial eugenics in the U.S. and Canada
(Guenther, 2016). Although the forms that these institutions have taken, and
the discourses that have been used to justify them, have been modified over
time, their fundamental purpose remains static. Police brutality and racial profiling at every level of the criminal punishment system have thus never been
aberrations but are rather intrinsic to policing and prisons in North America
since, or nearly since, their inceptions.

While these arguments have been rehearsed before, little attention has been
paid by critical prison studies scholars to the role of animals in this history.
Recently, however, a few studies have emerged tracing the lineage between
slave hounds and the contemporary police and prison dog (Parry &Yingling,
2020; Wall, 2016; Johnson, 2009), and between concentration camp dogs and
police dogs (Tindol, 2013); however, these works have not incorporated insights
from critical animal studies (CAS). The purpose of the current chapter is thus
to build on these recent histories of slave hounds, concentration camp dogs,
and police dogs, but to do so through the theoretical framework of scholarship that bridges critical race theory, postcolonial studies, and critical animal
studies (Kim, 2015; Ko, 2019). In what follows, we first trace the genealogy
of the police dog from slave hounds and concentration camp guard dogs to
their current deployment in the age of Black Lives Matter. In the final section

we consider the incongruence between the violent historical and contemporary deployment of canines as weapons of racial warfare and their use today as propaganda for the police.

Slavery hounds

Of the prevailing symbols and imagery of racial violence and white supremacist domination, Tyler Parry and Charlton Yingling (2020) observe that the lash and shackles remain seared in the memory of slavery (p. 70). Throughout different eras of intensified struggle over racial control, Tyler Wall (2016) notes the lasting power of other imagery, citing the noose on the bough in the Jim Crow era, and the police batons and crowd-control measures in the Civil Rights decades (p. 871, p. 862). As Parry and Yingling remind us, however, none of these tools have accomplished nearly as much, as consistently, and as effectively as dogs have throughout centuries in establishing racial domination (Parry & Yingling, 2020, p. 70). Indeed, the shift to canine power as a mode of warfare for different empires at the dawn of colonialism in the Americas marks a moment where the weaponization of animals functioned to entrench and enforce colonial racial order and the proliferation of the capitalist plantocracy (Parry & Yingling, 2020; Johnson, 2009).

To understand the nature of white supremacist mastery over Black bodies, both Claire Jean Kim (2015) and Aph Ko (2019) argue, from a critical animal studies (CAS) perspective, that the zoological dimensions of racism mean that violence against animals, like violence against racialized populations, is a powerful expression of white supremacy (Kim, p. 56; Ko, p. 106). Following the CAS literature, systems of white and human supremacy, along with the dominion over nature, exist in collusion and share a co-constitutional ideological matrix (Kim, pp. 277–8; Ko, pp. 71–2). Put otherwise, the discursive and material practices of violent dominion over animals bleed into the practices of racial domination (Kim, p. 32). Kim explicitly identifies the plantation as the site where the notions and terms of race, animality, and the human were under continual (re)production (Kim, p. 254).

Dating back to the 15th century, the Spanish empire's reliance on dogs in the suppression of revolt and insurgency among different colonies throughout the Caribbean has been documented in the novel regional historiographies of scholars such as Sarah Johnson (2009), Tyler Wall, and Tyler Parry and Charlton Yingling. In the early moments of contact between European colonists and Indigenous inhabitants of the Americas, the Spaniards cemented a legacy of deploying brutal attack dogs in accomplishing the conquest over and subsequent extirpation of Indigenous populations (Johnson, p.76; Parry & Yingling, p. 80). With the successful destruction of Indigenous communities, the Spanish unleashed the violence of dogs on the plantation, where slave hounds were crucial to the brutal management of slave economies. Dogs were deployed by plantation owners to track and hunt runaway slaves and rebels, and were routinely used to oversee and enforce labor operations (Parry & Yingling, p. 72; Johnson, p. 74). As Parry and

Yingling make evident, the canines in the colonists' arsenal constituted a form of biopower that scaffolded racial capitalism, and the handler-hound dyad was a terrifying "interspecies shaper of racial hierarchy and slavery" (p. 72).

Following the arrival of envoys from the British and French empires to the Americas, constellational colonies that came under insurgent threat were taken as an opportunity to wage campaigns of terror in bids to maintain a stronghold over respective territories. Johnson notes that in one account, as a response to the French Caribbean Saint Dominque colony's imperiled standing, commanders in the French army resorted to commissioning the purchase of famed Cuban bloodhounds from Spanish handlers in the region (p. 68). These pedigreed hounds were renowned for both their expert and unrivaled vicious conditioning (Johnson, p. 72). Establishing trans-imperial campaigns of terror and torture was indispensable to the commerce and trade networks that preserved the shared power among white colonists (Johnson p. 67, p. 72; Parry & Yingling, p. 84). Likewise, common to the satellite deployment of the dogs across different European empires was the staging of public executions and consumption of Black, living flesh, as a brute, yet effective, assertion of terror and fear upon those under colonial rule (Parry & Yingling, p. 86; Johnson, p. 76). Cuban bloodhounds eventually made their way into the ante-bellum American south around the early-mid 19th century. In this region, slavecatching became a lucrative way for non-slaveholding and landless whites to capitalize on the bondage of the enslaved, further spurring the professionalization of and demand for the handler-hound dyad (Parry & Yingling, p. 92).

The slave hound's infamy for brutality would further be intensified through accounts of handlers' incitement of grisly tactics that far exceeded what was required to re-capture and detain dissidents (Parry & Yingling, p. 78). Documented canine violence reveals gruesome accounts of dogs left to disembowel and shred the flesh of their victims. Other accounts tell of servants publicly sacrificed in making a mere spectacle of the brutal kill; and of butcher shops selling human meat for handlers to keep alive their hounds' taste for human flesh (Parry & Yingling, p. 78; Johnson p. 68, p. 76). Parry and Yingling recount one handler's penchant for having his dogs attack the genitals of the enslaved, in what Ko would rightly describe as "white supremacy's sexual, racist appetite for *nonhuman* death" (Parry & Yingling, p. 88; Ko, p. 50, emphasis in the original). Various slave narratives also tell of masters who flayed and smoked Black flesh for human consumption (Ko, p. 52).

Although slaveholders touted the dog's animosity towards the enslaved as an instinctual ability to detect racial inferiority, this idea dismissed the fact that training racial enmity, through Pavlovian conditioning, required severe abuse, mistreatment, and disciplining of the hounds (Johnson, p. 72). For this occupation, particular breeds were selected not only for their acute sensory capabilities but also for possessing structural integrity such that they could withstand savage beatings that might kill another breed (Johnson, p. 83; Parry & Yingling, p. 75). Black slaves were forced to regularly and severely beat the puppies who would grow up to be slave hounds, inculcating in them an aggression towards

Black people. Simply put, brutalized canines would go on to brutalize racialized human beings. While the literature sometimes describes handler-dog units relying on "collaboration" or "mercenary force," from a CAS vantage point, we have an imperative to dissociate the deliberate, white supremacist, human-driven weaponization of canines from any concept of interspecies unity or teamwork (Parry & Yingling, p. 94; Johnson, p. 73). Without a CAS framework, we miss seeing the ways that the brutalization and subjugation of non-white populations goes hand in hand with the brutalization and subjugation of animals.

The horrors of death at the literal jaws of slave hounds lead us to think carefully through the issue raised by scholars on the centrality of the rapacious hunger and consumption at the jaws of white supremacy, in both figurative and material ways. If, as Kim argues, the consumption of animals (and more specifically the animals permissible according to Western norms) is linked to notions of human supremacy, whiteness, masculinity, and nationalism, then this makes evident the significance of situating Black bodies as subhuman on the food chain as a mechanism of inscribing animality onto these racialized bodies (Kim, p. 56).

More acutely, Ko objects to labeling white supremacy as a system, or institution, and instead asserts that it is a "living, insidious, expansive, colonial force that works to 'get inside,' *consume* and destroy" (p. 3, emphasis added). Ko's intervention concerns white supremacy's insatiable appetite for nonhuman deaths, and how this is linked to a broader appetite for minoritized classes. She brands the practice of white supremacy "zoological witchcraft," where minoritized classes are consumed in physical and conceptual ways, hollowed out into "epidermal shells" and repurposed with the "definitions from the dominant class" (p. 54). This accomplishes a display of racial degradation that re-inscribes the myth of racial difference and white superiority (p. 99).

Both Megan Glick (2013) and Kim marshal arguments for a borderland conception of humanity under colonial constructs (Glick, p. 642; Kim, p. 272). Race, as a taxonomy of power, aggregates non-white populations and animals alike, casting them into a qualitatively liminal borderland realm (Kim, p. 22; Glick, p. 641). Likewise, in both of their accounts, being classified as human is a matter of gradation, rather than a dichotomy between inclusion and exclusion (Kim, p. 22; Glick, p. 642). Glick writes that in the eyes of a white supremacist state, there is an important distinction where disenfranchised classes, imagined outside of the notion of the human, are seen as "slaughterable but not murderable" (p. 641). To become disenfranchised is to become miscible with notions of animality, and to be open season for forms of violence deemed too abhorrent for humans (p. 642).

To be cast outside of the white, human prototype is to be shunted into these death-worlds, "racialized as prey" (Parry & Yingling, p. 76), and ultimately fated to be catabolized by a white supremacist state. With respect to the concept of the borderland and subhumanity, an important expansion is proposed. Beyond understanding the borderland as a space of exclusion where racialized and animalized beings are exiled, it must also be seen as an arena where fictive rivalries are set in motion and where inhabitants are turned against each other in struggles for survival. Ko observes this in the vehement rejection of the figure of the animal by racialized groups (p. 20). For racialized people, being compared to animals conjures associations of the brutal violence socially sanctioned against nonhumans. Interspecies hostilities, and a zero-sum view of rights to a life without violence, are a central feature of how white supremacy maintains the tautology of violence that feeds its survival. Pitting the dog against the enslaved is among countless precipitations of white supremacy's need for interspecies conflict.

Nazi dogs

In *The Best Friend of the Murderers: Guard Dogs and the Nazi Holocaust*, Robert Tindol observes that 200,000 dogs were used by the Nazis during World War II, compared to 6000 dogs who were deployed by the Germans during the first world war (Tindol, 2013, p. 105). Dogs of breeds that are known for friendliness were trained by the Nazis to terrorize, maul, and sometimes kill prisoners of the concentration camps (p. 105). As Tindol writes: "In regard to the use of guard dogs, the Nazi camps were examples of the modern prison that Foucault describes in such intricate detail, albeit a prison in which every prisoner is on death row and will sooner or later be executed" (p. 116). As in the modern prison, Tindol argues that dogs were used as a disciplinary tactic to terrorize prisoners into docile bodies and to maximize their productivity as laborers. Tindol notes that the hundreds of watchful eyes of the Nazi guard dogs added to the surveillance of the guards and the panoptic nature of the camps. Beyond their eyes, however, prisoners were aware that the dogs, unlike human guards, could "sense their movements and fear" and track them by their smell (p. 118).

Witness testimony from concentration camps invokes the terror instilled by the guard dogs. As one survivor recounts:

> We arrived in the middle of a pitch black night. Visions of horror. Visions of terror. The most tormented hours of my imprisonment. Cries of wild animals, unholy howling. What was it all about? The reception by the jailers, accompanied by their huge, well-trained wolfhounds. We were so afraid our legs buckled. We knew we would never leave this place.
>
> (Cited in Tindol, 2013, p. 106)

Another survivor recalls:

> The boxcars were forced open and the SS guards stormed in. Shouting wildly, they prodded us with rifle butts and bayonets and beat us with clubs, then set the dogs loose on us. Those who fell and could not get up were ripped apart. I was wearing a large cape which the dogs sank their teeth into, forcing me to submit.
>
> (pp. 106–7)

As in witness accounts of slave hounds, testimony from Maideneck includes examples of dogs eating their human prey. As a survivor from this camp reports:

> After endless torment the prisoners no longer had the strength to cover the 30 feet required to get back in line. Those who remained lying on the floor were taken to the camp kennels where they became the main course for the ravenous German shepherds. With their sharp teeth these vicious dogs tore apart the bodies of people who had been thrown into the cages still alive. We found out later that whatever scraps of human flesh were left over from this feeding frenzy were taken daily to the crematory. No trace was left. Everything was spotless, even pleasant.
>
> (p. 107)

At Buchenwald, 120–150 dogs were kept in kennels at the camp, and the dogs were conditioned to bite men in striped clothing (p. 108). A veterinarian survivor from the camp attests that "The dogs were trained exclusively to 'attack prisoners'" (p. 108). In particular, the dogs were trained to keep workers in line and to prevent them from resting. A survivor from Buchenwald recounts:

> With blows from the cane and the barking of dogs, the march to the infamous sewage facility in the gardening area began. And then a frightening drama unlike any that older prisoners had ever experienced began to unfold. At double time prisoners had to carry away heavy crates of excrement. The SS turned their dogs onto the exhausted men who had collapsed; the animals tore the clothes of the poor men into rags.
>
> (p. 108)

Yves Béon, a witness from the Dora camp, observes that prisoners feared the dogs more than the guns of the SS officers, and that this fear prevented them from evading the hell of their lives and the rule of the Nazis even by committing suicide.

> The dogs are here at Dora, as in all the camps. Held on leashes by their masters, they growl ferociously whenever a prisoner is near. One word or gesture from the SS and the dogs will tear the prisoner apart. They are really more efficient than their masters; a prisoner seeking death could cross the line without worrying too much about a bullet in the back or head, but the dogs are a terrifying, visceral fear.
>
> (p. 109)

Like police and prison dogs today, these same dogs who are so terrorizing to those they are trained to attack were the "best friends" of their "masters." Béon describes the affectionate play, games of catch, strokes, and caresses between SS officers and their hounds (Tindol, 2013, p. 109), much as police dog handlers describe the affectionate bonds they have with their "K-9 partners" (Wardell

& Barrett-Lee, 2018; Russell, 2012). Similarly, the veterinarian witness from Buchenwald describes the dogs having large kennels, running spaces, and good diets, and being well cared for when sick. This is similar to police and prison dogs today, in whom large sums of money and energy have been invested, and who in some respects have the status of quasi-officers, and who are therefore given the best possible veterinary care (Wardell & Barrett-Lee).

Rudolf Höss, the commandant of Auschwitz, notes that Himmler considered one dog to be the equivalent of two human guards, particularly at the women's camp of Ravensbruck; however, 150 dogs was "not enough" for the larger camp of Auschwitz (Tindol, 2013, p. 110). Höss is cited as having said "Himmler counted on the use of dogs to have a deterring effect on the prisoners" (p. 110). Höss recollected of the concentration camp guards, "When they were bored or just wanted to have some fun, they would sic the dogs on the prisoners" (p. 110). Other cases of guards using the dogs for sadistic pleasure have been recorded. One particularly sadistic SS officer, Kurth Franz, would let loose his dog Barry to attack prisoners arbitrarily (p. 111) and to herd prisoners into the gas chambers at both Treblinka and Sobibor. As one witness recounts:

> [T]here was a dog named Barry who was trained by the SS men to bite the Jews, especially when they were naked on the way to the gas chamber. The beatings, the biting of Barry, and the shooting and shouting of the guards caused the Jews to run through the "tube" and push themselves into the "baths," hoping to find some escape from the hell around them.
>
> (p. 111)

Similar to the sexual sadism of certain slaveholders discussed above, another SS officer, Otto Moll, who was in charge of the Auschwitz crematoria, had "a preference for setting his German shepherd loose on young, attractive Jewish women" (p. 111).

Despite these horrifying stories, Tindol observes that Nazi guard dogs were of breeds that are naturally affectionate and cooperative, and would not attack humans under normal conditions, but did so only on command and due to conditioning (pp.115–16). Tindol contends that although the dogs terrorized, maimed, and killed millions of prisoners, they did so out of an abused "love" and "loyalty" for their human masters (pp. 119–20). Nazi dog trainer Paul Henss justified his work with dogs by describing them as police dogs, used to capture escaping concentration camp prisoners much as police dogs are used to capture criminals and escaped convicts (Tindol, p. 105, pp. 115–16). Tindol follows Henss in using the comparison between camp and police dogs to exculpate. However, he does so to defend the innocence of the dogs rather than of the humans who deployed them. As he writes, "For Barry, the attacking of prisoners was likely a game" and "Barry was merely a normal dog that [sic] loved his human companion. Police dogs, after all, are trained to attack on a hair-trigger command as well" (p. 119). Again comparing the concentration camp dogs to police dogs, Tindol observes that:

the behaviors of the dogs were those normally instilled in police dogs everywhere through training. If police actions were appropriated by Nazi guards with the ultimate goal of extermination—which they were—then we should not fault the dogs for failing to reason out the moral implications of the routine guarding tasks they had been trained to perform. In all likelihood, Barry would have been a fine police dog in less chaotic times.

(p. 120)

As Tindol notes, the use of dogs in Europe by police and to control prisoners predated the Nazi concentration camps, and undoubtedly inspired the use of canine power in these spaces. The modern police dog must thus be situated in the history of power as it is deployed in concentration camps as well as in the institution of slavery.

Hunting and haunting as police ethos

With the 13th Amendment's seeming—if deceptively incomplete—foreclosure on Southern slavery, the slave patrols of the plantation, like the canine power deployed by the Nazis, may appear as relics of brutal regimes. Yet, the re-emergence of a similarly chimeric method of racial terror would not be far off. Writing of the legacy of slave hounds in modern K-9 police units, Johnson cautions that "disturbingly similar conversations about the use of this and other torture techniques are omnipresent two centuries later" (Johnson, 2017, p. 85). A history and genealogy of the modern police dog reveals the fundamental ways in which the figure of the dog—as a symbol, technology, and being of terror—is capitalized on by the law to police symbolic and material boundaries across racial lines (Wall, 2016, p. 871). Situating the modern-day police dog against the hounds of chattel slavery is not merely a simplistic overlaying of two discontinuous and distinct iterations of state power. Rather, as Wall and Yingling cuttingly note, it is to see the circulation of canine terror that began on the plantation has perfused the succeeding historical re-assertions of racial domination, culminating in our neoliberal present rooted in a ruthless colonial and capitalist past. Here, the police dog once again emerges as a central player for the white supremacist state in the present (Wall, 2016, p. 876).

The socio-cultural productions and logics that enable the use of police dogs sit against a backdrop of white bourgeois anxieties about Black disorder, revolt, and criminality (Wall, 2016, p. 863). While the first attempts to launch K-9 programs in departments across the U.S. are documented as far back as the early 1900s, it would not be until the height of the Civil Rights era that the key conditions would materialize for the widespread institutionalization of the police dog (p. 864). In the early 1950s, cities like Baltimore and St. Louis were pioneers of the K-9 programs. By the '60s these programs were operating in at least 24 departments across the country (p. 864). Proponents of instating K-9 programs specifically championed the police dog as an invaluable ally and technology that would suppress dissenting and unruly crowds and "administer public order" (p. 864). Broadly aligning crowds as threats to a safe and civil society functioned as a racially galvanizing dog-whistle for justifying the need to rein in Black citizens fighting for their civic freedoms (p. 869). This preoccupation with controlling crowds and securing social order was racially scripted through the white supremacist grammar that called for the preservation of "civilization" (p. 869). Wall sees these discursive terms that sanction brute violence as raced, much as they are classed. Thinking through Ko to see the centrality of animality to racism, we should also not miss how "*Animal* is part of the vocabulary of white supremacist violence" (Wall, 2016, p. 869; Ko, p. 99, italics in the original).

Images, like the oft-seen photograph of a white police officer at the helm of a snarling German shepherd, wielded against a peaceful demonstrator during the Birmingham, Alabama, protests in the '60s, provide a record of what Wall refers to as "animality harnessed" by the capitalist, racist state (Wall, 2016, p. 877). As a response to fears surrounding the excessive nature of the dog's force and their potential to inflict unbounded damage, K-9 advocates cast an image of the police dog as a controlled, measured, and proportionate law enforcement technology (p. 873). This framing oversold the degree to which "expert training" produced a near-perfect weapon that would only attack on command (p. 873). In one particular case of a police dog mauling in the UK, the victim recounted the dog clamping their jaws down on the victim's leg, and despite the screams of the canine's commanding officer, the dog did not relent. Only upon ramming the dog with his baton and "twist[ing] its head off" did the officer finally succeed in getting the dog to release, though not without the dog taking a chunk of the victim's flesh (Wall, 2014, p. 6). It stands to reason that brutalizing the canines for what they are trained to do is more likely than not a normalized practice, and that even in this role, they hardly benefit from any safeguards against police brutality.

With respect to the breeds that would dominate K-9 units across police departments, Wall marks the importance of the ill-named German shepherd and "Alsatian" breeds that filled this role (Wall, 2016, p. 865). Early in the 19th century, the breed became "Germanized" such that it became a canvas for the projection of attributes that were tied up with imperial and colonial conceptions of race, nationhood, blood, purity, and loyalty (p. 866). As seen in the previous section, the disturbing legacy of the racialization of the breed would further be intensified through the Nazis' extensive reliance on the breed during World War II, making the breed an "icon of state terror, highlighting its unstable, double image of obedient hero and vicious beast," a contradicting duality, that Wall argues, persists for the breed to this day (p. 866).

Kim points to pit bulls as another breed that has become the object of raced projections (see also Tarver, 2013; Guenther, 2020), reminding us of the porosity between the concepts of animality, species, and race. In the last several decades, the breed has been inseparable from racist notions of Blackness and associations of hyper-aggression and criminality in ways that have dramatically stunted their life expectancies and quality of life (Kim, p. 255). This much is evident in Stefano Bloch and Daniel Martínez's (2020) sociological overview of the incidence of lethal force by law enforcement that results in acts of "canicide" (p. 143). According to Justin Marceau, law enforcement officers in the U.S. kill an estimated 25 animals a day (Marceau, 2019, 276). Many dogs are killed, for instance, when police burst into residences and kill canines who try to guard and protect their homes and humans. Bloch and Martínez argue that a collision of racialized, classed, and speciesist histories create a pit bull–human nexus that results in the disproportionate maiming and killing of this breed by police officers (p. 149).

However, we should not take this to mean that breeds selected to do police work have fared much better. In Canada and the U.S. police dogs are bred and trained from birth for police work. Training for these dogs is divided into "narcotics searching" and "bite work," and entails terrifying experiences such as dangling in the air on a longline suspended from a helicopter, while the helicopter makes a "deafening" amount of noise (Rose, 2017, p. 124), and disciplining with an "electronic collar" to stop barking (Rose, pp. 67, 77).

When looking at the data and evaluations of the risk posed to K-9s in the line of duty, the emergent trend is that police dogs have not only been burdened with increasingly dangerous duties in comparison with their commanding officers, but have also not received the kinds of protections afforded to their commanding human officers (Barberi et al., 2019, p. 90). Police dog handlers are themselves eight times more likely to be in a shooting than a regular police officer (Rose, p. 89), and thus frequently send their dogs ahead into situations where shooting will occur (Ensminger, 2011; Allsopp, 2012; Wardell & Barrett-Lee, 2018). As Rose reports, "'For K9 teams, one out of one hundred have a lethal encounter with a firearm; for the average police officer, it's one out of one hundred thousand'" (p. 98). Police dogs who search for narcotics also run the risk of accidentally ingesting the drugs, as when a discovered stash of liquid heroine was splashed on a police dog's nose, which can quickly be fatal (Rose, p. 113). Needless to say, police dogs who are trained to search for explosives run the risk of dying when a bomb detonates. In addition to being blown up, poisoned, shot, stabbed, and sprayed with bear spray (Rose, 188), Rose describes police dogs being "choked, kicked, punched, and yelled at by people they've been commanded to attack" (p. 100), beaten with a backpack of tools, falling off a cliff in pursuit of a suspect, and even being bitten in the face by a suspect (p. 171). As a result of the inevitable abuse police dogs undergo in training and on the job, these animals develop a mistrust of anyone other than their handler. In return, one police dog handler is cited as stating: "Bad guy reaches for a gun and the dog is on him. Rookie cops try to shoot around the dog, but seasoned cops shoot through the dog" (Rose, pp. 104–5). Police dog handlers simultaneously refer to the dogs as their "partners" and their children, calling themselves "Dad" (Rose pp. 77, 88–9), yet will kill their own dogs in circumstances where they would not shoot their human partner or a human child.

In addition to being victims of trauma, assault, and deadly force, one of the most frequent causes of death for K-9s is heat exhaustion. Negligent abandonment of K-9s in police vehicles results in heat stroke-related fatalities that roughly mirror the rates of deaths attributed to gun-shot wounds and motor vehicle accidents (Barberi et al., 2019, pp. 90, 94). Despite being elevated into a racialized status of para-whiteness, we can thus see that under the human supremacist underpinnings of law enforcement, the life expectancy of these dogs is nevertheless curtailed. After all, they remain *animal* and thus disposable and consumable from the perspective of white and human supremacy. As Kim aptly asserts, "benevolent" dominance *remains* dominance (p. 271).

Canine terror in the time of BLM

In the era of Black Lives Matter (BLM), both the dynamics of deployment and the symbolism of the police dog as used against Black demonstrators continue to show remarkable fidelity to their original racial histories. Cue the protests that erupted in Ferguson, Missouri, in 2014, after the killing of Michael Brown, precisely 40 years after the passage of the Civil Rights Act. The imagery of police dogs unleashed on Black crowds uncannily harkened back to the disturbing images from the freedom struggle of the '60s in Birmingham. These are part of a stained track record where post-civil rights era police officers have analogized Black people to dog treats (Wall, 2016, p. 861). Contemporary police officers use social media to publicize their eagerness to have "bite work" for their K-9 units, and navy seals have come under investigation following the emergence of footage showing military canines attacking a stand-in wearing a Colin Kaepernick jersey (Wall, p. 876; BBC "Kaepernick Shirt," 2020). In *The Dog Lover Unit*, a book that is highly sympathetic to the police, Rose acknowledges that police dog handlers are nearly all white men (p. 2). Although at one point she meets a Black police dog handler, who expresses considerable internalized racism (p. 61), when describing the K-9 training in the U.S. Rose writes: "The troops gather round. There are no women on this division, no minorities that I can recognize; all the teams are white men." (p. 122) Rose asks one of these men why he likes being a police dog handler and, by way of reply, he quotes Hemingway: "There is no hunting like the hunting of man; and those who have hunted armed men long enough and liked it, never care for anything else thereafter" (Rose, p. 160).

In 2020, in the aftermath of George Floyd's abhorrent public execution by police officers in Minneapolis, newly re-ignited BLM protests spread from this epicenter, across 140 cities in the U.S., and reverberated into a decentered reckoning with racial injustice on a global scale (Bryson Taylor, 2020). These demonstrations aligned with the BLM movement's long-standing grammar: a denunciation of racist state violence, police brutality, and the charge of state impunity. Police suppression of the ensuing protests relied on harsh riot-control measures that culminated in the deployment of the national guard in Minneapolis within weeks of the killing (Bryson Taylor, 2020). Following a streak of peaceful protests outside of the White House, the then-president turned to Twitter to boast that the most "vicious dogs" would be waiting to "greet" any protestors who veered too close to the compound's gates (Trump, 2020). Invoking the police K-9 in this way has disturbing implications. On the one hand, it most evidently taps into the strong current of terror circulating via the dog as a symbol of long-standing racial domination. On the other, it underhandedly centralizes dogs as agents of violence, reifying human and white supremacist notions of animality that cordon off the nonhuman animal world as the locus of extreme violence and uncivilized atrocities. The emphatic incitement of canine terror is easily recognizable for many as a manifestation of the white supremacist kinds of violence seen in retaliation against previous racial justice movements. However, we are reminded by Johnson that we ought not to contaminate our critiques of systems of violence by focusing on the means deployed (the hounds), rather than the systems enlisting these means (p. 82). Otherwise, animals wind up bearing the weight of displaced blame for egregious and distinctly human acts of brutality (Johnson, p. 82). In the absence of a CAS perspective that challenges this instantiation of white supremacist notions of animality, we are liable to miss the crucial fact that animals are central vectors for white supremacist ends only through their own subjection to violent dominion.

Precisely what does it mean for an incumbent president, to borrow Kim's words, to be "clamoring for the punishment" of Black citizens protesting against a murderously racist state? Extending Kim's argument, there can never be a race-neutral narrative for sanctioning a violent method of state force that traces along a lineage of racial domination and continues a legacy of white-on-Black terror. Yet, this particular example is neither an outlier nor the exception to the fundamental project of continuing the spectacle of violent colonial, human, and white supremacist mastery. Police dogs, under the bondage of humans, continue the mauling of the racialized underclass of citizens. And the attacks that were, are, and will be, perhaps resound like an agonizing phantom limb syndrome to the racialized subjects who hear the stirring hunger of a white supremacist power eager to put its teeth to work.

In their physical state, teeth evoke the most primal and raw form of violence in the sanguine and disfiguring potential of their contact with flesh (Wall, p. 3). There is a violent seizing of flesh in the deployment of dogs, inflecting the meaning of the common aphorisms which describe a weaker side of the law as having no "bite," or a punishing and persecutory facet as having "teeth" (Wall, 2016, p. 878; Wall, 2014, p. 3). Wall states that in the act of devouring, there is power to order, and teeth, in metaphorical and material ways, come together to represent his notion of the "teeth of power" (Wall, 2014, p. 3). He turns to Derrida, who thinks the procurement of sovereignty through a "lexicon of devouring," and suggests that the notion of sovereignty itself perhaps rests in the "power of devouring" (p. 3).

Proceeding from Ko's argument that colonialism and white supremacy stand as a living and consumptive entity, Wall's analysis aids us in distilling an anatomical model of its body. If, as Ko puts it, white supremacy annexes the bodies of the racialized, fashioning "white appendages" for itself, then, to think through the notion of teeth as both figurative and material emblems of power, is to see how white supremacy has outfitted itself with razor-sharp canine teeth, all under the unrelenting veneer of a color-blind law and order (p. 107).

Following Grégoire Chamayou, Wall marks the reliance on patrol dogs as the embodiment of the police as a "hunting institution" (Wall, 2016, p. 874). A dynamic of predator and prey is established such that some humans are asymmetrically criminalized *and* animalized as prey, and the racist spatialization of redlined urban spaces has turned them into the grounds where the hunt takes place (p. 874). Officers of the law have long avowed that what makes dogs ideal suppressors of crowds and "hunters of men" is the "psychological effect" they engender (Wall, p. 868). This means that the German shepherd's cultural force of disseminating terror is made possible only through its cultural image as a vicious, snarling predator—directly countering any claims of dogs as a civilized and measured technology (Wall, 2016, p. 868; Wall, 2014, p. 6).

On the conceptual topographies of the canine-induced psychological terror, Wall reflects on the ways that the physical patrolling and hunting of Black bodies extends into a *haunting* where the terrors of being pursued by salivating and snarling beasts long outlive the physical chase (Wall, 2014, p. 6). Victims report recurring night terrors where they are devoured alive and recount the terrifying closeness to death at the time of the attack (p. 6). As Parry and Yingling hauntingly remark, the slave hounds' tormenting approach would have been among the last sounds in life heard by the enslaved (Parry & Yingling, 2020, p. 165).

While Wall refers to this terrorization as the "psycho-politics" of the police dog, Ko would frame it as one of the cannibalistic rituals of white supremacy that ingest the souls and consciousness of the oppressed, turning Black bodies into "extensions of whiteness" (Wall, 2014, p. 6; Ko, 2019, p. 107). Both Ko and Wall are tapping into the simultaneous physical, social, and psychological domains where terror is induced by the police dog and the ways that the internal world of Black subjects is under siege. When the police forthrightly avow their power as dependent on the dogs' psychological effects, it signals the profound importance of the aftershocks of terror and torment in maintaining racial domination. What the figure of the police dog successfully draws forth, then, is a multigenerational legacy of haunted victims. Wall includes Malcolm X's recognition that, while the Klan's uniform may have been upgraded, the hounds have consistently remained commissioned by a white supremacist state for the last 200 years (p. 877). Though police may make claims to tactical post-racial reforms or even "color-blind" practices, what remains salient is that the very power of one of its most disturbing programs is forged through the psychological torment that echoes across generations of the racially oppressed.

Police dogs and the indoctrinating of children

When we began researching this chapter, it came as a surprise that numerous recent books on police dogs are targeted at children. Perhaps less surprising is that many of these books are written by retired police dog handlers and family members of police officers. As we also learned, police dogs are frequently brought by law enforcement officers into schools to teach children—in the most positive light—about police work. Again linking police dogs and children, in Canada 12 police dog puppies are named through "the national Name the Puppy contest" each year, where school children across the country suggest names that are then selected for the young dogs (Rose, p. 22).

While the preponderance of children's books in the police dog literature was unexpected, in *The Dog Lover Unit* Rose provides an explanation for the genre. On one of the shifts that she spent with a police dog handler and his K-9 while researching her book, they went to a children's school, where Rose relates that the handler had the dog do obedience tricks to entertain the schoolchildren. Afterwards, the officer handed out trading cards and temporary tattoos, to the delight of the kids. Following the visit to the children's school, Rose cites herself as saying to the police officer: "'Each positive contact with the police, I'm sure it pays for itself." The officer replies: "Tenfold in the end"' (p. 183). Rose herself spends a considerable amount of her book examining the poor reputation of human police officers after years of media coverage of their racism and brutality. She reports discussing negative perceptions of the police by the public with each of the officers she spent time with, and cites at length their defenses of the profession, including consistent denials of structural racism. Rose's own book, focusing on the officers' love of their dogs, can be seen as an attempt to salvage the reputation of the police. *The Dog Lover Unit* is full of photographs of smiling police officers, shown in loving and noble poses with their dogs, as if these rosy images might eclipse widespread video footage of white policemen beating and murdering Black men, and media coverage of police murders and oppression of Indigenous people, such as the so-called "Starlight tours." What Rose never says—and what is never depicted in children's books—is that these very dogs have themselves been used and continue to be used by the police as weapons for purposes of racialized brutality. Given the extreme violence for which police dogs are deployed, and the histories of fascism, colonialism, and slavery in which this deployment is situated, it was disturbing to learn that police dogs are so widely used as a means to endear the police to children.

Several children's books about police dogs mention that guard dogs and police dogs have a long tradition in European history, and notably in Germany, but fail to mention the role such dogs played for the Nazi regime. Nor do children's books on police dogs mention their use in Euro-American slavery, or the history of dogs deployed against Indigenous persons in the Americas. For example, *Meet the Police Dogs: The K-9 Cops* (Judah, 2009) includes a section called "A brief history of police dogs," which traces the history of "guard dogs" as far back as ancient Greece and Rome, but never mentions slave hounds or concentration camp dogs, or the use of dogs to hunt and kill Indigenous people. Another children's book, *Officer Woof! Woof!*, commences by telling readers that dogs have been used by police in Europe since the Middle Ages. A few pages later, dogs are described being used for law enforcement in continental Europe, beginning in Paris, and then later in Belgium, Germany, and Austria-Hungary. Deceptively, however, this history is merely described as one in which dogs were used to "protect against criminal gangs roaming around at night" (Pets Unchained, 2017, n.p.). On the next page we are told that German shepherds were initially bred and trained specifically to be police dogs, and the author writes: "The dogs were trained systematically for obedience and respect to their officers as well as the tracking and attacking of the bad guys" (n.p.). The reader is not informed that in recent European history "the bad guys" were notably Jews, and no mention is made of the use of dogs to attack and control Jewish prisoners, and to herd them to their deaths. Similarly, the legacy of slave hounds in the U.S. and the use of dogs to exterminate Indigenous peoples goes untold in this telling of carceral canine history.

Children's books about police dogs deceive children on many other levels, including about the comfort of the lives these dogs lead and the reasons why they perform their jobs. One such book, *Police Dog Recruit: A Puppy's Dream to Become a Crime Fighter*, is written by a former U.S. police dog handler and current police dog trainer, Andy Falco, and his eight-year-old son, Kelly Falco (Falco & Falco, 2015). The son's writing is in large font that young children can read, and the father's writing is in smaller font, with information that might be of interest to older children and the adults who read to young children. The story is of a puppy, also named Falco, whose father and grandfather were police dogs, and who therefore dreams of being a police dog himself. To achieve this goal, he is said to "always listen to his mom and dad and does his best to stay out of trouble," goes to bed on time, and eats well. Illustrations show the puppy being hugged by his canine mother and father, being tucked into bed in an indoor bedroom by his dad dog and fed at a table by his mom dog, when in reality police dog puppies in North America are taken from their "breeding mothers" at six weeks old and kept in kennels while being trained, and generally sleep in outdoor kennels throughout their careers. As Rose describes:

> When I walk the row of kennels where the dogs are caged, they run to the fence, barking furiously, jumping on the wire that separates us. They scratch and whine, begging to be released, to go out and do something, anything. Their kennels are two little rooms with bare cement floors, open to the outside, easy to hose down and clean, but neither cozy nor stimulating. It is here, when the dogs are housed between assignments, that I pity them the most. No animal wants to live like that. I wish they didn't have to. But these animals are not pets; they are soldiers. They live in barracks as devoid of color or comfort as any army post.
>
> (Rose, 2017, p. 17)

Although during assignments police dogs live with their handlers, handlers are instructed to treat these dogs differently from pets, at least until retirement. For instance, in her description of Eryx, a police dog in training, Rose writes:

When he came to Nat at eight weeks old, he cried for two nights solid in his outdoor kennel. He wanted to come in and curl up by the fire with the family dog. But Eryx is not a pet. He is a police dog in training, and standard training policy for RCMP police dogs is that they sleep in kennels when they are not working. If he passes, he won't be curling up by the fire until his working days are through, in another decade or so.

(p. 28)

Although, as noted above, handlers regularly refer to themselves as "Dads" to their police dogs, they also stress that police dogs are not family dogs. For example, when one police dog handler had to move out of province, the police dog he had raised since puppyhood could not go with the officer, his family, and their other dog, and was instead assigned to another police officer (p. 77).

Another children's book, *K-9 Flash Becomes A Hero!*, tells a story about a puppy named Flash who, like Falco, longs to be a police dog when she grows up. Fortunately for Flash, "a police officer came to the animal shelter looking for puppies that wanted to become police dogs. Flash knew that being a K-9 was exactly what she was born to do. This was her big chance!" (Johnson, 2017, n.p.). *K-9 Flash* was written by another retired U.S. police dog handler, and, as noted above, in North America puppies are bred specifically to become police dogs. Although law enforcement would apparently like children to believe otherwise, police dogs in North America are not rescued from shelters and do not become police dogs because of their dreams or vocations.

Children's books also deceive children about the characteristics that are looked for in police dogs, masking the violence that is these dogs' purpose in law enforcement. For example, in *K-9 Flash Becomes A Hero!*, we are told that "Flash had to pass many tests to prove she was smart, fast, and strong," but there is no mention that she would be tested for a strong prey drive and aggressivity, and that few female dogs are selected to be police dogs because they are believed to be less aggressive than males. *Meet the Police Dogs: The K-9 Cops*, tells readers on the back cover to "Take the time to thank a canine cop today" and, like *K-9 Flash Becomes a Hero!*, describes police dog training in a deceptive manner. As the canine narrator of the book tells children, "We attend Police Dog School… Only the best are chosen for this job… the smartest, most loyal and those dogs willing to be trained and worked. During Police Dog School, we learn all kinds of obedience skills such as sit, stay, come, climb, jump, wait, crawl, and down" (Judah, 2009, n.p.). Again children are led to believe that dogs are selected for intelligence rather than aggression, and never learn that, unless they are narcotics search dogs, what they are trained to do is called "bite work."

Children's books lead children to believe that dogs help police "catch bad guys" without any mention of violence, and get to run, jump and climb, but do not dwell on other experiences that police dogs will have, such as being beaten, choked, stabbed, poisoned, shot, and otherwise assaulted by suspects, or being trained with "electronic collars" and left in hot cars by their handlers. *Dogs to the Rescue!* (Green, 2014) is one of the few books to mention the violent deaths of police dogs and the possibility that they will be hurt by suspects; however, the focus is placed on how honored the dogs will be for this "sacrifice."

> Police dogs are considered officers of the law. Judges severely punish people who hurt police dogs. Those found guilty of such a crime must pay large fines or go to prison. Police dogs killed in the line of duty receive a funeral ceremony with full police honors. Police officers gather from near and far to honor a fallen canine companion.
>
> (Green, 2014, p. 17)

In *Dogs to the Rescue!*, one police dog, Kenzo, is also described as saving two police officers and taking two bullets himself. However, "After two months of rest, Kenzo recovered. He returned to the sheriff's department a hero. For his bravery, Kenzo was awarded a Medal of Honor and a Combat Star. These are two of the highest police honors in the United States!" (Green, 2014, p. 21) Another children's book that provides children with some sense of the risks to which police dogs are subjected is *A Hero Lives in My Family: A Story for Kids of First Responders* (Hunt, 2015). Unfortunately, this book lumps police and military dogs together with fire dogs and medical dogs, implying that what the police and military do is similar to what doctors and firefighters do—each being "first responders" who simply and heroically save and protect lives.

Perhaps the most troubling and revealing of all the children's books we read for this chapter is *Police Dog Recruit: A Puppy's Dream to Become a Crime Fighter*, the book co-authored by a retired police dog handler and his son (Falco & Falco, 2015). In the Introduction, the eight-year-old co-author, Kelly, expresses amazement that police dogs can track suspects by their smell, writing, "I think it is amazing how they know the difference from the bad guy's odor and other people's odor... that is crazy to me." Later in the book Kelly writes, "One day, Falco and [his littermate] Fiona," who are young puppies with no police dog training, "go for a walk with their humans. They see local police and two men in handcuffs... Falco smells the men seated on the ground. Their scent is unique and different than the other human beings... As he walks away, Falco can't stop thinking about the smell of the two men in handcuffs." (n.p.) The way Kelly describes the situation, without being corrected by his father, suggests that dogs simply alert naturally to the peculiar scent of "bad guys." In reality, of course, when police dogs alert to a person based on their smell it is because they have been taken to a crime scene where that scent was found, or have been given an article of clothing or some other object with that person's scent and have been commanded to track it. Police dogs are also used to track humans the police do not consider "bad guys," such as lost or kidnapped children, runaway teens, and missing people with dementia. Although dogs track on command or based on training, Kelly's description misleadingly suggests to other children that "bad guys" have an inherently different smell from "good guys," indicating an evil or inferior essence. Kelly's narrative of a "different smell" obscures social factors that culminate in certain people being policed and incarcerated, including police racism and bias.

As the story continues, Falco—the untrained puppy—just cannot stop thinking about how the bad guys smelled different from good guys, and then he picks up the scent of something in the bushes that smells like the bad guys. Running to the bushes, he discovers money and a gun. At this point, "Falco barks to alert the police." Even though Falco is just a puppy with no police training who is out for a walk with his humans, when he barks "The police run to Falco. They look inside the bush and find the missing money and gun used in the robbery. This is all the police officers need to arrest the two men. Thanks to Falco, the crime is solved!" As Kelly's dad, Andy, explains: "To place a person under arrest, a law enforcement officer needs what is called probable cause and/ or solid evidence. Because a properly trained police dog's nose is so powerful and reliable, courts accept evidence gained through the use of a Police Dog." (n.p.) What he overlooks in this explanation is that Falco was not "a properly trained police dog," and so his barking would not in fact have brought police running, and nor would it have constituted probable cause or solid evidence. Again, the impression is given to children that just any dog can naturally smell "bad guys," because they belong to a category biologically separate from other humans. Although marketed as a book about police dogs, this book obfuscates the truths of police dog training and deployment, and the social construction of crime.

This narrative of a "different smell" recalls the belief of slaveholders that the slave hounds' supposed ability to "smell" slaves was proof of racial difference and hierarchy. As Johnson notes:

> Through breeding and training, slave hunters believed that they had conditioned enmity between their dogs and black people, premissed [sic] upon innate and perceptible racial difference. Racializing the animals' sensory capabilities, in which they could supposedly smell, hear or see racial difference, resonated with concepts of discernibly scented bodies posited by southern slave holders… Many white southerners considered that "blacks smell, sound, look, feel, even taste different."
>
> (Johnson, 2009, pp. 75–6)

Eight-year-old Kelly's explanation of police dogs' ability to track suspects is an historical echo of these racist beliefs, with "bad guys" substituting for the more transparent construct of "blacks."

The language of "bad guys" is ubiquitous not only in *Police Dog Recruit* but in other children's books about police dogs, such as *K-9 Flash Becomes A Hero!* (Johnson, 2017). Even more disturbingly, the childish phrase "bad guys" (and "baddies" in the U.K.) to refer to suspects is found throughout books about police dogs that are written for adults, and is found consistently in the discourse of police officers (Rose, 2017; Russell, 2012; Allsopp, 2015). Although *Police*

Dog Recruit is written for children and is co-authored by a child, its infantile and Manichean vision of a world divided into good and evil, cops and robbers, is characteristic of police dog handlers in all the countries in which Rose interviews them (Canada, the U.S., Britain, and France). The racialization of the "bad guys" is never made explicit in children's books, but some of these books, such as *Meet the Police Dogs: The K-9 Cops* (Judah, 2009), include photographs of police dog handlers and their canines, and without exception these depict white men with German shepherds. Interestingly, this book also includes photos of police handlers and their dogs doing school visits, and all the children in the photographs are also white, suggesting that the police might target predominantly white elite schools, rather than racialized inner-city schools.

Given the long-standing weaponization of dogs in the service of white supremacy, it is paradoxical that these same dogs would be used as propaganda to counter the negative publicity police receive due to their brutalization and execution of people of color. Nonetheless, in works such as Rose's, these connections are made explicit. As noted, Rose persistently discusses and does not deny the racism and violence of the police, and the generally negative reputation of the police for these reasons. As a "poet" and a "liberal," Rose even claims to have previously felt an anti-police "bias" herself, but her time with police dog handlers is a conversion experience, and she ultimately writes her book in defense of police. Rose's primary tactic is to demonstrate how much police handlers love their dogs, and thus must be good people, even while her book documents considerable abuse of these very animals within the police force, and the tremendous risks to which these animals are exposed without any possibility of consent.

However incongruous and selective, children's books, police dog visits to schools, and competitions that allow children to name police dogs are each used to teach youth to like, respect, trust, and even aspire to become police officers, because of the love of animals they share with children. This love is purportedly evidenced in the work handlers do with police dogs, which is presented to kids as vocational labor that honors dogs in ways that are meaningful to them, when it is not. Children are thus indoctrinated to understand police as "good guys," and to see policing as an attractive career in which they can grow up to not only catch "bad guys" but also work closely with animals.

Conclusions

The particular characteristics and capacities of canines have long been exploited by humans to hunt and control other animals, for instance in fox hunting, sheep herding, and the capture of wild and feral horses. It is no surprise, given the widespread harnessing of canine power to oppress other species of nonhuman animals, that they would also have been deployed so frequently against human beings who have been animalized, most often through racialization. Having used dogs to hunt animals, and to recapture feral animals, slaveholders and law enforcement alike would turn to this same species to hunt and recapture men and women who had been excluded from the category of the human by white supremacy. Since humans have long used dogs to herd sheep and goats, including to their slaughter, SS officers would think to use these same animals to herd dehumanized human beings into concentration camps and gas chambers. In this chapter we have focused on the use of carceral canines to terrorize, discipline, maim, and kill human beings who have been animalized by white supremacy, but further critical animal studies scholarship should explore the ways that these oppressed animals are themselves exploited so that humans can police and incarcerate other animals, as well as the continual imbrication of racial and animal oppression.

Acknowledgement

The phrase "carceral canines" was first heard several years ago by one of the authors, Chloë Taylor, in conversations with poet, scholar, and author Billy-Ray Belcourt. Moreover, it was discussions with Belcourt at that time—on the topics of decolonial studies, critical animal studies, and the use of dogs as tools of settler colonial law enforcement—that inspired the writing of this chapter.

References

Alexander, M. (2011). The new Jim Crow. *Ohio State Journal of Criminal Law, 9*(1), 7–26.

Allsopp, N. (2012). *K9 cops: Police dogs of the world.* Big Sky Publishing.

Barberi, D., Gibbs, J.C., & Schally, J.L. (2019) K9s killed in the line of duty. *Contemporary Justice Review, 22*(1), 86–100.

BBC. (2020, August 3). Kaepernick shirt was attack dogs' target at Navy Seal event. BBC. Retrieved August 20, 2020, from www.bbc.com/news/world-us-canada-53636098

Bloch, S. & Martínez, D.E. (2020). Canicide by cop: A geographical analysis of canine killings by police in Los Angeles. *Geoforum, 111*, 142–54.

Bryson Taylor, B. (2020, July 10). George Floyd protests: A timeline. *The New York Times.* Retrieved from: www.nytimes.com/article/george-floyd-protests-timeline.html.

Davis, A.Y. (2003). *Are prisons obsolete?* Seven Stories Press.

Ensminger, J.J. (2011). *Police and military dogs: Criminal detection, forensic evidence, and judicial admissibility.* CRC Press.

Falco, A. & Falco, K. (2015). *Police dog recruit: A puppy's dream to become a crime fighter.* Tactical Productions and Marketing.

Glick, M.H. (2013). Animal instincts: Race, criminality, and the reversal of the 'human'. *American Quarterly, 65*(3), 639–59.

Green, S. (2014). *Dogs to the rescue! Police dogs.* Bellwether Media.

Guenther, L. (2016). Life behind bars. In H. Sharp and C. Taylor (Eds.), *Feminist Philosophies of Life.* McGill-Queens University Press. 217–38.

Guenther, K. (2020). *The lives and deaths of shelter animals.* Stanford University Press.

Hunt, S. (2015). *A hero lives in my family: A story for kids of first responders.* Kids Hero Series of Social Motion Publishing.

Johnson, J.K. (2017). *K-9 Flash becomes a hero!* Social Motion Publishing.

Johnson, S.E. (2009). 'You should give them blacks to eat': Waging inter-American wars of torture and terror. *American Quarterly, 61*(1), 65–92.

Judah, C. (2009). *Meet the police dogs: The K-9 cops*. Coastal Books.

Ko, A. (2019). *Racism as zoological witchcraft: A guide for getting out*. Lantern Books.

Kim, C.J. (2015). *Dangerous crossings: Race, species, and nature in a multicultural age*. Cambridge University Press.

Marceau, J. (2019). *Beyond cages: Animal law and criminal punishment*. Cambridge University Press.

Mogul, J., Ritchie, A., & Whitlock, K. (2012). *Queer (in)justice: The criminalization of LGBT people in the United States*. Beacon Press.

Nichols, R. (2014). The colonialism of incarceration. *Radical Philosophy Review, 17*(2), 435–55.

Parry, T. & Yingling, C.W. (2020). Slave hounds and abolition in the Americas. *Past & Present. 246*(1), 68–108.

Pets Unchained. (2017). *Officer Woof! Woof!* Speedy Publishing LLC.

Rose, R. (2017). *The dog lover unit: Lessons in courage from the world's K9 Cops*. St. Martin's Press.

Russell, J.P. (2012). *Trust your dog: Police, firefighters, and military officers talk about their K-9 partners*. Lindholm Press.

Tarver, E. (2014). The Dangerous Individual('s) Dog: Race, Criminality, and the "Pit Bull", in *Culture, Theory, and Critique, 55*(3), 273–85.

Tindol, R. (2013). The best friend of the murderers: Guard dogs and the Nazi Holocaust. In R. Hediger (Ed.), *Animals and war: Studies of Europe and North America*. Brill Press. 105–22.

Trump, D. [realDonaldTrump]. (2020). May 30. …have been greeted with the most vicious dogs, and most ominous weapons, I have ever seen. That's when people would have been really badly hurt, at least. Many Secret Service agents just waiting for action. "We put the young ones on the front line, sir, they love it, and…[Tweet]. Retrieved from: https://twitter.com/realdonaldtrump/status/1266711223657205763?lang=en

Wall, T. (2014). Legal terror and the police dog. *Radical Philosophy*. Retrieved from www.radicalphilosophy.com/commentary/legal-terror-and-the-police-dog

Wall, T. (2016). 'For the very existence of civilization': The police dog and racial terror. *American Quarterly, 68*(4), 861–82.

Wacquant, L. 2009. *Punishing the poor: The neoliberal government of social insecurity*. Duke University Press.

Wardell, D., with Lynne Barrett-Lee. (2018). *Fabulous Finn: The brave police dog who came back from the brink*. Quercus Editions Ltd.

15 Trauma as a Möbius strip

PTSD, animal research, and the Oak Ridge prisoner experiments

Lauren Corman

Degradation of the patient or an undermining of their personal dignity and self-worth was not a side effect of the STU [Social Therapy Unit] programs. It was part of the design.
(Justice E.M. Morgan, Barker vs. Barker, p. 22)

…what can we say about subjects of violence who are rendered as not having a dignity to violate?
(Wadiwel, 2017, p. 389)

This chapter puts the torture and subsequent trauma resulting from the human experiments at the now infamous Oak Ridge psychiatric facility—a maximum security forensic hospital—in conversation with the torture and subsequent trauma resulting from PTSD (post-traumatic stress disorder) animal experiments. I draw on Dinesh Wadiwel's use of Agamben's notion of a "zone of legal exception" and his discussion of "black sites" to trace the cycle of trauma as it loops onto and reproduces itself. Wadiwel (2017) argues, "The 'black site' as a concept offers an imaginary for a space of social, political and juridical exception that hides extensive and intense violence against those who are captured within this zone of confinement" (p. 391).

In this chapter I argue that the Oak Ridge Division of the Penetanguishene Mental Health Centre (Oak Ridge) and the PTSD-focused animal laboratory represent two "black sites" that reinforce each other, both enacted under the guise of benevolence, in which harm is rationalized as necessary to treat harm. The torture of both the patients at Oak Ridge, often labeled "psychopaths" in particular and selected out for experimentation, and the rodents so commonly used in PTSD experimentation are among the most peripheralized subjects, cast into sites of invisibility where collective complicity regards them as abject debris. Indeed, Dr. Elliott Barker, a main facilitator of the programs, referred to the patients as "throw away people" (Morgan 2020, p. 304).[1] Journalist Colin Perkel (2019) also relates, "Barker, Rochon [the Plaintiff's co-lead trial counsel] said, knew society would be 'repulsed' by his methods, but believe he was justified because he was dealing with 'throwaway people' society rejected, [the] court heard."

Who or what is rendered a "throw away" is a matter of social construction and power, contingent on history and context. When we consider the experiments at Oak Ridge, we see it is not just patients generally who were tortured at Oak Ridge but those frequently categorized as psychopaths and the "criminally insane," targeted for "treatment" as such. When we consider PTSD animal experimentation, we see it is not just animals generally who are tortured in animal trauma-related experimentation, but most ubiquitously those categorized as rodents. These groups, "rodents" and "psychopaths" or the "criminally insane" dwell on the lowest rungs of Western "taxonomies of power" (Kim 2015), beyond the farthest reaches of "the human," the province of man. Indeed as Allen McMann, a former inmate at Oak Ridge, eloquently observes, "We were a society that existed outside of your society" (Fine, 2020, para 5). The patients tortured at Oak Ridge are among the most "animalized humans," and the lab rodents are among the most "animalized animals," to use Wolfe's (2003) terms.

To ground my theoretical argument, I provide a brief introduction to the Oak Ridge facility and the programs it conducted, primarily drawing on Justice Edward M. Morgan's recent 310-page judgement on the associated lawsuit. Next I offer a synopsis of contemporary PTSD research on rodents, using Perkins, Brothers, and Nemeroff's "Animal Models for Post-Traumatic Stress Disorder" (2018) from the authoritative collection *Post-Traumatic Stress Disorder* to anchor the discussion. Then I investigate the overlaps between Oak Ridge and animal laboratories. To make sense of these significant continuities, as noted, I apply Kim's "taxonomies of power" and Wadiwel's understanding of "black sites." Specifically, I consider Wadiwel's assertion that "black sites" are necessary to the creation of sovereign power. To conclude, I maintain that carceral human settings and animal laboratories are interlocked expressions of settler colonialism.

While a scholarly literature exists about Oak Ridge, including some condemnations, the research fails to employ Agamben's "black sites" as a crucial interpretive lens. Further, contextualization of the experiments remains profoundly anthropocentric, as evidenced in the 2019 opening of the trial, which drew historical continuities between Oak Ridge and human experiments infamously conducted on Jews by the Nazis (Perkel, 2019), yet did not mention animal experiments. Yet, I contend that we miss something vital about the Oak Ridge experiments if we fail to situate them within a broader analysis of the cojoined constructions of animality and humanity in the Western liberal tradition. One of the Plaintiffs, Reginal Barker, directly highlights the wrong committed against him through naming his animalization within the Total Encounter Capsule, one of the three programs scrutinized by the Oak Ridge lawsuit:

> The Clinical Records of the session indicate that it was a very uncomfortable 102 F in the Capsule for this session and that the patients were naked on a rubber floor and shared an open toilet. Mr. Barker is recorded as

having exclaimed, "You give us no shower, treat us like animals", and then, "Let us out of here, Dr. Barker."

(Morgan, 2020, p. 48)

Indeed, ideas about the Western conception of "the human" occupy the heart of the Oak Ridge case. Specifically, while the lawsuit revolves around a breach of fiduciary duties, the remedy to such a breach redresses not only physical and psychiatric harms, but also "…less tangible harms such as injury to a patient's right of inviolability and human dignity" (Morgan, p. 278). Justice Morgan comments on the Court of Appeal ruling, which

…described the programs in relatively strong terms favoured by the Plaintiffs: "[t]he Plaintiffs' claim involves very serious allegations of torture and degradation of human dignity." This more closely reflects the description contained in the Amended Second Fresh as Amended Statement of Claim which asserts, at para 173, that at Oak Ridge the Defendants subjected the Plaintiffs to "inhumane treatment and psychological and physical abuse and…experimentation."

(Morgan, 2020, p. 7)

The right of inviolability and human dignity are, like all legal rights, *exclusively* human. Until recently, the patients' claim hung in the balance, with four of the Plaintiffs dying as the case dragged on.

Degradation by design

Over the past two decades, beginning in 2000, more than two dozen patients have sued two doctors and the Ontario government for $25 million in damages. The claim asks whether the Oak Ridge doctors, Dr. Maier and Dr. Barker, along with the Crown, breached fiduciary duties owed to the Oak Ridge patients. The three impugned programs comprising the Social Therapy Unit (STU) at Oak Ridge are central to the claim:

a mind-altering drug regime called the Defence Disruptive Therapy ("DDT"), an isolation cell for group encounters, including hallucinogenic drug encounters, called the Total Encounter Capsule (the "Capsule"), and a strict physical disciplinary regime called the Motivation, Attitude, Participation Program ("MAPP").

(Morgan, 2020, pp. 5–6)

In his June 25, 2020 decision, Justice Morgan affirmed that indeed the two key doctors who ran the experimental STU programs and the government of Ontario breached their fiduciary duties and committed "assault and battery by subjecting these patients to unethical and medically meritless programs"

(Rochon & Genova, 2020). The trial is now set to enter phase two to determine damages, including possible damages against the Defendants, the Ontario government and two doctors Dr. Elliott Barker and Dr. Gary Maier.

Oak Ridge opened in 1933 as the "Criminal Insane Building," a specialized division of the Ontario Hospital in Penetanguishene. For over 81 years it functioned as the province's only maximum-security mental health care center (Waypoint Centre for Mental Health Care, "Origins", n.d.). Operating under a veil of benevolence, Dr. Barry Boyd (superintendent) in partnership with Dr. Barker implemented programs to create a "therapeutic community," in which patients would treat each other. Conceived as an opportunity to shift power, patients would set their own rules. Founded in 1965, those in the Social Therapy Unit (STU) participated in an intensive 80–100 hours a week of therapy; under Dr. Elliott Barker (who was hired by Boyd), council meetings, psychotherapy sessions, and the like became compulsory. Among his influences were British psychiatrist Dr. Maxwell Jones and theorist Martin Buber who believed that "full engagement with the other... could be the occasion for decisive personal transformation" (Weisman, 1995, p.43). Additionally, Barker visited China in 1965 to research "character-reshaping methods in prison camps" (Fine, 2020, para 6). Dr. Gary Maier, one of the other key doctors involved, regarded the STU programs as "the greatest experiment in psychiatry" (Fine, 2020, para 6). Conversely, expert witness Dr. Stephen Hucker lambasted them as a "blip in the history of psychiatry" (Morgan, p. 16). As Justice Morgan queries at the beginning of his judgement, "In other words, how can we characterize the impugned programs that the Plaintiffs were put through in the decade and a half beginning in the mid-1960s: were they medicine or were they abuse?" (p. 8).

These kinds of questions struck closer to home after I attended the Oak Ridge trial in May 2019, when Jane Marion, a dear friend and an estate representative for Plaintiff James (Jim) Motherall, testified on his behalf. Jim had died the year before. In her testimony, Marion threw the conditions of the Oak Ridge facility into sharp relief:

> [Motherall] felt that the violence done to him by the doctors and staff participants, could really only be seen as torture and he craved a judgment that would act not only to compensate those who had lost everything to this unusual and vile trauma, but would make judicial precedent that those who occupy positions of power and authority cannot be excused from culpability and complicity in treating human beings like "throw aways" and lab rats.
>
> (Marion, 2019, personal communication)

The day of Marion's testimony, a former patient shared his experiences at Oak Ridge, including the gruesome details of "the Capsule", a small, barren, and perpetually lit room where up to eight men were confined, restrained, and handcuffed together naked, conditions to which Motherall was also subjected. Between 1966 and 1983, these conditions were only part of a suite of experiments conducted on the patients, including forced mind-altering drug injections (such as LSD), solitary confinement, sensory deprivation, and physical restraints and mandatory immobility.

The Capsule STU program was especially startling given the uncanny similarity between the treatment of the patients and animal experimentation laboratories, which I was then researching, where animals are confined, retrained, and harmed in a variety of ways. What is a more paradigmatic image of animal experimentation than a rat in a cage, who is fed through a tube? Likewise, Justice Morgan describes the Capsule program, charged with the eerie echo of an animal lab:

> There was no solid food provided to the patients during their Capsule sessions; rather, they were made to ingest food and water from straws protruding through holes in the wall. Patients in the Capsule were subjected to sleep deprivation, were frequently restrained or strapped to each other, and were most often injected with DDT drugs to lower their inhibitions. They were often paired so that patients diagnosed with schizophrenia experiencing a chaotic range of emotions where [*sic*] placed together with patients with antisocial personality disorders—"psychopaths" in Dr. Barker's terminology—experiencing no emotions at all. In this state of forced polarity, they confronted each other, forming what Dr. Barker described in Buberian terms as "genuine dialogue…"
>
> (Morgan, 2020, p. 69)

The patients did not know why they were there, as they were not informed of the alleged therapeutic value of the treatments (Morgan, 2020). Justice Morgan notes that the Capsule program was "…specifically designed to be intense, disorienting, and stressful" (p. 264).

Intentional violence was a common theme throughout the STU programs. Various techniques were employed within this rubric of harm, framed by the doctors as necessary for treatment. Evident is the distorted logic of the doctors who believed the torment of the experiments was beneficial to the patients. Indeed, Dr. Barker openly admits the brutality of his therapies. For example, in 1968 Barker published an article (co-authored with a patient) in which he described the intrinsic violence of the Intensive Treatment Unit (later renamed, the STU). Barker argues, "The use of force is legitimate in treating patients for illnesses which they do not recognize, in settings where they will be incarcerated until they change" (Barker, quoted in Morgan, 2020, p. 11). He frames such force as preventative of even more insidious and greater harms. Barker bluntly states,

> While a bald report of the activities of a patient committee may suggest the weekend pastimes of Storm Troopers, our explanation would be that a seeming rape is attempted in order to impregnate the patient with ideas that may prevent a further, more subtle, and more menacing rape: the rape

that the illness perpetrates upon the patient, and the rape that a sick society perpetrates upon the patient, and the rape that a sick society maintains upon a few of its sicker members.

(Barker, quoted in Morgan, p. 12)

In his both vicious and patriarchal rendering of the STU, Barker plainly does not deny the violence inflicted upon the patients but instead elevates it to a higher purpose, one ultimately in service of his ward. Indeed, Barker conceives force as a *necessary* treatment, meted out to patients who are confined: "…force brough [*sic*] the patient to our hospital, physical force maintains him there, and this force will not be lifted until he changes his behaviour in a recognizable way" (Morgan, 2020, p. 12). Thus, force was not incidental but integral to the STU therapies, believed to be catalytic for change and, to use Barker's phrase, the "goad to freedom" (quoted in Morgan, p. 13). In other words, force brought them there and force will set them free. Harm is transfigured as care. Justice Morgan characterizes such views as emblematic of the coercive and authoritarian nature of Barker's approach. The Plaintiffs' lawyers similarly note,

The programs were designed to break down and change the Plaintiffs' personalities using techniques such as drug-induced delirium and hallucination, brainwashing and positional torture, with no apparent plan for reconstructing them once they had been broken down.

(Rochon & Genova, 2020)

Concluding phase one of the over 20-year legal battle, Justice Morgan dismissed the Crown's argument that it did not owe the Plaintiffs fiduciary duties because of its mandate to protect public safety. As co-lead trial counsel, Joel P. Rochon elaborates, "This landmark decision underscores the inviolability and the right to human dignity of every person, regardless of who they are—no one should be exposed to the dehumanizing and degrading treatment and experimentation" (Rochon & Genova, 2020). The court found that even those labelled "criminally insane" and diagnosed with psychopathy, anti-social personality disorder, schizophrenia, etc., are nonetheless human beings, and thus are entitled to inviolability and the right to human dignity. Notably, Kempers (2020) underscores that "dignity" has historically been used to differentiate humans from other animals, signaling their rational status and autonomy. While recent debates suggest a mobilization of "animal dignity" as a concept to promote animal flourishing, few legal examples use the concept and the idea remains peripheral.

Animal experimentation

Although the staggering and highly variable uses of rodents in lab research are widely documented, leading one author to characterize mice as "biomedical Swiss Army knives" (Shipani, 2019), the precise number of rodents used in

PTSD research is not collated. However, we know that they are the favored in PTSD animal models. Additionally, we know that animal research increased 5.7% in the United States from 2017 to 2018, to include 780, 070 animals used in public and private institutions (U.S. Statistics, 2020). However, this number excludes most fish, mice, and rats, who are not covered by the Animal Welfare Act. The number of animals used in experiments in Canada continues to increase, "reaching an all-time high of 4, 415, 467 animals in 2017," though this number only represents the statistics voluntarily provided by Canadian researchers accredited by the Canadian Council on Animal Care (Canadian Centre for Alternatives to Animal Methods, "Welcome to CCAAM", n.d.). The Humane Society International (2012) reports that 115 million animals are used globally in laboratory experimentation.

While many might believe that the modern animal experimentation lab takes every measure to avoid harm to animals, employing the "Replacement, Reduction, and Refinement" approach (Canadian Centre for Alternatives to Animal Methods "The Three Rs,", n.d.), we see that harm is considered necessary and is commonly inflicted upon animals in trauma-focused experiments. Indeed, precipitation of trauma is the central goal of animal-based PTSD research. Like the violence of the Oak Ridge experiments, harm is enacted as a kind of prophylactic against future harm. In their comprehensive review of current PTSD animal models, "Animal Models for Post-Traumatic Stress Disorder," Perkins, Brothers, and Nemeroff (2018) immediately emphasize a categorical difference between humans and other animals, which allows for experimentation on the latter, reasoning presented as so common sense as not to require justification:

> PTSD animal models hold the potential to provide invaluable sources of information on PTSD predisposition, onset, course, and treatment, with the opportunity to examine and manipulate the biology of the disorder in ways that are not always possible in humans. Given that animals are used in place of humans for such work, distinct differences between the two will invariably be observed, providing a number of challenges for animal work to address the human condition.
> (Perkins, Brothers, & Nemeroff, 2018, p. 422)

Shortly after, the authors parse specific relevant differences between human and animal experiences of trauma, which serve to both underscore the challenges of animal models as well as to suggest a *de facto* rationalization of their use:

> Trauma in humans is inevitably colored by the complexity of human thought. The type of complex stress experienced by humans following a traumatic event is often compounded by the ability to worry—the ability to envision the future and how to calculate how that future may be affected by the trauma—a trait that cannot be assumed in rodents.
> (p. 422)

Said differently, the authors assume that animals do not possess certain key traits and therefore, animal models remain lamentably imperfect. Yet, it is animals' supposed lack in comparison to humans which makes them available for such use. Interestingly, as a testament to their ubiquity within trauma research, at the beginning of their chapter, the authors presuppose rodents as the archetypal PTSD animal model. They then provide an overview of "PTSD Induction in Animal Models," including physical stressors such as Single-Prolonged Stress (SPS), Underwater Stress, Immobilization Stress (IMO), and Electric Shock, as well as psychological stressors including Predator Stress, Social Defeat Stress (SDS), and Early Life Trauma, all of which again assume a rodent model.

They first discuss Single-Prolonged Stress, an admittedly mischaracterized paradigm, which actually involves animals' subjection to numerous psychological and physiological stressors, thus compounding several acute ones (as common in human trauma). They write, "Typically, the animal (usually murine) is retrained for 2 hours, followed by a 20-minute forced swim and a 15-minute reprieve before the animal is exposed to ether vapors until unconscious" (Perkins, Brothers, & Nemeroff, p. 423). Next, they consider the "brief, natural, life-threatening situation" created through the Underwater Stress paradigm, in which rats swim in a water maze and then are "forcefully held underwater for 30 seconds" (p. 425). Immobilization Stress (IMO) entails placing animals within restricted spaces such as plastic tubes, or fully immobilizing them by restraint to wooden boards (p. 426). The Electric Shock paradigm, when used to induce fear conditioning, involves multiple trials with repeated shocks, commonly foot shocks. Predator Stress, one of the key psychological stressors used in animal models of PTSD, relies on a "natural unconditioned fear of predators by exposing rodents directly to predators or exposing them to objects marked with predator urine or odor" (p. 428). A more complex "psychosocial predator stress model" combines predator stress with "chronic social instability" through daily changing of cage mates (p. 428).

The Social Defeat Stress paradigm exploits the rodents' sociality to produce trauma. Rodents are placed as "intruders" within the cages of larger, more aggressive ones, "followed by a 24 hours of odor exposure to the aggressive resident" (p. 429). Over a period of 5–10 days, the experiment is repeated through exposure to multiple aggressive residents. "Animals exposed to SDS exhibit decreased motility and exploration, immobility on forced swim, and reduced sucrose preference (anhedonia)," state the authors (p. 429).

Perkins, Brothers, and Nemeroff (2018) note in their overview that although Early Life Trauma represents a risk factor in PTSD development, animal models frequently do not capture this characteristic. They offer a brief synopsis of the associated sparse literature, studies which include pairing periodic maternal deprivation of young rats with foot shocks as adults. Rats experiencing this potent combination of harms demonstrate "increased memory, emotional, and executive function impairment compared to rats exposed to foot shock alone" (p. 429).

Their research summary concludes with a description of genetic and epigenetic models, based on the genetic manipulation of mice and rats to produce PTSD vulnerability. These genetically modified rodents are then exposed to electric shock, including inescapable shock (IS), or predator scent stress. As one recent example of the fidelity of the PTSD animal model, Colucci et al.'s (2020) "Predicting Susceptibility and Resilience in an Animal Model of Post-Traumatic Stress Disorder," similarly relies on rodents. They opine that animal models facilitate "…development of more effective therapeutic strategies for humans. Although there are different rodent PTSD models, they however lack good translational value," which the authors claim to address in their study. Their work involves exposing the rats to electric shock and social isolation.

When considered alongside the Oak Ridge case, the parallels between contemporary PTSD animal models and human experimentation within the forensic hospital are striking. The violence done to the former is similarly intentional. The objective is to inflict harm to inspire negative effects that offer curative value according to the experimenters, one directed to the patients themselves and the other to those afflicted with PTSD. If the subjects of the Immobilization Stress paradigm were human, forensic psychiatrist Dr. John Bradford, Plaintiff expert in the Oak Ridge case, would likely regard their treatment as "positional torture," akin to "strict immobility" experienced by patients within the Motivation, Attitude, Participation Program (MAPP). Rodents' containment in tubes, part of the PTSD animal model Immobilization Stress paradigm, shares remarkable constancy with the treatment of patients in the barren and windowless 10-foot by 10-foot room of the Capsule, where the men languished for up to 11 days (Morgan, 2020).

The routinized and inescapable exposure to an aggressive cage mate, as conducted in the Predator Stress model, also finds a disturbing counterpart in the Capsule, where patients such as Danny Joanisse feared he would be abused by a "child murderer" or "pedophile" (Morgan, p. 275). Justice Morgan further elaborates on such conditions within the Capsule bearing a clear resemblance to the Social Defeat Stress (SDS) dyads used in PTSD animal models, in which a rodent is brought into the cage of a larger, aggressive one:

> This last point—that restraints were used to intentionally pair domineering with submissive patients—was related most graphically by Danny Joanisse. He testified as to being in the [STU] as a small 14-year-old boy. He related that his most vivid memory of the STU was having spent several days in the Capsule cuffed to a convicted pedophile murderer named George White. Dr. Hucker, in his testimony at trial, conceded that this would have provoked substantial anxiety and stress, and that it potentially could have caused lifelong harm.
>
> (Morgan, 2020, p. 44)

Commenting on the MAP program, Dr. Bradford testified, "…there were some people who were probably deliberately paired with individuals that caused them anxiety and distress, so it had a—a kind of a *coercive distress, traumatic-inducing component* to it as well" (emphasis added, quoted in Morgan, p. 44). As Justice Morgan concluded in his findings, Dr. Barker, Dr. Maier, and the Crown are liable for having caused substantial long-term harm and substantial short-term harm to Danny Joanisse. (Unfortunately, while Joanisse provided trial testimony, he died before Justice Morgan's judgement.)

For many Plaintiffs, the harm they experienced at Oak Ridge added to abuse they suffered as children. The early life trauma of the Oak Ridge Plaintiffs is thoroughly catalogued by Justice Morgan. Danny Joanisse, for example, suffered both physical and sexual abuse at the St. John's Training School. James Motherall was physically and verbally abused by his adoptive mother, and sexually assaulted by his hockey coach. Michael Pinet was sexually abused by a number of priests at the St. John's Training School. Samuel Shepherd was sexually and physically abused by his father. The list continues. Given that, as Perkins, Brothers, and Nemeroff (2018) indicate, early life trauma is a risk factor for the development of PTSD following adult trauma, the intentional infliction of harm on patients seems particularly cruel in light of their documented mental health conditions and difficult younger years.

Justice Morgan uses the language of vulnerability when describing the Plaintiffs generally, as "vulnerable patients… entirely under the control of the Crown" (p. 285), and "vulnerable, traumatized, and mentally ill individuals" (p. 306). Writing of particular patients, Justice Morgan asserts that "[Maurice Desrochers] was a vulnerable young man who, having been bullied as a youth, was again bullied by the very institution that was supposed to help him" (p. 106). Further, "[a]t the same time, [Dr. Maier] confirmed, in an almost flippant way, that placing a vulnerable and naked 15-year-old [Joanisse] in the Capsule with older criminals was indeed done and was an unusual approach to therapy" (p. 164). He further pronounces, "[Denis LePage's] pre-existing disorders made him particularly vulnerable to the oppressive environment and associated stretches of time in confinement that characterized his MAPP experience" (p. 195). In sum, Justice Morgan concludes,

> Given the scheduling of this trial, it suffices at this juncture to find that there is a valid claim against the Doctors for breach of fiduciary duties, and that the evidence establishes that those fiduciary duties have in fact been breached. On the record before me, both Doctors disregarded the ethical obligations that were on them to treat the patients in a way that did not cause them further harm, to ensure that they obtained truly voluntary and informed consent for treatment and/or experimentation, and to refrain from delegating their oversight and professional judgment to untrained persons (and especially to other patients likely to perpetrate abuse).
>
> (p. 278)

Like the Oak Ridge patients, the absolute vulnerability of rodents within PTSD experiments is evident. They are wholly objectified. They are violently forced into conditions that are meant to create persistent stress. Similar to the Oak Ridge patients, they are held captive and abused without consent, made involuntarily serviceable to some greater good unknown to them. How could the patients at Oak Ridge be harmed so intensely for decades? How is the large-scale use of rodents pervasively accepted? In other words, what cultural scaffolding exists that accounts for the durability of the Oak Ridge experiments, even though the program methodologies were incongruent with the ethical standards of the time (Perkel, 2019; Morgan, 2020)? How does animal experimentation persist despite an abundance of ethological evidence demonstrating animals' sentience and rich cognitive capacities (Bekoff, 2007), not to mention years of critique and availability of alternative medical research methods (Canadian Centre for Alternatives to Animal Models, "Current paradigm", n.d.)?

To answer these questions, I contend that the specificity of each group—rodents and patients who had committed crimes of rape, murder, and child abuse deemed (to use the language of the day) "criminally insane" and/or those branded as "psychopaths" (Weisman, 1995)[2]—are rendered violable through their culturally degraded and animalized status. That is, it is not just patients or inmates who were so flagrantly harmed at Oak Ridge, but particularly those labelled criminally insane and psychopathic. It is not just animals who are brutalized in PTSD laboratories, but those categorized as rodents. Recall counsel Rochon's reflections: "This landmark decision underscores the inviolability and the right to human dignity of every person, *regardless of who they are...*" (Rochon & Genova, 2020, emphasis added).

Taxonomies of power

To reflect on Rochon's comments, I turn to Claire Jean Kim's theoretical concept of "taxonomies of power," which illuminates hierarchies within groups produced as "subhuman, not human, less than human" by the Western settler colonial imagination (p. 283). Shifting from an understanding of interlocking dualisms often found within intersectional thought, we can consider "relationality, positionality and multidimensionality" suggested through Kim's taxonomical analysis of power (p. 17). "Who they are," to use Rochon's words, plunges them below the generic category of "criminals," to name those believed to be even lesser beings, the so-called "criminally insane" or those found not guilty by reason of insanity (Rochon & Genova, 2020). Such criminals are popularly understood as relinquishing any claim to humanity by virtue of the violent crimes they commit and the mental illness they suffer. The concurrent "image of the psychopath [as] that of a cold, heartless, inhuman being" (Martens, 2014) marks the popular landscape. Indicative of their denigrated social status, serial killers and other violent individuals are commonly labelled as "animals." They are, socially speaking, "throwaways."

Nonhuman species are also stratified within dominant Western thought. The lowly and abject status of rodents is not simply attributable to their generalized categorization as animals. Kim affirms, "...the concept of species cannot be reduced to a dualism (human/animal) but rather expresses itself as a taxonomy or complex hierarchical order of different animal kinds" (p. 17). To this end, she names rodents (alongside coyotes, wolves, and insects) as exemplary of animals deemed threatening and suitable for extermination. Comparatively, elephants are figured as "charismatic mega-fauna," deserving of special consideration. Leesa Fawcett (2016) notes that rats are disliked and deemed dangerous, as linguistically evidenced through metaphors such as "You dirty rat!" The cultural disdain for rats is likewise apparent in historical texts. For example, she cites the historical entanglement of Jewish and rat denigration within Nazi propaganda, such as the film *Der ewige Jude* that features the opening lines, "Just as the rat is the lowest of animals, the Jew is the lowest of human beings" (p. 462).

Fawcett also observes rats' profound disposability within the lab environment, despite the fact that ethological research complicates their pure objectification: For example, rats display a range of social behaviors, such as empathy toward restrained cage mates, which they attempt to free if given the opportunity. "If rats are empathetic at any level," she asks, "what does this mean for their ubiquitous use in intrusive experiments?" (p. 461). Of course, the scientific drive toward increasing standardization has created a powerful, self-rationalizing inertia around rodents' use and naturalized their objectification (Birke, Arluke, & Michael, 2007). While rodents remain strongly associated with disease, terror, and disgust (despite some pet-keeping), they are also identified as a "scientific tool" signaling medical progress. Indeed, it is rodents more than any other animal who became standardized and "now exemplify 'laboratory work'" (Birke, Arluke, & Michael, 2007, p. 29).

Rodents and the patients Oak Ridge share a marked debased status. My consideration of patients at Oak Ridge in tandem with rodents in PTSD research is not meant to suggest an equivalency between the experiences of these groups. Rather, following Kim's argument, I am interested in how power operates through dynamic and mutually contingent hierarchical ordering. In the dominant Western liberal tradition, "Othered" groups are constructed in ranked relation to "the human", represented as white, straight, able-bodied, cisgendered, etc. As Kim shows, this matrix has been integral to the production of racial categories in countries such as the United States, which are inextricably bound to colonial practices and processes. Both the rats of PTSD experimentation and the patients of Oak Ridge are cast outside of the realm of "the human," as animalized humans and animalized animals, respectively. Their animalization within and through the carceral setting of both the laboratory and the maximum-security facility enables the harms committed against them. This in turn expedites scientific inquiry, while it simultaneously legitimizes institutional power and authority.

Dinesh Wadiwel's work on "black sites" also helps us make sense of the subjugation of the Oak Ridge patients in the forensic hospital and the rodents in the PTSD lab. Wadiwel (2017) begins his article, "Disability and torture: Exception, epistemology and 'black sites'" with a brief description of the

Australian Government Senate Standing Committees on Community Affairs final report, published in 2015, on harms committed against people with disabilities. Specifically, the report indicated pervasive violence, abuse, and neglect inflicted upon people with disabilities, including electroshock, physical assault, forcible restraint, solitary confinement and routinized use of cages, but remained reluctant to name these violent acts as torture. This is remarkable, notes Wadiwel, because "[i]n another context, any of these practices could be understood as constituting torture" (p. 389). Wadiwel thus asks:

> If naming as torture assumes that the torture victim has an inherent dignity which is being violated through specific acts of violence, what can we say about forms of inflicted suffering that are not regarded as violating inherent dignities (forms of violence that are not granted signification as torture by social or legal institutions, including for example, organized State violence in the context of mass incarceration)? And simultaneously, what can we say about subjects of violence who are rendered as not having a dignity to violate? That is…what happens if torture is naturalized as a form of imperceptible violence? Does this epistemological violence constitute a different kind of torture 'by stealth'?
>
> (Wadiwel, 2017, p. 389)

To answer these questions, Wadiwel explores Giorgio Agamben's scholarship on sovereign exception and biopolitics. Agamben centrally argues that "political sovereignty is based upon the capacity to place life within a zone of legal exception" (Wadiwel, p. 389).

Agamben's theory is clearly applicable to the contexts detailed in this chapter. While Justice Morgan's judgement identifies a breach of fiduciary duty by both the Crown and the named doctors, after a decades-long legal battle, the violence against the patients nonetheless continued unabated for 17 years. What is groundbreaking in Justice Morgan's "landmark decision" (Rochon & Genova, 2020) is that it "underscores the inviolability and the right to human dignity of every person, regardless of who they are…" Returning to the point that, as the Plaintiffs' counsel claimed, the Oak Ridge patients were subjected to experiments similar to those conducted by Nazis, Agamben offers that Auschwitz was a key moment in the articulation of 20th-century biopolitical sovereignty. While the court's decision validates the human dignity of the patients, the Ontario government and the programs operated under legal sanction over many years. Wadiwel demonstrates that this kind of "lawful violence," named as such by Linda Steele, allowed the ongoing systemic violence against people with disabilities. Further, he claims the kinds of violence evidenced within the "care institutions" for people with disabilities finds unsettling parallels with conditions in Nazi camps. "Legal exception is crucial here. The law appears suspended…" (Wadiwel, p. 390).

Essentially, co-lead counsel Rochon welcomes Justice Morgan's finding that the patients at Oak Ridge are indeed human beings. That, despite "who they are," by virtue of their humanity, their dignity and inviolability must be acknowledged. The restraints, solitary confinement, and drug injections, and physical punishments at Oak Ridge are easily mapped onto similar conditions and practices found within institutions housing people with disabilities in Australia. In both instances, the systemic violence meted upon both groups becomes permissible because the institution functions as if the subjects have no dignity to violate and that their bodies are violable. While the violence cannot be undone in either circumstance, the Ontario Superior Court of Justice findings offer an initial remediation. By virtue of the anthropocentric legal regime, though, animals cannot be granted such recognition due to their exclusion from human species membership. Human exceptionalism becomes legal exceptionalism, the "law is suspended."

Wadiwel suggests that people increasingly condemn torture enacted within "black sites," specifically secret intelligence prisons operated and/or enabled by the United States (as part of the Global War on Terror). He aptly notes, "The 'black site' as a concept offers an imaginary for a space of social, political and juridical exception that hides extensive and intensive violence against those who are captured within this zone of confinement" (Wadiwel, p. 391). Visibility of this violence is hinged on the invisibility of other forms. Although the concept of the "black site" has engendered popular appeal in condemning torture, this is tied to the belief that such violence is anomalous and extraordinary rather than routinized and naturalized. Wadiwel disrupts this conceptualization to demonstrate that the notion of the "black site" is equally applicable to highly ubiquitous and normalized practices, such as mass incarceration, which is a manifestation of anti-Blackness essential to colonial advancement of modernity. Just as scholars have questioned Agamben's Eurocentrism in his positioning of the concentration camp as the "most refined example of political violence" (p. 393), Wadiwel reinterprets highly racialized "black sites" to show that such places are non-aberrant, instead representing the achievement of state power and political sovereignty.

Elsewhere, Wadiwel (2002) extends his conversation into nonhuman animal politics to consider how the modern industrial slaughterhouse might also illuminate sovereign exception, biopolitics, and its importance to the law. As this chapter and Wadiwel show, various groups of human beings nonetheless still struggle for recognition of dignity, by virtue of their animalization. I argue that Kim's "taxonomies of power" offers further insight into the related operation of "zones of legal exception," by illuminating the hierarchical ranking of certain categories of humans and animals in relation to colonial configuration of "the human", a process integral to racialization, imperialism, and the colonial project. As animals continue to be subjected to large-scale forms of violence within not only PTSD-focused animal experiments, but also within the numerous other "black sites" of industrial use, the collective refusal to recognize this violence as torture means their bodies, much like those of the Oak Ridge patients, continue "not [to be] coded by knowledge systems as having a dignity that can be infringed" (Kim, 2015, p. 393).

Conclusion

Recognizing violence and torture done to animals and those considered sub-human, inhuman, and animal-like helps us resist Western colonial epistemologies entrenched in the hierarchization of life. A posthuman conceptualization of trauma—posthuman trauma—suggests an understanding that all human and nonhuman animal bodies are inviolable, and all beings possess an inherent dignity. This reconceptualization of trauma defies the colonial logics of the Western liberal tradition, as we refuse both the splitting and binding of animal life into categories of worthiness in relation to "the human." Indeed, the colonial construction of "the human" serves as a category in which all designated Others—human and nonhuman—are prevented from arriving. This is why oppressed groups' proclamations of their humanity, despite the irrefutability of this biological fact, must be continually reasserted under European colonial regimes (Gosine, 2018). Recognition that the Oak Ridge patients are human, while legally vindicating, does not invite a more complex and critical consideration of what "the human" presupposes. The more difficult question is, "What does the category of the human authorize?"

Acknowledgement of posthuman trauma also turns the logic of the PTSD animal model against itself. Within PTSD animal modeling the rodents' sociality and capacity for pain, including their capacity for sustained stress, is what makes them candidates for use. Yet, the violation of bodies and numerous traumas inflicted can no longer be rationalized through a humanist framework that uses the tautology of species membership to perpetuate itself. Consequently, identification of posthuman trauma must necessarily be anti-colonial. The pervasive and ongoing violation of those considered beyond humanity's fringes, which subjects animal life (and humans considered animal-like) to such great mystification as to render them categorically exploitable and killable, is an expression of colonial machinations (Belcourt, 2015). The PTSD animal models bear cultural inheritances dramatically contra to numerous Indigenous worldviews grounded in equitable relations with nonhuman animals (see Corman & Robinson, 2016).

To struggle against nonhuman animal exploitation without connecting that harm to a broader anti-colonial analysis will inevitably treat the spoils of capitalism, appropriation of Indigenous land, extinction of wild species, racialized mass incarceration, and myriad other forms of violence as distinct phenomena without common cause. It will also mean that animal advocates will potentially not link the material and discursive violence done under and through the signifier of "the human" *to other humans* cast outside of its purview and damaged by its colonial calculations. Such activist silos forestall meaningful solidarity across movements and critical scholarship. Alternatively, to denounce the harms committed against the patients at Oak Ridge without considering that the experiments rested on not only the de-humanization, but also the animalization of those designated as the "criminally insane" and psychopaths, is to miss the deep speciesism of the colonial project.

Notes

1 Precisely, under cross-examination, Dr. Maier was queried: "Q. And what Doctor Barker said to you is society considers these throwaway people, anything we can do will be positive. A. Yes" (Morgan, 2020, p. 304).
2 Fine (2017, para 3) reports that some patients were "simply committed by their doctors."

References

Bekoff, M. (2007). *The emotional lives of animals: A leading scientist explores animal joy, sorrow, and empathy—and why they matter.* New World Library.

Belcourt, B. (2015). Animal bodies, colonial subjects: (Re)locating animality in decolonial thought. *Societies, 5,* 1–11.

Birke, L., Arluke, A., & Michael, M. (2007). *The sacrifice: How scientific experiments transform animals and people.* Purdue University Press.

Canadian Centre for Alternatives to Animal Models. (n.d.) Welcome to CCAAM / CaCVAM. University of Windsor. Retrieved September 29, 2020 from www.uwindsor.ca/ccaam/

Canadian Centre for Alternatives to Animal Methods. (n.d.). Current Paradigm. University of Windsor. Retrieved September 29, 2020 from www.uwindsor.ca/ccaam/299/current-paradigm

Canadian Council on Animal Care. (n.d.). The Three Rs—Replacement, Reduction, Refinement. ccac.ca. Retrieved September 29, 2020 from www.ccac.ca/en/three-rs-and-ethics/the-three-rs.html

Colucci, P., Marchetta, E., Mancini, G.F., et al. (2020). Predicting susceptibility and resilience in an animal model of post-traumatic stress disorder (PTSD). *Translational Psychiatry, 10*(243), 1–9.

Corman, L. [Interviewer] & Robinson, M. [Interviewee]. (2016). All my relations: Interview with Margaret Robinson. In J. Castricano & L. Corman's (Eds.), *Animal subjects 2.0* (pp. 229–47). Wilfrid Laurier University Press.

Fawcett, L. (2016). Rats! Being social requires empathy. In J. Castricano & L. Corman (Eds.), *Animal subjects 2.0.* Wilfrid Laurier University Press.

Fine, S. (2017, June 7). Doctors tortured patients at Ontario mental-health centre, judge rules. *Globe and Mail.* Retrieved September 30, 2020 from www.theglobeandmail.com/news/national/doctors-at-ontario-mental-health-facility-tortured-patients-court-finds/article35246519/

Fine, S. (2020, June 30). Court rules that Ontario mental-health program amounted to assault. *Globe and Mail.* Retrieved September 30, 2020 from www.theglobeandmail.com/canada/article-court-rules-that-ontario-mental-health-program-amounted-to-assault/

Gosine, A. (2018). Artefact: Animal. *C Magazine.* Retrieved August 31, 2020 from: https://cmagazine.com/issues/139/animal

Humane Society International. (2012, October 21). About Animal Testing. Hsi.org. Retrieved September 29, 2020 from www.hsi.org/news-media/about/

Kempers, E. (2020). Animal dignity and the law: Potential, problems and possible solutions. *Liverpool Law Review, 41,* 173–99.

Kim, C.J. (2015). *Dangerous crossings: Race, species, and nature in a multicultural age.* Cambridge University Press.

Morgan, E.M. (2020). *Barker v Barker.* ONSC 3766. Retrieved from www.rochongenova. com/Barker-v-Barker-2017-ONSC-3397.pdf

Martens, W. (2014). The hidden suffering of the psychopath. *Psychiatric Times.* Retrieved September 29, 2020 from www.psychiatrictimes.com/view/hidden-suffering-psychopath

Perkel, C. (2019, April 29). Former Oak Ridge psychiatric patients sue province, doctors over treatment. *The Star.* Retrieved Sept 29, 2020 from www.thestar.com/news/ canada/2019/04/29/former-oak-ridge-psychiatric-patients-sue-province-doctors-over-treatment.html

Perkins, E., Brothers, S., & Nemeroff, C. (2018). Animal models for post-traumatic stress disorder. In C. Nemeroff, & C. Marmar (Eds.), *Post-traumatic stress disorder.* Oxford University Press.

Rochon, V. & Genova, J. (2020, June 29). Oakridge. Rochon Genova Barristers. Retrieved September 29, 2020 from www.rochongenova.com/Current-Class-Action-Cases/oakridge.shtml

Shipani, S. (2019). The history of the lab rat is full of scientific triumphs and ethical quandaries. *Smithsonian Magazine.* Retrieved September 29, 2020 from www.smithsonia nmag.com/science-nature/history-lab-rat-scientific-triumphs-ethical-quandaries-180971533/

U.S. Statistics. (2020). *Speaking of Research.* Retrieved from: https://speakingofresearch. com/facts/statistics/

Wadiwel, D. (2002). Cows and sovereignty: Biopower and animal life. *Borderlands e-Journal, 1*(2). Retrieved September 30, 2020 from www.borderlands.net.au/vol1no2_ 2002/wadiwel_cows.html

Wadiwel, D. (2017). Disability and torture: Exception, epistemology and 'black sites'. *Continuum, 31*(3), 388–99.

Waypoint Centre for Mental Health Care. (n.d.) Remembering Oak Ridge: Digital Archive and Exhibit. Waypoint Centre. Retrieved September 29, 2020 from https:// historyexhibit.waypointcentre.ca/exhibits/show/origins

Weisman, R. (1995). Reflections on the Oak Ridge experiment with mentally disordered offenders, 1965–1969. *International Journal of Law and Psychiatry, 18*(3), 265–90.

Wolfe, C. (2003). *Animal rites: American culture, the discourse of species, and posthumanist theory.* The University of Chicago Press.

16 Coexistence as resistance

Humans and non-human animals in carceral settings

Calvin John Smiley

Introduction

Prisons are designed to cut individuals off from society by simultaneously removing physical, emotional, and verbal contact with people outside the prison, and structuring other forms of interaction inside. The earliest American prison models, the Auburn and Pennsylvania systems, both believed in the delivery of punishment that fostered silence and penitence (James, 2014). Eventually, the Auburn model became the standard form of corrections in the United States because it implemented "communal activities," namely the exploitation of prison labor (LeBaron, 2012). Due to the swelling of jail and prison populations beginning in the mid-20th century, the American prison system continues to exponentially grow with the extent of its social control commonly referred to as practices of "mass incarceration" (Garland, 2001). Additionally, the U.S. prison model has been globally exported (Garcia-Rojas, 2016).

Despite its growth, there remains active opposition to mass incarceration. The most obvious participants of prison resistance are justice-affected[1] individuals—those held within the gallows. This chapter examines how individuals within carceral settings exercise their agency by engaging in mutual associations with non-human animals. In so doing, they subvert the prison's draconian rules and maneuver within its silos in a manner that helps sustain their autonomy. Therefore, this chapter discusses existing literature surrounding human and non-human connections, particularly how relationships foster meaning, symbiosis, and resistance. Moreover, I use both fiction and non-fiction examples to highlight how the relationships developed between humans and non-humans cultivate enriching lived experiences through the sharing of mutual respect and spaces.

Meaning, symbiosis, and resistance

Relationships between humans and non-humans are ubiquitous and their importance continues to be well-documented. Furthermore, the field of critical animal studies is a burgeoning area of scholarship that attends to power relationships between humans and animals and theorizes what these relationships look like and how they manifest in society. More recently, an overlap between the fields of criminology and critical animal studies has placed them at the intersection of captivity, specifically prisons. Scholarship surrounding human-animal incarceration has been illustrated in at least three different ways: (1) human-animal programs; (2) human-animal performances; and (3) human-animal partnerships.

Human-animal programs

Scholar-activist Angela Davis notes in the documentary *Eyes on the Prize*, that "There is always a tendency to push prisons to the fringes of our awareness, so that we don't have to deal with what happens inside these horrifying institutions" (Hampton, 1987). In other words, prisons are out of sight and ultimately out of mind for many people in their day-to-day existence. While the deprivation of liberty is inherent in incarceration and meant to be *the* punishment, research has shown that an abundance of programs occur within captive spaces.

For example, Karen M. Morin (2016) has explored the carceral similarities and parallels between: the death chamber and slaughterhouse; bio-testing in labs and prisons; and prisoner and animal labor. Morin highlights the history of incarcerated individuals, similar to animals, being used for untested drugs and products. Lori Gruen (2014), a leading scholar in feminist and animal studies, has examined the role of dignity, particularly surrounding caging and experimenting on non-human animals and human prisoners. Here, Gruen's work has looked at the caging of chimpanzees who have been used in testing laboratories.

Beyond testing, literature surrounding human-animal prison programs, such as animal training, highlights specific goal-oriented instruction. Programs using a range of animals, particularly dogs and horses, are initiated with a purpose (Bachi, 2013; Britton & Button, 2005; Cooke & Farrington, 2016; Furst, 2006; Harkrader, Burke, & Owen, 2004; Huss, 2013). While the standard opinion is that many of these programs are used to assist and modify prisoner behavior for constructive outcomes, this work often either neglects or looks past the exploitative nature of these programs, which force animals to engage in various exercises and assignments. Additionally, these programs situate incarcerated humans in a place of authority over non-human animals, thus, reinforcing and replicating an authoritarian position within carceral settings.

Human-animal performance

Colin Dayan's (2011) book, *The Law is a White Dog*, examines racialization and incapacitation showing that legal definitions are detrimental to both humans' and non-humans' bondage. Yet, when thinking of human captivity, we typically think of incarceration, where the individual is confined for a period of time for a crime/legal infraction before being released.[2] However, non-human animals are also captive beings (Marceau, 2019) in locations that include animal agriculture, animal shelters, laboratories, and zoos. Kelly Struthers Montford (2016) has discussed how zoos are captive settings that appeal to the human gaze but simultaneously hide aspects of the living conditions of the non-human animals caged in these spaces.

Lori Gruen (2016), in an op-ed after the killing of Harambe, a male silver-back gorilla in Cincinnati Zoo, Ohio, discusses how these animals' lives are only valued to a point insofar as they do not infringe on human life. Her larger argument in this piece is not simply about the death of Harambe, but a critique of the larger structure that a human (a child in this instance) could even get so close to the large primate, which highlights that capitalism and not conservation is the reason why these animals are caged.

In both prisons and zoos, there is an expectation of performance. In the former, prisoners are expected to behave in a particular manner, which is subordinate to officials. Yet, in some cases, incarcerated humans are made to perform stereotypical acts of being imprisoned. The "Scared Straight" exercises bring non-incarcerated individuals inside prisons with the antici-pation of frightening a person out of committing crime (Unger, 1980). Here, incarcerated individuals must perform in a certain manner that fits the criteria outlined. Furthermore, in the latter, zoos often provoke animals to perform for human spectators. For instance, cologne such as Calvin Klein's "Obsession" is sprayed in big cat exhibits as part of "enrichment programs" to stimulate the animals (Petsko, 2018).

The convergence of human-animal performance is highlighted in Louisiana State Penitentiary's bi-annual rodeo, which brings together incarcerated humans and farmed animals in a multispecies spectacle of violence in the forms of both racialization and anthropocentrism that subordinates both incarcerated humans and animals (Gillespie, 2018).

More commonly known as "Angola," the state prison's rodeo highlights white supremacy and colonial settlerism as the prison is the site of a former slave plantation (Schrift, 2008). At this event, prisoners volunteer to take part in various rodeo-style activities involving farmed animals. Yet, the con-cept of volunteerism within a carceral setting seems dubious, as incarcerated people's freedoms are limited. Melissa R. Schrift (2008) notes that the majority of volunteers are white prisoners, despite the fact that the vast majority of incarcerated men are Black. Kathryn Gillespie (2018) argues this event is a way to showcase both patriotism and and masculinity that is deep-seeded within notions of whiteness.

Furthermore, farmed animals are forced to perform and are then slaughtered and sold in the private sector. Finally, Schrift (2008) and Gillespie (2018) dis-cuss the violence and harm that occurs to both the human and animal involved in these events. Often, the prisoners are not trained and the animals are prodded. In the end, this form of entertainment, for a mostly white audience, overshadows the potential consequences of injury or worse for the human and animal performers.

Human-animal partnership

While the majority of scholarship surrounding human-animal relationships has either been comparative or showcasing an aspect of exploitation, there is a minimal amount of work that highlights human-animal partnerships. In these relationships, there seems to be a mutual benefit between the human-animal within carceral settings.

Dominque Moran (2015) considers the parallels between prisoners and prison animals by looking at the animals within human-animal relationships not simply as therapeutic animals or as pests. Moran strives to broaden the discourse surrounding carceral geographies by incorporating animals. Beyond this, stories of human-animal relationships have emerged in popular journalism. *The Marshall Project* published a story entitled, "My Best Friends in Prison are Frogs, Turtles, and Racoons." In this piece, author Joseph Dole, who is serving a life-sentence, illustrates the various relationships he has forged with animals within and surrounding the various penal institutions he has resided in (Dole, 2017). Furthermore, the podcast, *Ear Hustle*, hosted by Earlonne Woods, Antwan Williams, and Nigel Poor at California State Prison-San Quentin, discusses various topics surrounding prison life. Season one, episode three, entitled, "Looking Out," highlights an incarcerated individual named, "Rauch" who is someone that has made animals part of his life in prison taking in critters such as moths, frogs, and spiders. Furthermore, Rauch explains that he does not consume animals as part of his lifestyle indicating solidarity with sentient beings (Woods, Williams, & Poor, 2017).

This chapter looks to expand and contribute to scholarship surrounding non-coerced human-animal partnerships and interaction within prison settings. Specifically, it looks to consider the positive connections between humans and animals rather than just comparing separate experiences of captivity or exploitation of one by the other. I argue that to circumvent the prison's logic, incarcerated individuals seek out ways to reclaim identity and autonomy in various ways, explicitly by interacting with non-human sentient life. These interactions with non-humans are acts of resistance, which simultaneously forge symbiotic relationships and create meaning for those incarcerated by offering new attitudes, roles, and outlets.

Solitary confinement

Human–non-human animal relationships were brought to my attention while I was conducting fieldwork on prisoner re-entry—the transition from incarceration to community. I was facilitating a weekly group with Black men returning to society that discussed the challenges they were experiencing. By chance, a conversation about the use of solitary confinement developed, as many of the regular attendees had experienced this form of punishment. Lisa Guenther (2013) argues that this form of intensive confinement—entailing 22 hours or more a day of in-cell isolation with few opportunities for meaningful contact—undermines an individual's sense of self both during the event, and following release from solitary. Guenther argues that both a process of "dehumanization" and "deanimalization" occurs within these confined spaces, which attempts to take away dignity from all living beings, human and non-human. Despite this, solitary confinement is routinely used in contemporary American jails and prisons. The case of Kalief Browder, who was held at New York City's Rikers Island jail, is a prime example of how solitary confinement is used by prison administrations. Arrested for robbery in May 2010, Browder was jailed as a pre-trial detainee for more than three years because his family could not afford his bail. Approximately two of these years were spent in solitary confinement (Gonnerman 2015). Browder's case was eventually dismissed, yet the impact of prolonged isolation likely caused Browder to develop severe mental and emotional traumas that culminated in him taking his own life in June, 2015 (Gonnerman, 2015).

Men in the re-entry group described being sent to solitary confinement for reasons unrelated to the crime for which they were charged or convicted. Instead, it was often for minor infractions—a reaction they understood as the subjective and arbitrary exercise of power by correctional staff. In fact, the use of segregated housing has increased over the last four decades, particularly as a form of prison management (Browne, Cambier, & Agha, 2011). Malik[3] described being sent to solitary confinement for possessing "various weapons" which were in fact art supplies that included pencils and felt tip pens. Others discussed being sent to solitary for disagreeing with corrections officers. Lamont explained that he was sent to the SHU (segregated housing unit) for asking why he was not allowed to go to "chow" (i.e. dinner). The experiences of these men are not unique and many others said they experienced the same or similar treatment. These individuals had common experiences of solitary confinement that centered on physical and mental pain and anguish. Some noted that they lost weight and/or a sense of time. Many of the men discussed dealing with depression or paranoia post-solitary confinement. As one explained, "solitary is a prison within a prison and it's meant to break you."

Despite the hardships solitary confinement had caused to members of the group, one participant, Jerome, added an interesting anecdote to the conversation stating, "The only people you can talk to in there [solitary confinement] are the roaches and the rats." After his comment, others in the group laughed and agreed by either nodding their head or verbally affirming his statement with "that's right" or "you right about that." Another participant added, "Yea, at least you got someone to talk to."

I noted this statement, but at the time did not know what to make of it. Yet, the statement, the reaction of the group, and a response from another participant lingered in my mind. At first, I thought of the unsanitary conditions that would create an environment rife with vermin and insects. But the more I thought about this comment and delved into critical animal studies literature, particularly that at the intersection of race, crime, animality, and animals, I took this to be a profound statement. Despite being in arguably one of the most desperate situations in his life, Jerome was able to subvert and resist his conditions of extreme isolation by creating a relationship with another living being: Jerome circumvented his situation, if only fractionally, by engaging with the "rats and roaches." Furthermore, it is important to note that Jerome humanized these non-human animals by saying, "*the only people*," which elevates the status of the rats and roaches to subjects instead of their typical categorization as invasive, pestilential, and nuisance creatures. While many humans seek to "exterminate" or try to avoid these animals, Jerome was inviting them in.

Additionally, in gangster culture and prison vernacular, to call someone a "roach" or "rat" is degrading and insulting, and reserved for an individual who has spoken to law enforcement or has been accused of "snitching" (Smiley, 2015). Therefore, the idea of being able to, "speak to a roach and rat," takes on a whole new meaning in this context, as an individual would not generally speak to a human who was perceived to be a "rat" or "roach" in prison. Yet, to undermine the pains of imprisonment and to resist the prison's severing of relationships of one's choosing, speaking to sentient creatures such as actual rats and roaches becomes a way to reclaim autonomy, agency, and sanity. This next section observes the many ways fictional and non-fictional representations take up human and non-human interactions within carceral settings.

Interaction in carceral spaces

Fiction

When it comes to human and non-human animal contact in fiction, two films come to mind. First is the 1994 drama, *Shawshank Redemption*, which focuses on the conviction of an innocent man who is sentenced to life for the murder of his wife and her lover in the 1940s. Within this overarching story arc are secondary plots that focus on other convicted men, such as Brooks Hatlen. Convicted of murder at the beginning of the 20th century, Brooks, a white male, is the oldest and longest serving prisoner. While working in the prison library, Brooks begins to take care of a fledging crow, whom he names "Jake." After serving nearly 50 years, Brooks is granted parole. Before being released, Brooks and Jake share a final scene, where Brooks gently carries Jake towards the window in the prison library and says, "I can't take care of you no more, Jake, you go on now, you're free...you're free" (Marvin & Darabont, 1994). Brooks reluctantly lifts Jake between the bars of the window and releases him to fly away. In between Brooks telling Jake that their relationship is coming to an end, Jake lets out a series of loud "caws" which Brooks is saddened by, highlighting his distress over the inevitable end of their relationship.

Brooks has anthropomorphized this crow by giving him a human name (Jake), and by setting this bird "free" at the same time that he was preparing to leave prison. The scene represents the end of Brooks' time at Shawshank prison, which means that the things he holds closest to him inside, such as Jake, cannot go with him to the outside world. Brooks and Jake had shared a symbiotic relationship and had comforted each other throughout the film. In one instance, Brooks is shown in the cafeteria feeding the small bird that he has hidden in his prison uniform so as to not be caught by guards. While crows have typically been designated as "bad luck" or foreshadowers of death, for Brooks, Jake's presence was the opposite. Jake was the closest relationship Brooks had inside, and his storyline ends as he commits suicide as a free man who does not have his closest friend, Jake, to save him.

The second film, *The Green Mile*, released in 1999, centers around a large Black man, John Coffey, who is convicted of the murder of two white girls, and subsequently placed on death row in Louisiana in the 1930s, despite his actual innocence. While on death row, Coffey performs miracle acts taking away pain from other characters. One act was the revival of Mr. Jingles, the pet mouse of another inmate, Eduard Delacroix, simply known as Del. In the film, Mr. Jingles arrives on the death row cellblock and evades capture by the prison guards, eventually reaching Del's cell. Upon learning of the mouse's whereabouts, the guards reluctantly allow Mr. Jingles (the name given by Del) to stay after seeing the positive impact he has on Del's disposition. A prison guard, Percy, who has already shown a dislike towards Del, crushes Mr. Jingles under his foot after the mouse left the cell to retrieve a spool that Del had been using to play fetch. This scene is extremely difficult to view as Del is physically and emotionally distressed witnessing the murder of the mouse. Additionally, this unnecessary killing also saddens the other prison guards, as they too had grown fond of the mouse, and the lightheartedness his presence had brought to an otherwise tense environment. The death of Mr. Jingles highlights a disruption in the harmony and community the mouse engendered in the death row unit. However, because of John Coffey's miraculous powers, he is able to revive Mr. Jingles, giving the mouse life again. Del's disposition instantly changes from sadness to relief to joy. Percy, on the other hand, is perplexed as he returns to the unit to find an unharmed mouse.

When it is Del's time to be executed, he makes the guards promise to protect the mouse. Before Del is taken to the death chamber, he turns and looks at Mr. Jingles, who is being held by Coffey and states, "Au revoir, mon ami. Je t'aime, mon petit," which translates to "Goodbye, my friend. I love you, my little one" (Darabont & Valdes, 1999). Mr. Jingles, a mouse who, like rats and roaches, is typically categorized as an invasive creature, brings a certain level of levity to death row by creating joy for the men.

While these two films provide powerful examples of human–animal relationships in prisons, U.S. prison history has also documented these forms of relating.

Non-fiction

Perhaps the best-known and enduring example of human–animal relationships inside is that of Robert Stroud, who was incarcerated from 1909 until his death in 1963. Better known as "the Bird Man of Alcatraz," Stroud was respected for his contribution to ornithology (Sifakis, 2003). While incarcerated at the Leavenworth Federal Penitentiary, Stroud first cared for three injured sparrows. This first relationship with the sparrows sparked a lifelong interest in birds; over the time of his incarceration he cared for roughly 300 canaries and conducted bird-related research while imprisoned. In 1933, he published the *Diseases of Canaries*, a comprehensive work spanning anatomy, feeding, and injuries, amongst other topics (Stroud, 1964). Having a reputation as a violent prisoner, Stroud was eventually transferred to the Alcatraz Federal Penitentiary, where he was forbidden to keep and research birds, yet the moniker lasted.

More recently, the MSNBC docu-series, *Locked Up*, which profiles various jails and prisons around the United States, featured relationships forged between human and non-human animals. For example, in California's Corcoran prison, men have established relationships with gophers in the prison yard. In one episode, a man says to the camera, "It's like anything, you treat them with love and respect and they will treat you with love and respect right back" (Maynardcat, 2016). In prison, respect is a vital necessity that entails the mutual understanding of giving and receiving. Here, the men are applying the same principles they would use for each other to their interactions with the gophers. In the scene, the men are viewed practicing this principle of respect as they intentionally give the gophers a certain amount of distance, and are also conscious about the amount of time they spend petting and feeding the gophers. These human-gopher relationships help the incarcerated individuals reinforce their own guidelines surrounding space, touch, and affection.

In another example at San Quentin prison in California, an incarcerated man by the name of Mike Miller—commonly referred to as "the Birdman of San Quentin"—describes that on his first day at the prison the birds flocked towards him. Embracing his new friends, his prison cell has become a shrine to birds with various cut outs, magazine pages, and other pictures that seem more fitting for the Audubon Society than for a California state prison. On the prison yard, a sign reads, "Feeding pigeons will result in CDC #115 issued"—a rules violation. Despite the regulation, the staff and corrections officers seem to allow Miller to feed the birds in plain sight without repercussion. Relationships such as these become part of a larger prison stability that researchers such as David Skarbek (2014), who studies California prison gangs, describe as keeping order through a delicate balance between rule enforcement and looking the other way. In his interview, Miller states, "It's a good way to release a lot of tension and anger… Only friends I got is [sic] these birds, I can't trust nobody else" (Maynardcat, 2016). Miller acknowledges his predicament and the precarity of prison spaces as violent and stressful. Yet, he finds solace in being able to provide for the birds and to resist prison rules. In a way, there is a double nourishment occurring. For the birds, they are provided seed that nourishes their hunger. For Miller, this act nourishes his soul by giving him an outlet and purpose while incarcerated.

In other facilities, such as in Kentucky, men have developed relationships with feral cats. A correctional officer notes, "These cats is [sic] their kids, if you mess with one these cats...these cats is their family, it's like messing with one of my kids at home. These cats is [sic] all they got" (Maynardcat, 2016). As featured in *Locked Up*, the men discuss the joy they experience raising the cats, particularly in holding and petting them. They also share photos of their favorite cats with viewers. The producers of the show have explained that the unplanned introduction of cats has resulted in a calmer prison yard: namely, that men are careful to not break rules in fear of being sent to segregation, where they would be prevented from caring for the cats. One such prisoner, who was convicted of murder and for the killing of his cellmate, took pride in holding and petting "his" cat. Interestingly, men would pay for toys, food, and vet bills to ensure a high quality of life for the cats. Many of the men can be seen holding, petting, and even kissing the cats, showing outward affection, something typically unseen in prison contexts. In these hyper-masculine spaces that breed extreme violence, the introduction of non-human animals allowed the men to let their guard down, even if just for a moment.

In another scene, a male prisoner is holding a cat, while another prisoner is petting the feline orange tabby. The second man at one-point leans in towards the cat and in a gentle voice says, "I wish you cats would get together and get rid of some of these rats we got running around this yard. The people rats [sic], you leave the itty bitty mice alone" (Maynardcat, 2016). This interaction highlights the paradoxical nature of anthropomorphization as the man is humanizing the mice but animalizing certain humans. The term rat, as explained earlier, does not just refer to rodents but to humans who speak to law enforcement. Furthermore, the man does not want to see the cat harm the rodent mouse but the human "rat." Moreover, by placing a hierarchal stance of both importance and distinction, the man is suggesting that the mice are better than the (human) "rats." Instances such as these show that terms are complex and have meanings that are contextually specific. Here, the mice and cats should be protected, whereas humans who have committed a violation of the convict code should not be.

Finally, the documentary *The Farm* released in 1998, profiles several individuals incarcerated at Louisiana State Penitentiary, the site of the prison rodeo and former slave plantation. Death row inmate John A. Brown, convicted of murder, described how he is in his cell for 23 hours a day and cannot come into contact with people unless handcuffed, stating, "It's kind of weird because after a while you develop into that and then when you get around people it's kind of strange, kind of like an animal I guess" (Garbus, Stack, & Rideau, 1998). Brown likens his own conditions to that of a non-human animal. Moreover, his description is reminiscent of slaughterhouses, which confine farm animals to small spaces while awaiting execution. Additionally, Brown described having a big window across from his cell where he could see the hills, stating, "I seen [sic] some deer back there one day for the first time I see some live deers [sic] back there that wasn't in the zoo" (Garbus, Stack, & Rideau 1998). In a passing comment in a larger documentary about conditions of one of the most notorious American prisons, Brown highlighted his delight in seeing deer through his window. This, assumingly, fleeting moment of joy, is a profound instance of resistance to his current condition. Death row is not designed for delight or pleasure but to inflict pain, both psychologically and physically, as death is imminent. Yet, for Brown, to see deer created meaning beyond the death chamber. Brown was executed in 1997.

Conclusion

Non-human animals have a profound influence on the human condition. Humans are in constant and omnipresent relationships with animal others, used for food, companionship, experimental bodies, entertainment, and fashion. The various examples discussed in this chapter highlight the unique experiences of those who are incarcerated and their relationship to non-human animals. For many, to keep, protect, share, and watch non-human animals is an act of simple resistance. For Jerome, when coming out of prison, speaking to the rats and roaches was a way to subvert the isolation of solitary confinement. For John Brown on death row, seeing the deer was a means to see beyond his execution. In other instances, human-animal relationships exemplified a symbiosis that began as mutual sharing. For the men in Kentucky, the feral prison yard cats provided emotional support and physical aid; petting was not merely a substitute for human companionship, but represented genuine connection. The cats were provided with food, toys, and vet checkups, as well as physical interaction that ensured they had a better quality of life overall. Finally, these symbiotic relationships give meaning in settings that are often defined and experienced as isolating and brutal. Whether the fictitious roles of Brooks or Del who saw themselves as protector and provider, or the real life situation of Robert Stroud who dedicated his life to the study of birds, these relationships produce meaning and roles, which come with their own sets of tasks, duties, and obligations. This in turn produces a sense of agency, purpose, and belonging.

Human and animal relationships do not just occur in rural prisons. On the contrary, prisoners also find ways to interact with non-human animals in urban prisons, highlighting again the significance and importance of interspecies relationships formed within carceral settings. In the spring of 2019, while volunteering at Rikers Island, I spotted a creature in the wooded-area next to the bridge onto the island. At first, I thought it was a dog, but quickly noticed this canine was not a household pet. Its grey markings, wolf-like face, big ears, and large paws indicated she was a wolf, coyote, or hybrid. I began to exclaim about what I was seeing but quickly muffled my voice when a correctional officer walked by. Yet, the officer had already seen my expressive face and remarked, "They are all around here." When I got to the classroom, I told the participants what I witnessed. After class, a student told me that he knew which "wolf-dog" I was describing as his work detail brought him outside the jail to clean up trash in the area. He told me that he would occasionally smuggle small pieces of bread to leave behind for her and her pups. When I asked if he was ever afraid, he shook his head and said, "Nah that's the homie."

Notes

1 As a note, throughout this paper, various terms are used to refer to justice-affected individuals. In some cases, it is either a direct quote or description. I try to refrain from using negative impact terms to describe this population throughout. Yet, some terms might make it through. For that, I apologize.
2 Over 95% of individuals who are incarcerated in the United States are released (Travis, Solomon, & Waul, 2001).
3 All names are pseudonyms.

References

Bachi, K. (2013). Equine-facilitated prison-based programs within the context of prison-based animal programs: State of the science review. *Journal of Offender Rehabilitation, 52*(1), 46–74.

Britton, D.M. & Button, A. (2005). Prison pups: Assessing the effects of dog training programs in correctional facilities. *Journal of Family Social Work, 9*(4), 79–95.

Browne, A., Cambier, A., & Agha, S. (2011). Prisons within prisons: The use of segregation in the United States. *Federal Sentencing Reporter, 24*(1), 46–49. doi:10.1525/fsr.2011.24.1.46

Cooke, B.J., & Farrington, D.P. (2016). The effectiveness of dog-training programs in prison: A systematic review and meta-analysis of the literature. *The Prison Journal, 96*(6), 854–76.

Darabont, F. [Director, Producer] & Valdes, D. [Producer] (1999). *The Green Mile.* Warner Bros.

Dayan, C. (2011). *The law is a white dog: How legal rituals make and unmake persons.* Princeton University Press.

Dole, J. (2017, January 13). My best friends in prison are frogs, turtles, and raccoons. The Marshall Project. Retrieved September 15, 2020, from www.themarshallproject.org/2017/01/12/my-best-friends-in-prison-are-frogs-turtles-and-raccoons

Furst, G. (2006). Prison-based animal programs: A national survey. *The Prison Journal, 86*(4), 407–30.

Garbus, L. (Director, Producer), Stack, J. (Director, Producer) & Rideau, W. [Director] (1998). The Farm: Angola, USA [documentary film]. Seventh Art Releasing.

Garcia-Rojas, C. (2016, August 15). Incarceration nations: On the dangers of exporting US prison systems. TruthOut. Retrieved September 1, 2016, from https://truthout.org/articles/incarceration-nations-on-the-dangers-of-exporting-us-prison-systems/.

Garland, D. (Ed.). (2001). *Mass imprisonment: Social causes and consequences.* Sage.

Gillespie, K. (2018). Placing Angola: Racialisation, anthropocentrism, and settler colonialism at the Louisiana State Penitentiary's Angola Rodeo. *Antipode, 50*(5), 1267–89.

Gonnerman, J. (2015, June 07). Kalief Browder, 1993–2015. *The New Yorker.* Retrieved May 24, 2019, from www.newyorker.com/news/news-desk/kalief-browder-1993-2015

Gruen, L. (2016, June 1). The Cincinnati Zoo's problem wasn't that it killed its gorilla. It's that it's a zoo. *The Washington Post.* Retrieved June 2, 2016, from www.washingtonpost.com/opinions/the-cincinnati-zoos-problem-wasnt-that-it-killed-its-gorilla-its-that-its-a-zoo/2016/06/01/a44015e8-27ea-11e6-b989-4e5479715b54_story.html.

Gruen, L. (Ed.). (2014). *The ethics of captivity.* Oxford University Press.

Guenther, L. (2013). *Solitary confinement: Social death and its afterlives*. University of Minnesota Press.

Hampton, H. (Producer) (1987). A Nation of Law? (1968–1971), Episode 12. *Eyes on the Prize* [TV documentary series]. PBS.

Harkrader, T., Burke, T.W., & Owen, S.S. (2004). Pound puppies: The rehabilitative uses of dogs in correctional facilities. *Corrections Today, 66*(2), 74–9.

Huss, R. (2013). Canines (and cats) in correctional institutions: Legal and ethical issues relating to companion animal programs. *Nevada Law Journal, 14*, 25.

James, Kirk A. (2014, November 18). The history of prisons in America. Medium. Retrieved August 11, 2017, from https://medium.com/@kirkajames/the-history-of-prisons-in-america-618a8247348.

LeBaron, G. (2012). Rethinking prison labor: Social discipline and the state in historical perspective. *WorkingUSA, 15*(3), 327–51.

Marceau, J. (2019). *Beyond cages: Animal law and criminal punishment*. Cambridge University Press.

Marvin, N. [Producer] & Darabont, F. [Director] (1994). *The Shawshank Redemption*. Columbia Pictures.

Maynardcat. (2016, February 7). Prisoners and their cats. *YouTube*. Retrieved from www.youtube.com/watch?v=i8xIwiPk0G8&t=176s.

Moran, D. (2015). Budgie smuggling or doing bird? Human-animal interactions in carceral space: Prison (er) animals as abject and subject. *Social & Cultural Geography, 16*(6), 634–53.

Morin, K.M. (2016). Carceral space: Prisoners and animals. *Antipode, 48*(5), 1317–36.

Petsko, E. (2018, October 11). Why Tigers Find Calvin Klein's Obsession for Men Cologne So Irresistible. Mental Floss. Retrieved September 15, 2020, from www.mentalfloss.com/article/560127/why-tigers-find-calvin-kleins-obsession-men-cologne-so-irresistible

Schrift M (2008) The wildest show in the South: The politics and poetics of the Angola Prison Rodeo and the Inmate Arts Festival. *Southern Cultures 14*(1), 22–41.

Sifakis, C. (2003). *The encyclopedia of American prisons*. Facts on File crime library. Facts on File.

Skarbek, D. (2014). *The social order of the underworld: How prison gangs govern the American penal system*. Oxford University Press.

Smiley, C.J. (2015). From silence to propagation: Understanding the relationship between "Stop Snitchin" and "YOLO". *Deviant Behavior, 36*(1), 1–16.

Stroud R. (1964). *Stroud's digest on the diseases of birds*. TFH Publications.

Struthers Montford, K. (2016). Dehumanized denizens, displayed animals: prison tourism and the discourse of the zoo. *PhiloSOPHIA, 6*(1), 73–91.

Travis, J., Solomon, A. & Waul, M. (2001). From prison to home: The dimensions and consequences of prisoner reentry. Urban Institute Press.

Unger, A. (1980, November 05). "Scared Straight!" How the media can exploit a social program. *The Christian Science Monitor*. Retrieved September 15, 2020, from www.csmonitor.com/1980/1105/110501.html

Woods, E., Williams, A., & Poor, N. (Hosts). (2017, July 12). Looking out [episode. *Ear Hustle* [podcast series]. www.earhustlesq.com/episodes/2017/7/12/looking-out

Afterword: Building abolition in pandemic times

Justin Piché

Ejaz Choudry—an elderly Muslim man living with schizophrenia—was shot and murdered by police during a wellness check requested by his family (Nasser, 2020). Joyce Echequan—an Indigenous woman and mother—laid in a hospital bed screaming in pain from a stomach condition and mustered the strength to livestream the racist taunting she endured from medical staff who ridiculed "her poor choices" and asked "what would your kids think of seeing you like this?" during the final minutes of her life (Shingler et al., 2020). Moka Dawkins—a Black trans woman and sex worker who was imprisoned for four years following a manslaughter conviction for defending herself against a client who was trying to kill her—was again arrested, this time for allegedly uttering threats, committing assault and breaching probation conditions in the midst of a dispute with a roommate (Laurenco, 2020). Seth MacLean—a young man living with mental health and drug use issues—died from fentanyl poisoning in a downtown homeless shelter and was buried in a distant suburb without his family's knowledge (Gibson, 2020). Perhaps more mundane to more people, but no less shocking are the countless women who have sacrificed their careers to take care of their kids at home, while other women continued to work precarious jobs including as care providers in long-term care homes, without being provided the necessary protective equipment by their employers, which in far too many cases cost them their lives (Wright, 2020).

The above are just a few of the unsettling scenes that have gotten mainstream attention in so-called Canada during the COVID-19 pandemic which have laid bare the insecurity that plague the lives of many pushed to the margins by colonialism, capitalism, racism and white supremacy, patriarchy, cis-heteronormativity, ableism, and other violent structures of power, often under the guise of "care." It has been well-documented that this acutely felt insecurity—the lack of access to adequate water, food, housing, income support, education, health and mental health care, mobility, corporeal safety and/or other necessities of life—that has become further entrenched with every passing day is not an accident. This is not unique to pandemic times. This is not the work of a few "bad apples." Rather, this—the lives constrained, the lives maimed, the lives lost—is by design (Ware et al., 2014) and enforced by cops, courts, and cages of different kinds within and beyond the penal system (Piché and Larsen, 2010).

As it becomes apparent to more and more people that most forms of "care" are control and rooted in state and corporate commitments to necropolitics (Mbembe, 2003) and racial capitalism (Robinson, 2000), rather than life and the pursuit of equality, it should not be surprising that there appears to be increasing support for "kite-ideas" (see Zurn, this volume) that (a) break with present structures and relationships of violence and (b) open the horizons to a world where we continually strive to find new ways to keep each other safe in all facets of our lives. Thanks in large part to the steadfast work of a new generation of BIPOC community organizers, scholars and public intellectuals who are inspiring abolitionist work (e.g. Walia, 2013; Jones, 2014; Maynard, 2017; Diverlus et al., 2020), calls for defunding the police, abolishing prisons, and transformative justice remain radical pursuits, but are no longer fringe ideas deemed unthinkable and unspeakable in mainstream debates in this country. This is a moment where—as the Toronto Prisoners' Rights Project reminds its members at the close of each of their meetings—abolishing the police, prisons, and other forms of carcerality in order to reallocate resources to build-up people and communities is not only necessary, but inevitable.

At this time of great pain and hope, how can those committed to building abolition usher in inevitable abolitionist futures sooner than appears to be currently possible? The contributors to *Building abolition: Decarceration and social justice* offer much insight into how to (a) make sense of the present carceral moment, (b) reimagine what is possible both in the immediate term and generations from now, and (c) engage the terrain that has yet to be forged.

A necessary starting point, borrowing from Lisa Guenther's (this volume) reflections on the role settlers can play in decolonization struggles, of which abolitionism is a part, is to "Get out of the way." At this critical time when Indigenous, Black, and other racialized and otherwise marginalized people continue to be systematically oppressed and subject to carceral violence, Guenther's advice to fellow privileged travelers to avoid "insisting that" the efforts of the oppressed to survive, resist and resurge "take a form that is acceptable to the settler state" is prescient. It is not for scholars, particularly ones in positions of privilege, to set boundaries around what is reasonable both in terms of process and outcomes. After all, it is dominant strands of reason that inform the exercise of power which have led the world to its profoundly unequal present. If we are to engage in struggle to dismantle and build the world anew, this necessarily implies "becoming different kinds of subjects, in relation to different organizing logics, motivated by the desire for a more just and beautiful world, structured not by the logic of elimination, replacement, and racism, but by the promise of decolonization, whatever that looks like and whatever it demands of us" (Guenther, this volume). Seen in this light, working toward abolitionist futures requires abolishing violent structures within ourselves in addition to external oppressive forces.

Building abolition also demands intellectual labor to make sense of shifts and continuities in the deployment of carceral logics and power, including in these times of intersecting pandemics of inequality in which policing (McClelland et al., 2020), punitive injustice (Deshman et al., 2020), and confinement (Maynard and Piché, 2020) are being deployed in stated efforts to enhance public health and safety. As contributors in the volume remind us, to unsettle carceral common sense we need to sharpen our analyses to mount critiques against, build alternatives to, and dismantle the normalization and proliferation of carceral control.

First and foremost, this requires centering the experiences and insights of people subject to carceral violence, who Isabel Scheuneman Scott, Fran Chaisson and Bobbie Kidd (this volume) show us have amassed the strength and wisdom to guide how past and present regimes of confinement ought to be remembered in order to imagine a future free from their destruction. Through the work of Chaisson, Kidd and others involved in the P4W Memorial Collective that are seeking to create a memorial garden at the Prison for Women in Kingston, forgetting about the women they did time with is impossible and their efforts will ensure that future generations do not suffer from the collective amnesia that allows for atrocities to persist. In building abolition in ways that center the "carceral other" (Chartrand, 2017), Calvin Smiley's (this volume) examination of interactions between human and non-human animals in sites of confinement highlights the critical importance of fostering moments within carceral spaces that "produce meaning and roles, which come with their own sets of tasks, duties, and obligations," which also generate "a sense of agency, purpose, and belonging." Such insights are critical, reminding us that, as we strive towards abolitionist futures, we must also attend to the immediate needs of those presently confined for whom escaping isolation, even temporarily, is often a pressing concern.

Escaping carceral logics and practices in the future also requires building ways of attending to the needs stemming from conflicts and harms premised on knowledge and processes that collectively break us free from the desire to control and punish. For Sol Neely, this break can be realized through "situating abolitionist endeavors in the concreteness of oral literary traditions, their protocols, and their ceremonies," an "Indigenous cosmopolitanism" that engages "both descendants of victims and perpetrators of settler colonialism, the colonized and the colonizers." He adds that this approach, which departs from the "permanent war against Indigenous bodies" waged by colonial states, requires building abolition in a way that erects "phenomenological and micrological sites of decolonial intervention… that restore ancestral wisdom to both descendants of perpetrators and victims of colonization." Such transformative interventions stand in sharp contrast to the "Indigenization" efforts of state prison agencies, which Danielle Bird (this volume) demonstrates are an approach that "reifies the centuries-old 'Indian Problem' by constructing Indigenous women's criminalization as 'Indigenous' problems, requiring 'cultural' solutions, rather than settler colonial societies and institutions" in need of "total transformation."

Confronting collective forgetting (Scheuneman Scott et al., this volume) and making room for approaches to justice in the wake of conflicts and harms that are rooted in Indigenous knowledges which move us beyond punitive injustice rooted in "white supremacy" that "fails to account for its own impoverishment" (Neely, this volume), also requires confronting the "carceral enjoyments" derived from the subjugation of the carceral other (Dilts, this volume). As Andrew Dilts notes, working towards abolitionism obligates us to confront the fact that many derive "material, psychic, and symbolic benefits and privileges" from carceral power and violence. He adds that so long as people are allowed to engage in "parasitic forms of social life, 'purchased' through the racialized social deaths of others, effected in our contemporary moment by the practice of incarceration," abolitionists will be unable to move past a way "social life produced by the social death of confinement." From the consumers of penal spectacles pervading popular culture (Brown, 2009) to the many profiteers of imprisonment (Christie, 2017), along with the vast numbers of people and entities that produce and consume "penal pornography" (Wacquant, 2009, p. xi) in the many spaces in between, Dilts (this volume, original emphasis) argues that "supporting killjoys, becoming killjoys ourselves, and above all, ceding the floor to those best situated and able to disrupt the flow of the 'good feelings' of carcerality, *including the good feeling of 'reform'*," must be a necessary part of the work abolitionists do.

Pushing back against carceral enjoyments that manifest themselves in progressive politics that rhetorically softens the various forms of subjugation that are most acutely felt by racialized people requires abolitionists to be attentive to "how law is integral to white supremacy" (Avila and Bundy, this volume). As Fernando Avila and Jessica Bundy note, such a focus allows for "the associations among racism, capitalism, white supremacy, settler colonialism, and state-organized violence via the criminal justice system" to be "starkly revealed." Moreover, as Sarah Turnbull (this volume) illustrates in her examination of immigration detention in the United Kingdom, decisions about inclusion in and exclusion from the nation state are premised in manners similar to decisions in the punitive injustice realm in that they are "fundamentally about race—as it intersects with gender, class, and other social relations of power." Given that the "[i]mmigration detention" is "an increasingly vital part of the carceral state that also produces and maintains systemic racism and white supremacy," it is vital that abolitionists across the board take up the call of groups like Solidarity Across Borders for status for all, alongside demands to free them all.

Anti-carceral feminist analyses of the kind chronicled by Jennifer Kilty and Katarina Bogosavljevic (this volume) that "challenge the use of incarceration" and reject the state deployment of "additional heteropatriarchal and racist harms" as a means of recognizing and ending gender-based violence are also central to working towards abolitionist futures. Building on the insights of pioneering critical feminist criminologist Carol Smart concerning the limits of law, Kilty and Bogosavljevic note the important role feminist killjoys can play in illuminating "the fantasy that carceral logics adequately nurture our emotional state and keep us safe," as well as the need to channel "emotions that underpin calls for carceral punishment toward an abolitionist ethos" in the pursuit of liberation and social justice. Moreover, as Dawn Moore and Vered Ben-David (this volume) note, in a context where "women who fail to conform to trauma scripts are more likely to be even more deeply pathologized, criminalized, incarcerated and also lose custody of their children" when subject to state gender-based violence responses developed in the global northwest and exported elsewhere, it is critical that the construction of abolitionist alternatives involve insights from the global south and east where many states have more limited capacity for carceral intervention. Among the insights gleaned from such contexts noted by Moore and Ben-David are the centering of the will of survivors, community-based efforts to ensure access to care and basic life necessities, pursuing reconciliation where possible, and an emphasis on eradicating the cultural norms that normalize the violence of men against women. By taking "into account the ecology of the problem and the real needs of the victims," they conclude that "a more comprehensive response that acknowledges the impact of social disadvantages will represent a more effective approach" than the model at work in the global northwest that far too often positions those impacted as the "deviant/dismissed female victim." Such work demonstrates that not only are alternatives imaginable, they are already in existence (also see Dixon and Piepzna-Samarasinha, 2020), and could significantly flourish if given even a fraction of the material and symbolic resources currently invested in punitive approaches to gender-based violence.

Strategic abolitionist insurgencies must also multiply in other spaces where the carceral has become further entrenched. As Megan Gaucher and Alexa DeGagne (this volume) highlight, such forays are needed in queer communities that have often turned carceral "solutions" like creation of "hate crime" laws to end the violence they endure despite historical and contemporary forms of organized oppression and abandonment by various "state institutions—police, carceral, immigrant, medical and legal—which have regulated, threatened and shortened LGBTQ2S life." Noting that "Racially neutral narratives of queer marginalization—specifically in the context of police at Pride," who have historically targeted racialized LGBTQ2S refugees for repression and removal, fails to account for the "deep-rooted interconnectedness between colonialism, xenophobia, racism, capitalism and heterosexism." This requires those engaged in building abolition and decolonization to engage in the "simultaneous deconstruction of these multiple systems of power." It also demands an investment of energy in constructing "long-running practices of mutual "aid" and "communities of solidarity" that have roots in LGBTQ2S mobilizations around Pride parades," including "providing supports for mental distress, establishing community-safety-patrols, and providing free legal advice and defense funds." Importantly, Gaucher and DeGagne highlight that practices such as "Self-marshalling and safety-patrols during Pride parades provide a micro example of what future space could be without the incursion of state institutions in queer spaces," which ought to inform abolitionist alternatives more broadly.

Carcerality is also at work in other self-styled marches towards progress. For instance, Kelly Struthers Montford and Eve Kasprzycka (this volume) explore how the so-called animal protection movement in the United States centers calls for criminalization and harsh punishments in the development of animal cruelty laws, which perversely "elevate the animal through the subjugation of blackness—now enacted by the prison system rather than the institution of slavery." This manifestation of white supremacy is also all too evident in what Paula Cepeda Gallo and Chloë Taylor (this volume) refer to as the "widespread harnessing of canine power" that has been used not only "to oppress other species of nonhuman animals," but also for carceral purposes "to terrorize, discipline, maim, and kill human beings who have been animalized." We can add to this animalized subjugation the normalization of torture experienced by people, like Oak Ridge patients who were frequently deemed psychopaths, and non-human animals, like rodents, whom Lauren Corman (this volume) notes are "among the most peripheralized subjects, cast into sites of invisibility where collective complicity regards them as abject debris" in the pursuit of medical discovery. It is through such analyses that it becomes clear "that carceral human settings and animal laboratories are interlocked expressions of settler colonialism" underpinned by "co-joined constructions of animality and humanity in the Western liberal tradition" that legitimate the caging of living creatures. Seen in this light, for freedom to not be parasitic, Struthers Montford and Kasprzycka (this volume) argue that abolitionists must at once make "schemas of life that uphold the human-subhuman-animal triad…inarticulable," while insisting on "forms of political subjectivity that are creaturely." Without such work, dignity will continue to be denied to the subjugated, enabling caging to continue under the pretext of benevolent interventions.

Perhaps nowhere is the politics of progressive disposability most insidiously at work then when "carceral ableism" is allowed to perpetually "mark (disabled) bodies at the intersections of difference as pathologically dangerous and/or paternalistically innocent" (Meiners et al., this volume). As Erica Meiners, Liat Ben-Moshe and Nirmala Erevelles observe, in both scenarios the consequences are grave, funneling "people away from prisons into institutions, psych facilities and life-long surveillance, leaving the brutal logic of carcerality intact." This being the case, invoking "innocence" to free people in the short term is unlikely to lead to liberation for all (also see Gilmore, 2017).

If this is the case, then taking-up the provocative call from Debra Parkes (this volume) to foreground "everyone convicted of murder" and those deemed to be the "dangerous few" in abolitionist struggles, "to start with these stories and not leave them for another day," might be the key to undercutting the perceived need for carceral control writ large. It may also be key to revealing the "liberal lie that the criminal punishment system [or any carceral system for that matter] is actually about protecting people from violence and harm." The alternative is to continue to fail to displace the individualization of responsibility for violence in ways that "leave untouched the structures and cultures that facilitate and perpetuate it, such as heteropatriarchy, colonial dispossession, white supremacy, capitalism, and the like." Parkes asserts that when abolitionists adopt an approach diametrically opposed to engaging in the politics of innocence, we can reveal that "The brunt of punitive sentencing policies aimed at addressing violence, and murder in particular, is felt most harshly by those who are Indigenous and racialized," along with their loved ones and communities. She further notes that "By centering people living under life sentences we do not allow official stories that are told about them to stand unchallenged", while advancing "different stories, ones that locate the particular event that led them to be criminalized in context of state and structural violence." In so doing, we point to the need for structural change that is necessary for the freedom and safety of everyone without exceptions.

Taken together, the various approaches to abolitionist engagement brought into conversation in this edited collection reveal both the need for and import of "contextualized and situated socio-historical analyses of carceral power" that Fernando Avila and Jessica Bundy (this volume) call for to "dismantle systems of subjugation" and build "more just and ethical communities." Coupling such analyses with praxis that builds power through the redoubling of community organizing efforts to form, sustain, and deepen coalitions that cut across trans-formative movements for social justice (Dixon, 2014) is necessary to contend with state and corporate forces abundantly equipped to pacify and fragment resistance through carceral violence and progressively packaged, but nonetheless life-taking, reformism. As people in increasing numbers are coming to the realization that they are on the wrong end of the pandemics of inequality that pervade all of our lives, carceral abolition is more within our reach than ever. If we continue to build a world where we can envisage and create the material conditions to free us all we will win. Losing is not an option.

References

Brown, Michelle (2009) *The Culture of Punishment: Prison, Society, and Spectacle*, New York: New York University Press.

Chartrand, Vicki (2017) "Penal Tourism of the Carceral Other as Colonial Narrative", in Jacqueline Z. Wilson, Sarah Hodgkinson, Justin Piché and Kevin Walby (eds.), *The Handbook of Prison Tourism*, London: Palgrave-Macmillan, pp. 673–687.

Christie, Nils (2017) *Crime Control as Industry: Towards Gulags, Western Style*, New York: Routledge.

Deshman, Abby, Alexander McClelland and Alex Luscombe (2020) *Stay Off the Grass: COVID-19 and Law Enforcement in Canada*, Toronto and Ottawa: Canadian Civil Liberties Association and the Policing the Pandemic Mapping Project.

Diverlus, Rodney, Sandy Hudson and Syrus Marcus Ware (eds.) (2020) *Until We Are Free: Reflections on Black Lives Matter in Canada*, Regina: University of Regina Press.

Dixon, Chris (2014) *Another Politics: Talking Across Today's Transformative Movements*, Berkeley: University of California Press.

Dixon, Ejeris and Leah Lakshmi Piepzna-Samarasinha (eds.) (2020) Beyond Survival: Strategies and Stories from the Transformative Justice Movement, Oakland: AK Press.

Gibson, Victoria (2020, October 1) "Seth MacLean was one of nine fatal overdoses in Toronto shelters in July—during one of the system's deadliest summers. His family wants changes made so it can't happen again", *Toronto Star*. Retrieved from www.thestar.com/news/gta/2020/10/01/seth-maclean-was-one-of-nine-fatal-overdoses-in-toronto-shelters-in-july-during-one-of-the-systems-deadliest-summers-his-family-wants-changes-made-so-it-cant-happen-again.html

Gilmore, Ruth Wilson (2017) "Abolition Geography and the Problem of Innocence", in Gaye Theresa Johnson and Alex Lubin (eds.), *The Futures of Black Radicalism*, New York: Verso, pp. 225–240.

Jones, El (2014) *Live from the Afrikan Resistance!* Halifax: Fernwood.

Laurenco, Denio (2020, July 31) "Toronto activist Moka Dawkins release from police custody after protests from anti-racism groups," *CTV News*. Retrieved from www. ctvnews.ca/canada/toronto-activist-moka-dawkins-released-from-police-custody-after-protests-from-anti-racism-groups-1.5047987

Maynard, Robyn (2017) *Policing Black Lives: State Violence in Canada Slavery to the Present*, Halifax: Fernwood.

Maynard, Robyn and Justin Piché (2020) "No One is Disposable: Depopulating Carceral Sites During the COVID-19 Pandemic and Beyond," in Between the Lines Editorial Collective (eds.), *Sick of the System: Why the COVID-19 Recovery Must Be Revolutionary*, Toronto: Between the Lines, pp. 105–115.

Mbembe, Achille (2003) "Necropolitics," *Public Culture*, 15(1): 11–40.

McClelland, Alexander, Alex Luscombe and Nicholas Buhite (2020) *Criminal Enforcement Report*, Ottawa: Policing the Pandemic Mapping Project.

Nasser, Shanifa (2020, June 22) "Family of Ejaz Choudry demands firing of officer who fatally shot him during mental health crisis," *CBC News*. Retrieved from www.cbc. ca/news/canada/toronto/ejaz-choudry-1.5622160

Piché, Justin and Mike Larsen (2010) "The Moving Targets of Penal Abolitionism: ICOPA, Past, Present and Future", *Contemporary Justice Review*, 13(4): 391–410.

Robinson, Cedric (2000[1983]) *Black Marxism: The Making of the Black Radical Tradition*, Chapel Hill: University of North Carolina.

Shingler, Benjamin, Julia Page and Sarah Leavitt (2020, October 1) "Racism at Quebec hospital reported long before troubling death of Atikamekw woman", *CBC News*. Retrieved from www.cbc.ca/news/canada/montreal/quebec-joliette-hospital-joyce-echaquan-1.5745150

Wacquant, Loïc (2009) *Punishing the Poor: The Neoliberal Government of Social Austerity*, Durham: Duke University Press.

Walia, Harsha (ed.) (2013) *Undoing Border Imperialism*, Oakland: AK Press.

Ware, Syrus Marcus, Joan Ruzsa and Giselle Dias (2014) "It Can't Be Fixed Because It's Not Broken: Racism and Disability in the Prison Industrial Complex", in Liat Ben-Moshe, Chris Chapman and Allison C. Carey, *Disability Incarcerated: Imprisonment and Disability in the United States and Canada*, New York: Palgrave-Macmillan, pp. 163–184.

Wright, Teresa (2020, May 23) "COVID-19's impact on women investigated by Canadian government," *Toronto Star*. Retrieved from www.thestar.com/news/canada/2020/05/23/covid-19s-impact-on-women-investigated-by-canadian-government.html

Index